Gender and the Long Postwar

Gender and the Long Postwar

The United States and the Two Germanys,
1945–1989

Edited by
Karen Hagemann
Sonya Michel

Woodrow Wilson Center Press
Washington, D.C.

Johns Hopkins University Press
Baltimore

EDITORIAL OFFICES
Woodrow Wilson Center Press
Woodrow Wilson International Center for Scholars
One Woodrow Wilson Plaza
1300 Pennsylvania Avenue, NW
Washington, DC 20004-3027
www.wilsoncenter.org

ORDER FROM
Johns Hopkins University Press
Hopkins Fulfillment Services
P.O. Box 50370
Baltimore, MD 21211-4370
Telephone: 1-800-537-5487
www.press.jhu.edu/books/

Library of Congress Cataloging-in-Publication Data

Gender and the long postwar : the United States and the two Germanys, 1945–1989 / editors, Karen Hagemann, Sonya Michel.
    pages cm
Includes bibliographical references and index.
ISBN-13: 978-1-4214-1413-3
    1. Women—Germany (West)—Social conditions. 2. Women—Germany (East) —Social conditions. 3. Women—United States—Social conditions—20th century. 4. Sex role—Germany (West) —History. 5. Sex role—Germany (East)—History. 6. Sex role—United States—History—20th century. 7. Social change—Germany (West) —History. 8. Social change—Germany (East) —History. 9. Social change—United States—History. 10. World War, 1939–1945—Social aspects—United States. 11. World War, 1939–1945—Social aspects—Germany. I. Hagemann, Karen. II. Michel, Sonya, 1942–
    HQ1623.G446 2014
    305.40943—dc23
                            2014004601

Wilson Center

The Wilson Center, chartered by Congress as the official memorial to President Woodrow Wilson, is the nation's key nonpartisan policy forum for tackling global issues through independent research and open dialogue to inform actionable ideas for Congress, the Administration, and the broader policy community.

Conclusions or opinions expressed in Center publications and programs are those of the authors and speakers and do not necessarily reflect the views of the Center staff, fellows, trustees, advisory groups, or any individuals or organizations that provide financial support to the Center.

Please visit us online at www.wilsoncenter.org.

Jane Harman, Director, President, and CEO

Table of Contents

II. The Military, Politics, and Changing Masculinities

III. Restoring Families and Recasting Welfare States

Acknowledgments

The book at hand is the result of extensive transatlantic cooperation. It began with a conference of the same name held at the German Historical Institute (GHI) in Washington, DC, in May 2008, organized by the editors in cooperation with Corinna Unger (GHI). The starting point for this endeavor was Tony Judt's book *Postwar: A History of Europe Since 1945*, in which he analyzes the period after World War II as a time of new beginnings. As gender historians, we wondered how these conditions affected women and men, and since Hagemann and Unger worked on Germany and Michel on the United States, we had an opportunity to compare developments on both sides of the Atlantic. By extending the investigation to 1989, we sought to trace both continuities and change over a long expanse of time, sorting out the impact of the war itself from other factors that came into play during the period. With the kind hospitality of the GHI, we invited 45 scholars to come together to explore these questions. Once we had the exciting results of the conference before us, the organizers decided to publish a book. Corinna Unger bowed out to pursue other research, and we went ahead, selecting a number of the conference papers and inviting several American and German scholars to write new chapters for the volume on subjects that were clearly missing.

For their generous support, the editors wish to thank the sponsors of the initial conference: the GHI, the German Academic Exchange Service, and the Department of History at the University of Maryland, College Park. The staff of the GHI coordinated the conference with their usual expertise and cordiality, and as a result, it ran very smoothly, allowing the participants to focus on what turned out to be two days of very productive intellectual exchange.

It was a pleasure to work with our enthusiastic co-organizer, Corinna Unger, and with all of conference participants, whose knowledge and ideas enlivened the project as a whole.

We thank the authors for their willing collaboration and patience in the process of writing and editing the chapters presented here. And finally, we thank the staff of Woodrow Wilson Center Press, particularly the director, Joseph Brinley, for their work in shepherding this volume through the publication process.

Karen Hagemann and Sonya Michel
Chapel Hill, North Carolina, and College Park, Maryland
January 2013

Gender and the Long Postwar

Introduction: Gender and the Long Postwar: Reconsiderations of the United States and the Two Germanys, 1945–1989

Karen Hagemann and Sonya Michel

Historians have long understood that wars can serve as catalysts for change. Many focus on the aftermath of sustained death and destruction; others—while not denying the depth of pain and suffering—emphasize the openings for progress that appear on the social, political, and economic horizons at these moments. In his penetrating synthesis, *Postwar: A History of Europe Since 1945*, Tony Judt, for example, argues that "World War II created the conditions for a new Europe."[1] To be sure, the war itself shredded the social fabric of all the belligerents, upending rigid hierarchies and sweeping away outmoded conventions in the process, but without the defeat of Nazism and fascism, it would have been politically impossible for a new Europe to emerge.

The possibilities for change were especially apparent in the realm of gender relations. While in Europe, the immediate aftermath of the war brought with it continuing privations, dislocations, family separation, and, for women especially, the risk of bodily danger; peace—or at least the rhetoric of peace—held out the prospect of new opportunities. Both communism and liberal democracy promised equality for women and well-being for them and their families. Yet the demands of rebuilding nations and restoring social and political order took immediate precedence. The tensions between the political and economic needs of nations; the promises of the new social orders; women's ongoing struggles for recognition, autonomy, and equality; and men's efforts to recast masculinity in the wake of unprecedented violence—these constitute one set of themes in *Gender and the Long Postwar*.

1

Judt's study implies that conditions for creating "the new" were more propitious in Europe than in the United States. Was this in fact the case? From the perspective of gender, the war and its aftermath opened up possibilities for women and men on both sides of the Atlantic. But the extent to which those possibilities were realized varied across societies. The present volume explores why this was so. By examining in detail and then comparing gender developments in the United States and the two Germanys during "the long postwar," the essays collected here allow us, on the one hand, to see how gender relations developed in two types of political systems: market democracies (the United States and the Federal Republic of Germany, or FRG) and communist regimes (the German Democratic Republic, or GDR). On the other hand, we can see how the developments and policies in each of these three states were bound up with and influenced each other. The postwar transformation of West Germany was first greatly shaped by the occupation policies of the Western Allies and later by the Cold War; as the major power the United States played an important role in both. Similarly, developments in East Germany are impossible to understand without recognizing the influence of the Soviet Union. Furthermore, the two German states were, until unification in 1989, connected by a relation of "entanglement and demarcation."[2]

Judt's chronology, extending from 1945 to 1989, affirms an insight that was first advanced by gender historians, namely that the periodization of any war changes when historians begin to consider its long-term extra-military consequences.[3] Instead of dating a conflict from the onset of hostilities through truce, gender historians have argued that war may entail a *longue durée* that continues well after the fighting ceases, with the wartime dislocations of gender relations reverberating for years, even decades, after hostilities end. During the fighting, belligerents' economic, military, and social needs may bring women into unaccustomed positions of authority, but the determined postwar search for "normality"—often defined in terms of the prewar gender order—can have the reverse effect. Because of the impact of war itself, however, efforts to return to normality often become frustrated.[4] While entire populations become caught up in demobilization and reconstruction, women bear specific burdens—maintaining their families and households, waiting for missing and imprisoned soldiers, caring for veterans with mental and physical disabilities, adjusting to widowhood.[5] At the same time, the sudden prevalence of "unattached" women and the overall gender imbalance give rise to economic as well as social anxieties.

2

At such moments, the "double helix" of gender relations (to use Margaret and Patrice Higonnet's famous term) appears to structure relations between women and men as societies—or at least some forces within them—seek to restore forms of male dominance that became eroded through men's absence, injury, death, or defeat. As the Higonnets point out, while a hierarchy that privileges masculinity seems to persist, gender definitions themselves do not remain stable over time, but readjust according to circumstances.[6] This process certainly occurred during the Second World War and its postwar period. In West Germany, for example, both political leaders and the occupying forces rejected the deeply entrenched martial ideals that were at the core of Germany's hegemonic concept of masculinity of the past. They attempted to recast men as caring husbands and fathers. But to retain the gender (im) balance, they urged women to put their wartime roles behind them as well, to give up any paid work and devote themselves once again to their domestic responsibilities, thereby stabilizing the social order and with it, the gender hierarchy. As men returned from the battlefield, either in glory or in defeat, women were supposed to retreat into the home, mimicking a kind of Arthur Murray diagram for dancing the foxtrot, with the male partner stepping forward and the female backward (not unlike Fred Astaire and Ginger Rogers).

Yet the war itself, its aftermath, and reflections on male militarism and heroism and female sacrifice were not alone in shaping gender relations in the three societies. The Cold War, the economic surge and growth of consumerism, demographic shifts, and the rise of the New Left also had major impacts. These factors—common nodes of inquiry in the mainstream historiography of the period—undergo revisionist examination from the perspective of gender in this volume too. The Cold War had important implications for gender roles in the two Germanys insofar as each deployed images of ideal womanhood and especially motherhood as political foils against the other.[7] Similarly, East German officials used images of American masculinity as negative models for East German manhood. This dynamic of political-cultural triangulation drew in sexualities as well as gender relations.

But the Cold War does not fully define the period, nor did it completely determine sexual identities or gender relations. Change in these areas became most visible in the 1960s, when first the New Left and later the new women's movement forcefully challenged both militarism and gender relations in the United States and West Germany. This radical political agenda did not spring up de novo, but in both societies arose from social, cultural, and political conflicts that had been roiling since 1945.[8] The essays gathered in this volume

3

offer new perspectives on the origins of social and reform policies and the new movements that started in the 1960s. A chapter on masculinity in the American civil rights movement, for example, shows how race and gender worked together to both advance and inhibit social change. Several other chapters compare the impact of the antiwar movement and postwar feminism on concepts of masculinity as well as femininity in the United States and West Germany, while one on East Germany examines how the relative absence of a New Left and a grassroots women's movement inhibited change in gender relations in that society. While most of the previous research on the two postwar Germanys and the United States uses gender as one analytical category among several at best, the present volume's primary focus on gender allows us to undertake a comprehensive interrogation and revision of much of the social, economic, and political historiography of the period from a fresh perspective.[9] Our volume also extends comparisons presented by other women's and gender historians that focus on Europe by adding the United States to the mix.[10] Using a comparative and transnational perspective, we build on the increasing number of single-country studies of gender and postwar in both East and West Germany and the United States, emphasizing the relations and interactions between the FRG and the GDR as well as between the two Germanys and the United States.[11] During the Cold War these societies represented the most distinct and at the same time entangled extremes of governmental family and gender policy.[12] In the following, we summarize the content and some of the main insights of the volume, which is structured in four parts.

Gendering the Aftermath of War

May 8, 1945 formally marked the cessation of hostilities in Europe, but the suffering was not over; indeed, for many—civilians and soldiers alike—it had just begun. Instead of disappearing, ethnic hostilities flared up anew as former victims sought to settle scores with their now-vanquished oppressors.[13] The Allies forced millions of German-speaking residents from southern and central Europe to relocate to a homeland many had not seen for generations. Tens of millions more, refugees of the war itself, including thousands of children, languished in camps for "displaced persons," awaiting word of lost relatives and assignment to new homes.[14] And everywhere, home, shops, farms, schools, and businesses lay in ruins, creating massive shortages of food, clothing, medicine and other basic necessities.

4

As the first section of this volume, "Gendering the Aftermath of War," demonstrates, the hardships of postwar fell disproportionately on women, not only because they now outnumbered men in populations decimated by wartime losses, but also because tradition assigned them the role of caring for their families, regardless of the circumstances. The risks and challenges they faced differed greatly across the different German occupation zones, and between Germany and the United States. Especially in occupied Germany, but also elsewhere in Europe, the exigencies of daily life, such as seeking basic supplies, continually and unavoidably exposed women to the risk of sexual predation. While some voluntarily sought sexual partners among the occupiers—for protection as well as material goods—many more became victims of rape.[15]

Both in wartime and afterward, sexual violation was rampant on all sides. During the war the German Wehrmacht ravaged in eastern Europe, while American GIs preyed on French women, incited by their supposed passionate nature.[16] But in the postwar period, it was the Soviet army that became notorious for such practices. As Atina Grossmann reports in her chapter, "The 'Big Rape': Sex and Sexual Violence, War, and Occupation in German Post–World War II Memory and Imagination," scholars estimate that up to half a million women—one third of Berlin's female population—were attacked by members of the Red Army, despite official prohibitions by the Soviet Military Administration. It is customary, in the post-feminist West, to view rape as a particularly heinous crime, but because of its prevalence in the Soviet sector of postwar Berlin, Grossmann argues, rape became somewhat normalized in the memory of those who lived through it. "The story of sexual violence," she found, "was told as part of the narrative of survival in ruined Germany."[17] For this reason, Grossmann believes it is important to "take seriously women's own portrayals of themselves as resourceful agents and not merely helpless victims (or villains) in a tumultuous historical moment."

Although the risk of rape was not as high in the other zones of occupation, material privations and losses among the male population were just as common, compelling women to resort to black-market negotiations for everyday necessities and seek employment to support their families, sometimes through arduous work as *Trümmerfrauen* (literally translated as "rubble women"). In the chapter "Gender Roles in Ruins: German Women and Local Politics under American Occupation, 1945–1955," Rebecca Boehling shows how these conditions as well as their experiences in the war itself prompted women to challenge gender norms, questioning "men's inherent ability to lead either families or society as a whole." This brought them into conflict with the American occupiers as well as the postwar West German government, both of whom regarded those norms as essential to stabilizing postwar society. Examining the policies of the Office of Military Government, United States (OMGUS) and its effect on gender policies in the American zone in general and the local example of Munich's municipal government, Boehling shows that German female activists and the American occupiers were working at cross-purposes. While the first cohort of leftist German women who became active in postwar politics often ignored political party lines (much to the consternation of the parties' leaders) in pushing for feminist policies such as equal pay for equal work, OMGUS sought to steer them into apolitical "community activities" that would serve as extensions of—and reinforce—their familial roles. Because many of the most active women identified with the left, they became vulnerable to the Cold War politics that came to dominate both the United States Military Government (USMG) in the American occupation zone and, after 1949, the Christian-conservative government of the newly established FRG. Isolated within and in some cases expelled from their parties, the first feminist cohort fell away, to be replaced by a younger generation of women who readily accepted their role as housewives in the new Germany.[18]

Shortages, particularly of housing, also plagued the postwar United States, although American conditions were nowhere as dire as those in Europe. Nevertheless, to women expecting some sort of "peace dividend," the difficulties they encountered came as a bitter pill as they sought to restore homes and reunite families. In the chapter "A Women's Peace Dividend: Demobilization and Working-Class Women in Chicago, 1945–1953," Laura McEnaney reveals that long-standing racial and ethnic as well as class cleavages, temporarily papered over during the Depression and war years, reemerged as the war came to an end, at a time when most Americans believed that their sacrifices had earned them a share of the long-deferred "good life." In contrast to the usual narrative of comfortable suburbanization and prolific reproduction, McEnaney offers a story, or rather, multiple stories, of women struggling, individually and together, against gender and racial discrimination, to find decent dwellings, keep jobs without access to child care, and budget for household expenses as prices rose. What distinguished this period from earlier times of hardship, such as the Depression, was the widely shared assumption that government should take responsibility for ensuring social and economic equity. When it came to housing, for example, women called for federal policies to underwrite their postwar prosperity through rent control, a statist demand made by female citizens who thought their wartime labors deserved recompense. This, in McEnaney's view, points to the emergence of a working-class, multiracial base of support for the liberal state, "forged not on the shop floor but in the postwar apartment."

While listening to the mellifluous tones of paeans to peace and prosperity, women in the postwar United States and West Germany stayed alert to openings for gender shifting. In their search for gender equality they faced numerous obstacles: not only physical threats but also social and economic injustice and political resistance from both entrenched parties and occupation forces. As noted above, Rebecca Boehling demonstrates how the Western Allies, especially the United States, targeted not only German men but also German women with their reeducation projects, which included visions of a gender order based on the breadwinner-housewife family, and sought to contain female political postwar activism according to their agenda of Cold War politics. But this was a difficult and ambiguous enterprise, as Ulrike Weckel shows in her chapter, "Teaching Democracy on the Big Screen: Gender and Reeducation of Postwar Germans in *A Foreign Affair* and *The Big Lift*." Weckel analyzes two American films (the first made in 1948, the second in 1950) that are particularly rich sources of insight into the complex gender politics of the period. Shot against the backdrop of war-torn Berlin, both depict romantic relationships between American military men and German women. Despite the unique setting, these transatlantic stories follow the conventional lines of the Hollywood romantic genre, but they also serve as metaphors for American efforts to inculcate democratic principles in a German political population deemed bereft of appropriate values. In a clever bit of turnabout, Weckel explains, the films end up subverting that message, as the German women on the screen repeatedly upstage the American male characters who are supposedly their moral and political superiors. Apparently, however, patriotic Americans were not ready to criticize either the democratization project or US gender norms. Not only did the films fail to draw American audiences, but authorities barred their distribution in Germany for decades.[19]

The Western Allies were not, of course, alone in seeking to restabilize the German family and re-Christianize German society; they were joined by West German politicians and the Catholic and Protestant churches. Despite their efforts, however, nontraditional gender images and relations persisted at least into the first postwar decade. The Christian-conservatives, glorifying the family as the basis for social reconstruction "unsullied" by National Socialism and as a haven of continuity and stability, tried to turn marriage and the family into private arenas for coming to terms with the past.[20] But opposition grew, especially on the left. By the early 1950s, signs of incipient gender consciousness and the building blocks of female political solidarity were already becoming visible. The phrase "men and women are equal" appeared—with nearly the same wording—in the 1949 provisional constitutions of both the FRG and GDR. The antithetical political and economic systems of the liberal democratic West and the communist East notwithstanding, the legal rhetoric of both nations promised *Gleichberechtigung von Frauen und Männern* (the equality of men and women) as a fundamental right. Each constitution further guaranteed its implementation in all subsequent legislation. As a result, "gender equality" remained a highly contested term in the legal and political discourses in the two Germanys during the 1950s and 1960s.[21] In both states, women especially pushed for reform—a fact that was long overlooked by the activists of the new women's movement that started in West Germany in the late 1960s and continues to be ignored by many researchers.[22] Academia and media were part of a Cold War culture that suppressed even the collective memory of any activities by the "Old Left" to which many of the first generation of postwar feminists had belonged.

Ironically, while the American authorities were rhetorically promoting gender equality in their zone of occupation in Germany, gender *in*equality characterized the postwar United States. The so-called "GI Bill" (Servicemen's Readjustment Act of 1944), which provided veterans substantial housing and educational benefits as well as low-interest loans to start up businesses, both implicitly and explicitly favored male veterans—implicitly because service members were overwhelmingly male, and explicitly because of specific benefits that only men could access.[23] Through both trade union practices and legally imposed preferences for male veterans in hiring, the legions of women who had joined the US labor force during the war were driven out or forced to shift from lucrative manufacturing to less well-paid "pink-collar" jobs.[24] Federal support for child care—a major innovation of America's wartime welfare state (and a policy similar to that developed in the Third Reich)—was withdrawn over the protests of wage-earning mothers around the country.[25] Meanwhile, a wide array of social and cultural forces directed women to focus their energies on their homes and families, not only as a locus of reproduction but as the principal site of pleasure and security in the still-uncertain postwar world.[26]

8

The Military, Politics, and Changing Masculinities

Men's roles in postwar societies were also being recast, as traditional forms of manhood, especially their linkage with martial qualities, came under scrutiny. Even though Allied military strength had succeeded in vanquishing the Axis, the scope of the war's devastation prompted many—ordinary citizens as well as cultural and political leaders—to challenge the long-standing coupling of military and masculinity. The section "The Military, Politics, and Changing Masculinities" explores this process as it unrolled across the United States and West Germany. These chapters show that as the war receded into memory, the idea that men could (only) prove their manhood through military service met with increasing opposition on both sides of the Atlantic.

Signs that the military-masculinity dyad might be crumbling could be found in political rhetoric, everyday exchanges between women and men and, as Weckel shows, in postwar cinema.[27] Meanwhile, away from the silver screen, both American occupation officials and West Germans were determined to extirpate all traces of militarism from German culture. According to Kathleen Nawyn, the Americans feared that unless Germany's "militaristic spirit" was vigorously addressed, it might lead to yet another conflict. Accordingly, officials developed specific policies to eliminate all sources and symptoms of militarism. This effort only added to the "crisis of masculinity" many German men themselves were already experiencing.[28] In "Banning the Soldier Hero: American Regulations, German Youth, and Changing Ideals of Manhood in Occupied Württemberg-Baden, 1945–1949," Nawyn explains that "German soldiers had learned that war was hardly a heroic enterprise . . . . They had failed as defenders of their families and fatherland, millions were dead or captive, and many who did return home were physically or psychologically broken and incapable of caring for their loved ones." Focusing on German-run youth groups in Württemberg-Baden, Nawyn demonstrates that American demilitarization efforts complemented the Germans' own rejection of heroic masculinity, opening the way for "new prescriptive ideals that presented men as morally strong, devoted fathers." Moreover, she notes, in the decades that followed, opposition to martial ideals remained popular, fueled in part by the antimilitarization protest of the 1950s, the antiwar demonstrations of the 1960s, and the peace movement of the 1980s.[29]

In the next chapter, "Sending Young Men to the Barracks: West Germany's Struggle over the Establishment of New Armed Forces in the 1950s," Friederike Brühöfener picks up the story of German demilitarization where Nawyn leaves off. Brühöfener analyzes the public debate about West Germany's rearmament, which came to a head over the issue of drafting young men into the Bundeswehr (German Federal Armed Forces, founded in 1955) when they came of age. Politicians of all parties, military representatives, concerned citizens, and the media quarreled over the positive as well as negative effects of military training on West Germany's male population. The perils of drill notwithstanding, the majority believed in the educational value of military training, contending that it could turn young men into proper male citizens. But many were concerned that all-male life in barracks would corrupt young draftees and deprave their conduct toward women. Thus the debates over the draft turned on the question of acceptable gender roles for men in uniform and how they could be made compatible with the social expectation and beliefs of the 1950s and early 1960s—while simultaneously enabling a break from the National Socialist past. Although similarly comprehensive research on masculinity and militarism has not been undertaken for the Soviet-occupied zone and the former GDR, an exploratory article by Christine Eifler indicates that the East German National People's Army (Nationale Volksarmee), established in 1956, nourished a far more militaristic concept of masculinity for its soldiers than the FRG.[30]

In the United States, opposition to militarism peaked somewhat later, in the 1960s and 1970s, but there, too, it emerged from a trend that had been gaining momentum since the immediate postwar period, despite the persistent glorification of "the Greatest Generation" of Americans who had served in World War II.[31] According to Amy Rutenberg in "Service by Other Means: Changing Perceptions of Military Service and Masculinity in the United States, 1940–1973," three factors—the decaying public image of the American soldier, the selectivity of federal military manpower policies, and activists' vocal rejection of military service—helped decouple military service from male citizenship obligations in the United States over this period. As a result, many men ceased to understand service in the armed forces as their responsibility and sought ways to avoid conscription. Competing modes of masculinity offered them ways to define their own manhood, whether through occupational means, domestic responsibilities, or protest. Rutenberg demonstrates that a decline of military masculinity in American popular culture, combined with two decades of manpower policies by the military that deemphasized the need for universal service, the disappointing course of the Vietnam war, unbroken pacifist opposition to the draft, and the spread of the idealistic, individualistic values of the New Left, finally created in the late 1960s and early 1970s a situation in which young men,

10

regardless of their commitment to the peace movement, could openly reject the claim that military service was necessary to their masculine identity.

For African Americans, however, the disavowal of militarized masculinity did not come as a matter of course. In his chapter "Man the Guns: Race, Masculinity, and Citizenship from World War II to the Civil Rights Movement," Steve Estes argues that the new sense of pride gained by African American men who served in the military prompted them to fight for and defend their rights more assertively than ever before, leading, ultimately, to the Civil Rights Movement of the 1950s and 1960s.[32] Military service altered white perceptions of black manhood for the better in some places, but in others it created fear on the part of whites that hardened into opposition to the growing demand for black rights, producing virulent racial conflict. For both blacks and whites, the postwar baby boom created a new emphasis on fatherhood, but the racialized and gendered assumptions underpinning the GI Bill reinforced the ideal of white fatherhood, while subsidizing white flight from America's inner cities and underwriting the de facto segregation that continues to define the country's housing patterns to this day.

The link between war and male prowess made the post–World War II period a particularly propitious moment for challenging masculine ideals. As details about the brutality of the war became known, populations on both sides began seeking ways to decouple these two values. Yet, as these chapters show, the process did not necessarily lead to greater gender equality, as the new democracies opened up different ways for men to claim social, economic, and political dominance. Moreover, in the United States, race and ethnicity significantly complicated postwar gender politics, and these complications spilled over into the US occupation zone in Germany.[33]

Restoring Families and Recasting Welfare States

Postwar changes in the images of femininity and masculinity went hand-in-hand, and were, in turn, connected to the (re)construction of class, race and ethnicity, as well as generational belonging, sexual orientation, and family status. The entanglement of all these factors becomes visible once more in the third section on "Restoring Families and Recasting Welfare States," which examines the three societies as families were reunited and the "peace dividend" came to fruition. As its chapters reveal, the situation of families changed dramatically during the first two postwar decades. On the one hand, economic

11

recovery led to improved living conditions for many. But on the other, gender politics became increasingly complicated by the Cold War, which informed education, labor, social, and family policies—in short, the different forms of welfare-state building in the FRG and GDR as well as in the United States.[34] As a result of these changes, while the first postwar year was the "hour of women," with large numbers waiting for the return of their fiancés and husbands from the front and prisoner-of-war camps, while hundreds of thousands of others were mourning their losses, the 1950s and early 1960s became a kind of "golden age" for the male-breadwinner/female-homemaker family in the United States and West Germany. In both societies, more adult men and women than ever before married, and more married couples were able to live this ideal because of the "economic miracle" of the postwar era. At the same time, however, the proportion of women who continued to work after marriage, mainly through part-time employment, increased beginning in the early 1950s.

The situation in East Germany was quite different. Without the financial support of the European Recovery Program (also known as the Marshall Plan) established by the United States in 1947 and ended in 1951, economic restoration in the GDR went much more slowly. The exigencies of a "command economy," along with an extreme labor shortage, which led in August 1961 to the closing of the borders to West Germany and the construction of the Berlin Wall; an authoritarian-paternalist welfare state; and communist gender ideals resulted in full-time employment for women, including mothers, taking family life and society in a different direction. At least rhetorically, the GDR propagated "full equality" for men and women, but in practice, the gendered division of labor in the economy, society, and the family changed very little. In addition to paid labor, East German women continued to carry the burden of housework and family.[35]

On both sides of the Atlantic, one important theme of the public discussions about postwar families was their "health." All three societies wanted "healthy" and "normal" nuclear families, which they considered to be fundamental for the thriving of state and nation. But in many cases, the terms "healthy" and "normal" were used as euphemisms to criticize the social, racial and ethnic composition of families. In West Germany, this public debate focused on the relations between African American soldiers of the occupying forces and German women—and their "offspring," the so-called *Mischlingskinder* (mixed-race children) or "brown babies."[36] In the United States, the racial and ethnic composition of the national populace also became an issue, reviving long-standing tensions within the society. As Angela Tudico demonstrates in her chapter, "White on Departure? Race and War Bride Immigration to the United States after World War II," US authorities used racial and ethnic categorizations to broker the immigration process for war brides seeking to enter the country. Tudico argues that although Congress honored male soldiers' service by passing special legislation to allow their foreign wives and even fiancées to immigrate, many of these women encountered barriers in the immigration process—barriers that were racially and ethnically specific. Tudico's discovery that immigration officials insisted on classifying European war brides by ethnicity challenges other historians' argument that World War II was a turning point in the "whitening" of second-wave immigrants to the United States.[37] Rather than eradicating distinctions and leaving the country with the broad, roughly equal categories of white, black, and Asian, Americans continued to differentiate among immigrants on the basis of race and ethnicity.

The remaining chapters in this section focus on the role of the family and gender images in the shaping of welfare states in the two Germanys and the United States. In "Hot Lunches in the Cold War: The Politics of School Lunches in Postwar Divided Germany," Alice Weinreb demonstrates the importance of the politics of food for the two countries' gender and family ideals and national self-conceptions. Her chapter compares the trajectory of school lunch programs in the FRG and the GDR during the occupation period and the Cold War. In both German states during the early postwar years, communities and welfare organization provided school meals to hungry children. But starting in the late 1940s, school lunch policies on the two sides of the Iron Curtain began to diverge. The East German government systematically extended school meals programs, resulting, by the 1980s, in one of the world's highest school lunch participation rates. From the 1950s on, the GDR's economy required the full-time employment of all women. Thus the Socialist Unity Party (Sozialistische Einheitspartei Deutschlands, or SED) supported an extensive expansion of policies to facilitate mothers' employment, including afterschool care to complement half-day school education in the morning, and the provision of school meals.

In West Germany, by contrast, communities and welfare organizations quickly abolished school meal programs as the economic recovery set in; by 1950, school lunches had become an exception. One main cause for this development was the half-day time policy for child care, preschools, and schools in the FRG. Here, unlike the GDR, the ideal of the male breadwinner family drove not only the family policy of the Christian-conservative federal government, but also the education policy of the federal states (*Länder*),

13

which were responsible for it, as well as the communities and private welfare organizations that organized child care and social welfare, including school meals.[38] For different reasons, the policies in both states (developed within the context of their fierce Cold War effort to differentiate themselves from one another) were highly controversial among the populations—particularly mothers—of the two German states. Weinreb describes the economic, political, and cultural contexts for these different food policies, showing how the presence or absence of a lunch program helped determine women's identity as both mothers and Germans.

Although controversial, the East German school lunch program fit squarely within the broader context of that country's welfare state development. In her chapter "Women, Family, and 'Postwar': The Gendering of the GDR's Welfare Dictatorship," Donna Harsch traces the arc of communist rhetoric from 1949 to 1989. Initially, the SED promised a glorious future built on socialist "productivism," but toward the end, it was making only muted claims about providing East Germans with "social safety and security" in the here and now. Over time, funds were shifted from disproportionate investment in heavy industrial production to expensive outlays for consumer goods, apartments, maternity leave, and universal child care. Harsch argues that the transition to a more socially oriented dictatorship was driven by the interaction between the strict gender equality dictated by orthodox communism,[39] on the one hand, and intensifying Cold War economic competition over the ability to satisfy demands for private consumption, on the other.[40] Because of its proximity to its western counterpart, East Germany was confronted with this rivalry more directly than other communist states.[41] The SED tried to ignore the challenge but could not because of the population's lingering attachment to the idea that women should only perform unpaid domestic labor—this at a time when the GDR desperately needed them as wage workers. Consumer goods and social services became the payoff.[42]

In terms of welfare state generosity, it would be difficult to find a greater contrast than that between East Germany, with its universal child care and maternity leave policies, and the United States, with its grudging public provisions restricted to the poor and those with disabilities.[43] As Jennifer Mittelstadt's chapter shows, however, this pattern changed markedly in the mid-1970s, as the United States shifted from conscription to all-volunteer armed forces, using generous welfare provisions such as health care and housing as an incentive to enlistment. In "The Soldier-Breadwinner and the Army Family: Gender and Social Welfare in the Post-1945 US Military and Society," Mittelstadt identifies this transition as a pivotal moment in the construction of gender and the function of the military—and in the construction of the American welfare state. To an unprecedented degree, the volunteer force relied on married male soldiers. Their needs as male breadwinners prompted the army to expand its existing benefits and services as well as create wholly new ones to support soldiers' families. In so doing, the army significantly enlarged its social welfare functions, reviving the historic but neglected ideal of an "Army Family" that "took care of its own" and embedding the volunteer force in a distinctive gendered, paternalistic notion of family and social welfare. At the same time, military benefits added a new layer to what had been heretofore a "reluctant welfare state," but it established military service (rather than, say, citizenship per se) as the basis for entitlement. As in the private welfare state, this made women's access to social benefits largely dependent on marriage to an eligible spouse.[44]

The chapters in this section suggest that the shape and constituencies of postwar welfare states depended on both internal national priorities and their positioning in the Cold War. Immediately after the war, both the GDR and FRG, recognizing the need to ensure the very survival of the precious next generation, provided school lunches to combat children's hunger. But as the countries' priorities diverged, so too did their attitudes toward this policy. The GDR continued to offer school lunches and developed special benefits for women because they were needed as paid labor, while in the FRG, such benefits were rejected as part of the time policy of child care and schooling by the federal government, the *Länder,* and the municipalities as well as the different welfare organizations. All of them supported only child care facilities, preschools, and schools that were open half day, a policy intended to uphold the male-breadwinner family by preventing the full-time work of mothers.[45] This development proceeded hand in hand with a labor market policy by the federal government, the Confederation of German Employers (Deutscher Arbeitgeberverband), and the German Trade Union Federation (Deutscher Gewerkschaftsbund) that fostered part-time work for mothers, which, starting in the 1960s, became accepted as a form of "modernization" of the male-breadwinner family model and as a result steadily increased.[46] Like West Germany, the United States withdrew benefits that encouraged maternal employment (in this case, child care) in an effort to restore the male breadwinner ideal, and it was not until several decades later, as the government sought to build an all-volunteer military, that federal support for such provisions was expanded, but then only for enlistees and their families, or as part of anti-poverty policy.

15

Forging New Sexualities and Creating New Gender Identities

The final section, "Forging New Sexualities and Creating New Gender Identities," listens for the resonances of war at the most intimate level. Here the question of whether or not the war opened up new opportunities for individual self-expression comes in for close scrutiny, and as these chapters show, national political contexts offered different degrees of latitude. In the United States, wartime had led to the formation of gay and lesbian communities within the same-sex environments of the military, along with a general loosening of sexual mores.[47] But many historians argue that the postwar period brought a dramatic reversal, as Cold War fears led to a crackdown on the "homosexual menace"—while emphasizing greater sexual satisfaction for heterosexuals, as long as it remained within the confines of marriage.[48] New research, including the chapters in this section, challenges the long-held assumption that the 1950 and early 1960s were a thoroughly prudish era. At the same time, these studies emphasize the ambiguities in postwar development, which can only be understood in a long-term perspective—for the two Germanys, one that includes Weimar and Nazi Germany.[49]

Joanne Meyerowitz challenges the notion that the postwar era in the United States was a time of ascendant sexual conservatism. In her chapter "The Liberal 1950s? Reinterpreting Postwar American Sexual Culture," she argues that at least some Americans in the postwar years were in fact much more broad-minded on issues of sexuality than has usually been understood. Focusing on new studies addressing obscenity, homosexuality, and interracial sex and marriage, Meyerowitz contends that instead of sexual "containment," there was vocal debate, mostly within the middle class, marked by conflicting positions on sexuality. Long-term economic, intellectual, and political trends, she concludes, favored sexual liberalism more than sexual conservatism, framing the postwar years as an early iteration of the current (local and global) battles over the meanings of sexual expression and sexual display—one that has vacillated between greater permissiveness and new rights for sexual minorities, on the one hand, and harsh repression, on the other.

West Germany also witnessed vigorous debates over sexuality in the postwar decades, but the range was not as great. One example is presented in Elizabeth Heineman's recent study, *Before Porn was Legal: The Erotica Empire of Beate Uhse*. The focus of the study, Uhse, was a former Luftwaffe pilot, war widow, and young mother who turned to selling a self-penned guide to the rhythm method that found many buyers on the black market. She built a

16

mail-order business in the 1950s that sold condoms, sex aids, self-help books, and more, soon becoming the world's largest erotica entrepreneur and even expanding into the East. On her way she battled restrictive legislation, conservative churches, and prudish mores.[50]

The struggle against these forces is also a theme in Robert Moeller's chapter "Private Acts, Public Anxieties: The Fight to Decriminalize Male Homosexuality in Postwar West Germany." He traces the controversy over the decriminalization of same-sex sexual activity between men in West Germany in the 1960s. Paragraph 175 of the Penal Code (Strafgesetzbuch), the criminal statute prohibiting sex between men, had been the law of the land since 1871. Its provisions were significantly intensified by the Nazis in 1935, and in this expanded form, it remained on the books in the FRG. In the 1960s, many doctors, lawyers, psychologists, religious leaders, and politicians argued forcefully that the state's attempt to regulate consensual sex between men violated a fundamental right to privacy, and in 1969, a majority in the West German parliament, the Bundestag, voted to reform Paragraph 175 by setting the age of consent at 21. In 1973, it was lowered to 18. This more liberal legal consensus did not, however, lead to popular embrace of same-sex desire as an acceptable alternative to heterosexuality. Many West Germans agreed that the state should not dictate morality, but even supporters of reform conceded that most people would continue to view homosexual acts as abhorrent. The essay explores the tension between the acknowledgement of a right to privacy and clearly articulated public anxieties that homosexuality was morally unacceptable and potentially a threat to West Germany's male youth and the foundations of civil society.

A similar debate in the GDR during the same period produced more liberal laws but again not necessarily more liberal practices. In 1950, East Germany abolished Nazi amendments to Paragraph 175, in 1968 limited its scope to sex with youths under 18, and in 1988 terminated it entirely. Jennifer V. Evans roots her chapter, "Homosexuality and the Politics of Masculinity in East Germany," in the still-underdeveloped history of the persistence of Nazi jurisprudence and homophobia after the demise of the Third Reich. Exploring the shifts and changes in regulatory mechanisms through the prism of gender, youth, and sexuality, she engages assertions made most recently by Dagmar Herzog in her important contribution to postwar sexual mores regarding the slow liberalization of German attitudes toward sex and sexuality.[51] Specifically, Evans questions the notion that the decriminalization of same-sex sexuality in East Germany represented a triumph of the sexual revolution. Instead, she highlights the difficulty of postwar negotiations of intimacy and identity in relation to gay male sexuality. Decriminalization, while realizing a private sphere of intimacy for adult men, came at a cost for youths, whose actions, relationships, and identities were subjected to invasive monitoring via age-of-consent regulations and protective discourses of containment. Although homosexuality had become a public subject of debate by the 1970s, hard-fought changes in the law did not always serve to counterbalance lingering homophobia. In exploring the tension between liberalization and reform in East Germany, Evans, mindful of the Nazi past, situates legality against the backdrop of reticence in state and society to deal with the intimacies of ordinary citizens.

Thus, while the cultural crack-up brought on by the wars in Korea and Vietnam led to a loosening of sexual mores in the United States, far less dramatic changes occurred in the two Germanys, where the laws changed, but popular attitudes toward sexuality, most notably homosexuality, remained conservative, particularly in the Federal Republic, where marital heterosexuality was closely linked to a return to postwar social normalcy.[52]

Conclusion

Taken together, the chapters in this volume demonstrate that, in different ways, the Cold War and reactions to it drove gender politics in all three countries. In the United States and the Federal Republic of Germany, this cycle of cause-and-effect led initially to efforts to restore conventional gender orders but subsequently to challenges to those same norms, while in the German Democratic Republic, it produced more radical changes in rhetoric and policies, but also to continuities in everyday life, especially with respect to the gendered division of labor in the family. Because they had to carry the triple burden of wage work, family, and housework, East German women valued certain welfare state programs very highly: full-time child care, after-school care and school meals, as well as the *Hausarbeitstag*, a monthly day off granted to married women to carry out their household duties. Weary of having to line up for hours to get rare consumer goods, East German women also welcomed unlimited access to new household technology, food, and clothing. But as the 1959 "kitchen debates" in Moscow revealed, the Soviet Union and the other state socialist societies like the GDR remained vulnerable when it came to living up to promises of greater consumer choice.[53]

At the same time, consumerism and the good life that were, presumably, meant to tamp down gender unrest in the United States and West Germany were floundering; already in the first postwar years women were becoming restless, and signs of feminist resistance beginning to emerge. Not all American women withdrew quietly behind the picture windows of their suburban homes. Instead, they joined together to demand better schools and living conditions and oppose residential segregation, their efforts drawing the attention of Senator Joseph McCarthy and his infamous anti-communist minions.[54] In the Federal Republic of Germany, feminist demands had little chance against the policies of the American occupation authorities, who sought to promote an "apolitical and womanly" approach to "women's policy." Leftist women and their socialist-feminist ideas became victims of Cold War politics, their approach firmly rejected as "communist," pushed to the margins or even, as in the case of the 1957 ban of the Democratic Women's League of Germany (Demokratische Frauenbund Deutschlands), the largest women's organization in the FRG, simply forbidden.

It is interesting to compare the impact of the American occupation on the Civil Rights Movement and on the women's movement. Maria Höhn and Martin Klimke argue that African Americans' participation in the occupation force, with its emphasis on promoting democracy and equality in Germany and eradicating all traces of racism under the banner of "denazification," sharpened their awareness of racial injustice at home and added momentum to the Civil Rights Movement.[55] But American women's participation in the occupation did not have the same effect. As Boehling shows, the few American women who were recruited to work with their West German counterparts were selected precisely because of their gender-conservative politics. Their assignment was to reinforce the message about conventional gender roles that the American authorities wished to convey, and few, if any, seemed to note the irony of the fact that while the Americans insisted on formal gender equality in the Federal Republic's new constitution, American women at home had— and still have—no such general protection.

The impact of the Cold War on sexuality was somewhat different. In reaction to what was perceived as widespread sexual immorality during the war, American social and cultural leaders sought to reimpose conventional sexual order in the 1950s and 1960s. But underneath, as Meyerowitz argues here, there was a strong trend toward liberalization—in practice as well as in cultural debates. However, it would not be until the 1970s that abortion became legal, and not until 2003 that homosexuality was fully decriminalized in the United States. In the two Germanys, developments followed a reverse trend. As both Moeller and Evans show, homosexuality was decriminalized relatively early—in 1968 under the new GDR Penal Code, and in 1969 and 1973 under the FRG Penal Code—but deeply entrenched conservative social and cultural trends continued to police behavior and drive homosexuality underground. Abortion was legalized in the same decade in both German states—1972 in the GDR and 1974 in the FRG—but to a different extent. The GDR allowed abortions in the first three months of pregnancy (*Fristenlösung*). The West German Bundestag had approved a similar law in 1974, but the Federal Constitutional Court demanded a change in this law and allowed abortions only in the case of four documented and approved indications: medical, criminal, eugenic, and social.[56]

We began by asking whether or not the postwar period opened up opportunities for gender equality and sexual liberation, and if not, why. The essays collected here suggest that this question must be framed more broadly. From the perspective of the governments of the three countries themselves, gender equality and sexual liberation, while perhaps goals in themselves for the individual women or sexual minorities involved, were, for officials, more of an instrument, a means to pursue other priorities, namely victory in the Cold War. But these two sets of goals were not always in concert; indeed, gender and sexual equality were sometimes regarded by male-dominated political establishments as inimical or antithetical to their geopolitical agenda. Thus if we pull back and view gender politics and sexual liberation in a more transnational or international context, we can see why those goals remained elusive. At the same time it becomes apparent that issues of gender, the family, and sexuality were by no means trivial "hullabaloo" as Gerhard Schröder, the former Social Democratic chancellor of the FRG, stated dismissively in 1998. On the contrary, these issues were highly contested, especially in the first three postwar decades, and they played a crucial role in the conflict between East and West. The role of women, the place of the family in society, and the treatment of alternative sexualities became key markers of difference between authoritarian communist states and liberal market societies.[57]

Within this context, it was not so easy for women, sexual minorities, or even men seeking new ways to redefine their gender roles to mobilize. Yet, as the very controversies of the late 1940s and 1950s reveal, the forces of change could not be fully suppressed. The disruptions of the war itself, coupled with the lofty promises of postwar rhetoric on both sides, opened the way for ongoing struggles for gender and sexual equality. In the United States and West Germany, incipient feminism and redefinitions of masculinity became complementary and mutually reinforcing, and both lent support to the push for gay and lesbian liberation. Although all of these movements proceeded only in fits and starts, they were driven by a powerful momentum that would soon spread around the globe.

In East Germany, too, women's postwar experience left its mark. Even though women were de facto forced to work outside the home because paid work was regarded as the duty of every "socialist citizen" while continuing to shoulder responsibility for household and family, after unification they attempted to remain in full-time work and rejected the usual half-day child care and schooling of West Germany. Recent surveys show that former East German women continue to regard full-time employment for mothers as "normal." In one survey conducted in 2003, only 37 percent of East German women working part-time stated that they did so for "personal or familial reasons," as compared to 85 percent of women in the West. On the contrary, 47 percent of the East German female part-timers wanted to work full-time but had not yet found a full-time job, while in West Germany this was the case for only 4 percent of female part-timers.[58]

Ten years later, the women in the West are catching up. As a recent study by the Berlin Social Research Center (Wissenschaftszentrum) shows, today 91 percent of the women under age thirty-five in both parts of Germany believe that having a "job and their own money" is crucial, and they are calling for different family and labor market policies by the government that would allow them to combine family and work.[59] In the United States, too, women continue to address the same issues, although many of the most vocal protagonists look to women themselves as well as business, rather than to the government, to make changes.[60] While the sites of international conflict have shifted since the end of the Cold War, in both Germany and the United States, domestic struggles around equal social citizenship for women and equal rights for sexual minorities—struggles that took root in the political spaces opened up during the long postwar—persist.

Notes

1. Tony Judt, *Postwar: A History of Europe Since 1945* (London: Pimlico, 2005, 2007), chap. 1.

2. Christoph Kleßmann, "Abgrenzung und Verflechtung: Aspekte der geteilten und zusammengehörigen deutschen Nachkriegsgeschichte," *Aus Politik und Zeitgeschehen*, B 29–30 (1995): 30–41, 30.

3. Margaret Higonnet, Jane Jenson, Sonya Michel and Margaret Weitz, eds., *Behind the Lines: Gender and the Two World Wars* (New Haven, CT: Yale University Press, 1989).

4. See Karen Hagemann and Stefanie Schüler-Springorum, eds., *Home/Front: The Military, War and Gender in Twentieth-Century Germany* (Oxford and New York: Berg Publishers, 2002).

5. See, for example, Deborah Cohen, *The War Come Home: Disabled Veterans in Britain and Germany, 1914–1939* (Berkeley: University of California Press, 2001); and Marina Larsson, *Shattered Anzacs: Living with the Scars of War* (Sydney: University of New South Wales Press, 2009).

6. Margaret Higonnet and Patrice Higonnet, "The Double Helix," in Higonnet et al., *Behind the Lines*, 31–50.

7. See Robert G. Moeller, *Protecting Motherhood: Women and the Family in the Politics of Postwar West Germany* (Berkeley: University of California Press, 1993).

8. Here we disagree with Bonnie G. Smith, who argues that "the 1960s were a time when both male and female activists suddenly confronted the Cold War order directly"; Introduction, *Women and Gender in Postwar Europe: From Cold War to European Union*, ed. Joanna Regulska and Bonnie G. Smith (London and New York: Routledge, 2012), 7. For examples of earlier routes of protest, see for example, Kristina Schulz, *Der lange Atem der Provokation: Die Frauenbewegung in der Bundesrepublik und in Frankreich 1968–1976* (Frankfurt/M. and New York: Campus, 2012); Carol Giardina, *Freedom for Women: Forging the Women's Liberation Movement, 1953–1970* (Gainesville: University Press of Florida, 2010); and Martin Klimke, *The Other Alliance: Student Protest in West Germany and the United States in the Global Sixties* (Princeton, NJ: Princeton University Press, 2010).

9. See Ulrich Herbert and Axel Schildt, eds., *Kriegsende in Europa: Vom Beginn des deutschen Machtzerfalls bis zur Stabilisierung der Nachkriegsordnung 1944–1948* (Essen: Klartext, 1998); Klaus Naumann, ed., *Nachkrieg in Deutschland* (Hamburg: Hamburg Edition, 2001); Richard Bessel and Dirk Schumann, eds., *Life After Death: Approaches to a Social and Cultural History of Europe during the 1940s and 1950* (Cambridge, UK: Cambridge University Press, 2003); Konrad H. Jarausch, *After Hitler: Recivilizing Germans, 1945–1995* (Oxford: Oxford University Press, 2006); Richard Bessel, *Germany 1945: From War to Peace* (New York: Harper Collins, 2009); and Frank Biess and Robert Moeller, eds., *Histories of the Aftermath: The Legacies of the Second World War in Europe* (New York: Berghahn Books, 2010).

10. One early example is Claire Duchen and Irene Bandhauser-Schöffman, eds., *When the War Was Over: Women, War and Peace in Europe, 1940–1956* (Leicester, UK: Leicester University Press, 2000); a more recent one is Regulska and Smith, *Women and Gender in Postwar Europe*.

11. Important studies on the postwar women's gender history for the two Germanys include Erica Carter, *How German Is She?: Postwar West German Reconstruction and the Consuming Woman* (Ann Arbor: University of Michigan Press, 1997); Uta Poiger, *Jazz, Rock, and Rebels: Cold War Politics and American Culture in a Divided Germany* (Berkeley: University of California Press, 2000); Moeller, *Protecting Motherhood*; Frank Biess, *Homecomings: Returning POWs and the Legacies of Defeat in Postwar Germany* (Princeton, NJ: Princeton University Press, 2006); Marianne Zepp, *Redefining Germany: Reeducation, Staatsbürgerschaft und Frauenpolitik im US-amerikanisch besetzten Nachkriegsdeutschland*

(Göttingen: Vandenhoeck & Ruprecht, 2007). For the postwar United States, see Elaine Tyler May, *Homeward Bound: American Families in the Cold War Era*, rev. ed. (New York: Basic Books, 2008); Joanne Meyerowitz, ed., *Not June Cleaver: Women and Gender in Postwar America, 1945–1960* (Philadelphia: Temple University Press, 1994); Jessica Weiss, *To Have and to Hold: Marriage, the Baby Boom, and Social Change* (Chicago: University of Chicago Press, 2000); Emilie Stoltzfus, *Citizen, Mother, Worker: Debating Public Responsibility for Child Care after the Second World War* (Chapel Hill: University of North Carolina Press, 2003); Steve Estes, *I Am a Man! Race, Manhood, and the Civil Rights Movement* (Chapel Hill: University of North Carolina Press, 2005); and Natalie Fousekis, *Demanding Child Care: Women's Activism and the Politics of Welfare, 1940–1941* (Urbana Champaign: University of Illinois Press, 2011). Several studies also focus on US occupation forces: Petra Goedde, *GIs and Germans: Culture, Gender and Foreign Relations, 1945–1949* (New Haven, CT: Yale University Press, 2003); and Maria Höhn and Seungsook Moon, eds., *Over There: Living with the U.S. Military Empire from World War Two to the Present* (Durham, NC: Duke University Press, 2010)

12. See Karen Hagemann, Konrad H. Jarausch, and Cristina Allemann-Ghionda, "Children, Families, and States: Time Policies of Childcare and Schooling in a Comparative Historical Perspective," in *Children, Families, and States: Time Policies of Child Care, Preschool, and Primary Education in Europe*, eds. Karen Hagemann, Konrad H. Jarausch, and Cristina Allemann-Ghionda (Oxford and New York: Berghahn Books, 2011), 3–50.

13. Keith Lowe, *Savage Continent: Europe in the Aftermath of World War II* (New York: St Martin's Press, 2012); R.M. Douglas, *Orderly and Humane: The Expulsion of the Germans after the Second World War* (New Haven, CT: Yale University Press, 2012).

14. Atina Grossmann, *Jews, Germans, and Allies: Close Encounters in Occupied Germany* (Princeton, NJ: Princeton University Press, 2007); Tara Zahra, *The Lost Children: Reconstructing Europe's Families after World War II* (Cambridge, MA: Harvard University Press, 2011); Gerard Daniel Cohen, *In War's Wake: Europe's Displaced Persons in the Postwar Order* (New York: Oxford University Press, 2011); and Lowe, *Savage Continent*, chap. 3.

15. Dagmar Herzog, ed. *Brutality and Desire: War and Sexuality in Europe's Twentieth Century* (Basingstoke: Palgrave Macmillan, 2009); Grossmann, *Jews, Germans, and Allies*.

16. See Regina Mühlhäuser, *Eroberungen: Sexuelle Gewalttaten und intime Beziehungen deutscher Soldaten in der Sowjetunion, 1941–1945* (Hamburg: Hamburg Edition, 2010); and Mary Louise Roberts, *What Soldiers Do: Sex and the American GI in World War II France* (Chicago: University of Chicago Press, 2013).

17. Michael Wieck, *Zeugnis vom Untergang Königsbergs: Ein "Geltungsjude" berichtet* (Heidelberg: Heidelberger Verlagsanstalt und Druckerei, 1990), 261.

18. See also Irene Stoehr, "Der Mütterkongreß fand nicht statt: Frauenbewegung, Staatsmänner und Kalter Krieg 1950," *WerkstattGeschichte* 17 (1997): 66–82. For similar efforts on the part of American occupation officials in Japan, see Mire Koikari, *Pedagogy of Democracy: Feminism and the Cold War in the U.S. Occupation of Japan* (Philadelphia: Temple University Press, 2009).

19. For the role of cinema in the reconstruction of the postwar gender order, see also Ulrike Sieglohr, ed., *Heroines without Heroes: Reconstructing Female and National Identities in European Cinema, 1945–1951* (London and New York: Cassell, 2000).

20. See Moeller, *Protecting Motherhood*.

21. On the struggle in the 1950s, see for example, Donna Harsch, *Revenge of the Domestic: Women, the Family, and Communism in the German Democratic Republic* (Princeton, NJ: Princeton University Press 2007); Elizabeth Heineman, *What Difference Does a Husband Make?: Women and Marital Status in Nazi and Postwar Germany* (Berkeley: University of California Press, 1999); Christine Franzius, *Bonner Grundgesetz und Familienrecht: die Diskussion um die Gleichberechtigung von Mann und Frau in der westdeutschen Zivilrechtslehre der Nachkriegszeit, 1945–1957* (Frankfurt/M.: Klostermann Verlag, 2005); Carola Sachse, *Der Hausarbeitstag: Gerechtigkeit und Gleichberechtigung in Ost und West, 1939–1994* (Göttingen: Vandenhoeck & Ruprecht, 2002).

22. See for example, Ute Frevert, "Frauen auf dem Weg zur Gleichberechtigung—Hindernisse, Umleitungen, Einbahnstraßen," in *Zäsuren nach 1945: Essays zur Periodisierung der deutschen Nachkriegsgeschichte*, ed. Martin Broszat (Munich: Oldenbourg, 1990), 113–30; also Schulz, *Der lange Atem*; as a comparison of West Germany and the United States, Stefanie Ehmsen, *Der Marsch der Frauenbewegung durch die Institutionen: Die Vereinigten Staaten und die Bundesrepublik im Vergleich* (Münster: Westfälisches Dampfboot, 2007).

23. In practice, the policy also discriminated against homosexuals; see Margot Canaday, *The Straight State: Sexuality and Citizenship in 20th-Century America* (Princeton, NJ: Princeton University Press, 2011), chap. 4.

24. Alice Kessler-Harris, *Out to Work: A History of Wage-Earning Women in the United States*, 20th anniversary edition (New York: Oxford University Press, 2003), chaps. 10–11.

25. Sonya Michel, *Children's Interests / Mothers' Rights: The Shaping of America's Child Care Policy* (New Haven, CT: Yale University Press, 1999), chaps. 4–5; Stoltzfus, *Citizen, Mother, Worker*; and Fousekis, *Demanding Child Care*.

26. See May, *Homeward Bound;* and Lizabeth Cohen, *A Consumers' Republic: The Politics of Mass Consumption in Postwar America* (New York: Vintage Books, 2003).

27. See also Robert Moeller, "Winning the Peace at the Movies: Suffering, Loss, and Redemption in Postwar German Cinema," in Biess and Moeller, *Histories of the Aftermath*, 138–55.

28. See also Biess, *Homecomings*; Svenja Goltermann, *Die Gesellschaft der Überlebenden: deutsche Kriegsheimkehrer und ihre Gewalterfahrungen im Zweiten Weltkrieg* (Munich: Deutsche Verlags-Anstalt, 2009).

29. See Alice Holmes Cooper, *Paradoxes of Peace: German Peace Movements since 1945* (Ann Arbor: University of Michigan Press, 1996); and Thomas Kühne, ed. *Von der Kriegskultur zur Friedenskultur? Zum Mentalitätswandel in Deutschland nach 1945* (Münster: LIT, 2000).

30. See Christine Eifler, "Bewaffneter Friede: Zum Konzept der Friedenssicherung in der DDR und seinen geschlechterpolitischen Implikationen," in *Frieden, Gewalt, Geschlecht: Friedens- und Konfliktforschung als Geschlechterforschung*, ed. Karen Hagemann, Jennifer Davy and Ute Kätzel (Essen: Klartext, 2005), 205–21.

31. In *What Soldiers Do*, Mary Louise Roberts seeks to undermine this myth.

32. Serving in the occupation forces also strengthened African American men's resolve to claim their civil rights; see Maria Höhn and Martin Klimke, *A Breath of Freedom: The Civil Rights Movement, African American GIs, and Germany* (New York: Palgrave Macmillan, 2010).

33. See Poiger, *Jazz, Rock, and Rebels*; Höhn, *GIs and Frauleins*; Heide Fehrenbach, *Race After Hitler: Black Occupation Children in Postwar Germany and America* (Princeton, NJ: Princeton University Press 2005); and Höhn and Klimke, *Breath of Freedom*. The intersections of race and gender politics were foreshadowed when the US military established forward bases in Hawaii during the war; see Beth Bailey and David Farber, *The First Strange Place: Race and Sex in World War II Hawaii* (Baltimore, MD: Johns Hopkins University Press, 1994).

34. On the family and the West German welfare state, see Heineman, *What Difference*; Moeller, *Protecting Motherhood*; Merith Niehuss, *Familie, Frau und Gesellschaft: Studien zur Strukturgeschichte der Familie in Westdeutschland 1945-1960* (Göttingen: Vandenhoeck & Ruprecht, 2001); Christiane Kuller, *Familienpolitik im föderativen Sozialstaat: Die Formierung eines Politikfeldes in der Bundesrepublik 1949–1975* (Munich: Oldenbourg, 2004); on East-Germany, see Gesine Obertreis, *Familienpolitik in der DDR, 1945–1980* (Opladen: Leske + Budrich, 1985); Heike Trappe, *Emanzipation oder Zwang?: Frauen in der DDR zwischen Beruf, Familie und Sozialpolitik* (Berlin: Akademie Verlag, 1995); Harsch, *Revenge of the Domestic*; for a comparison of East and West Germany, see Sachse, *Hausarbeitstag*. For the impact of the Cold War on American families, see May, *Homeward Bound*; and Weiss, *To Have and to Hold*.

35. See Harsch, *Revenge of the Domestic*.

36. See Maria Höhn, *GIs and Frauleins: The German-American Encounter in 1950s West Germany* (Chapel Hill: University of North Carolina Press, 2002); and Fehrenbach, *Race After Hitler*. For an interesting cinematic portrayal of this situation, see the 1952 West German feature film *Toxi*, directed by Robert Stemmle.

37. See, for example, Gary Gerstle, *American Crucible: Race and Nation in the Twentieth Century* (Princeton, NJ: Princeton University Press, 2001); Thomas A. Gugliemo, *White on Arrival: Italians, Race, Color, and Power in Chicago, 1890–1945* (New York: Oxford University Press, 2004); and David R. Roediger, *How American Immigrants Became White: The Strange Journey from Ellis Island to the Suburbs* (New York: Basic Books, 2006).

38. For a comparative study of thirteen European countries, including East and West Germany, see Hagemann et al., *Children, Families, and States*; as a direct comparison of the FRG and the GDR, see Karen Hagemann, "Between Ideology and Economy: The 'Time Politics' of Child Care and Public Education in the Two Germanys," *Social Politics* 13, no. 1 (2006): 217–60. The American school lunch program had very different roots; see Susan Levine, *School Lunch Politics: The Surprising History of America's Favorite Welfare Program* (Princeton, NJ: Princeton University Press, 2010).

39. Dictated, but seldom realized; see Wendy Z. Goldman, *Women, the State, and Revolution: Soviet Family Policy and Social Life, 1917–1936* (New York: Cambridge University Press, 1993); and Alena Heitlinger, *Women and State Socialism: Sex Inequality in the Soviet Union and Czechoslovakia* (Montreal: McGill-Queen's University Press, 1979).

40. On the rivalry between the United States and the Soviet Union on this score, see Greg Castillo, *Cold War on the Home Front: The Soft Power of Midcentury Design* (Minneapolis: University of Minnesota Press, 2010).

41. Kleßmann, "Abgrenzung und Verflechtung"; for the complicated relations of East and West Germany, see Jarausch, *After Hitler*.

42. See also Harsch, *Revenge of the Domestic.*

43. On American welfare state development, see Alice Kessler-Harris, *In Pursuit of Equity* (New York: Oxford University Press, 2003); and Premilla Nadasen, Jennifer Mittelstadt, and Marisa Chappell, eds., *Welfare in the United States: A History with Documents, 1935– 1996* (New York: Routledge, 2009).

44. The overwhelming majority of service members in the all-volunteer army are male. In 1983, the percentage of women was 9.8 percent; in 2009, this had risen to 15.5 percent; see Bernard D. Rostker, "I Want You! The Evolution of the All-Volunteer Force," *Rand Corporation Monograph*, MG 265 Santa Monica, CA: Rand Corporation, 2006), http://www.rand.org/pubs/monographs/MG265.html, retrieved January 28, 2013.

45. See Karen Hagemann, "A West-German 'Sonderweg'? Family, Work, and the Half-Day Time Policy of Childcare and Schooling," in Hagemann et al., *Children, Families, and States*, 275–300.

46. See Christine von Oertzen, *The Pleasure of a Surplus Income: Part-Time Work, Gender Politics, and Social Change in West Germany, 1955–1969* (New York: Berghahn Books, 2007).

47. John D'Emilio, *Sexual Politics, Sexual Communities* 2nd ed. (Chicago: University of Chicago Press, 1998), chaps. 2–3.

48. See, for example, John D'Emilio, *Making Trouble: Essays on Gay History, Politics, and the University* (New York: Routledge, 1992), chap. 3, "The Homosexual Menace: The Politics of Sexuality in Cold War America."

49. Dagmar Herzog, *Sex after Fascism: Memory and Morality in Twentieth-Century Germany* (Princeton, NJ: Princeton University Press, 2005).

50. Elizabeth Heineman, *Before Porn was Legal: The Erotica Empire of Beate Uhse* (Chicago: University of Chicago Press, 2011); also Sybille Steinbacher, *Wie der Sex nach Deutschland kam: Der Kampf um Sittlichkeit und Anstand in der frühen Bundesrepublik* (Munich: Siedler, 2011).

51. Herzog, *Sex after Fascism*; also Herzog, *Sexuality in Europe: A Twentieth-Century History* (Cambridge and New York: Cambridge University Press, 2011.

52. See Herzog, *Sex after Fascism*, chaps. 5 and 6.

53. On the GDR, see Castillo, *Cold War*, chaps. 3-4.

54. See Rosalyn Baxandall and Elizabeth Ewen, *Picture Windows: How the Suburbs Happened* (New York: Basic Books, 2001); more generally for the United States, see Meyerowitz, *Not June Cleaver.*

55. Höhn and Klimke, *Breath of Freedom.*

56. Myra M. Ferree, William Gamson and Jürgen Gerhards, *Shaping Abortion Discourse: Democracy and the Public Sphere in Germany and the United States* (Cambridge and New York: Cambridge University Press, 2002).

57. Here we are extending an argument originally made in Moeller, *Protecting Motherhood.*

58. Statisches Bundesamt, "Mikrozensus 2003: Müttererwerbstätigkeit steigt," news release no. 191 (April 28, 2004).

59. Sarah Schaschek, "Studie zu Frauen, Familie und Beruf Junge Frauen stehen unter großem Druck," *Tagespiegel*, September 11, 2013.

60. Consider, for example, the popularity of books like Facebook executive Sheryl Sandberg's *Lean In: Women, Work, and the Will to Lead* (New York: Knopf, 2013), which was endorsed by Anne-Marie Slaughter, former US State Department Director of policy planning, in her review, "Yes, You Can," *New York Times Sunday Book Review*, March 7, 2013; see also Slaughter, "Why Women Still Can't Have It All," *The Atlantic* (July-August 2012), 84–102.

Part I

Gendering the Aftermath of War

Chapter 1

The "Big Rape": Sex and Sexual Violence, War, and Occupation in German Post–World War II Memory and Imagination[1]

Atina Grossmann

The defeated Germany that the victors encountered in spring 1945 wore a predominantly female face. German men had been killed, wounded, or taken prisoner, leaving women to clear the ruins, scrounge for material survival, and serve the occupiers, often as sexual partners and victims.[2] After years of remarkable inattention since the 1950s, and provoked in part by the sexual violence associated with the conflicts in the former Yugoslavia in the early 1990s, Red Army rapes became the subject of vigorous scholarly and feminist debates on German women's role in the Third Reich. The sixtieth anniversary of the end of World War II, with its new emphasis on publicly recognizing—and legitimizing—German suffering, as well as a growing popular awareness of rape as a war crime in civil and ethnic conflicts, brought renewed attention to German women's victimization, albeit in a less carefully contextualized manner than the broader and long-overdue international political and legal activism about contemporary sexual violence in conflict zones which began in the 1990s.[3] The numbers reported for these rapes vary wildly, from as few as 20,000 to almost one million or even two million altogether as the Red Army pounded westward. A conservative estimate might be about 110,000 women raped, many more than once, of whom up to 10,000 died during or as a result of the assaults; others suggest that perhaps 1 in 3 of the approximately 1.5 million women in Berlin fell victim to Soviet rapes.[4]

Whatever the figures, it is unquestionably the case that mass rapes of civilian German women signaled the end of the war and the defeat of Nazi Germany.[5] Soviet rapes secured a particularly potent place in postwar memories of victimization, because they represented one instance in which Goebbels' spectacular anti-Bolshevik propaganda turned out to be substantially correct. Millions of Germans were trekking westward in flight from the Red Army and millions of German soldiers were marching eastward as prisoners of war (POWs), but as Berliners—primarily women, children, and the elderly—emerged from their cellars during the piercingly beautiful spring of 1945, the Soviets did not kill everyone on sight, deport them to Siberia, or burn down the city. As the musician Karla Höcker reported with genuine surprise, in one of the many diaries composed by women at war's end, "the Russians, who must hate and fear us, leave the majority of the German civilian population entirely alone—that they don't transport us off in droves!"[6]

In fact, the Soviet Military Administration (SMA) moved quickly and efficiently to organize municipal government, restore basic services, and nurture a lively political and cultural life. In regard to violence against women, however, the Nazi horror stories (*Greuelgeschichten*) were largely confirmed. Official Soviet policy, however, obstinately refused to acknowledge that soldiers, who had sworn to be "honorable, brave, disciplined, and alert" and to defend the "motherland manfully, ably, with dignity and honor," would engage in atrocities on anything more than the level of "isolated excesses."[7] Ilya Ehrenburg, having quickly assimilated Stalin's new more conciliatory line toward compliant Germans, insisted, "The Soviet soldier will not molest a German woman . . . . It is not for booty, not for loot, not for women that he has come to Germany."[8] "'Russian soldiers not rape! German swine rape!'" a Soviet interrogator bellowed at the actress Hildegard Knef when she was captured after having disguised herself as a soldier in an effort to escape the female fate of the defeated.[9]

Clearly, however, that new message did not impress troops engaged in a costly final battle, who had been told that "every farm on the road to Berlin was the den of a fascist beast."[10] As exhausted, brutalized Red Army troops— "a raucous armada of men with their trousers down" as one officer described his men during their "hour of revenge"—finally crossed into Germany, they entered not only the fascist lair but also a still capitalist world of "butter, honey, jam, wine, and various kinds of brandy."[11] Shocked at the continuing

32

affluence of the society they had so determinedly defeated, and the contrast to their own decimated country, Russian soldiers told their victims, "Russia my homeland, Germany my paradise."[12]

For German women in 1945—certainly in Berlin and to its east—these Soviet rapes were experienced as a collective event in a situation of general crisis, part of the apocalyptic days of Berlin's and Nazism's fall. "Rape had," many noted, "become routine"; the story of sexual violence was told as part of the narrative of survival in ruined Germany.[13] A certain matter-of-factness (*Sachlichkeit*), in some ways still reminiscent of the pre-Nazi Weimar New Woman, pervades many of these accounts. Margret Boveri, a journalist who had continued working throughout the Nazi years, was laconic about the Soviet "liberators" in her Berlin "Survival Diary" for May 8, 1945: "The usual rapes—a neighbor who resisted was shot. . . . Mrs. Krauss was not raped. She insists that Russians don't touch women who wear glasses. Like to know if that is true . . . the troops were pretty drunk but did distinguish between old and young which is already progress."[14] Others accepted their fate as an inevitable, to-be-expected consequence of defeat, almost like a natural disaster that could not be changed and must simply be survived: "In those days I endured the Russians as I would a thunderstorm."[15]

This article analyzes the remarkably open, both unsentimental and sensationalized, descriptions, by both Germans and occupiers, of sexual violence and sexual fraternization in defeated Berlin, as recorded by a wide variety of observers and participants, themselves often an overlapping category. It relies on contemporary reportage, diaries, memoirs, and film as well as later popular literature and cinema. Portrayals of Berlin's wild trade in coerced, instrumental, and voluntary sex—along with reflections about how to name, define, and distinguish among those experiences—constitute a pervasive and changing theme in memories and imaginings of the chaotic, immediate postwar years. This chapter considers the multiple ways that Red Army sexual violence was parsed and understood, reflects on the rather different narrations of American "sexual antics," and concludes with a consideration of the fraught and complex connections between sexual violence and fraternization in both West and East Germany, especially as it was, and remains, inflected by categories of nation, ethnicity, and race. Above all, the analysis seeks to take seriously women's own portrayals of themselves as resourceful agents and not merely helpless victims (or villains) in a tumultuous historical moment.

Surviving and Narrating Rape

In diaries composed at the time as well as in reworked diaries, memoirs, and oral histories recorded years later, women reported extremely diverse experiences of what they variously named as rape, coercion, violation, prostitution, or abuse. Indeed, the more one looks at the diaries, memoirs, and novels of the postwar years, the more one sees that rape stories are omnipresent, told matter-of-factly, told as tragedy, told with ironic humor and flourish. In a recurring trope, women are gathered at water pumps in bombed-out streets, exchanging "war stories" with a certain bravado. Sometimes women recounted stories of surprising escape or reprieve; often they resorted to generalities and passive voice (the awful scenes went on all night, we all had to submit), or referred specifically to the horrific experiences of neighbors, mothers, and sisters which they themselves had supposedly been spared. "But many fewer escaped than was later claimed," journalist Curt Riess asserted a few years later.[16]

In a compelling diary edited and published by a popular German writer in the 1950s, an anonymous "woman in Berlin"—now identified as Marta Hillers, another young journalist who had continued to work in the Third Reich—recounted how, after a series of brutal rapes during the first chaotic week of April-May 1945, she decided, "It is perfectly clear. I need a wolf here who will keep the wolves away from me. An officer, as high as possible, Kommandant, General, whatever I can get."[17]

Such unsentimental directness in reporting and dealing with sexual assaults or efforts to elude them was quite typical. Curt Riess, a Berlin Jew who had returned, with deeply "mixed feelings," as a reporter with an American passport, was both horrified and cynical: "But it was strange, when the horrific had happened five or six times, it was no longer so horrific. That which one had thought one could not survive, was survived by many twenty—or thirty times."[18] Another younger Berlin Jew, who had returned from Auschwitz, recorded with bittersweet amusement an exchange between two women in the familiar rough (and quite untranslatable) Berlin dialect that, almost despite himself, he was happy to hear again. Justifying her usurpation of a space on an overcrowded train, one loudly announced, "We Berliners had to let the bombs whip around our heads. I sat in a bunker for almost two weeks, was bombed out four times, and the Russians didn't exactly treat me with kid gloves either; in fact they raped me three times if you really want to know." This revelation provoked her equally loudmouthed competitor to an often-reported retort: "She actually seems to be proud that at her age the Russians would still take her."[19]

In a peculiar way, women's apparent sangfroid in the face of mass sexual assault became part of the story (and myth) of "Berlin *kommt wieder*," of the city's irrepressible irreverent spirit. Their self-preserving sexual cynicism can be attributed, at least in part, both to the modernist *Sachlichkeit* of Weimar culture and to the loosened mores of the Nazis' war, including women's experience of fraternization with foreign laborers recruited or forced into the war economy. Even more broadly, the fraying of bourgeois morality that had alarmed cultural conservatives at least since World War I and the Weimar Republic clearly continued into the Third Reich and the Second World War, albeit in complex and selective ways—a process recently delineated by Dagmar Herzog in her provocative study of sexuality during and "after fascism." The war had inevitably and paradoxically led to a loosening of domestic bonds and an eroticization "of public life," unevenly prosecuted, sometimes denounced, and sometimes accepted by the populace. Indeed, as Annemarie Tröger argued in an important 1986 essay, the dissociative endurance with which women survived rape as well as their instrumental fraternizing affairs bore an uncanny resemblance to the matter-of-fact encounters in the Weimar "new woman" novels of Irmgard Keun or Marieluise Fleisser. German women, Tröger contended, had been trained into a sexual cynicism "freed *from* love," which served them well during the war and its aftermath.[20] In Annemarie Weber's autobiographical postwar novel *Westend*, the main character narrates her rape with precisely the cool distant tone associated with New Woman writers: "He carried out the act which he perhaps saw as a kind of self-imposed duty coldly and without interest. She felt sorry for the man on top of her."[21]

The Russian (*Russe*), whose arrival had been so desperately anticipated by victims and opponents of Nazism and so dreaded by most Germans, became, in Berlin, an object not only of terror but of intense fascination and bewilderment. In keeping with the images provided by Nazi propaganda, he appeared as the drunken, primitive "Mongol" who descended on Germany like a vengeful "hungry locust" in an "orgy of revenge." These "slanty-eyed ravagers" from the Far Eastern steppes demanded watches, bicycles, and women; they had no clue that a flush toilet was not a sink or a refrigerator, and were astounded that the wurst they had stored in the tank disappeared when a handle was pulled. They loaded expensive precision instruments for transfer to the Soviet Union as if they were potato sacks, only to have them rust on blocked roads or train tracks.[22]

The Soviets baffled their conquests with their strange behavior. As one woman remembered, "we never could quite make sense of the Russians, sometimes they were mild-mannered, sometimes sadistic."[23] They assaulted women but were tender and protective toward children and babies. They brazenly ripped a watch off someone's arm or grabbed a bicycle, and then offered a big bear hug, two kisses on the cheeks, and a friendly farewell. Women reported that their attackers could be distracted or even cowed, like a child or puppy, by firm commands. Or they seemed genuinely convinced that looting constituted proper restitution, and that rape too was merely part of their due. Both Germans and the other Allies were intrigued by the Soviets' capacity for drink, debauchery, and eye-popping portions of caviar. "We went to Berlin in 1945, thinking only of the Russians as big, jolly, balalaika-playing fellows, who drank prodigious quantities of vodka and liked to wrestle in the drawing room," US Commander Frank Howley recalled.[24] They had arrived not only with tanks and deafening cannons (the *Stalinorgel*, or Stalin's organ, that figures in so many memoirs) but with horse- and even camel-drawn vehicles; they quaffed gasoline and 4711 cologne in their endless search for alcohol. A Jewish youth remembered his first glimpses of his liberators, "They were dressed in olive-brown, high collar blouses and had rope belts around their waists. Their pants were stuffed into their boots. I had never seen anything like them. If they hadn't been so terrifying, they might have funny."[25] These contradictory impressions reflected the generally schizoid quality of the Soviet occupation: "By day they put the Germans, both men and women, to work in dismantling commandos, clearing up rubble, removing tank barricades; and by night they terrorized the city," even as some officers were moved to shoot offending soldiers on the spot.[26]

The rapacious "Ivan" was accompanied by the cultivated officer who spoke German, recited Dostoyevsky and Tolstoy, and deplored the excesses of his comrades, even as he used the threat of their assaults as a lure to attract "consensual" sex. Germans frequently counterposed these "cultivated" Soviets from European Russia to the equally if differently fascinating American occupiers who—rehearsing images of American POWs in Nazi newsreels—were categorized as vulgar, gum-chewing primitives. GI conquests, however, came primarily via nylons and chocolate, rather than rape. "The difference," Berliners quipped, "is that the American and the British ask the girls to dinner and then go to bed with them, while the Russians do it the other way round."[27] Yet the remarkably frank diary entries of one Ukrainian Jewish Red Army officer, who professed himself horrified by the depredations of his comrades, differed little from the pleased descriptions of their "fraternization" experiences by American occupiers: German women in Berlin begged him,

36

"I'm willing, just fuck me (*fick-fick*), I'll do anything you want, just rescue me from all these men."[28]

In the end perhaps, the many negative but also confused interpretations of the Soviets' behavior helped women to distance themselves from the horror of their own experience. The narrative of the Russian primitive or exotic curiously absolved him of guilt, as it also absolved women themselves. Such uncivilized, animal-like creatures could not be expected to control themselves, especially when tanked up with alcohol. Nor could women be expected to defend themselves against an elemental force, backed up, of course, in most cases by rifle or revolver. As one woman remembered, after the initial panic about a fate worse than death, "It became clear to me that a rape, as awful as it might be, had nothing to do with loss of honor."[29]

Not a few women favorably compared Russian officers to contemptible, defeated German men who either abetted women's humiliation or sought to punish them for it, sometimes to the point of killing them to preserve their male honor. Pathetic parodies of the manly Teutonic genus valorized by Nazi propaganda, preoccupied with saving their own skin, they were not above pressuring women to submit in order not to endanger themselves; rape, after all, was a less horrific fate than being sent to Siberia or getting shot. The anonymous narrator of *Ein Frau in Berlin* (*A Woman in Berlin*) wrote of the Soviet officer whom she finally cornered into her bed, hoping that he would fend off rivals: "On the other hand, I do like the Major, I like him the more as a person, the less he wants from me as a man . . . . Because among all the male creatures of the last several days he is the most tolerable man and human being.[30]

In the 1951 potboiler *The Big Rape*, American war correspondent James W. Burke's "composite" heroine Lilo describes her (temporary) protector Captain Pavel Ivanov in remarkably similar terms. He "was all that she had bargained for. He was kind, he was considerate, he was gallant. And he safeguarded her from wanton attack." Lilo in turn was determined not to have "painstakingly preserved her life thus far to foolishly lay it down at the altar of such a spurious and pretentious virtue."[31]

The turn of the millennium explosion of memory (and memory politics) about German suffering during and after the war relies in part on the nagging sense that this victimization was never adequately expressed or recognized and always overshadowed in both West and East Germany by the demand for a recognition of collective guilt for Germany's crimes. This insistence on what historians have called "the silence that never was" certainly applies to popular perceptions that German women's massive and collective experience of sexual assault was quickly and profoundly silenced or treated as taboo. It is indeed the case that the ubiquitous stories of rape were downplayed or "normalized" by virtually everyone, including, in many ways, by the victims themselves. Depending on who was talking, rapes were presented as the inevitable byproduct of a vicious war, or, in the "antifascist" narrative, as understandable retribution or exaggerated anticommunist propaganda.[32] In no way, however, did these framings mean that rape stories were denied or silenced. On the contrary, in the direct aftermath of the war, there was no lack of speech or documentation about rape. If anything, we find a plethora of talk in many different voices and venues, although it is indeed difficult to measure those expressions against our current expectations of treating and "working through" trauma.

Given the realities of mass rape, German communists and SMA authorities could not, particularly during the immediate postwar years of 1945 through 1947, impose a total silence around Red Army actions. They sought instead to find ways of containing both the massive incidence of rapes and the conversation about them. They denied, minimized, justified, and shifted responsibility. They freely admitted violations, excesses, abuses, and unfortunate incidents and vowed to bring them under control (or to demand that the Soviet army do so). But they also trivialized rape, as an inevitable part of normal brutal warfare, as comparable to Allied violations, and as understandable if not entirely excusable in view of the atrocities perpetrated on the Russians by the Germans. In a common pattern of simultaneous acknowledgment and denial, party memos and press reports referred frequently and openly to (purportedly unjustified) rumors of rape by Red Army soldiers, thereby reproducing and disseminating stories that, their coding as rumors or pernicious anti-Soviet propaganda notwithstanding, everyone presumably knew to be true. The *Berliner Zeitung*, which often resorted to cartoon characters speaking in Berlin dialect to explain unpopular positions (such as unwillingness to take responsibility for having profited from "aryanized" Jewish property), even ran a cartoon strip satirizing women's fears while encouraging their labor as *Trümmerfrauen* (rubble women). Under the headline, "Mongols in Berlin, the latest rumor" (*Flüstergeschichte*, literally, whispered story), the sensible Frau Piesepampel informs her hysterical neighbor Frau Schwabbel that she has "no time for such nonsense" and no intention of worrying about "Mongols" now that the war was finally over. There was cleanup work to be done and she would not be distracted.[33] And while Soviet officers did sometimes exact summary punishment by shooting soldiers accused of rape, few worried as did the dissident Lev Kopolev in his memoirs of life as a political officer in the Red

Army, "Why did so many of our soldiers turn out to be common bandits, raping women and girls one after another—on the side of the road, in the snow, in doorways? How did this all become possible?" His "bourgeois human[ist]" compunctions led to his arrest for being pro-German.[34]

All protestations notwithstanding, it was generally if not explicitly acknowledged that the Communist party's embarrassing loss to the Social Democratic party in Berlin's first open elections in 1946 was due in no small part to a heavily female electorate remembering and responding to the actions of the Soviet "friends."[35] The Soviets had worked hard to present themselves as liberators, organizing city services, licensing newspapers and political parties, and promoting cultural revival, but in many ways their efforts came too late; the damage of the first few weeks could not be undone. In his report to the London paper *The Observer*, Isaac Deutscher had predicted, "Next Sunday the women of Berlin will take their revenge against the humiliations that were forced upon them during the first weeks of occupation." The election results indicated that he was right.[36]

Rape continued to figure in German narratives of victimization for many years. Public conversation, however, so common in the immediate postwar period, despite all communist and SMA efforts to block the discussion, was indeed curtailed in both East and West once conditions had somewhat normalized. With the return of POWs and the "remasculinization"[37] of German society, the topic was suppressed, deemed humiliating for German men and too risky for women who feared—with much justification, given the reports of estrangement and even murder—the reactions of their menfolk. But rape stories continued to circulate and indeed were repeatedly invoked or alluded to by contemporary chroniclers, both German and occupier. In immediate reports and in later memoirs, women reported over and over that the cry "*Frau komm*" still rang in their ears.[38] Moreover, the importance of Berlin as the conquered capital and the millions of refugees from the east who poured into western Germany assured the centrality of rape stories in memories of defeat, even in areas where there had never been a Red Army soldier.

Rape and American Conquerors

The continuing prominence of rape in German narratives of victimization in the period 1945–1949 was not, however, as suggested by East German communists, due to propaganda by the Western Allies. When Colonel Howley, who had served as the first US commander in Berlin, published his virulently anticommunist memoirs in 1950, he wrote at length about the horrors of the Soviet regime of rape, murder, and looting.[39] But in his earlier official military reports from Berlin, he had downplayed German anxieties about crime, disorder, and hunger. With a touch of sarcasm, he noted that the per capita crime rate in 1945–46 Berlin was lower than that of most cities in the United States, especially New York![40]

Even among the Americans, therefore, where such tales might have served as useful anticommunist propaganda, the discussion was restrained. In the early occupation years, US officials were far from seizing on rape stories to discredit their Soviet allies and competitors, whom they viewed as "hard bargaining, hard playing, hard drinking, hard bodied, and hard headed."[41] Russians might be barbarian rapists, but they were also tough fighters and exotic celebrators who could drink, eat, and copulate prodigiously—often to the admiring frustration of US colleagues unable to match their levels of activity. Nor were Americans necessarily unsympathetic to Soviet "excesses." Shortly before the war ended, a *Newsweek* reporter had no trouble explaining a rape "behind the barn" by a liberated Soviet POW who had been "badly treated, particularly by a farmer's daughter who was a Hitler Maiden and took delight in trying to prove the Russians were second class human beings," as an act of "justice."[42] More than ten years later, in his lurid 1956 novel, *fräulein*, the American writer James McGovern sneered, "Poor Frau Graubach. When she had voted *ja*, she had not bargained for this."[43]

On September 6, 1945, US Military Government officer John Maginnis noted, "We had another incident tonight. . . . The MPs were called in by the German police on an attempted rape by two Russians which ended in a shooting contest. Captain Bond went along to see the fun [sic] and almost got himself killed. The Russians were subdued but one of the MPs was shot in the thigh. I gave Captain Bond a good dressing down for getting mixed up in such a brawl; he should have known better."[44] This generally lighthearted tone of American reporting about Soviet abuses surely had something to do with the fact that the US forces had their own problems, not only with fraternization and prostitution, but also with sexual violence.[45] When William Griffith took over as a denazification officer for the Military Government in Bavaria, where there were many more American troops than in divided Berlin, he discovered that an important military police task was "largely to parade weeping German rape victims past their suspected GI assailants for identification." Luckily for the GIs, "the poor girls, I regret to say, never identified any of our soldiers."[46]

As American reporters Bud Hutton and Andy Rooney smirked about Soviet rapes, "The great novelty for the United States Army was, however, that for the first time in the history of living man someone was behaving worse than the American soldier."[47]

If German communists worried about the effects of Red Army behavior on support for the occupation and the Socialist Unity Party they had established in April 1946, American officials and journalists certainly also debated the corrupting effects—on both occupier and occupied—of servicemen's looting, brawling, raping, and general "sexual antics."[48] Defeat and military occupation, with their enormous pressures to engage in instrumental sex, make it in many cases difficult to disentangle coercive, pragmatic, and what might be called genuinely consensual sex. Kay Boyle captured this ambiguous state well in one of her "Military Occupation Group" short stories, when an American occupier declares, "Let me tell you that Berlin's the territory for the man who's got a flair. They're still pretty hungry there, so they come to terms without too much of an argument."[49] Thomas Berger's fiercely comic (and presumably somewhat autobiographical) 1958 novel *Crazy in Berlin*, begins with a GI shouting at a woman in a Berlin park, "Honey . . . *schlafen mit* me, oh won't you *schlafen mit* me!" and concludes with the lesson learned in occupied Germany: "Organize your sex life and all else followed, the phallus being the key to the general metropolis of manhood, which most of the grand old civilizations knew but we in America had forgotten."[50]

Certainly, the many American fictionalizations of postwar Berlin—a genre in itself, often written by men who served there—stressed the unique advantages of the GIs' sexual bonanza; what a historian of the US occupation summarized as the "general willingness on the part of German women" and the American Jewish writer Meyer Levin described, more bitterly, as "the lustful eagerness of the German girls to fulfill their roles as conquered women."[51] In McGovern's *fräulein*, the jaded women survivors of the Battle of Berlin hopefully await the American conquerors: "The Americans had not suffered in the war. Their homes had not been bombed, their women raped, their industries razed. Their casualties in Europe had been smaller than those of the *Wehrmacht* at Stalingrad alone. They would be free from the spirit of revenge for which the French, British and Russians could hardly be blamed." Cynically, the women repeat the dominant American view, "Rape? They don't have to rape. All those women who swarm outside their barracks would rape them for a carton of cigarettes or a chocolate bar." American privilege also assured a more benign general level of exploitation and looting: "The Russians steal power plants and cranes and whole factories, while the Amis are content to ship Meissen china, Zeiss cameras, and family heirloom jewels through their Army Post Office." [52]

Fraternization: Sexual, Political, and Racial Border Crossing

The "other" but frequently difficult-to-disentangle side of the rape story was sexual fraternization. The bans imposed with all serious intent by the Americans (and British) very quickly showed themselves to be utterly and hopelessly unenforceable, "an immense and sordid joke." In one of the many apparently autobiographical novels published in the years right after the war, an officer, marveling at the sudden bounty of "guns, wine, silver, paintings, women, and various combinations thereof" greeting the Americans, tells his men, "In this outfit we stand on Patton's unofficial ruling that it is not fraternization if you don't stay for breakfast. Sleep with 'em but don't shake hands."[53] With everyone agreeing that "surely it is necessary to go back to Prohibition to find a law so flagrantly violated and so rarely enforced," General Eisenhower eased the ban on July 7 just as the Americans were taking up their positions in Berlin, and then essentially lifted it by officially permitting public conversations between Germans and Americans on July 15, 1945.

Technicalities notwithstanding, any political fraternization suggested by a handshake was clearly not the major issue; as an American observer bluntly put it in 1946, "Fraternization is strictly a matter of sex. An American with a German woman is with her because she is a woman, not because she is a German."[54] The American Jewish intelligence officer Saul Padover noted the obvious when he wrote, "The dictionary" may have "define[d] fraternization as 'bringing into brotherly love,' but the relations between Americans and Germans did not belong in that category" and it quickly "came to have the exclusive signification of fornication." It was no accident that the ever-creative German joke-makers nicknamed the military government "government by mistresses."[55]

Over and over again, using virtually identical phrases, reporters highlighted occupied Germany's ubiquitous *Fräuleinwunder*. "There is nothing like it this side of Tahiti," they marveled about the accessibility of young German women. When a young officer inquired about bringing his wife to his Berlin posting, he was greeted with incredulity, "Wife? You must be nuts!" said the general. "You're bringing a sandwich to a banquet."[56] Or as one decidedly not amused female American reporter sniffed about German women who treated "all American women with contempt and all American men as gods": "If there was any rape, it certainly wasn't necessary."[57] Particularly titillating was the picture of German women quickly shedding all the "baggage" of racial indoctrination, at least in matters sexual or romantic. Initial reports highlighted fraternization with both Jewish and African American soldiers as ironic racial transgressions: "The Negro troops are doing particularly well with the Fräuleins . . . . It is also true that Jewish boys are having a field-day."[58]

Field day or not, the politics of fraternization was particularly fraught for Jewish Allied soldiers. In a report on a "ride through Berlin," posted to the refugee weekly *Aufbau* in July 1945, a German Jewish master sergeant reflected on how hard it was to resist the temptations of well-dressed, well-fed, and appealing Fräuleins. He described his own painful discipline of staring into their eyes and visualizing Buchenwald and Dachau.[59] For US occupation official Moses Moskowitz, the fact that "German women have been known to be on intimate terms with Jewish men who only a year ago were behind concentration camp gates" was one of the most difficult and inexplicable aspects of the German "enigma of irresponsibility."[60] Kurt Hirsch, the Czech Jewish American GI whom the actress Hildegard Knef married, was excruciatingly explicit about this clash of memories and identities. On their first date in bombed-out Berlin, he took her to the movies in the Russian sector to watch the Soviet newsreel about the liberation of Auschwitz. "I lost sixteen relatives" he told her on the way home.[61]

The combustible mix of race and sex played out in different but—for occupation policy in a still-segregated military—even more tense ways for African American troops. William Gardner Smith, a reporter for the *Pittsburgh Courier*, an African American newspaper, echoed black GIs' own highly ambivalent feelings about fraternization in his semi-autobiographical 1948 novel *Last of the Conquerors*. Drinking with "sultry looking" German women, a GI remarks, "Two years ago I'd a shot the son of a bitch that said I'd ever be sittin' in a club drinking a toast with Hitler's children . . . . The same people we're sittin' with tonight is the ones that burned people in them camps and punched the Jews in the nose." One of the girls retorts angrily, "How can you talk? What about the white Americans? In your country you may not walk down the street with a white woman." Musing on his initially carefree love affair with a "white girl" named Ilse, the narrator notes "bitter[ly]" how "odd, it seemed to me, that here, in the land of hate, I should find this one all-important phase of democracy." He remembered the pleasures of postwar

Berlin, border crossing through the sectors, strolling along the Wannsee in the summer, or going to the opera in the eastern side of the city with his girlfriend, even as they "could still smell the bodies of the dead buried beneath the rubble as we walked." Not wanting to face the reality that Ilse's dream of marriage could never be fulfilled in Jim Crow America, he has no ready response to the buddy who blurts out, "I like this goddamn country, you know that . . . . It's the first place I was ever treated like a goddamn man . . . . You know what the hell I learned? That a nigger ain't no different from nobody else . . . . I hadda come over here and let the Nazis teach me that."[62]

Women had their own reasons for making themselves sexually available, as the sharp-eyed sociologist Hilde Thurnwald surmised in her report on family life in postwar Berlin. Aside from the bare necessities provided by American foodstuffs and supplies, the Fräuleins were perhaps lured less by sexual interest than by a general postwar yearning for life's pleasures (*Lebenshunger*). If soldiers' rations could ease "the hunger which had replaced the bombs in making life into hell," as Curt Riess put it, then Berlin's women were also seeking a bit of warmth, a bar of chocolate, an ice cream from the American club, some untroubled hours. The *Amis*, they said, in a reference to the Weimar enthusiasm for American efficiency and rationalization, were "so streamlined." And indeed the crack 82nd Airborne, which had marched into Berlin in July, was well fed, well groomed and fragrant, as many recalled, with aftershave lotion; quite a contrast to the ragged German men returning from the front or POW camps (and in most cases the feared Russians).[63] Their entry into the destroyed capital was limned rather contradictorily in Burke's *The Big Rape*: "giants of men—tall, huge, powerful . . . . They were giants—all! In contrast to the Russians there was something immediately sharp and commanding about these troops. Their uniforms were neat, clean and trim . . . . Their faces were uniformly bright and clean. All seemed to be happy. There were no dark brooding faces. They were like a bunch of kids, away on a lark or outing."[64]

Yet by July when the Americans entered Berlin, the experience of Red Army rapes shadowed the fraternization phenomenon that accompanied them. Indeed, the very experience of rape may have made embittered women less resistant to the casual prostitution that also characterized fraternization, while simultaneously making them more open to the pleasures offered by the 82nd Airborne. It was no secret in postwar Berlin that a politics of guilt, revenge, and punishment had been recently enacted on the bodies of German women. The "furlines" and Veronikas, as depicted in the politically and physically infected cartoon character *Veronika Dankeschön* (an allusion to VD, or venereal disease) in *Stars and Stripes*, as well as the stolid cleaner-uppers and self-sacrificing mothers designated as *Trümmerfrauen*, were both desirable and dangerous. They were freighted with the shame and horror of rape and the guilt of Nazism as well as emblematic of the victims that war produces. In James McGovern's 1956 novel, he professed to capture this mood: "The cook had lost one son at Orel, another at Kasserine pass, her husband and small apartment in a Liberator raid on Prenzlauer Berg, her modest life savings in the black market chaos, had narrowly escaped being raped by a Russian, and she stubbornly muttered that if she were going to feel guilty, or sorry for any-body, it would be for herself."[65]

Berlin's women appeared, however, not only as victims and villains but also as shameless sexually available Fräuleins and determined, unsentimen-tal, do-whatever-it-takes survivors. James Burke's fictional Lilo personified this tougher version: in July 1945, having made it through the initial Soviet occupation, she walked into the US military government press office to offer her services. She had after all worked for the Nazi press, the Americans needed people with skills and experience, they could denazify her "later." Her motto was "Survival! Above all things she must survive. . . . She had survived the rape of Berlin. Surely she could manage from here on."[66] "One has long since lost the habit of pathos" (*Jedes Pathos hat man sich längst abgewöhnt*), the Berlin journalist Ursula von Kardorff, better known than Martha Hiller's *Anonyma*, who also continued to work in the Third Reich, noted in her journal on January 29, 1945.[67]

Conclusion

It is indeed this lack of pathos, this insistently matter-of-fact tone, laconic, resigned, but determined to endure, sometimes laced with gallows humor—so evident in women's contemporary testimony—that challenges our under-standings of both the victimization caused by, and inflicted on, German women as the Nazi empire collapsed. The decades of the "Long Postwar" both before and after 1989–90 have profoundly changed our understandings of sexual violence in wartime or conflict zones and simultaneously produced a more complex analysis of the gendered and racialized workings of postwar German reconstruction in both East and West and women's crucial role in stabilizing these postwar societies.[68] Whether and how the highly particular and historically contingent manner in which German women confronted, contained, and articulated their experience of sexual coercion and consent in the aftermath of a genocidal war can be relevant to more current explosions of gendered violence in conflict zones seems to me to be an entirely different and very open question.

Notes

1. This article is a slightly revised version of Atina Grossmann, "The 'Big Rape': Sex and Sexual Violence, War, and Occupation in Post–World War II Memory and Imagination," in *Sexual Violence in Conflict Zones: From the Ancient World to the Era of Human Rights*, ed. Elizabeth D. Heineman (Philadelphia: University of Pennsylvania Press, 2011), 137–51.

2. One Berlin district counted 1,873 women for every 1,000 men in August 1945, and the city ratio was 169 to 100. In August, the total population was counted at 2,784,112 (1,035,463 male, 1,748,649 female) vs. 4,332,000 in 1939. The male population had been halved, female population reduced by a quarter. The 100 men, 169 women figure compared to 100 to 119 in 1939. *Berliner Volk-, Berufs- und Arbeitstättenzählung*, August 12, 1945, in *Berliner Zeitung* 1:91 (August 29, 1945): 1. On the meaning of the female "surplus" at war's end, see Elizabeth D. Heineman, *What Difference Does a Husband Make?: Women and Marital Status in Nazi and Postwar Germany* (Berkeley: University of California Press, 1999), 10.

3. For a summary of the international discussion and developments in international law, see Rhonda Copelon, "Toward Accountability for Violence Against Women in War: Progress and Challenges," in Heineman, ed. *Sexual Violence in Conflict Zones*, 232–56. On Red Army rapes, see the well-received and publicized but controversial publication in Germany, Britain, and the United States of a revised and retranslated text about mass rapes in Berlin, Anonyma, *Eine Frau in Berlin: Tagebuchaufzeichnungen vom 20 April bis zum 22 Juni 1945* (Frankfurt/M: Eichborn, 2003); in English, *A Woman in Berlin: A Diary: Eight Weeks in the Conquered City*, by Anonymous, trans. Philip Boehm, with foreword by Antony Beevor (New York: Metropolitan, 2005). This interest was preceded by the positive response to Beevor's discussion of rape in *The Fall of Berlin 1945* (New York: Viking, 2002). Research published in the 1990s includes Norman Naimark, *The Russians in Germany: A History of the Soviet Zone of Occupation, 1945–1949* (Cambridge, MA: Harvard University Press, 1995); *Heimatmuseum Charlottenburg Ausstellung: Worüber kaum gesprochen wurde: Frauen und alliierte Soldaten. 3 September bis 15 Oktober 1995* (Berlin: Bezirksamt Charlottenburg, Abt. Volksbildung, 1995); and the text accompanying Sander's film on the topic, Helke Sander and Barbara Johr, eds., *BeFreier und Befreite. Krieg, Vergewaltigungen, Kinder* (Munich: Antje Kunstmann, 1992). For earlier feminist analyses, see Ingrid Schmidt-Harzbach, "Eine Woche im April. Berlin 1945. Vergewaltigung als Massenschicksal," *Feministische Studien* 5 (1984): 51–62; Erika M. Hoerning, "Frauen als Kriegsbeute. Der Zwei-Fronten Krieg. Beispiele aus Berlin," in *"Wir kriegen jetzt andere Zeiten" Auf der Suche nach der Erfahrung des Volkes in antifaschistischen Ländern. Lebensgeschichte und Sozialkultur im Ruhrgebiet 1930 bis 1960*,

ed. Lutz Niethammer and Alexander von Plato, 3 vols. (Berlin: J.H.W. Dietz, 1985), 3:327–46; and Annemarie Tröger, "Between Rape and Prostitution: Survival Strategies and Chances of Emancipation for Berlin Women after World II," in *Women in Culture and Politics: A Century of Change*, ed. Judith Friedlander et al. (Bloomington: University of Indiana Press, 1986), 97–117. For an even earlier feminist consideration of sexual violence in World War II, including attacks by Soviet liberators on German women, see Susan Brownmiller, *Against Our Will: Men, Women, and Rape* (New York: Simon and Schuster, 1975), 48–79. On the thorny problems of historicizing rape at war's end and the controversy about Sander's film, see Atina Grossmann, "A Question of Silence: The Rape of German Women by Occupation Soldiers," *October* 72 (1995), 43–63; reprinted in Robert Moeller, ed., *West Germany Under Construction: Politics, Society, and Culture in the Adenauer Era* (Ann Arbor: University of Michigan Press, 1997), 33–52.

4. Barbara Johr, "Die Ereignisse in Zahlen," in Sander and Johr, eds., *BeFreier und Befreite*, 48, 54–55, 59. See also Erich Kuby, *Die Russen in Berlin 1945* (Bern and Munich: Scherz, 1965), 312–313 and especially Naimark, *The Russians in Germany*, 69–90.

5. Naimark, *The Russians in Germany*, 132–3, 79–80, 106–7, 86. Beevor's *The Fall of Berlin* presents much of the same material.

6. Karla Höcker, *Beschreibung eines Jahres. Berliner Notizen 1945* (Berlin: Arani Verlag, 1984), 42.

7. Harold J. Berman and Miroslav Kerner, *Soviet Military Law and Administration* (Cambridge, MA: Harvard University Press, 1955), 48.

8. Ilya Ehrenburg, *The War: 1941–1945*. Vol. 5: *Of Men—Years—Life* (Cleveland, OH: World Publishing Company, 1964), 175. See also Hoerning, "Frauen als Kriegsbeute," 327–46.

9. Hildegard Knef, *The Gift Horse: Report on a Life* (New York: McGraw-Hill, 1971), 95.

10. *The Economist*, October 27, 1945, in Isaac Deutscher, *Reportagen aus Nachkriegsdeutschland*, (Hamburg: Junius Verlag, 1980), 130.

11. For a careful and sensitive discussion of the rage and frustration as well as sheer exhaustion, brutalization, and alcohol that fueled Red Army rapes, see Catherine Merridale, *Ivan's War: Life and Death in the Red Army, 1939–1945* (New York: Henry Holt Metropolitan, 2006), 299–335, 302, 309, 307.

12. Gabrielle Vallentin. "Die Einnahme von Berlin Durch die Rote Armee vor Zehn Jahren. Wie ich Sie Selbst Erlebt Habe," 1955, 37. Landesarchiv Berlin, Acc 2421.

13. Michael Wieck, *Zeugnis vom Untergang Königsbergs: Ein "Geltungsjude" berichtet* (Heidelberg: Heidelberger Verlagsanstalt und Druckerei, 1990), 261.

14. Margret Boveri, *Tage des Überlebens: Berlin 1945* (Munich: Piper, 1985, first published 1968), 126, 121–22.

15. Interview with G.C, conducted in early 1990s, quoted in Heimatmuseum Charlottenburg, "Worüber nicht gesprochen wurde," 22.

16. Curt Riess, *Berlin Berlin 1945–1953* (first published c. 1953, reprint, ed. Steffen Damm, Berlin: Bostelmann & Siebenhaar, 2002), 19.

17. My translation from Anonyma, *Eine Frau in Berlin*, 78. See the republished version, *Anonyma* (2003) and subsequent debates about the legitimacy of "outing" Anonyma's name and identity as the journalist Marta Hillers, a kind of Nazi "new woman" who had written

minor texts for Goebbels' ministry before the war (*Kleinpropagandistin*), played out on the *Feuilleton* pages of major newspapers among male scholars and journalists. See especially Jens Bisky, *Süddeutsche Zeitung*, September 24, 2003. See also the enthusiastically received 2005 American edition, *A Woman in Berlin*, and the 2009 film version. On the controversy about the German republication, see Elizabeth Heineman, "Gender, Sexuality, and Coming to Terms with the Nazi Past," *Central European History* 38 (2005): 41–74, 53–56.

18. Riess, *Berlin Berlin 1945–1953*, 23, 26, 19.

19. Hans Winterfeldt memoir, Leo Baeck Institute archives, ms. 690, p. 438.

20. Tröger, "Between Rape and Prostitution," 100. As Heineman observes, a "regime obsessed with racial purity had become the catalyst of an unprecedented number of relationships between Germans and foreigners." *What Difference*, 58. See also Dagmar Herzog, *Sex after Fascism: Memory and Morality in Twentieth Century Germany* (Princeton, NJ: Princeton University Press, 2005).

21. Annemarie Weber, *Westend* (Munich: Desch, 1966), 104.

22. Deutscher, *The Observer*, October 7, 1945, and *The Economist*, October 27, 1945, in *Reportagen*, 122–24, 129–30.

23. Margarete Dörr, *"Wer die Zeit nicht miterlebt hat . . . " Frauenerfahrung im Zweiten Weltkrieg und in den Jahren danach* (Frankfurt/M.: Campus, 1998), 408.

24. Frank Howley, *Berlin Command* (New York: G.P. Putnam & Sons, 1950), 11.

25. Bert Lewyn and Bev Saltzman Lewyn, *On the Run in Nazi Berlin* (Berlin: Xlibris, 2001), 277.

26. Eugene Davidson, *The Death and Life of Germany: An Account of the American Occupation* (New York: Alfred A. Knopf, 1959), 74.

27. Anne-Marie Durand-Wever, *Proceedings of the International Congress on Population and World Resources in Relation to the Family. August 1948.* (London: H. K. Lewis and Co., n.d.), 103.

28. Wladimir Gelfand, *Deutschland Tagebuch 1945–1946: Aufzeichnungen eines Rotarmisten* (Berlin: Aufbau, 2005), 78–79.

29. Gudrun Pausewang, in Heinrich Boll, ed. *NiemandsLand. Kindheitserinnerungen an die Jahre 1945 bis 1949* (Bronheim-Merten: Lamuv Verlag, 1985), 62.

30. *Eine Frau in Berlin*, 138.

31. James Wakefield Burke, *The Big Rape* (Frankfurt/M.: Friedrich Rudl Verleger Union, 1951), 145, 197. The similarities between Lilo and the Anonyma of *A Woman in Berlin*, first published three years later, are striking and worth further study.

32. Consider the contentious discussions surrounding Helke Sander's film *BeFreier und Befreite,* which explicitly claimed to "break the silence" around Soviet rapes of German women. On the 1990s debates, see the special issue of *October* 72 (Spring 1995) on "Berlin 1945: War and Rape, 'Liberators Take Liberties,'" particularly Grossmann, "A Question of Silence," 43–63.

33. *Berliner Zeitung* 1:10 (30 May 1945): 2.

34. Lew Kopelew [Lev Kopelev], *Aufbewahren für alle Zeit*, afterword by Heinrich Bö (Munich: DTV, 1979, first published in Russian, 1975), 19, 51, 137.

35. According to the West Berlin women's magazine *sie*: 45 (October 13, 1946), 3; women outnumbered male voters 16 to 10.

36. Deutscher, *The Observer*, October 13, 1946, in *Reportagen*, 187. The communist Socialist Unity Party received only 19.8 percent of the vote. See Donna Harsch, "Approach/ Avoidance: Communists and women in East Germany, 1945–9," *Social History* 25 (2000): 156–82, and in general, among many sources, Naimark, *Russians in Germany*, 119–121.

37. I borrow the term "remasculinization" from Robert Moeller; he refers to Susan Jeffords, *The Remasculinization of America: Gender and the Vietnam War* (Bloomington: University of Indiana Press, 1989).

38. See for example, LAB Rep 2651/2/184/1, report by Erna Kadzloch.

39. Howley, *Berlin Command*, 65–66.

40. *6 Month Report*, 4 January–3 July 1946 (US Army Military Government, Report to the Commanding General US Headquarters Berlin District.), 8.

41. *6 Month Report*, 8. By 1950, with the Cold War in full swing, Frank Howley, who had been the American commander in Berlin, had changed his relatively benign, bemused view of the "jolly" Soviets, asserting that, "we know now—or should know—that we were hopelessly naive." Howley, *Berlin Command*, 11.

42. Bill Downs, *Newsweek*, April 16, 1945, 62.

43. James McGovern, *fräulein* (New York: Crown, 1956), 79. Here too, similarities to *The Big Rape* and Anonyma's *A Woman in Berlin* are worth investigating.

44. John J. Maginnis, *Military Government Journal: Normandy to Berlin*, ed. Robert A. Hart (Amherst: University of Massachusetts Press, 1971), September 6, 1945, 294.

45. See for example, William L. Shirer, *End of a Berlin Diary* (New York: Knopf, 1947), 148.

46. William E. Griffith, "Denazification Revisited," in *America and the Shaping of German Society 1945–1955*, ed. Michael Ermarth (Providence, RI: Berg, 1993), 155. On American sexual violence in Bavaria, see Heide Fehrenbach, *Race After Hitler: Black Occupation Children in Postwar Germany and America* (Princeton, NJ: Princeton University Press, 2005), 54–55.

47. Bud Hutton and Andy Rooney, *Conquerors' Peace: A Report to the American Stockholders* (Garden City, NJ, and New York: Doubleday, 1947), 67.

48. Harold Zink, *The United States in Germany, 1944–1955* (Princeton, NJ: Van Nostrand, 1957), 138. Among numerous contemporary sources, see also Julian Bach Jr., *America's Germany: An Account of the Occupation* (New York: Random House, 1946), especially "GIs Between the Sheets," 71–83.

49. Kay Boyle, "Summer Evening," in *Fifty Short Stories* (New York: New Directions, 1992), 405–6 (first published in *New Yorker*, June 25, 1949).

50. Thomas Berger, *Crazy in Berlin* (New York: Ballantine, 1958), 6, 236, 405.

51. Harold Zink, *American Military Government in Germany* (New York: Macmillan, 1947), 173; Meyer Levin, *In Search: An Autobiography* (New York: Horizon, 1950), 179. For a recent fictionalization, see Joseph Kanon, *The Good German: A Novel* (New York: Henry Holt, 2001).

52. McGovern, *fräulein*, 118.

53. David Davidson, *The Steeper Cliff* (New York: Random House, 1947), 63, 33.

54. Bach, *America's Germany*, 71–72, 75.

55. Saul K. Padover, "Why Americans Like German Women," *The American Mercury* 63:273 (1946): 354–57

56. Drew Middleton, *Where Has Last July Gone? Memoirs* (New York: Quadrangle, The New York Times Book Co., 1973), 148.

57. Judy Barden, "Candy-Bar Romance—Women of Germany," in *This is Germany*, ed. Arthur Settel (New York: William Sloane, 1950), 164–65.

58. See Cedric Belfrage, *Seeds of Destruction: The Truth about the US Occupation of Germany* (New York: Cameron & Kahn, 1954), 67–68.

59. "Fahrt durch Berlin. Aus einem Brief von Master Sgt Charles Gregor," *Aufbau* (August 17, 1945): 32.

60. Moses Moskowitz, "The Germans and the Jews: Postwar Report: The Enigma of German Irresponsibility," *Commentary* 2 (1946), 7.

61. Knef, *Gifthorse*, 120–123. The marriage did not last.

62. William Gardner Smith, *Last of the Conquerors* (New York: Farrar, Straus, 1948), 35, 44, 57, 67–68. On Smith, see also Fehrenbach, *Race After Hitler*, 35–39; and Petra Goedde, *GIs and Germans: Culture, Gender, and Foreign Relations, 1945–1949* (New Haven, CT: Yale University Press, 2003), 109–12. See also Maria Höhn and Martin Klimke, *A Breath of Freedom: The Civil Rights Struggle, African American GIs, and Germany* (New York: Palgrave Macmillan, 2010).

63. Riess, *Berlin, Berlin*, 60, 59. See also Hilde Thurnwald, *Gegenwartsprobleme Berliner Familien: eine soziologische Untersuchung an 498 Familien* (Berlin: Weidman, 1948), 146.

64. Burke, *The Big Rape*, 258.

65. McGovern, *fräulein*, 129.

66. Burke, *The Big Rape*, 10, 259.

67. Ursula von Kardorff, *Berliner Aufzeichnungen aus den Jahren 1942 bis 1945*, rev. ed. (Munich: Bilderstein, 1962).

68. See for example, Rita Chin et al., eds., *After the Nazi Racial State: Difference and Democracy in Germany and Europe* (Ann Arbor: University of Michigan Press, 2009).

Chapter 2

Gender Roles in Ruins: German Women and Local Politics under American Occupation, 1945–1955

Rebecca Boehling

The aftermath of the defeat of the Nazi regime was characterized by social upheaval and German disillusionment with familiar social and political institutions presumed to be responsible for the rise of Nazism. The collapse of the Third Reich, military occupation, and demographic shifts made an immediate restoration of old structures and hierarchies, including those within a traditional male breadwinner-headed family and society, rather unlikely. At the time of the first postwar German census in 1946, 56 percent of the German population was female.[1] Many were war widows; others had husbands who returned from the front or from prisoner-of-war camps, in particular in the Soviet Union, not only physically but often also emotionally impaired and unemployable. In the early postwar period, the number of marriages fell, while the average age of marriage and the divorce rate rose dramatically,[2] increasing the number of women heading single-parent families.[3] By 1949, only 43 percent of all West German women were married,[4] and by 1950, barely 60 percent of the entire population of the new Federal Republic of Germany lived in what sociologists would call "traditional families,"[5] and a "surplus of women" were functioning on their own. Despite these stark realities, conventional marriage and family continued to be propagated as the ideal, both by occupiers and many Germans themselves, in the western zones of occupation. The model of the "male-breadwinner family" found more political and cultural support than ever before, reflecting a desire for "normalcy" in response to defeat, military occupation, and growing Cold War tensions.

This push for a return to conventional gender roles was not, however, the whole postwar story. Some women questioned men's inherent ability to lead either families or society as a whole. In 1945 and 1946 a number of prominent leftist women such as Else Wendler and Maria Pfeifer, but also more conservative leaders of the women's movement like Agnes von Zahn-Harnack, chairwoman of the Federation of German Women's Associations (Bund Deutscher Frauenvereine, or BDF) from 1931 to 1933 and co-founder of the German Women's League of 1945 (Deutsche Frauenbund 1945), stated publicly that they considered men more culpable for the war because of the misogyny of Nazi ideology and culture and the many restrictions the Nazi regime had placed on women. Such women had often been influenced by the separate-but-equal gender ideology of the BDF, the pre-Nazi mainstream middle-class women's umbrella organization founded in 1894,[6] an ideology that was also shared in Weimar Germany by the female leaders of the German Social Democratic Party (Sozialdemokratische Partei Deutschlands, or SPD).[7] Questioning whether men should continue to exercise political dominance and feeling that women endured a great deal during and after the war, these and other women, such as the Stuttgart Social Democrat Anna Haag, argued that they had earned the right to equality with men in the public sphere[8] and contested attempts to reassert German men's hegemonic role in both politics and the family.[9]

The realities of the socioeconomic realm also made it difficult to uphold the ideal of the male breadwinner family. German women's employment was necessary because so many men continued to be absent, large numbers of women were heading households, and more labor was needed for German economic recovery, to which the Western Allies had fundamentally committed themselves by late 1946. Often the sole breadwinners in their families, women in the western zones frequently found themselves bartering on the black market or directed to employment as *Trümmerfrauen* (rubble women), toiling in the ruins of bombed cities and towns.[10] After being coerced into wage labor during the war, German women resented being forced by either Allied occupation or German authorities to register with labor exchanges for manual work. Women's labor was also needed in industry, crafts, and trade in positions previously dominated by men but which women had already held during the First and Second World Wars.

The situation prompted considerable debate in the western zones about whether women should get equal pay for equal work if they did perform "male" jobs, with German government officials from across the political spectrum and even a majority of male trade union members opposed. Many asserted that even if women were hired in comparable jobs, the level and standard of their work were qualitatively and quantitatively inferior to that of men. The many women now heading households did not benefit from the oft-stated argument that because men were the primary wage-earners and supporters of the family, they were entitled to a family wage. Neither German private employers nor local government officials supported the principle of equal pay for equal work, regarding women's employment in "male" jobs as an anomaly—a temporary expedient or stopgap until the return to gender "normalcy" in society and the economy.[11] And although the Office of Military Government, United States (OMGUS) insisted that the principle be included in state (*Länder*) constitutions in its occupation zone, it made no attempt to put it into practice.[12]

The United States, as the hegemonic power in the western zones of occupied Germany, pursued various policies to democratize German society, while seeking to limit the potential economic appeal of communism and thus pushing for economic reconstruction. Democratization initiatives not clearly tied to anticommunist goals took a back seat as US-Soviet relations became increasingly tense in the years 1946 to 1948, culminating in the Soviet blockade of western access to Berlin followed by the US-British airlift and the division of the country in 1949. As the Cold War heated up, OMGUS come to realize how key German women, as the majority of the population, could be to US occupation goals, in particular fighting the appeal of communism.

This essay brings together three interrelated themes: the push and pull of American and German attempts at democratization in early post-WWII western Germany; a significant questioning of gender roles in the midst of social upheaval, gender imbalance, and the aftermath of defeat; and the impact of the early Cold War on gender politics. I begin by providing the social and political context of US-occupied Germany, in which OMGUS's Women's Affairs Section (WAS) sought to "bring democracy" to German women[13] in a way that favored women's nonpartisan civic engagement over their political activism. Moving to the local level of German self-government, I analyze German women's political activities and concerns and the response of both OMGUS and German local officials. I then zero in on the microcosm of the Munich city council during the first postwar decade in order to consider the reaction of US occupation officials to the election of a significant number of German women city councilors from a variety of political parties.

Female politicians in a major city like Munich tended to transcend partisan politics and operate along feminist lines on various issues, including equal pay for equal work, while opposing top-down party politics and overly simplified Cold War dichotomies that labeled peace activism as procommunist and antidemocratic. These positions dismayed male party leaders, who, with the exception of those in the German Communist Party (Kommunistische Partei Deutschlands, or KPD), did not hesitate to use Cold War rhetoric to reprimand women who failed to toe the party line. Discouragement and redbaiting by political leaders and the lack of OMGUS support for women in politics, in conjunction with growing societal pressure for a return to conventional gender roles, made it difficult for politically active women to prevail. As this cohort, many of them single, widowed, or divorced, aged in their fifties and sixties during the decade of the 1950s, they were less able to serve as role models for a younger generation of women in their thirties and forties, who more easily fell into the ideology of separate spheres for men and women that framed women's civic and political support roles as an extension of their familial roles.

Bringing Democracy to German Women

Ever since 1946, OMGUS and the US government in Washington, D.C., had been hearing about the need to take the problems of German women seriously and promote policies in their interest. Pressure was coming from American women journalists and trade unionists, as well as representatives from American women's organizations, such as the League of Women Voters and the Young Women's Christian Association (YWCA), who had visited postwar Germany.[14] By early 1947, OMGUS had taken note of the fact that women staff members of the Education and Religious Affairs (ER&A) Branch and two officers from the Women's Army Corps (WAC) on detached service with the Youth Activities Section were volunteering their time to work with German women's groups, who appealed to OMGUS for information about democratic methods of organization, background on the "cultural, educational, social, and civic interests of women in USA and elsewhere," and "how to understand public affairs through study and discussion of a nonpartisan nature." The German women, representing a wide range of political, economic, and professional interests from some forty-four women's organizations, who initiated and attended the first interzonal women's conference in Bad Boll in May 1947, asked American women from the ER&A Branch for their "assistance in regaining positions of responsibility in education, the professions, and in public life."[15]

At the behest of various women in OMGUS and visiting experts returning from Germany, in late September 1947 the president of the US League of Women Voters, Anna Lord Strauss, asked the US Zone's military governor to form a headquarters office of select women "experienced in the formation of women's organizations" in order "to implement a program devised to activate, develop, and lend moral support to the democratic potentials awaiting such help and leadership."[16] Apparently in response to this plea, OMGUS's Political Affairs Division conceded that the US zone "should no longer overlook the support for our political principles that could be mobilized in the ranks of German women," at a time when the British zone already had a competent staff handling women's affairs and the Soviet zone was making "strenuous efforts to establish military government and encourage women's groups favorable to Communism."[17]

The OMGUS women advocating for a women's affairs section buttressed their arguments with anticommunism, claiming that OMGUS should form the section in order to "do much to combat the expansion of the DFD in the US-Zone."[18] The Democratic Women's League of Germany (Demokratische Frauenbund Deutschlands, or DFD) had been founded in March 1947 by communist, social democratic, and independent women who were active in the antifascist women's committees that had started their work as early as in October 1945 in the Soviet zone and at about the same time in the western zones. OMGUS agreed to form a women's affairs section in large part to strengthen noncommunist women's organizations, in particular nonpartisan ones, and thus minimize the appeal of the DFD, which it considered a communist-front organization. The two other large parties in postwar Germany, the SPD and the Christian Democratic Union (Christlich Demokratische Union, or CDU), also set up women's groups. The SPD founded its Women's Office (Frauenbüro) in 1946 and the CDU established its National Women's Committee (Bundesfrauenausschuss) in 1951, but both were far less active than the women's group of the KPD.[19] The DFD's more overt politicization served to feed OMGUS's distrust of German women's overtly political activism. Although OMGUS did come around to the idea of encouraging women's democratic consciousness, they intended to promote more civic than political consciousness—and activities.

In March 1948 OMGUS created the Women's Affairs Section within the Education and Cultural Affairs Branch, the branch with the most women on staff, and also, not coincidentally, the least powerful branch of OMGUS.[20] Its first chief, Lorena B. Hahn, had been a child welfare officer within OMGUS's Public Welfare Branch. She was replaced less than a year later by Ruth F. Woodsmall, who worked as a women's affairs advisor after serving as the general secretary of the YWCA since 1935.[21] Appointed as the special advisor on women's issues to US military governor General Lucius D. Clay was former Connecticut Congresswoman Chase Going Woodhouse, president of the Connecticut Federation of Democratic Women's Clubs from 1943 to 1948. Woodhouse insisted that feminists not be hired to work with the WAS, implying that they would be unable to cooperate with men; "the job is not one for a feminist," she stated. "Much of the work is with men."[22]

Given the background of this core leadership, it is perhaps not surprising that the WAS was most interested in supporting nonpartisan women's groups and shaping them to resemble women's civic organizations in the United States, rather than promoting overtly political roles for women or a feminist agenda, equality of the sexes, or even equal pay for equal work. The WAS did hope to reverse the negative legacy of the Nazi era's impact upon women, which in its view had limited German women's sphere to that of the three Ks: *Kinder, Küche, Kirche* (children, kitchen, church). Unaware of the fact that more than three-quarters of all single women had been employed in Nazi Germany in 1939, or of the role many had played in the Nazi organizations for women like National Socialist Women's League (NS-Frauenschaft) or the League of German Girls (Bund Deutscher Mädel), or as wartime female auxiliaries of the Wehrmacht and the civil aerial defense or Red Cross nurses,[23] most Americans at home viewed German women primarily as Nazi victims who had been forced to give up control of their families and their work roles. They thus felt that postwar German women would need to be encouraged to regain control of the private sphere.[24] Until American occupation officially ended in May 1955, the WAS, as an arm of the American democratization program, would sponsor activities to help German women influence their husbands and children in order to instill democratic behavior within the family. This effort was intended to empower women, albeit primarily in the private sphere.

To strengthen women's maternal influence within the private sphere and help extend it into what it called either "community affairs" or the "civic sphere,"[25] the WAS arranged for a variety of visiting experts representing the YWCA, civic clubs, the League of Women Voters, and professional women's organizations to meet with German women and encourage them to undertake volunteer work. These visits were intended to restore German women's moral superiority, which the Nazis had allegedly repressed. Instead of encouraging German women to run for public office or play prominent public roles, the idea was to bring more peaceful, maternal values into the public sphere, ensuring that all women voted and influenced how men voted and behaved. Thus the WAS preferred to have German women serve as representatives on nonpartisan so-called community councils, which resembled American civic organizations, rather than on city councils or in other elected parliamentary bodies,[26] and the WAS director prided herself on making "it a practice not to work with political groups."[27] One American visiting expert, who was sent to Germany because of her role in American women's civic clubs, observed that, as a result of the WAS's efforts, German women were finally beginning to understand "that what happens, or can happen, in the home depends on what happens in the community and in the world and that women must learn to fulfill their responsibility as citizens by helping to choose their officials, shape policies and make public opinion."[28]

These well-intentioned American women did not realize that attempts to broaden German women's civic horizons might actually restrict their public roles. Before the war, German women had achieved a certain professional status by working as social workers within the Weimar welfare structure; volunteer work could reverse what limited gains they had made. The WAS did acknowledge that because of the shortage of men, some German women would be unable to marry and have children, and probably need to work— an unfortunate but inevitable fate, given the demographics. As the Women's Affairs Branch (the WAS became a branch after 1949) put it, "Unless those women, who would normally be absorbed into family units, can be drawn into public life or private businesses a serious sociological problem is inevitable which will undoubtedly create a significant dislocation in the structure of community life."[29] But the branch stopped short of stating the obvious: that many of them, especially single women, often working class, would need to earn a living to support themselves, just as they had done in the past.[30]

Uncritical of its own middle-class bias against female employment, OMGUS officially professed to oppose any discrimination against women in political life and in employment and took credit for any strides toward gender equality in its zone. As early as October 1947, the Civil Affairs Division (CAD) remarked on all that OMGUS had already done "to remove the psychological and legal barriers against the participation of women in public life," including the fact that the state constitutions within their zone, which OMGUS approved and helped shape, all "guarantee[d] the equality of the sexes." Indirectly taking credit, CAD drew attention to the fact that, except in Bavaria, there were proportionately far more women delegates in German state parliaments in their zone than in the US House of Representatives.[31]

But beyond ensuring that such principles were included in the state constitutions and trying to get women to take their civic responsibilities seriously, OMGUS made no attempt to put equal rights into practice in Germany. When the West German Parliamentary Council, after considerable debate, did guarantee equality of the sexes in all walks of life in Article 3 of the federal constitution (the Grundgesetz, or Basic Law) in May 1949, the equal rights provision came into direct conflict with the definition of the roles of wives as subordinates within the family in the Civil Code (Bürgerliches Gesetzbuch) of 1900, which remained in effect. The Basic Law required a revision by 1953 of all laws that came into conflict with Article 3, but the Christian-conservative government worked against any fundamental reform, which the KPD and SPD and many West German women demanded. The Americans, whose homeland continued to discriminate against women in politics, education, and employment, also did not push for German legal reforms, which only gradually came into effect between 1957 and 1975.[32]

Although OMGUS took some credit for supporting German legislation against gender discrimination, it did little to advance German women's active roles in political life. Already in the Weimar Republic the active integration of women into politics, as indicated by the number and size of women's associations, their party and union membership and representation in the parliaments, was much more developed than in the United States; yet the WAS did not seem cognizant of this. The WAS's emphasis on women influencing politics behind the scenes, whether in the home or in civic clubs, rather than by actually holding office, blinded it to German women who played direct political roles after 1945. Women such as those serving in municipal city councils or state parliaments could have used OMGUS support to encourage their male colleagues to take equality issues seriously and could have profited by contacts with the League of Women Voters or the US Department of Labor, both of which sent advisors over to assist the WAS and sponsored exchange visits with selected German women. But the WAS did little to support female politicians, because the majority of them were on the liberal or leftist side of the political spectrum.[33]

The fact that the Soviet zone of occupation and, after 1949, the German Democratic Republic touted women's social and economic equality along with the expectation that women would be gainfully employed influenced how both the American occupiers and West German politicians approached women's role in the labor force, society, and politics. Cold War propaganda in West Germany began to warn that the model of women's social and economic equality propagated in the East would lead to the destruction of the family and the loss of femininity. As the American occupiers targeted German women for democratization, neither the Americans "bringing them democracy" nor the early postwar Germans in positions of authority, especially in the mainstream Protestant and Catholic churches and the conservative Christian parties, the CDU and the Christian Social Union (Christlich Soziale Union, or CSU), wanted women to have or to aspire to real social, economic, or political equality with men. They continued to propagate women's "equality" based on difference and emphasized their role as mothers and housewives.[34] The propaganda reinforced traditional biases against women not only in the workforce but also in the political realm, where conservative family policies stymied the realization of gender equality, despite legislation at the state and the national level, and kept women second-class citizens.[35] German and American interests also seemed to merge in the general belief that a return to the prewar gender order with male breadwinners and supportive, subordinate wives would facilitate the demobilization and reintegration of returning soldiers and prisoners of war into civilian society, just as they had after World War I.[36]

Gender and German Municipal Politics

The postwar challenges to traditional gender roles,[37] and then the backlash against them, was particularly visible in local German politics, where women's early postwar political activism manifested itself in various ways. Once political activity was permitted in the western occupation zones in late August 1945, some women formed their own political parties, including the Frauenpartei in Stuttgart,[38] the Soziale Frauenpartei in Würzburg, and a women's party in Frankfurt am Main, but they either failed to make significant electoral gains or were denied licenses by OMGUS.[39] Those operating within male-dominated political parties did, however, have electoral success on the local level. Women's representation on municipal councils in a number of towns and cities in the US zone was higher by 15 to 20 percent in the mid-to-late 1940s and early 1950s than any time previously. The significant number of German women—typically those with fewer family obligations, such as those who were single or had grown children—elected to the early postwar municipal councils frequently exhibited activist, independent political behavior, but this trend petered out after less than a decade. Elected female politicians became less assertive and by the mid-1950s began to disappear altogether, as Cold War ideological imperatives about gender roles intensified. Few managed to ascend, as might have been expected, from municipal politics into state (*Land*) or federal politics, and when they did, they lasted only for one term.[40]

The local level thus provides an interesting lens into the interplay of postwar gender politics between local politicians and American occupiers in their mutual quest for democratization and reconstruction. Already before the first postwar municipal elections in the spring of 1946, some German women's organizations attempted, without any support from the American authorities, to promote women's active involvement in local and state decisionmaking. In Munich a women's organization passed a resolution about the need to include women in responsible posts in state and local administrations.[41] In Stuttgart, Social Democrat Anna Haag, one of the few women appointed to the advisory city council in 1945, called attention to the fact that in the Franconian village of Korbersdorf, the local council was made up exclusively of women. This was, she said, not only of local significance, but "symptomatic for the new position that women of our day are beginning to take on in political life."[42] Haag, who became an elected SPD state representative in Baden-Württemberg from 1946 to 1950, appeared to be foresighted, but in reality, political openings for women proved to be narrower than she imagined and considerably shorter lived.

The experience of the women who served on the Munich city council in the immediate postwar years illustrates why and how the window of opportunity was so brief. Their challenges to the gender status quo were neither propelled nor supported by the Americans, despite the WAS's official mandate to encourage women's political and civic involvement to further German democratization. By promoting women's rights beyond both the confines of the American civic club model of women's public activism and the ideal of republican motherhood—in which women influence society only indirectly, by raising good citizens[43]—the female city councilors defied the vision of OMGUS and the WAS.

In 1945, the OMGUS-appointed mayor of Munich, Karl Scharnagl, a member of the former and then revived Bavarian People's Party (Bayrische Volkspartei), called on the leaders of the old pre-1933 non-Nazi parties in Munich to present him with lists of representatives from whom he would choose a thirty-six-member advisory city council. The former party leaders did not include a single woman on their lists, although women had indeed been represented in the pre-1933 city councils in Munich. The mayor eventually appointed one woman from his own party, which was the regional and generally more conservative wing of the German Catholic party and the predecessor of the CSU, but only at OMGUS insistence.[44] In this period before the founding of the WAS and before political parties could exert direct political influence, the initiative to include a woman on the Munich advisory council came from the American male officers charged with restoring local German government.

In the first postwar elections in Munich, those of May 26, 1946, five of the thirty-nine seats on the city council went to women, of whom four came from the left.[45] Except for a thirty-three-year-old KPD member, these women (three SPD and one CSU) ranged in age from forty-six to fifty-nine; only one was married, and none had small children. Four of the five, the representatives of the SPD and KPD, had been persecuted and incarcerated by the Nazis, and all were employed at the time of their election.[46] In many ways they mirrored the so-called "abnormal family situation" that was in fact the sociological immediate postwar norm, but that had also been typical of many, especially SPD, female parliamentarians during the Weimar Republic.[47]

These women initially had difficulty in making their voices heard on the council, as the debate over pay equity illustrates. OMGUS had issued a directive ordering equal pay for equal work, which was incorporated into the new Bavarian constitution,[48] yet Munich's city personnel director sought to avoid implementing the policy by arguing that the constitution really meant equal pay for equal *performance*, and that women did not perform the same as men. As the issue was discussed in the city council, Scharnagl, the now-elected CSU Lord Mayor, noted the dangers of interpreting the Bavarian Constitution literally, warning that male workers would feel indignant if the policy were to be implemented. The motion to implement equal pay was defeated soundly.[49] OMGUS, which monitored council decisions and at this stage of the occupation could have insisted that the directive be followed, remained silent.

Overall on this first elected postwar city council, women were given minor committee assignments, mainly in those fields deemed "especially suited" for women, such as education, health, youth, and welfare, and played only minor roles in debates. After all five women were reelected two years later and were joined by several new women, the entire group became much more vocal. The number of women on the 1948 council doubled, reaching 20 percent of its fifty members and constituting a third of the factions of four parties—the KPD, SPD, the liberal Free Democratic Party (Freie Demokratische Partei) and the Reconstruction Alliance (Wiederaufbau-Vereinigung)—while the Christian conservative CSU and the Bavarian Party (Bayern Partei) each had at most 10 percent female representatives in their faction. The proportion of women city councilors was the highest in Munich's history until then and would remain so for many years thereafter, at least until the 1982 municipal elections. In terms of their marital status and family situations, as well as employment and experience under the Nazis, the women elected in 1948 resembled the 1946 cohort, as well as their Weimar predecessors.[50] They were independent women, largely in nonconventional gender roles, who apparently were not regarded as so exceptional or abnormal by Germans at the time. Indeed, they had been elected by voters, at a time when the major-ity of the electorate was female, who singled them out from slots relatively low on the party lists, proving that their party's popularity alone did not account for their success.[51]

Once in office, most started out somewhat shy, but rather quickly they began to speak with ease and self-confidence. The overall atmosphere in the council became quite a bit livelier, and gender issues moved to the fore. Notably, the recently formed American WAS was not a factor here, as it appar-ently never contacted any of these city councilors. To the dismay of male party leaders, the 1948–52 Munich women councilors, across the political spec-trum, frequently ignored traditional party discipline by introducing numerous cross-party women's motions and actively promoting equal rights for women, whether their own parties supported them or not. Like the four women on the Parliamentary Council—Elisabeth Selbert and Friederike Nadig (SPD), Helene Weber (CDU) and Helene Wessel (Catholic Zentrum)—who pushed the sixty-one members of the Parliamentary Council hard to get the equality clause included in the Basic Law, the Munich women took particularly strong stands on equal pay issues and on the promotion, training, and continuing education of women in city employment. For a few of the SPD women coun-cilors, their "independence" led to conflicts with the party hierarchy, result-ing in penalties ranging from being barred from running for reelection to ejection from the party altogether. Some of these cases involved charges of association with communists and peace groups, but sources indicate that the independence and strong character of these particular women singled them out as "troublemakers" whom the party wanted to purge.[52] In addition to get-ting them thrown out of the SPD, the charge of associating with communists alienated the Americans; US intervention on their behalf, even if it had been requested, would not have been forthcoming.[53]

OMGUS also failed to intervene on women's behalf when they did not receive equal pay for equal work, despite its insistence that the principle be included in the Bavarian constitution. But the large number of women in the Munich city council did draw the attention of the OMGUS detachment for Bavaria. Shortly after the 1948 election the (male) detachment officers arranged for individual interviews with the women.[54] The data the women provided are less telling than the response of the American male interviewers, who made comments such as: "The interviewee makes an excellent impression, bright and charming" and "The interviewee is uncertain (as concerns her city council post; otherwise she is elegant and quite [a] pretty-type exclusive fashion boutique manager); she apparently doesn't quite know herself how she got to be a city councilor." In this latter example, the city councilor being interviewed was accompanied by the male head of her party, who constantly interrupted and corrected her as she tried to respond. Although the interviewer noted the man's comments verbatim, he did not seem to connect the woman's "uncertainty" with her party leader's presence and behavior.[55] This episode reveals that individual OMGUS officers often showed little understanding of or sensitivity to gender politics, while projecting their understanding of American political culture onto Germans.

The next two Munich city councils, those of 1952–56 and 1956–60, included just fewer than 20 percent women. This was still a considerable proportion, yet the number of cross-party women's initiatives and discussions of women's issues decreased considerably. This was not because the women who had previously played active roles had now changed their behavior, but because of a generational shift that was clearly supported by the male party leadership. The younger women entering the council in the 1950s, perhaps influenced by the WAS and Cold War ideology, were more likely to identify themselves as housewives, whether they worked outside the home or not, and to defer to party discipline. Unlike their older female colleagues, who had often already been active in Weimar politics, these young women entered politics only after the war and tended to play more passive roles. The older, politically active women had been unable to establish a precedent for having women as a major political presence in municipal government. Their more independent, even confrontational style was not emulated by most of those of the younger generation. Societal pressure for a return to "normal" gender roles, as well as a lack of appreciation for politically active women,[56] combined

63

with the US occupation authorities' failure to support their political quest, and the rise of Cold War propaganda criticizing East Germany's commitments to gender equality, greatly aggravated this situation.[57]

Gender Role "Normalization" and the Loss of Political Power

As German prisoners of war gradually returned home and currency reform brought with it economic normalization, women felt growing pressure to leave their jobs and return home to their families. Urged to be apolitical and concentrate on consumption and restoring their homes, many women seemed to have felt a sense of responsibility to bring order to the household and the family. Although many women remained employed and, in fact, their employment rates continued to rise, their jobs were publicly portrayed as substitute or interim in character. At the same time, discussions surrounding efforts to reform labor, social and family law to make it comport with the Basic Law's principle of "equality between men and women," as stated in its Article 3, elicited loud pronouncements about women's primary role as housewives and mothers. These reactionary pronouncements discouraged even professional women from defining themselves publicly as anything beyond this primary role. Women working in previously male-dominated fields remained frozen in subordinate positions and were rarely given a chance for further training or promotion.[58] Unmarried women were treated as outcasts in public, both at work and in social situations,[59] and the WAS view of single German women as unfortunates did little to alleviate this marginalization.

The social biases against women's public presence gradually affected the extent and character of their political activism. Starting in 1952, as younger, less assertive women were elected to the councils, members of the older female cohort began retiring as the result of age or ill health or were labeled as "troublesome" and marginalized by their parties. As a result, gender politics in municipal government in Munich and elsewhere in the former US zone of occupation changed. As traditional gender roles for women no longer came under challenge, the model of the male-breadwinner family once again took hold.

Meanwhile Cold War rhetoric in the West condemned what was regarded as a loss of femininity among East German women because of the GDR regime's stress on gender equality. West German propaganda increasingly referred to East German women as *Hosenweiber* (women in pants)—a denunciation of women who "wore the pants" and thus transgressed their feminine roles.[60] The OMGUS WAS continued to support nonpartisan groups, such as those that had participated in the first interzonal women's conference in May 1947, and in October 1949 it helped them form the German Women's Circle (Deutsche Frauenring e.V.), an umbrella organization of West German women's associations in the tradition of the BDF. The Frauenring was more inclined to stress gender difference alongside demands for equal rights and cooperation with men, rather than fundamental gender equality. Like the BDF, it embraced a maternalist political approach, propagating the slogan "equal but not the same." In the interim, more activist grassroots groups had emerged in large cities in both the British and US zones, and they were committed to working for women's political, social, and economic equality as well as setting up special offices for women's concerns.[61] These groups objected to the less politicized tenor of the Frauenring, as they watched their continued pacifist and egalitarian movement get swallowed up when they worked within the Frauenring's larger bureaucratic structure.[62] The South German Women's Working Group (Süddeutsche Frauenarbeitskreis, or SFAK), for example, defined itself as antifascist and antimilitarist and advocated for women's representation on all levels of parliamentary government. Its more progressive politics and spokeswomen's ideological closeness to the SPD limited its appeal to more conservative Bavarian women and prevented it from gaining the support of the WAS.[63]

After the founding of the Federal Republic in May 1949, the national women's organizations lacked the ability to mobilize support to implement the equal rights clause of the West German constitution, which key female politicians, along with the early local and regional women's groups, had struggled to include in the Basic Law.[64] Women's organizations, the media, political parties, and the government urged women to be supportive of men rather than take political initiatives of their own.[65] Christian Democrat Dorothea Karsten, the first head of the West German Interior Ministry's women's section, promoted separate spheres for men and women, while warning women that they risked sacrificing the special identity granted them by their role in the family if they tried to enter the public world of men. Such women, she felt, would become a mirror image of men and lose their emotionalism, their special way of relating to people, their acquiescence, and their ability to self-sacrifice; ultimately they would have to give up having a family.[66] The WAS had not pushed for this extreme version of the separate-spheres ideology, but its approach had done little to discourage such attitudes or to support more progressive women to become more politically influential.

65

Women's groups that continued to agitate actively for gender equality and other feminist concerns, even into the 1950s, ran the risk of being labeled communist, and after the KPD was banned in 1956, of being banned as well, especially if they supported antimilitarist causes such as holding a referendum on the issue of German rearmament, which many of them did. The largest German women's postwar organization, the DFD, grew out of various antifascist women's committees, which in March 1947 had sent some 2,000 delegates, half of them from the Soviet zone, to a German Women's Congress for Peace in Berlin.[67] The DFD, which was not officially founded in the FRG until 1951 but then was banned as a communist organization in 1957, took strong stands in favor of equal rights for women and against militarism. These positions earned the opposition of Gabrielle Strecker, the CDU politician who became the first head of the women's radio station (*Frauenfunk*) in the state of Hesse. Appointed by OMGUS and advised by the WAS, she used polemical Cold War rhetoric in her critique of the DFD, associating the organization with the kind of women's emancipation found in East Germany, which she considered antithetical to the womanly (*fraulich*) essence of women. Like the WAS, Strecker publicly promoted a nonpartisan women's movement while overtly red-baiting pacifist women activists and their organizations, whether or not they were affiliated with the DFD.[68]

Conclusion

US occupation authorities were certainly not solely responsible for the 1950s retreat of German women into the private sphere or their return to more traditional gendered behavior. But OMGUS did not intervene to support the implementation of equality provisions in either the state constitutions or the Basic Law, despite its official espousal of gender equality. The WAS emphasis on driving more women into the civic sphere, especially via nonpartisan civic organizations, rather than into active political participation and electoral politics, did little to help further German women's direct political influence. The rhetoric of maternalism and anticommunism, along with the antifeminist bias of the WAS, limited rather than encouraged German women's opportunities for emancipation.

German women faced many obstacles when they tried to pursue apparent emancipation opportunities. Together with anticommunist rhetoric, the restriction of women's employment options as a result of long-held biases about women's abilities and alleged inferior performance compared to male workers, and views about the primacy of the family and the household for married women, created a self-fulfilling prophecy: many women seemed to accept and probably internalize a sense of inferiority in the workplace due to poor pay and treatment as well as a sense of guilt about working outside the home because of the possible detrimental effects on the domestic sphere. In the 1950s, the majority of West German women, at least overtly, gave top priority to their homes and family, which, of course, public and political discourse encouraged them to do. Nevertheless, many found themselves having to work in menial, unskilled, or semiskilled occupations with little job security, chance for advancement, financial compensation, authority, or recognition. The closing-off of career opportunities limited women's public influence and created a poor public self-image even for single women, making it less likely that they would seek active participation in political life.[69] If women could play only subordinate roles at work, how could they imagine important roles for themselves in the even less traditionally female sphere of public life and politics? Yet, without women's active participation in political life, the pattern of discrimination was unlikely to be changed, whether socially or judicially.

As the example of the Munich women city councilors in the first decade following World War II shows, there were women who, given the chance, were quite eager to participate in political life. But these were usually older, often unattached, women who could draw on their pre-1933 political and professional experiences and party connections to reenter politics. Even they, however, were rarely able to ascend into state and national parliaments, nor were they able to alter fundamentally the political party system and its antifemale and antifeminist bias. When it came to the younger women who were often married and in many cases still had children at home but nevertheless ran and won elections in the 1950s, they found themselves confronted with a combination of the ever-strengthening resurgence of traditional German gender expectations and the Cold War and antifeminist politics of the US occupation authorities and the CDU/CSU-led federal government.

Notes

1. Robert G. Moeller, *Protecting Motherhood: Women and the Family in the Politics of Postwar West Germany* (Berkeley: University of California Press, 1993), 27.

2. Hermann Korte, "Bevölkerungsstruktur und -entwicklung," in *Die Bundesrepublik Deutschland*, ed. Wolfgang Benz (Frankfurt/M: Fischer Taschenbuch Verlag, 1983), 2:17.

3. *Frankfurter Allgemeine Zeitung*, March 13, 1953, as quoted in *Aufstieg aus dem Nichts: Deutschland von 1945 bis 1953*, ed. Kurt Zentner (Cologne: Kiepenheuer & Witsch, 1954), 1:88.

4. *Frankfurter Allgemeine Zeitung*, November 8, 1950, as quoted in Zentner, *Aufstieg aus dem Nichts*, 1:54. See also Angela Vogel. "Familie," in *Die Bundesrepublik Deutschland*, ed. Wolfgang Benz (Frankfurt/M.: Fischer Taschenbuch Verlag, 1983), 2:99.

5. Vogel, "Familie," 99–100.

6. Annette Kuhn, ed., "Frauen suchen neue Wege der Politik," in *Frauen in der deutschen Nachkriegszeit*, ed. Annette Kuhn (Düsseldorf: Schwann, 1986), 2:14–21. Wendler reached the public by publishing in the US-controlled *Die Neue Zeitung*, while Maria Pfeifer wrote in the women's magazine *Der Regenbogen* and von Zahn-Harnack spoke in Berlin on various occasions to the German Women's League in 1945.

7. See Irene Stoehr, "Cold War Communities: Women's Peace Politics in Postwar West Germany, 1945–1952," in *Home/Front: The Military, War and Gender in Twentieth-Century Germany*, ed. Karen Hagemann and Stefanie Schüler-Springorum (Oxford: Berg, 2002), 311–16.

8. See, for example, statements by the head of an alliance of women's organizations in Stuttgart, Dorothea Groener-Geyer, as cited in Moeller, *Protecting Motherhood*, 55. See also Kuhn, "Frauen suchen neue Wege der Politik," 14–18.

9. Kuhn, "Frauen suchen neue Wege der Politik," 15.

10. Vogel. "Familie," 99. See Moeller, *Protecting Motherhood*, 25; and Nori Möding, "Die Stunde der Frauen? Frauen und Frauenorganisationen des bürgerlichen Lagers," in *Von Stalingrad zur Währungsreform*, ed. Martin Broszat et al. (Munich: Oldenbourg Verlag, 1990), 619–32, 622.

11. Moeller, *Protecting Motherhood*, 25–6. Moeller argues that German labor officials steadfastly tried "to limit and label as temporary women's access to jobs held largely or exclusively by men." Examples of local government officials contesting equal pay for equal work will be provided later in this chapter.

12. It is worth noting that such rights were not even formalized in principle in the United States at this time.

13. Hermann-Josef Rupieper coined the term "bringing democracy to the Frauleins" in his article with the same title, "Bringing Democracy to the Frauleins: Frauen als Zielgruppe der amerikanischen Demokratisierungspolitik in Deutschland 1945–1952," *Geschichte und Gesellschaft* 17 (1991): 61–91.

14. National Archives and Records Administration, Washington National Records Center (NARA), RG 260, ECR, CEB, WAS (hereafter WAS Records), Box 156, File "Visiting Experts' Reports". See also Marianne Zepp, *Redefining Germany: Reeducation, Staatsbürgerschaft und Frauenpolitik im US-Amerikanisch besetzten Nachkriegsdeutschland* (Göttingen: Vandenhoeck & Ruprecht, 2007), 220–25.

15. WAS Records, Box 157, "Women's Affairs Policy (activities within OMGUS)."

16. Ibid., Anna Lord Strauss to Lucius D. Clay, September 29, 1947.

17. Ibid. The memo is entitled: "The Needs and Problems of German Women with Suggested Proposals from Military Government Offices."

18. Archiv des Instituts für Zeitgeschichte-München (IfZ), OMGUS Files, RG 260, ECR, *5/297-1/1*, 1 of 4. These archival designations are based on the original NARA

citation system indicating box, folder, and file in effect at the time the German microfilming project took place. Unfortunately, there was never a concordance developed once NARA moved these files to College Park and created a new filing system, so microfilmed OMGUS files in German archives retain the original NARA designations. OMGUS official Rebecca G. Wellington wrote an undated report about the DFD, in which she stated: "There has recently been established a Women's Affairs Branch of OMGUS which . . . should do much to combat the expansion of the DFD in the US-Zone. But it is highly unlikely that the non-Communist women's organizations can successfully compete with the DFD unless they are given material assistance at least in some degree comparable to that afforded to the DFD."

19. See Gisela Notz, *Frauen in der Mannschaft: Sozialdemokratinnen im Parlamentarischen Rat und im Deutschen Bundestag, 1948/49–1957* (Bonn: Verlag J.H.W. Dietz Nachf., 2003); and Petra Holz, *Zwischen Tradition und Emanzipation: CDU-Politikerinnen in der Zeit von 1946 bis 1960* (Königstein: Ulrike Helmer Verlag, 2004).

20. The Education and Cultural Affairs Branch was the successor agency to the Education and Religious Affairs Branch.

21. Zepp, *Redefining Germany*, 242.

22. WAS Records, Box 156, File "Visiting Experts' Reports." Press Release from Mrs. C. G. Woodhouse, September 5, 1948. Woodhouse apparently did not consider either Hahn or Woodsmall feminists but wanted to be sure that the WAS hired no feminists.

23. Karen Hagemann, "Mobilizing Women for War: The History, Historiography and Memory of German Women's War Service in the Two World Wars," *Journal of Military History* 75, no. 3 (2011): 1074–75.

24. Loc. cit., press release from Mrs. Chase Going Woodhouse re: German Women's Activities.

25. Ibid. Woodhouse stated that the "good mother tradition can be used in an appeal for more participation in public affairs." I use the term "civic sphere" rather than public sphere, because it was the term the WAS employed and its dimensions differ from that of the public sphere, or in what philosopher Jürgen Habermas would term "civil society."

26. WAS Records, Box 11, File "General Correspondence VII B," May 17, 1949 Community Education Branch meeting minutes.

27. Ibid., Box 156. File "Daily Correspondence (from March 1, 1948 on)," May 27, 1948, biographical information on Mrs. Lorena Hahn.

28. Sophia Smith Collection, Smith College, Ruth F. Woodsmall Papers (hereafter Woodsmall Papers), Box 52, Folder 2, Report of Mrs. Bartlett B. Heard, Visiting Expert, Women's Affairs Section when she visited Germany from May 27 to August 28, 1950. Cited by Toni Mortimer in "Officially Speaking: United States Policies Regarding Family Roles for German Women, 1945–1952" (paper presented at the ninth Berkshire Conference on the History of Women, Vassar College, Poughkeepsie, NY, June 11–13, 1993), 3. Under the Allied High Commission (HICOG) in 1949, the WAS was reclassified as a branch.

29. Woodsmall Papers, Box 50. Folder 5, Memo on Women's Affairs, Basis of Organization and Program, by Ruth Woodsmall, Sept. 9, 1949, cited in Mortimer, "Officially Speaking," 7–8.

30. In 1952, the Women's Affairs Branch hit upon a solution to the problem of what to do with women who did not fit into conventional family roles: it set out "to create a

politically educated group of German [women] leaders as a bulwark against communist infiltration and pernicious communist propaganda." See Woodsmall Papers, Box 57, Folder 1, HICOG Cultural and Exchange program, Program Area N. WA 525–Women's Affairs.

31. WAS Records, Box 157, "Women's Affairs Policy (activities within OMGUS)." Since the German states were the highest level of German government at the time, the comparison of the gender composition of the state parliaments in the US zone was made with that of the composition of the proportionately elected representatives in the US House of Representatives.

32. See Eva Kolinsky, *Women in West Germany: Life, Work and Politics* (Oxford and New York: Berg Publishers, 1989), 42–3.

33. See Moeller, *Protecting Motherhood*, 37, where Moeller argues: "Perhaps more so than any other aspect of social and political recovery, West Germans were left on their own when it came to defining policies to re-shape gender relations in the aftermath of fascism and defeat."

34. See Rupieper, "Bringing Democracy to the Frauleins," 61–91; and Rebecca Boehling, "Mütter in die Politik: Amerikanische Demokratisierungsbemühungen nach 1945: Eine Antwort auf Hermann-Josef Rupieper," *Geschichte und Gesellschaft* 19 (1993): 504–11.

35. See Kolinsky, *Women in West Germany*, 43.

36. See, for example, Maureen Healy, "Civilizing the Soldier in Postwar Austria," in *Gender and War in Twentieth-Century Eastern Europe*, ed. Nancy M. Wingfield and Maria Bucur (Bloomington: Indiana University Press, 2006), 47–69.

37. Some would argue that gender roles were already intensely challenged during World War II, perhaps even more so than in the postwar period. See Hagemann, "Mobilizing Women for War," 1055–93.

38. German political activity was permitted in the US zone as of August 27, 1945.

39. For Stuttgart, see Hermann Vietzen, *Chronik der Stadt Stuttgart, 1945–1948* (Stuttgart: Ernst Klett Verlag, 1972), 126 and 178–182. In 1948, women initially made up nearly 12 percent of Stuttgart's sixty-member city council; after various replacements, the proportion rose to 15 percent. For Würzburg, see Bayrisches Hauptstaatsarchiv, RG 260, OMGBY, ID, 10/90·1/20, 1 of 3, 18 April 1946 Würzburg Detachment Report. For Frankfurt am Main, see *Frauenalltag und Frauenbewegung. 1890–1980*, Katalog des Historischen Museums, Frankfurt am Main (Frankfurt/M.: Roter Stern, 1981), 135.

40. Möding, "Die Stunde der Frauen?", 626.

41. Michael Schattenhofer, ed., *Chronik der Stadt München 1945–1948* (Munich: Stadtarchiv München, 1980), 166.

42. Anna Haag, "Frauen in Parlamenten und Kabinetten," in *Frauenbuch*, eds. Lisa Albrecht and Hanna Simon (Offenbach: Bollwerk-Verlag Karl Drott, 1947), 44–45, as cited by Möding, "Die Stunde der Frauen?," 619. Either Möding or Haag or both mistakenly referred to this unique village as Kobersdorf, when in fact it was Korbersdorf. The town was incorporated into Marktredwitz in 1975. See letter from Bavarian State Interior Ministry to author, May 25, 1994, in response to inquiry about the town's records.

43. This idea was first developed by Mary Wollstonecraft in her 1792 treatise, *A Vindication of the Rights of Woman*. For the spread of this concept to the United States, see Linda Kerber's discussion of "republican motherhood" in *Women of the Republic: Intellect and Ideology in Revolutionary America* (Chapel Hill: University of North Carolina Press, 1980).

44. Stadtarchiv München, Bürgermeister und Rat (hereafter BuR) 1537, "Bildung des beratenden Stadtrates." The Munich detachment of the US military government had insisted on two, but only one was actually appointed.

45. Schattenhofer, *Chronik*, 170–71.

46. Stadtarchiv München, BuR 2528, Zeitungsauschnittsammlung Personen, Ratskartei der Mitglieder des Stadtrates.

47. See Karen Hagemann, *Frauenalltag und Mannerpolitik: Alltagsleben und gesellschaftliches Handeln von Arbeiterfrauen in der Weimarer Republik* (Bonn: Verlag J.H.W. Dietz Nachf., 1990), 574-577. This was the case not only for SPD female Weimar parliamentarians but also for female party and trade union leaders.

48. At this point in 1946, the new state constitutions represented the highest level of German law, since there was no federal government.

49. Stadtarchiv München. RP *72011,* Stadtratssitzungsprotokol, June 10, 1947, 1349ff. One of the KPD representatives was the party spokesperson within the council, and the other was Adelheid Liessmann, the director of the office of the municipal pawnshops, whose performance two years later the new Social Democratic lord mayor, Thomas Wimmer, would describe as such an exception to normal female performance.

50. Stadtarchiv München, BuR 2528, Zeitungsauschnittsammlung Personen, Ratskartei der Mitglieder des Stadtrates.

51. The political parties submitted lists of candidates to the voters. Voters could simply vote the party ticket or single out individuals from the list. The higher one's place on the list, the more likely one was to be elected as long as voters selected the ticket. Thus being singled out from low on the list indicated a genuine selection of the individual.

52. Stadtarchiv München, BuR 2528/4 (alt); ZA·Personen, *Abendzeitung*, February 1, 1956; *Die Südpost*, 10 May 1950; Author's interview with Felicitas Füss, August 30, 1991, München. Füss was the only woman to have served as the head of the local SPD district committee (*Bezirksausschussvorsitzende*) from the time the party was refounded after the war until 1960.

53. The fact that different communist-led organizations and especially the DFD, which OMGUS managed eventually to restrict to the Soviet zone, committed themselves to the peace and anti-rearmament movements resulted in the word "peace" being regarded by the US occupation authorities and some Germans as a code word for communism. This was despite the fact that others, including Christian groups, did so as well. See Möding, "Die Stunde der Frauen?" 634.

54. OMGUS detachment officers were always male and often career military.

55. Archive of the Institut für Zeitgeschichte-München, OMGUS files, RG260, OMGUSB·ID, 10/70–112.

56. See, for example, the SPD female parliamentarian biographies in Gisela Notz, *Frauen in der Mannschaft: Sozialdemokratinnen im Parlamentarischen Rat und im Deutschen Bundestag 1948/49–1957* (Bonn: Verlag J.H.W. Dietz Nachf., 2003).

57. Nori Möding argues that after 1945 all the politically engaged women in prominent positions were born before 1915 and that there was a striking void of politically active women, even in "staatsbürgerlichen Frauenverbänden" in the cohorts born after 1920. Möding, "Die Stunde der Frauen?," 639.

58. Ibid., 622.

59. See Elizabeth Heineman, *What Difference Does a Husband Make?: Women and Marital Status in Nazi and Postwar Germany* (Berkeley: University of California Press, 1999).

60. See Lutz Niethammer, *Bürgerliche Gesellschaft in Deutschland* (Frankfurt/M.: Fischer, 1990), 602.

61. Vogel, "Frauen," 82–3.

62. Ibid., 83.

63. Zepp, *Redefining Germany*, 157–164. Else Reventlow, the head of the SFAK, was an SPD member and worked for the OMGUS German language newspaper *Die Neue Zeitung*, at least until 1948, when she disagreed with the more nationalist course she felt the newspaper was taking. Her departure may well have also made it difficult for her to curry favor with the WAS.

64. Hagemann, *Frauenalltag*, 134.

65. See Antonie Cordemann. "Die Frau muss mithelfen," in *Der Bürger im Staat,* 1951, 10; See also Institut für Zeitgeschichte-München, ED 145/24, Sattler Nachlass, Nov. 6, 1950 CSU Landtagswahl Rednerdienst Nr. 3, "Die CSU und die Frau;" Ibid., ED 117176. Eberhard Nachlass, SPD, Bezirk Württemberg-Baden. Referenten-Material 7. June 1946, "Frauenfrage"; Ibid., ED 117175, Eberhard Nachlass, Befragungen des Institut für Demoskopie, Sept. 3, 1949.

66. Vogel, "Frauen," 85.

67. Ingeborg Nödinger, "'Mitwissen, mitverantworten und mitbestimmen': Zu den Anfängen des Demokratischen Frauenbundes Deutschland," in *Frauen in der deutschen Nachkriegsgeschichte,* ed. Annette Kuhn (Düsseldorf: Schwann, 1986), 2:122–26.

68. Kuhn, *Frauen in der deutschen Nachkriegsgeschichte*, 2:82.

69. Various works have tried to get at what women were thinking and feeling in this period with interviews, surveys, and oral histories. See, for example: Sibylle Meyer and Eva Schulze, eds., *Wie wir das alles geschafft haben: Alleinstehende Frauen berichten über ihr Leben nach 1945*, (Munich: Beck, 1985, 3rd ed.); Meyer and Schulze, *Von Liebe sprach damals keiner: Familienalltag in der Nachkriegszeit* (Munich: C.H. Beck, 1985); and Rita Polm *". . . neben dem Mann die andere Hälfte eines Ganzes zu sein?!": "Frauen in der Nachkriegszeit": zur Situation und Rolle der jüngeren Frauen in den Städten der Bundesrepublik (1945–1949)* (Münster: Unrast, 1990).

Chapter 3
A Women's Peace Dividend: Demobilization and Working-Class Women in Chicago, 1945–1953

Laura McEnaney

World War II began for most Americans not with Pearl Harbor, but with a train trip. Millions boarded trains in a "great defense migration," as one journalist called it, headed for boot camp, internment camp, or a new job. The war came to a close that way, too. As the United States demobilized, veterans, civilian workers, internees, and family travelers all boarded trains to reunite and start anew. No American city saw as much train traffic as Chicago during or immediately after the war. Since the mid-nineteenth century, Chicago's location between east and west made it a national wartime crossroads—"the place where Americans changed trains." The Travelers Aid Society (TAS) estimated that more than nine million people passed through Chicago's six major terminals from Pearl Harbor through early 1946.[1] Uniformed men, of course, made up much of this human traffic, but women were also in motion. During and after the war, they were domestic migrants of various kinds: workers, wives, mothers, fiancées, girlfriends, armed forces members, volunteers, or adventurers. Their travel, like everyone else's, bent to the necessities and opportunities of war and postwar.

One of these migrants was twenty-eight-year-old Japanese American Kaye Kimura, who in 1943 left her Manzanar, California, internment camp to resettle in Chicago. A former domestic servant, music teacher, and then office clerk, she had accepted a job in a factory that made gambling dice, despite her view that "nice girls" did not do such work. Like so many earlier settlers, Kimura came with expectations. While in camp, she told an interviewer, she "had read in books what an exciting place Chicago was. . . . There was supposed to be a sort of electrical energy in the atmosphere there." But when her train pulled in, she was disheartened: "The dirtiness of this city sounded exciting in poems but it was a big disillusionment in real life. Everything seemed so grim and cheerless." Little by little, family members joined her, and in the war's final year, they fantasized about opening their own business. Kimura, especially, sought economic independence after the war so she could finally "taste the cultural things which are obtainable to most middle-class Americans."[2]

Situated at the moments of departure and arrival in people's lives, TAS staff heard similar tales of longing from millions who passed through terminals across the country. This chapter uses Kimura's arrival as a point of departure for exploring urban, working-class women's demobilization—or reconversion, as it was also called—from World War II. Her story highlights the complexities and paradoxes of the war's aftermath, the central concern of this volume. The war had taken everything from her, but then it created new possibilities for economic and social autonomy. The outcome of her journey, though, would depend on a whole range of variables, all of them shaped by World War II's long reach into everyday life. As this collection reminds us, women's military timelines are not tidy, for women do not march away and then home again, the usual demarcation between war and peace. War's effects on women are uneven, too, often depending on geography. In Europe and Asia, women endured on multiple and shifting "fronts," while American women remained largely insulated from the carnage. Still, war's violence and disruption found them, stealing family members "for the duration" and leaving them with the consequences. As an internee, Kaye Kimura's trajectory from desert prison camp to urban apartment was unusual, but after settling in Chicago, her experiences resembled those of most postwar citizens. Her journey from pleasant anticipation to grudging accommodation to determined ambition for the "cultural things" of the middle-class matched the experiences of other urbanites as the United States went from making war to making peace.

This chapter examines that shift from war to peace in terms of a series of small household grievances that reveal much about the gender and class politics of demobilization after armed conflict. Chicago's crowded North Side neighborhoods offer a case study of how diverse groups—African American women from the South, Japanese American women freed from internment, and working-class white women one generation away from the turn-of-the-century wave of

European immigration—encountered demobilization's daily grind. Their post-war trials reveal that working-class women's reconversion was less a definitive break and more an extension of wartime calculations about financial and family welfare. To be sure, they shared the task of rebuilding with the men who had disappeared and now returned, but demobilization in the United States happened on a smaller scale than in Europe. It was less national reconstruction than home repair: the mending and maintenance of family and household. This was women's work before the war, and now after, it was a task laden with great national import, assigned to every American woman. As one scholar argues, the war's dislocations "put a high premium on the preservation of social order," and the "rudder" against instability was the family.[3] Blue-collar women faced this oversized charge with meager resources. In fact, war's end both augured new opportunities and resurrected old vulnerabilities for them. They worried about affordable housing, wages and prices, racial discrimination, child care, and other matters over which they had little control. And yet, despite their distance from the battle, they had a keen sense of what they saw as war's entitlements, a consciousness that came from both prewar and wartime identities. They were survivors—of a long Depression and a big war; they were paid urban workers and unpaid managers of splintered or overcrowded households; they were consumers and tenants; they were indignant victims in substandard flats, segregated housing, or internment camps; and they were citizens of both a nascent welfare state and a warfare state, which encouraged them to see their federal government as a benefactor in the transition to peace. Indeed, they saw demobilization as a negotiation in which those who had given to the war effort would now get something in return. In sum, they wanted a peace dividend.

Working-class women's struggle to assemble the ingredients of the postwar "good life" challenges a still-powerful narrative about American women after World War II: that they married, moved to the suburbs, had children, and grew quiet. Although decades of scholarly research has complicated this story, the notion that the wartime Rosie the Riveter became television's archetypal housewife June Cleaver persists. In fact, we still know too little about what happened to urban working-class women between V-J Day and their much-touted middle-class suburban entrenchment, a gap that stems not only from the difficulties of tracking war's timelines for women, but also from a wider scholarly silence on the history of demobilization. The conversion to peace was itself a *historical process*, fraught with the same kind of intricate planning dilemmas as making war, yet the postwar epoch has not been dissected as carefully as that of the war. As one historian has remarked, scholars "have simply leap-frogged over this war-to-peace transition."[4]

This essay pauses in that transition, chronicling working-class women's postwar stories from the end of World War II into the early 1950s, for that was how long women felt the war's impact. Alternating between national policy and local experience, the chapter traces how American cities like Chicago absorbed the demands of a population recovering from conflict. A focus on housing will show how single "girls" and married women, moving from train station to city apartment, asked their government to underwrite their postwar prosperity through federal rent control, a statist demand made by female citizens who thought their wartime home-front labors deserved recompense. Although attachment to a veteran was not a prerequisite for help, soldiers' wives gained a slight advantage through marriage, as the government fast-tracked returning soldiers' claims. But working-class women from around the city pressed their case for rent control as Americans who had survived—and helped win—a war. As historian John Bodnar has shown, this notion of reciprocal citizenship—the idea that citizens "served the nation because they believed the nation would serve their democratic interests in return"—permeated American political culture during the war.[5] The stories in this chapter attest to the resilience of that notion in the postwar, even as a nascent Cold War antistatism emerged, revealing a female, working-class, and multiracial support base for the liberal state, forged not on the shop floor but in the postwar apartment.

Women on the Move

From a railway lobby, the demarcation between war and peace looked fuzzy indeed. As the self-proclaimed first responders of the home-front war, the TAS predicted that demobilization would mark the onset of a "restless era" and warned that "serious problem cases loom larger on the horizon." In fact, as early as 1944, TAS staff lamented that they were already seeing "'postwar problems,'" which, they said, "took most of our time . . . [and] professional skill." Just weeks before victory in Europe, the TAS's 1945 annual report featured its own gloomy take on peace: "Workers Lose Residence," "Youthful Migrants Have No Ties," and "Wounded Veteran is 'All Mixed Up.'"[6]

These headlines were drawn from the TAS's own case records from the first phase of demobilization, and their reports show a fascinating variety of people walking through Chicago's train stations, from Mexican American migrant workers to French war brides. These armies of travelers signaled the start of a complex transformation that began before World War II ended and lasted even into the next war in Korea. The "shock of peace," as one scholar calls it,[7] was felt across the country, just as the jolt of Pearl Harbor had pulled everyone into the business of war. In truth, demobilization was less a shock than a process that happened in stages and at different intensities, depending on a city's role in the defense effort. The relationship "between the city and the sword," in historian Roger Lotchin's words, was determined by the dispersal of federal government contracts, which had concentrated war production in many older metropolitan areas, such as Chicago, along with newer urban areas in the West and Southwest.[8] Tearing down the war, so to speak, in these locales involved engaging in layers of economic planning, federal-municipal coordination, and political wrangling and compromise. At the highest levels, President Harry S Truman feared a return of the inflation and unrest that had followed World War I, and there were fierce debates within his administration over precisely how to keep unemployment low and consumer confidence high. Similarly, at the state and municipal levels, politicians, urban planners, labor leaders, and social reformers all advanced different visions of how to capitalize on their regions' wartime fortunes. They worried as much as federal officials about reconversion, knowing that any problems would surface first where they lived.[9]

The political alignments of demobilization formed around the question of what government's reach and function should be in a postwar era. Wartime expansions of state power, on the heels of Great Depression–era interventions, had been decried by conservatives as "big government," and peace liberated them to condemn even more stridently any extension of New Deal–style statism. Liberals, in contrast, sought to use government to create urban renewal programs, hoping to harness the spirit of New Deal and wartime innovations to address longstanding housing and infrastructure problems now exacerbated by wartime migrations. Some cities initiated their own plans as a hedge against demobilization's coming upheavals, but the implementation of any program, local or federal, was hamstrung by the larger question of how much or how little government to activate. Still, local demobilization efforts reflected a widespread view that government's rational planning could address gloomy postwar forecasts, such as those advanced by TAS staff and other front-line responders.[10]

On the ground, those who lived through demobilization "probably thought it was far from a planned affair," as one scholar observed.[11] In Chicago's working-class neighborhoods, where the war had taken loved ones overseas and sent others to work, residents experienced demobilization as a tangle of hope and despair. They had heard many of their leaders—politicians, union leaders, media figures, and local boosters—use the word "postwar" in the same breath as "renewal" and "prosperity," but their first encounters with peace amounted to an intensification of urbanization's worst features. The speed of wartime migrations meant that "the growing pains" of American cities at mid-century "were compressed into a relatively brief span of time," argues historian Philip Funigiello.[12] Cities that had received the most defense contracts, such as Chicago, were now the most stressed in housing, transportation, and welfare services. Along with the millions passing through the city, wartime migration had added about a quarter of a million new residents to Chicago. Even more than a year after V-J Day, one Chicago official complained, "The housing situation . . . is very acute. . . . People coming into the city still exceed those going out."[13]

TAS volunteers were the first to see this urban stress in the train terminals as they shepherded female travelers through reconversion's initial phases. According to a TAS survey of lobby traffic after the war, 42 percent of those passing through were women, and almost 60 percent of train travelers, male or female, were "unattached"—traveling with neither friends nor family. What they all needed most was temporary housing, almost impossible to find on weekends, especially for a woman alone. Propriety guided TAS assistance to single women, as it had since the late nineteenth century, reflecting the view that female newcomers to the city had to be shielded "from mishap." Station workers were warned, for example, that one hotel "may be perfectly satisfactory for a single man, but under no circumstances suitable for young women." Only one hotel in Chicago catered exclusively to women, and though volunteers acknowledged it was "not a first rate hotel," lone female travelers stayed there because they felt "insecure in a strange city, or [had] limited funds."[14]

Often, the solo female traveler was not really "single." She was connected to a serviceman as girlfriend, fiancée, or wife and mother, but this connection brought her no advantages on the road. Near the end of the war, the sole nursery at Chicago's main terminal, according to its manager, was being "used almost exclusively by wives of the lower paid service men who are still following their husbands from camp to camp or who are visiting around among relatives." These women, many of them mothers, arrived "tired, dirty, and irritable," and they found it too tough to leave the station—with babies and sometimes luggage in tow—to locate diapers and milk. "They are definitely in need of someone to help them," the manager reported.[15] After the war, they showed up in TAS case reports, arriving in Chicago to reconnect with their husbands, but they faced the same shortages as single women. One woman with her toddler came to be near her husband as he was discharged, but according to the report, this "young mother . . . could not afford $2 per night for the only room available," so she and her child got back on the train and went home.[16]

As this initial wave of female nomads passed through Chicago's terminals from V-E through V-J Day, the TAS began to notice that the second wave presented more complex challenges. "Travelers reflect the state of the nation, economically and sociologically," one staffer noted, and if true, then the state of the nation was fragile.[17] TAS president Byron Harvey reported in mid-1946 that volunteers were already seeing more intractable problems, and some of these were so delicate that he asked Chicago's railway station managers for private interview space to enable staff to give the kind of attentive care they could not provide in a bustling lobby.[18] In a sense, train passengers were evolving into "clients," and it was hard for volunteers not to see each arriving train car as a big, worrisome welfare caseload. Although it was impossible from a train lobby to really quantify what the war had wrought, TAS staffer Fern Lowry analyzed 1,500 cases during the last month of 1947 and surmised that peacetime had brought "no new or significant trends" but "more of everything numerically." TAS planners for 1949 confirmed her findings, recasting the demobilization as a "peace time mobilization," not as large as wartime, of course, but with "some of the same elements . . . present."[19]

The Economics of Postwar Morality

The necessary elements of this "peace time mobilization" were really quite simple: affordable housing, a good job, and consumption of necessities, even some luxuries—essentially, what Kaye Kimura wanted when she got to Chicago. But assembling these components would take some doing. While the TAS had been a "trusted friend" in the station, once a woman headed into the city, she would have to find some new chums to help her get by. And though every woman, whether urban greenhorn or old hand, faced what TAS staffer Lowry had called the "chaotic conditions" of postwar, she did so with different resources and liabilities. Race determined where a single woman passing through the city could stay the night or whether a veteran's wife could find anything from an apartment to health care. The housing crisis affected all working-class women, but by war's end, only white female European immigrants and their daughters and granddaughters had the "luxury" of renting second-rate housing in a wide range of neighborhoods. Race also affected a woman's chances of finding work in the postwar labor market. As former internees, Chicago's Japanese American women could now sell their labor in a diverse urban market, but only a narrow range of industries were buying—and for low wages. And, of course, these two elements—housing and jobs—determined where and how much a woman could participate in the bountiful postwar "consumers' republic."[20] Kimura's chance to realize her poetic dreams rested, then, on her ability to surmount these urban challenges. As she put it, "life was real" in the city, "and it went at a much more rapid pace . . . I had to look after myself or else go under."[21] And so as she and her female cohort set off to find the postwar good life, they left the train station with different baggage.

Moving from downtown train stations into Chicago's North Side areas, women had to navigate neighborhoods that were a varied mixture of residential and industrial, with railway lines either bordering or slicing through them. By 1950, these areas were populated by white ethnics, newly freed Japanese Americans, and African Americans, most of them renters. Overall, only 30 percent of Chicago's dwellings were owner occupied by 1950, but in sections immediately north of the city's downtown, the proportion of owner-occupied units was less than 15 percent. The war had left its imprint on these neighborhoods, but unevenly. Walking through them, one could find both seriously blighted areas and high-income zones, humming industry and abandoned lots, high-end shopping and a variety of "cheap amusements."[22]

The war had changed the workplace geography as well, with more men on the daily commute and in factories and offices, even as jobs were still largely segregated by sex. Women did not always regard this as a disadvantage; those who were single saw a workplace with more men in it as a new space to find a mate. As one office worker wrote to the *Chicago Tribune*, "Our office reconversion plans included men at desks again. . . . Our smiles abound with males around!"[23] Although World War II had sparked much hurried matchmaking, and the media began the marriage drumbeat even before the war ended, the sex ratio in 1945 was not in women's favor. The war had finally tipped it toward a surplus of women, and though the percentage of women who married was still rising, it may have been a good thing that single women were poring over fantasy magazines about future marital bliss rather than reading their government's grim analysis of their marriage prospects. A 1946 Labor Department study predicted "a largely permanent increase in the earning responsibilities" of American women, not only for war widows and wives of disabled veterans, but for single women with no connection to a soldier. In a

clinical tone, researchers argued that a "[re]duction in the numbers of mar-
riageable men," due to wartime death and serious injury, "operates to raise the
numbers of women who will never marry and who must support themselves
and in many cases other dependents as well." And this situation, they said,
would "continue over a long period of years."[24]

For many of Chicago's young, single women, this reality meant that a stay-
at-home suburban life probably would not materialize anytime soon. So they
faced the demobilization years exposed to the city's economy as solo earners but also poised to exploit its delights as unattached "girls." Although a
relatively small percentage of Chicago's population, single women of every
race loomed large as a postwar cultural phenomenon. The Young Women's
Christian Association (YWCA), which ran women's dormitories throughout
the city, noted a "decided change" in their residents in 1946: "We have the
problem of the young girl having money to travel for the first time in her life,
and having her first experience of city night club life." Interestingly, the staff
saw, too, a new breed of "single" woman: "the middle aged woman who is
finding her returned service husband and her home life unsatisfactory, coming to the city for a gay life to get away from what she thinks unbearable."
A dormitory director expressed frustration and confusion in "dealing with
girls these days," citing "petting parties" and alcohol among the troubles. Her
counterparts across Chicago, in white and African American areas, reported
similar problems, all agreeing it was a worrisome postwar trend.[25]

It is always hard to sort out these reports of young people's behaviors, because
adults (observing young singles as a kind of novel and strange tribe) were the
source, and because social welfare organizations saw potential benefit in foment-
ing a postwar morals emergency. The American Social Hygiene Association, for
instance, justified aggressive fundraising by projecting a marked increase in sexual depravity. Its postwar reports—all the way up to the Korean War—peddled
more fear than news about demobilization's ripple effects on urban communities: "VD [venereal disease] rates are rising, prostitution threatens again. Are the
gains made in wartime to be lost? Does peace mean license?"[26]

Single women themselves did not define their postwar plight in such terms.
To them, respectability was less about social conduct than about social worth,
as measured in housing conditions. And as troubled as they were about morals,
social welfare folk were just as concerned with single women's financial well-
being—that is, whether they had jobs and decent housing. In fact, they saw
a link between demobilization's economics and its sexual climate. According
to the Labor Department, for a single woman to live "in health," she had to

be paid enough to live in "a respectable neighborhood" and eat "nourishing food, properly prepared." Intangibles were important, too. The single woman "participates in the life around her," taking advantage of city recreation. She "eats candy and sodas and smokes cigarettes [and] . . . exchanges gifts with her friends." Social welfare workers knew that rising prices would make this postwar ideal hard to grasp, especially finding "respectable" housing. Labor Department figures show that nationally, Chicago had the sharpest rise in rents in 1947, and the price of clothing—not incidental to a single woman— had spiked as well.[27] Without adequate wages, single women might depend on men's favors to fund their postwar good life; without suitable housing, they might turn city streets into living rooms.

Housing Headaches: Women Petition the State

As it became clear that wartime housing shortages would persist, driving up rents, hampering economic reconversion, and, worse, stoking veteran discontent, Congress tried in piecemeal fashion to offer some relief by extending federal rent control, first administered in 1942 by the Office of Price Administration (OPA) as part of its rationing and price regulation system. By May 1946, an increasingly fiscally conservative Congress charged the new Office of the Housing Expediter (OHE) with administering *postwar* rent control, grudgingly admitting that there was still "a housing emergency" requiring "certain restrictions on rents" to continue. This extension was aimed primarily at softening demobilization's economic blows to veterans, but since the legislation applied to all of Chicago's renters (a majority of the city's population), any tenant could benefit.[28] Whether happily single, married and expecting, raising children alone, or supporting an elderly parent, female renters could rely on federal rent control. For a group of Chicagoans who could otherwise obtain the state's most generous housing benefits only by marrying a vet, it was an especially useful buffer against peacetime's economic jolts.

Federal rent control records show that women leaned heavily on this government regulation to lower rents and raise the standard of decency. Female complainants appeared in 55 percent of the OPA/OHE case files reviewed. Whether they lived in higher-end buildings or in more industrial sections, women wrote to federal officials about filthy bathrooms and negligent landlords, their voices unmediated by TAS or YWCA advocates. Case records suggest that tenants often informally coordinated their complaints, in both language and timing, and that they chose to frame their rights as members of a new, postwar renter class. At 1100 North LaSalle, occupied mostly by single white working women, more than half of the building's 307 tenants fought their management company's 1949 attempt to raise rents based on "substantial hardship," a claim landlords could make legitimately if rents were not meeting reasonable maintenance expenses. After the landlord filed a petition with the OHE, the largely white-collar tenants exposed their own balance sheets. Francis Ryan put it succinctly: "I too plead a hardship." Stella Barr tried to explain the blue-collar realities of her white-collar job: "I am among the 'white collar' class of workers, getting along on a small salary. More than 26 percent of my salary is used for my rent. I also support my aged father and another raise in rent would mean doing without many essentials." Frozen in apartments and wage structures that did not deliver prosperity as quickly as they had hoped, these sole breadwinners had monthly budgets with little give. Although office work brought some degree of social status, these clerical workers lived a precarious comfort. "I have no Union to look after my interests," said one.[29] North Side tenant Elsie Ries spoke for many when she wrote on New Year's Eve, 1949: "Everyone is waiting for the day when conditions will make it possible to move to a better place." In the meantime, though, there was falling plaster and failing heat to contend with. As one frustrated renter put it, "I would not call this the 'MORE ABUNDANT LIFE.'"[30]

These single women were clearly a class-conscious group, but in complicated ways. Tenants who lived and worked in more prosperous areas saw themselves as a higher class of working women and were careful to draw lines between their situation and those who lived in grittier areas. One tenant, who for five weeks lacked a working refrigerator, grumbled about her rising food costs, but worried as much that the number of tenants chilling their dairy on the window sill made "the apartment look like the tenement district."[31] Such statements were a poke at nearby slum areas, inhabited by a shrinking, older, European immigrant population and growing African American and Japanese American populations. Japanese American newcomers, though, shared the racial elitism of their white working-class cohort. Racism funneled them into rundown rooming house neighborhoods, but their own racial and class aspirations prompted them to distance themselves from the stereotyping aimed at their African American neighbors. Kaye Kimura, for example, insisted that the Nisei (second-generation Japanese Americans) "really want to improve their standards of living," so it upset her "when stories are passed around that we lower the standards . . . when we go into a new area."[32]

Demobilization brought similarly heightened aspirations and sobering realities for Chicago's married women. Here, too, race could intensify the challenges of a tenant-housewife, but rent records show a surprising consistency in married women's complaints. As managers of more complex households and budgets, they, too, encountered demobilization as a series of housing headaches, but their frustrations were compounded by the daily trials of trying to make a "home" out of a hovel for immediate and often extended families. Their sense of entitlement to something better was sharpened in Chicago's deteriorating and still scarce housing stock, 63 percent of which had been built before 1920.[33] Neglect during the Depression and war had turned decent housing into barely passable, and passable into slums. The rate of new construction skyrocketed after the war, but most of this was for single-family homes outside of cities. Around Chicago, and across the country, the trend toward increased home ownership for both white and nonwhite families was clear, and yet the wartime practice of "doubling up" continued nationwide, with about two million married couples or single parents still living with relatives well into the 1950s.[34] Urban, working-class housewives in former wartime "boom towns" thus found themselves in cramped postwar flats—spaces that brought too much of the celebrated nuclear family togetherness.

Married women's correspondence with the OPA/OHE can be read as a catalog of immediate postwar needs and long-term fantasies. Housewives advanced the argument that peace should, at the very least, deliver a baseline housing standard below which no self-respecting *postwar* family should be forced to live. Maybe shabby shelter was tolerable during the war, but after, it seemed unnecessary—even unjust. While single women pled their cases as vulnerable, solo earners, married women made claims based on attachments to veterans and children. In fact, sometimes they even wrote in their veteran husband's voice. Veteran status on a rent petition promised speedier processing, since it was never good public relations for an already controversial price control program (extended well after the war had ended) to be caught idle when a GI's rights were at stake. Rent records suggest that veterans' wives tried to leverage their marital mergers, hoping their husbands' status might infuse their plea with the cultural capital of warrior service in a demobilizing but not completely demilitarized culture. For example, when tenant Annette Harrison learned that veterans could get priority review, she concluded her letter by saying (as her husband): "I'd like to state again that I am a veteran. The rent is more than I can afford."[35]

Claims based on children—current and future—appeared throughout married women's correspondence, too. One expectant mother asked the OPA to investigate her landlord's misdeeds, saying: "I'm in a family way and don't want to bring a baby up in such a filthy place which is full of roaches."[36] Another, told recently by her landlord that she would be evicted for getting pregnant and thus adding another tenant to the lease, asked: "My husband is a World War II veteran. Can they put us out just because we have a child?"[37] Here, too, women tried to trade on the privileged meaning of childbearing, which carried weight in any era, but particularly in a postwar moment focused on regeneration after global devastation.

Housing insecurities affected everyone, but the remedies for African American and Japanese American women were more limited than for their white working-class peers. The war had pulled thousands of African Americans north to Chicago, almost doubling the city's black population in the 1940s. By 1950, African Americans made up almost 14 percent of Chicago's inhabitants, up from 8 percent in 1940. On the Near North Side, they comprised 20 percent of the population and climbing, but they lived cheek by jowl in its industrial quarter, marooned there by racially restrictive covenants and the prohibitive cost of housing elsewhere in the city.[38] Wartime Chicago also witnessed a significant Asian migration. The size of its Japanese American population had made it a "second city" to Los Angeles. Over 20,000 freed internees headed to the "Windy City," drawn there by the same reasons as other migrants: booming industry, plentiful jobs, and high wages. And just as important, according to the War Relocation Authority (WRA), the city's "metropolitan atmosphere" could offer "a cloak of indifference" for former internees anxious about their reception.[39] However, as the WRA pointed out, Japanese American resettlers were arriving in Chicago just as the housing crisis was worsening, so locating an apartment became their "first and increasingly desperate concern."[40] Racism restricted their choices, relegating them to "transition zones" where whites and blacks were already fighting over shifting racial boundaries.[41]

Rent case files did not record race, but surnames or snippets of migration stories show that Japanese Americans turned to the federal government for assistance soon after that same government had forcibly "relocated" them. In fact, varied evidence suggests that Japanese American attitudes about the government's role in social provision were in flux after the war. A 1947 WRA study found that "many times more Japanese Americans are now receiving public welfare assistance," in contrast to very low prewar levels. Most of those on public aid on the West Coast were the elderly Issei (first-generation Japanese immigrants), but even large Nisei families who could not find housing expected help from the state. The WRA concluded, "The feeling of stigma

85

attached to acceptance of public assistance has been greatly weakened by the evacuation experience; ill fortune was caused by public action, they believe, and many have come to accept the idea that assistance is a public responsibility properly to be accepted."[42] Certainly, Chicago's resettlers continued to lean on their own mutual aid groups, as they had for decades, but their internment, ironically, gave them a new sense of both their government's cruelty *and* capacity.

This attitudinal shift may be why we find Japanese American resettlers in the rent records asserting the same claim to federal intervention as white ethnics and African Americans. In 1948, for example, eighteen-year-old Christine Shishida and her family complained that their landlord charged more than the federally mandated price and then cheated them out of a refund. Pressing this case required real determination, because Shishida's mother was the original victim of the landlord's ruse, but she did not speak English. Christine, a high school student, had to push through her mother's claim, which required affidavits, legal help, meetings, and paperwork. Aided by a dogged OHE team of investigators, the family finally got their refund.[43] Although resettlers' relations with federal agencies were strained and still evolving after the war, the intensity of the postwar housing crisis and rent control's tangible relief led families like the Shishidas to overcome whatever reluctance they may have felt about relying on the state. In fact, as demobilization unfolded, Japanese American leaders increasingly lamented a *lack* of government in their lives, complaining in 1947 that there was still "no collective effort by either government or private agencies to meet even the most urgent needs" of resettlers.[44]

In Chicago's North Side neighborhoods, African American residents echoed this complaint. The city's Council of Social Agencies exposed glaring gaps in postwar health and welfare services for black residents, especially in those categories that would have most helped mothers—or inspired newlyweds to start families after the war. In 1947, for example, only seven of the city's forty privately run child care facilities were located in black neighborhoods, and merely fourteen of seventy-five private welfare agencies offered the kind of after-school programming that would have helped younger African Americans (and, by extension, their parents) cope with continued poverty and peacetime transitions.[45] African American parents also had a harder time keeping their families healthy. Higher rates of infant death and death from tuberculosis plagued black families, who lived in crowded, filthy housing, where they were most susceptible. Such "conditions are fulfilled notoriously in the Negro residential districts," according to public health reports, such as on Chicago's Near North Side, where researchers found "that the tuberculosis death rate increases as the rents paid for housing decrease."[46]

Black women's rent petitions confirm and chronicle this misery in painstaking detail: failing heat, broken fixtures, drafty windows, assorted bugs, and lots of dirt. Garbage (and the pests it attracted) was a perennial problem. African American housewife Mrs. Henry Grier complained that she had no hot water in the winter and her back stairway was so "covered with rubbage [*sic*]" that it presented a fire hazard. Her neighbor, Mrs. Lafayette Goins, became so fed up with dirty halls and stairways that she began to clean them herself; the landlord rewarded her not with reduced rent but with a compliment: she was "a nice lady."[47] Of course, some renters were messy and careless, but it was the manager's responsibility to provide proper containers for waste removal. Most did not do this, though, making garbage a postwar women's issue. In 1946, Chicago's sanitation commissioner found that at 85 percent of the stops, garbage crews drove up to find either faulty containers or none at all.[48] In the meantime, housewives like Mrs. Goins had to keep battling roaches and rats, and they could do little about it except tidy their own spaces and complain. The power of their grievance lay in the mundane details of women's work—no hot water, broken toilets, sick babies, and stubborn dirt. These were legitimate war-related claims, petitioned to the state by women who felt the war's consequences most intimately as caretakers of others, and whose racial experiences demobilization had yet to alter.

Postwar Women in a Postwar State

For women like Mrs. Shishida, Mrs. Goins, and thousands of others, it took initiative and determination to "complain" (a word with inflections of the postwar nagging housewife). To research, write, telephone, commute downtown to agency offices, track family budgets, and prove landlord negligence amounted to serious work, layered on top of other women's work, paid and unpaid. Chicago's working-class women did this work because they wanted long-term material and social stability, something they had lacked since the 1930s. Their search for a peace dividend, for some recompense after years of sacrifice, begs a reconsideration of how to periodize war and how to evaluate its outcomes for women. War's totality includes the years following the conflict, as civilians recover, regroup, and plan for the future. Extending wartime narratives to include that aftermath points to train stations, rooming houses, family apartments, and settlement houses as war-related urban spaces where America's female working class rebuilt their lives into the 1950s. Thus it becomes important to rethink not only war's timelines but its geographies, too. Much of the history of postwar women moves hurriedly from city to suburb, but if this spatial account can be altered—or at least slowed down—new stories of working-class women in their city neighborhoods, just starting their campaign for war's spoils, can enrich the larger narrative of the American postwar era.

What these women wanted was simply what President Franklin Roosevelt had promised during the war to both men and women: a good wage, a fair price, a decent life. Indeed, as historian Meg Jacobs points out, "government propaganda during World War II actually fueled popular expectations that abundance was not only a reward for winning the war but the essence of American life."[49] Working-class people had heard something like this before. Roosevelt's New Deal, too, had promised consumer abundance through government activism. Voices from the rent records are mostly silent about the financial cataclysm just past and barely survived; it was the weight of the war that anchored women's claims, not any particular strain of liberalism. But anticipation of—or even a sense of entitlement to—government assistance had been bred in the financial crisis that preceded the military one. So when working-class women turned to federal and local agencies for help, they were merely asking the state to make good on earlier promises, now intensified by a war that had derailed them in all kinds of ways—mostly in the short term, but sometimes, depending on the war's personal price, for good. Whatever their prewar political leanings, a crowded and gritty urban geography shaped and sharpened women's postwar liberal demands for a safety net that would cushion the blows of demobilization and finally set them on a path to affluence.

The stories here thus suggest that war can be a stimulus for postwar liberalism—at least, the belief that government can and should provide a safety net beneath those affected by a country's shared hardships. War is violence, sacrifice, and loss, but it is also an *experience of governance* that can alter, deepen, or radically reconfigure ordinary Americans' views about the state's operation in their lives. In the late 1940s, after almost two decades of Depression and war, "the state" was an entity both abstract and tangible to citizens. And whites, Japanese Americans, and African Americans each had their own, very different encounters with that state. Now in peacetime, how did they perceive it? How did they *experience* it? If the war had shaped expectations, now the postwar helped working-class women articulate what they wanted from the state to fix what the war had broken. They did not frame their demands for state intervention as welfare dependents but as entitled and battle-tested citizens. Understanding that veterans were the privileged class of the moment, married women, even fiancées, positioned themselves in relation to those who had served. And whether single or married, women used an array of strategies to mitigate their losses, including dependence on kin, private charities, municipal welfare, and their own racial or ethnic advocacy groups. Whatever the target—federal or local—the tone was the same: they needed it, they deserved it, and they would use it wisely to put them on a path to "the more abundant life."

It may be a sign of a robust democracy when female citizens hear and believe in their government's promises. This is not, however, a story about an upstart postwar women's movement—a precursor to second-wave feminism. Tracking working-class women from Chicago's train stations into their neighborhoods and flats, we find a political consciousness but not a collective strategy. Yet, Chicago's working-class women, both single and married, came from working-class spaces and cultures that gave them a collective class consciousness not very far from what we have seen in other studies of postwar women around the country—organized at the workplace or "unorganized."[50] And their middle-class striving did not obviate a worker-consumer perspective. Indeed, in almost every rent dispute examined, female tenants saw federal regulation as a springboard to future prosperity—whether that was home ownership in the city or in the suburbs. Implicit in their written complaints was an avowal of faith in government, the possibility that citizen grievances could be heard and acted upon. Some even resembled political fan letters. As one woman wrote, "I was a hard worker for continued rent control writing to many congressmen in favor of it, every year." Another told the OHE: "Keep up the good work, what would we do without you?"[51]

This support for government regulation represents an important political moment, before Cold War economic policies and political moods hostile to a larger state (except for defense) congealed in the United States. Republican Party victories in the 1946 congressional elections have been understood partly as a vote to end "big government" price controls, but these snapshots from Chicago's demobilization point to a robust postwar liberalism that was shaped by global war but rooted in local circumstances. These women—renters, workers, consumers, housewives, and mothers—constituted an important female, multiracial support base for the statist path as postwar policy. The longevity and trajectory of their liberalism, as they suburbanized or were ghettoized, as they stayed at home or joined the workforce, as they moved to the left or to the right in subsequent decades, is simply not yet clear, which may be why the Rosie-to-June arc is so resilient. Their political support, though, along with the mundane but important work of household reconstruction, should not be missed in our postwar narratives. All of it helped to reconstitute a Depression- and war-weary working class, to revive and renew it, and to create anew the vaunted but, yes, complicated "postwar family," whether it stayed in the city or went to the suburbs for a full kitchen and a picture window.

Notes

1. Perry R. Duis and Scott LaFrance, *We've Got a Job to Do: Chicagoans and World War II* (Chicago: Chicago Historical Society, 1992), 3, 97, 103; Mrs. A. L. Tidball to Statistical Department, April 12, 1946, folder 15, Travelers Aid Society of Chicago Papers, Department of Special Collections, Richard J. Daley Library, University of Illinois at Chicago, Chicago, IL (hereafter TAS Papers, UIC).

2. Dorothy Swaine Thomas, *The Salvage* (Berkeley: University of California Press, 1952), 498, 502. Kaye Kimura is a pseudonym for an evacuee interviewed by a researcher under the auspices of the Evacuation and Resettlement Study, an exhaustive two-volume work on the "social aspects" of the Japanese American wartime experience, from evacuation to release and resettlement. *The Salvage* is the second volume, focused on resettlement.

3. Susan M. Hartmann, "Prescriptions for Penelope: Literature on Women's Obligations to Returning World War II Veterans," *Women's Studies* 5 (Fall 1978): 224. Many historians since have both echoed and complicated Hartmann's claims.

4. Jack Stokes Ballard, *The Shock of Peace: Military and Economic Demobilization after World War II* (Washington, DC: University Press of America, 1983), vii, 203. On demobilization, see, for example, Lizabeth Cohen, *A Consumers' Republic: The Politics of Mass Consumption in Postwar America* (New York: Knopf, 2003), chaps. 2–3; Michael W. Flamm, "Price Controls, Politics, and the Perils of Policy by Analogy: Economic Demobilization after World War II," *Journal of Policy History* 8 (1996): 335–55; Meg Jacobs, *Pocketbook Politics: Economic Citizenship in Twentieth-Century America* (Princeton, NJ: Princeton University Press, 2005), chaps. 5–6; George Lipsitz, *Rainbow at Midnight: Labor and Culture in the 1940s* (Urbana: University of Illinois Press, 1994); Laura McEnaney, "Nightmares on Elm Street: Demobilizing in Chicago, 1945–1953," *Journal of American History* 92 (2006): 1265–91; Mark D. Van Ells, *To Hear Only Thunder Again: America's World War II Veterans Come Home* (Lanham, MD: Lexington Books, 2001), vi. Revisions to postwar women's history include Daniel Horowitz, *Betty Friedan and the Making of* The Feminine Mystique*: The American Left, the Old War, and Modern Feminism* (Amherst: University of Massachusetts Press, 1998); Sylvie Murray, *The Progressive Housewife: Community Activism in Suburban*

Queens, 1945–1965 (Philadelphia: University of Pennsylvania Press, 2003); Joanne Meyerowitz, ed., *Not June Cleaver: Women and Gender in Postwar America, 1945–1960* (Philadelphia: Temple University Press, 1994); Megan Taylor Shockley, *"We, Too, Are Americans": African American Women in Detroit and Richmond, 1940–1954* (Urbana: University of Illinois Press, 2004).

5. John Bodnar, *"Saving Private Ryan* and Postwar Memory in America," *American Historical Review* 106 (2001): 806–7. See also John Bodnar, *The "Good War" in American Memory* (Baltimore: The Johns Hopkins University Press, 2010).

6. TAS, "A Report to the Community," April 1946, folder 15; memo for Mr. Harvey— Statements on services given by agency in 1944, April 9, 1945, folder 14; TAS, "Report to the Community," April 1945, folder 14, in TAS Papers, UIC.

7. Ballard, *Shock of Peace.*

8. Roger W. Lotchin, *Fortress California, 1910–1961: From Warfare to Welfare* (New York: Oxford University Press, 1992), 1–2.

9. On postwar economic policy, see for example, Ballard, *Shock of Peace*; Alan Brinkley, "The New Deal and the Idea of the State," in *The Rise and Fall of the New Deal Order, 1930–1980*, ed. Steve Fraser and Gary Gerstle (Princeton, NJ: Princeton University Press, 1989), esp. 100–12; Cohen, *Consumers' Republic*, chaps. 2–3; Flamm, "Price Controls, Politics, and the Perils of Policy by Analogy"; Jacobs, *Pocketbook Politics*, chaps. 5–6.

10. Ballard, *Shock of Peace*, 57–8, 125–28. On debates over postwar liberalism, see Jonathan Bell, *The Liberal State on Trial: The Cold War and American Politics in the Truman Years* (New York: Columbia University Press, 2004); Richard O. Davies, *Housing Reform During the Truman Administration* (Columbia: University of Missouri Press, 1966); Philip J. Funigiello, *The Challenge to Urban Liberalism: Federal-City Relations during World War II* (Knoxville: University of Tennessee Press, 1978), chaps. 4–5, epilogue.

11. Ballard, *Shock of Peace*, 59.

12. Funigiello, *Challenge to Urban Liberalism*, 5.

13. Chicago Plan Commission, "Housing Goals for Chicago," 1946, p. 4, Municipal Reference Collection, Harold Washington Library Center, Chicago, IL (hereafter MRC-HWLC); Tighe E. Woods to Tom Tippett, et al., November 5, 1946, folder: Narrative Reports, July/Dec. 1946, box 6, entry 107, Narrative Reports of Area Rent Offices, 1942–1951, Records of the Office of the Housing Expediter, RG 252, National Archives and Records Administration—Great Lakes Region, Chicago, IL (hereafter OHE Records).

14. TAS, Report Pertaining to Weekend Housing Survey of November 9–11, 1945, folder 156; TAS, Volunteer's Work Letter, #17, November 1945, folder 156, in TAS Papers, UIC.

15. Gladys Rideout to Mrs. Aneita L. Tidball, April 4, 1945, Brief History of the Nursery Situation in the Chicago Terminals, April 5, 1945, in folder: 406-3, box 406, Travelers Aid Society Papers, Welfare Council of Metropolitan Chicago Collection, Chicago History Museum, Chicago, IL (hereafter WCMC Collection).

16. TAS, Report Pertaining to Weekend Housing Survey, TAS Papers, UIC.

17. *Chicago Daily Tribune*, April 6, 1948, clipping in folder 158, TAS Papers, UIC.

18. Letter, Byron Harvey, Jr. to Mr. O. H. Frick, June 14, 1946, folder 157, TAS Papers, UIC.

19. Memo, Fern Lowry to Mrs. Tidball and Mrs. Chiles, April 5, 1948, and Minutes, Meeting of the Service Committee of the TAS of Chicago, September 13, 1948, in folder 158, TAS Papers, UIC. On the rise of psychological expertise as a new kind of postwar cultural authority, see Ellen Herman, *The Romance of American Psychology: Political Culture in the Age of Experts* (Berkeley: University of California Press, 1996).

20. This term comes from Cohen, *Consumers' Republic*.

21. Thomas, *The Salvage*, 499.

22. Philip M. Hauser and Evelyn M. Kitagawa, eds., *Local Community Fact Book for Chicago, 1950* (Chicago: Chicago Community Inventory, University of Chicago, 1953), 4-5, 30, 34, 38; Kathy Peiss, *Cheap Amusements: Working Women and Leisure in Turn-of-the Century New York* (Philadelphia: Temple University Press, 1986).

23. Elsie Muriel Farr, printed in Ruth MacKay's column, "White Collar Girl," *Chicago Daily Tribune*, October 19, 1945. This was written as a poem, and I have altered only the lines and capitalizations, not the words.

24 *Monthly Labor Review*, Serial No. R. 1821 (February 1946), 1–6. In Chicago, this sex ratio is confirmed by census data from 1950—there were 469,058 single men and 542,590 single women—but it should be noted that single women were a varied group: the never married, the separated and divorced, and the widowed. See *Local Community Fact Book, 1950*, 7.

25. Annual Report, McCormick, 1946, folder 7, box 31, Minutes, Residence Directors, November 21, 1945, folder 14, box 41, in YWCA Papers, Department of Special Collections, Richard J. Daley Library, UIC.

26. "To Victory and Beyond"; Walter Clarke, M.D., *1946—A Year of Transition from War to Peace: Annual Report of the American Social Hygiene Association*, 17-18, folder 20:2, box 20; Ray Lyman Wilbur, M.D., to "Dear Friend," n. d., folder 20:2, box 20, both in American Social Hygiene Association Papers, Social Welfare History Archives, Elmer L. Andersen Library, University of Minnesota, Minneapolis, Minnesota.

27. Clothing costs rose 42 percent between 1945 and 1947. On rents and consumer prices, see Hazel Kefauver, "State Budgets for Single Women Workers," *Monthly Labor Review* 66 (February 1948): 182–83; Bruno Schiro, "Residential Rents under the 1947 Housing and Rent Act," *Monthly Labor Review* 66 (1948): 15; and "Current Labor Statistics," *Monthly Labor Review* 65 (December 1947): 730.

28. On the history of rent control, see for example, Neil H. Lebowitz, "'Above Party, Class, or Creed': Rent Control in the United States, 1940–1947," *Journal of Urban History* 7 (1981): 439–70; McEnaney, "Nightmares on Elm Street"; Wendy Plotkin, "Rent Control in Chicago after World War II: Politics, People, and Controversy," *Prologue* 30 (1998): 111–23.

29. Notice to Tenant and Tenant's Statement, for Francis Ryan, March 16, 1949, Stella Barr, n.d., but received March 21, 1949, Edith Eminger, March 18, 1949, in folder: 1100 N. LaSalle (12 of 16), box 35, Entry 110B, OHE Records. Barr's estimate matches my calculations of average salaries for Chicago's office workers and average median rent for units in North Side neighborhoods. See Kermit B. Mohn, "Salaries of Office Workers in Large Cities," *Monthly Labor Review* 67 (1948): 240–243; *Local Community Fact Book, 1950*, 31, 35, 39.

30. Notice to Tenant and Tenant's Statement, for Elsie Ries, December 31, 1949, Agnes Weidenherner, December 31, 1949, in folder: 215 E. Erie, box 17, Entry 110B, OHE Records.

31. Marge McCarthy to OPA, February 3, 1947, folder: 23-25 East Delaware Place-6, box 10, Entry 110B, OHE Records.

32. Charlotte Brooks, "In the Twilight Zone between Black and White: Japanese American Resettlement and Community in Chicago, 1942–1945," *Journal of American History* 86 (2000): 1655–1687; Thomas, *The Salvage*, 502. On Japanese Americans' relations with African Americans, see Jacalyn D. Harden, *Double Cross: Japanese Americans in Black and White Chicago* (Minneapolis: University of Minnesota Press, 2003).

33. In the three North Side neighborhoods in my case records, more than 70 percent of dwelling units had been built before 1920. See *Local Community Fact Book, 1950,* 5.

34. By 1955, two years after wartime (and then Korean War era) rent control ended in Chicago, 55 percent of all nonfarm families owned their homes, with 40 percent renting. But ownership rates for those in the unskilled and service occupations were lower. For statistical analyses of postwar housing, see Glenn H. Beyer, *Housing: A Factual Analysis* (New York: Macmillan, 1958), 16, 152, 158-160; Davies, 103.

35. Letter, [Annette as] Lester E. Harrison to OPA, January 23, 1946, folder: 4635-37 Malden, box 37, Entry 110B, OHE Records.

36. Statement of Complaint, Mrs. Harry Nakis, Jan. 29, 1945, folder: 1016 N. LaSalle, box 33, Entry 110B, OHE Records.

37. Letter, Mr. E. Radtke to Mr. O'Connor, March 5, 1946, folder: 4322 N. Kenmore Ave, box 29, Entry 110B, OHE Records.

38. *Local Community Fact Book, 1950,* 2, 39. By 1960, they were 23 percent—almost one quarter—of the city's total population. See Evelyn M. Kitagawa and Karl E. Taeuber, *Local Community Fact Book, Chicago Metropolitan Area, 1960* (Chicago: Chicago Community Inventory, University of Chicago, 1963), 2; Otis Dudley Duncan and Beverly Duncan, *The Negro Population of Chicago: A Study of Residential Succession* (Chicago: University of Chicago Press, 1957).

39. United States Department of the Interior, *People in Motion: The Postwar Adjustment of the Evacuated Japanese Americans* (Topaz Japanese-American Relocation Center Digital Collection, War Relocation Authority Reports and Documents, http://digital.lib.usu .edu, accessed variously throughout July and August 2007), 8, 11–12, 145–46. There is some disagreement about how many Japanese Americans went to Chicago. Some estimate almost 20,000, others cite 30,000. See, for example, Brooks, "Twilight Zone"; and Masako Osako, "Japanese Americans: Melting into the All-American Melting Pot," in *Ethnic Chicago: A Multicultural Portrait*, 4th edition, ed. Melvin G. Holli and Peter d'A. Jones (Grand Rapids, MI: William B. Eerdmans Publishing, 1995), 422–23.

40. *People in Motion,* 9.

41. Brooks, "Twilight Zone," 1674–1677. See also Harden, *Double Cross*, chap. 3.

42. *People in Motion,* 49–50. Charlotte Brooks has wisely pointed out that historians "tend to identify immigration and naturalization policy as the sole point of Asian American contact with the state," but she shows that the history of "housing reveals more extensive Asian American interactions with the emerging welfare state than most historians have recognized." See Brooks, *Alien Neighbors, Foreign Friends: Asian Americans, Housing, and the Transformation of California* (Chicago: University of Chicago Press, 2009), 2–3. In her earlier work on Chicago, however, Brooks suggests that Japanese Americans, post-internment, "relied on each other for support and assistance," carving out a new path for

postwar Japanese American identity "that neither resembled the prewar Little Tokyos of the Issei nor welcomed government interference." See Brooks, "In the Twilight Zone," 1657.

43. See folder: Mann, Harold (1 of 2), box 50, entry 110, Sample Rent Enforcement Case Records, OHE Records. My evidence does not suggest, as Brooks argues for the years 1942–1945, that resettlers shunned "government interference" in the postwar years. See Brooks, "In the Twilight Zone," 1657.

44. Chicago Resettlers Committee, Chicago Resettlement, 1947, A Report, Welfare Council of Metro Chicago, folder 719-10, Welfare Council, box 719, in Chicago Resettlers Committee Papers, WCMC Collection.

45. Council of Social Agencies of Chicago, Report of the Committee on Minority Group Relationships, June 18, 1947, folder 157, TAS Papers, UIC. Significantly, black migration nationwide peaked in 1945, putting more pressure on city services at the start of demobilization. Funigiello, *Challenge to Urban Liberalism*, 22.

46. See "Public Health in Chicago-Cook County," 463, "Maternal and Child Health," 612, "Tuberculosis Control," 502, in United States Public Health Service, *The Chicago-Cook County Health Survey* (New York: Columbia University Press, 1949).

47. Statement of Tenant, Mrs. Henry Grier, Mrs. Lafayette Goins, Mrs. Erie Taylor, September 1949, folder 353-355 West Chicago, box 6, Entry 110B, OHE Records.

48. *Chicago-Cook County Health Survey*, 166–173. The city tried to impose an ordinance mandating standard containers for sanitation workers, but wartime material shortages delayed implementation until January of 1945.

49. Meg Jacobs, "'How About Some Meat?': The Office of Price Administration, Consumption Politics, and State Building from the Bottom Up, 1941–1946," *Journal of American History* 84 (1997): 912.

50. On working- and middle-class women's class and political aspirations after World War II, see, for example, Shockley, "*We, Too, Are Americans*"; Murray, *The Progressive Housewife*; there are some parallels between my arguments and Lisa Levenstein's in *A Movement without Marches: African American Women and the Politics of Poverty in Postwar Philadelphia* (Chapel Hill: University of North Carolina Press, 2009).

51. Gertrude Vogel to Thye [*sic*] Woods, May 19, 1951, folder: 23–25 East Delaware Place-3, Helen Gilday to Housing Expediter, January 16, 1950, folder: 23–25 East Delaware Place-2, in box 10, Entry 110B, OHE Records.

Chapter 4

Teaching Democracy on the Big Screen: Gender and the Reeducation of Postwar Germans in *A Foreign Affair* and *The Big Lift*

Ulrike Weckel

Recent work on the history of West Germany unanimously concludes that the liberal democracy installed at the demand of the Western Allies has proven to be remarkably stable in the long run.[1] Yet the early, ambitious initiatives of the American occupiers to teach Germans democracy have long met with criticism.[2] There may be three main reasons for this. First, in light of how thoroughly the Nazi regime had discredited itself by the unprecedented extent of its crimes against humanity, many contemporary observers, as well as researchers up to the present, developed unrealistically high hopes for spontaneous political conversion on a broad scale—hopes that could only be disappointed. Second, since the democratization of the Germans was gradual and neither as obvious nor as widespread as one could wish, it is easy to find shortcomings that prevent one from declaring it an overall success. Finally, there is the paradox of prescribing and teaching democratic self-determination, especially as victors toward the vanquished. Although many American reeducators were well aware of this predicament, it has always been easy for critics to accuse them of self-righteousness or even of violating their own democratic ideals.

Much more interesting than the question of the success or failure across the board of early reeducation efforts in postwar Germany would be micro-historical case studies that would show that specific reeducation measures produced spectra of responses and reveal the conditions that made each of these varying responses more or less likely. Different primary sources for such analyses may come to mind: controversial articles and letters to the editors on German guilt in the licensed German press, reactions to the Nuremberg trials, and the popularity of books at public libraries and Amerika-Häuser (centers for Germans to learn more about American politics and culture) as determined by checkout data, to name just a few. This chapter shows how fruitful it can be to analyze fictional depictions, in this case films, of reeducation efforts. In addition to educational documentaries, which the Information Control Division (ICD) of the Office of the Military Government, US (OMGUS) screened in cinemas in its occupation zone,[3] several contemporary American feature films addressed the topic of German reeducation, in particular Billy Wilder's *A Foreign Affair* (1948) and George Seaton's *The Big Lift* (1950).[4] By telling stories about fictitious German characters' political attitudes in the immediate postwar period, these films invited their audiences to consider the project of reeducation in new ways. Since they were not screened in Germany during the Allied occupation, they can hardly be considered part of the American reeducation project per se. But both were based on the filmmakers' knowledge of the situation (in Wilder's case his own immediate postwar experience in Germany; in Seaton's through filming on location in Berlin and the casting of actual military personnel). Thus, read closely and within the broader context of the period, they provide historians insights into the complexities of reeducation.

Feature films are ambiguous and need viewers to make sense of them. The stories they tell are conveyed not so much explicitly in words but through the composition and succession of images. In reading these images, viewers must constantly fill in what is not said and not shown and thereby understand a movie in individual and sometimes idiosyncratic ways. Movies thus constitute events of social communication, yet many historians hesitate to use them as primary sources of their research. It is true that in their interactive complexity, feature films are hard to interpret historically, and historians' training in interpreting primarily written texts does not suffice for the task. Yet by shying away from analyzing feature films, historians lose a chance to glean valuable insights into what people at a given time and place were ready to think and feel, what they hoped for, and what they feared. Especially for gender historians there is much to gain. Most feature films tell stories about women and men and their relations to each other, and because of the need to show much more than written or spoken texts express, filmmakers, along with actors and actresses, compose telling pictures that include many details of which they themselves might be unaware. Therefore, even films that do not intentionally deal with questions of gender offer gender historians rich material for analysis.

The two films in question deal intentionally with gender relations; more precisely, with heterosexual romance. This is, to be sure, a very common theme in feature films, yet what makes *A Foreign Affair* and *The Big Lift* remarkable for gender historians of the postwar period is the fact that they situate their love stories in the context of American attempts at reeducating postwar Germans. The American architects of reeducation programs were by no means insensitive to the fact that their target group consisted of both men and women, but the documentary record suggests that they did not particularly consider how their measures might affect the gender dynamics of the occupation period. The feature films, by contrast, depict reeducation efforts as enacted through male and female characters and portray the effects as influenced by the characters' perceptions of each other. Moreover, the films' gender relations can be read as metaphors for certain modes of reeducation.

Before introducing and interpreting the films, I must consider the historical context of their stories. The predominantly male American occupation troops encountered a German population in which women, especially those between the ages of twenty and forty, were visibly in the majority. This did not make their job of reeducation any easier. Intelligence reports on Germans' nazification regularly hypothesized that next to youngsters, who had been subjected to Nazi indoctrination in their formative years and had experienced nothing but dictatorship since then, women were the group most resistant to democratization.[5] The basis of this hypothesis was not always spelled out, but most analysts seem to have assumed that women were politically less mature, that their views were more emotional than rational, and that Nazi propaganda had appealed primarily to emotions. Analysts also may have had in mind girls' and women's roles in the notoriously authoritarian German family as well as the idea of a specifically female conservatism or provincialism arising from women's primary interest in preserving home and family. Interviews with Germans in the areas first occupied appeared to confirm these assumptions. It was found, for example, that women were more likely than men to accept Nazi crimes against humanity as atrocities inevitable in war.[6] Despite such differences, however, reeducation plans did not initially include any gender-specific efforts.[7]

Officials did begin to employ a gendered rhetoric regarding reeducation once it became obvious that the US military was unable to enforce its ban on "fraternization." Issued during the fighting as a security measure, the prohibition of GIs' social contact with Germans beyond what was absolutely necessary was not lifted with the cessation of hostilities because, first, the military feared that incorrigible Nazis would turn to guerrilla warfare and, second, the discovery of hundreds of concentration and work camps on German soil made the American public call for a harsh peace. This demand was not, however, supported by the majority of American GIs. They seem to have had no problem maintaining a stern attitude toward German men,[8] but their sexual relations with German women were so frequent that "fraternizing" (or "going frattin'") soon took on the meaning of searching for sex.[9] Warnings that German *Fräuleins* might be fanatical Nazis who would lure soldiers into their misguided world view and give them venereal diseases— both fears were combined in the famous cartoons of *Veronika Dankeschön* in *Stars and Stripes*—seem to have deterred hardly anybody.[10] Soldiers insisted that their sexual activities and romantic interests were personal, nonpolitical matters. Since not even officers always refrained from erotic adventures with Germans, many enlisted men mocked the official ban as designed "to give the brass the first crack at all the good looking women."[11] If the Army did not want to further embarrass itself—especially in the eyes of Germans—by being unable to prevent widespread violations of its own regulation, it had to loosen the strict ban.

This, however, was delicate, since the American public was already alarmed about the allegedly lenient treatment of the German population, and many could not have been pleased by the idea that their husbands, fiancés, and sons were promiscuously engaging in easily available sex. The first easing of the prohibition against fraternizing in June 1945, therefore, allowed contact only with young children, a move that suggested that it was this consequence of the rigorous policy to which soldiers most objected. Soon after, *Life* reported, GIs would often greet German women with "Good-day, child."[12] When, one month later, "conversations with adult Germans on the streets and in public places" were permitted, soldiers gaily dubbed this "the fraternization order," and on October 1, 1945, the ban was ended entirely with the exceptions of marrying Germans and being billeted in their homes.[13]

While unofficially the US military mostly tolerated sexual encounters between German women and soldiers, not least in order to encourage them to seek medical treatment after contracting venereal diseases,[14] it had to find better reasons for liberalizing its restriction on fraternization when it came to convincing the American public. Linking fraternization to denazification and reeducation appeared to be the best argument. When General Dwight D. Eisenhower, military governor of the US occupation zone, announced the first easing of the ban in mid-July 1945, he claimed this had been decided "in view of the rapid progress which has been made in carrying out Allied de-Nazification policies."[15] Not only was there supposedly less to fear from the Germans, but fraternization, it was now argued, could actually serve a positive goal—as a means of reeducation. In late May 1945, Douglas Schneider of the Supreme Headquarters Allied Expeditionary Force's ICD pointed out that the ban on fraternization prevented occupation forces from contributing to ICD's main goals of eradicating Nazi ideology and encouraging a peace-loving, democratic spirit. Schneider asserted that soldiers should be allowed to pursue informal interactions with German civilians so that they could work as "ambassadors for our country and her ideals."[16] In the probably-invented conversation that *Life* correspondent Percy Knauth reported to have had with some GIs, one of them complained that nonfraternization was "against human nature." "After all," he continued, "we are supposed to educate these Germans back to be normal citizens and this way we are just raising a barrier between us and them."[17]

The chances for, and limits of, reeducating Germans in romantic relationships with members of the American occupation force are playfully investigated in *A Foreign Affair* and *The Big Lift*. Neither film found the broad audiences in the United States and Germany that their makers had hoped for. *A Foreign Affair*, which premiered on June 30, 1948, was given a divided reception by American critics. Some liked this daring black comedy about denazification and fraternization, while others deemed it tasteless. Congress denounced *A Foreign Affair*, which satirically portrayed six of its members, as a "rotten movie," and the Defense Department issued a statement saying that it gave a false picture of the decent and honorable army of occupation. The production company apparently received further protests and decided some weeks into the Berlin blockade to withdraw the film quietly from distribution despite its commercial success.[18] In Germany, where OMGUS did not authorize the film's release, *A Foreign Affair* could not be seen before 1977, when West German television broadcast the movie. It finally reached German movie theaters in 1991.[19] *The Big Lift* premiered in the United States on April 26, 1950, not quite one year after the Berlin blockade and the airlift it portrays had ended.[20] It failed to excite much interest with American audiences.[21] In the Federal Republic of Germany, however, a significantly shorter version of the film, entitled *Es begann mit einem Kuß* (*It Started with a Kiss*), came into cinemas in May 1953. The unannounced removal of certain scenes spared German viewers the revelation that one of the film's two *Fräuleins*, who are dating US sergeants, is an incorrigible Nazi and, instead, allowed the couple a nonpolitical happy end (as the title suggests). The resulting harmless story line denied German viewers a motivation to think critically about obstacles to democratization in their society.[22]

Though it is telling that the one movie was so unpopular with patriotic Americans that it was not released in Germany while the other one provoked German patriots (or perhaps the production company out of fear of the reactions of such Germans) to remove certain scenes before its screening in their country, it is not so much the *actual* audience reception that makes these two feature films so potentially interesting for historians. They are most useful as primary sources for a history of mentalities if historians consider different *possible* ways for contemporaries to have read them. Far from artificially separating the public and the private, the political and the personal, both movies invited their audiences to think about politics by watching the romantic entanglements of American men and German women.

Billy Wilder's Bid for Another Kind of Reeducation

Soon after the Nazis took power, Billy Wilder, who was Jewish, fled Berlin, where he had worked as a reporter, authored some film scripts, and enjoyed its vibrant metropolitan culture. By the end of World War II, he had become a successful screenwriter and director in Hollywood. In the summer of 1945, the US Army sent Wilder to Germany to investigate the state of the German film industry and make recommendations for its denazification and reorganization. He was also consulted in the production of a documentary compiled from footage of the liberation of concentration camps that the ICD was preparing to screen throughout its occupation zone.[23] Although rumors that Wilder had little interest in this atrocity film and ordered its editors to cut it down significantly do not stand up to close inspection,[24] there can be no doubt that he had his own ideas about reeducation through film. In a memorandum titled "Propaganda through Entertainment," which Wilder submitted to the ICD Film, Theater and Music Branch on August 16, 1945, he set forth a dilemma for its current film policy. The ICD was gradually reopening movie theaters in the US zone but had so far allowed the screening of only newsreels and documentaries to German moviegoers.[25] Wilder acknowledged that attendance was satisfactory and audiences appeared to respond favorably to the seriously reeducational and, at least in the case of the British-American newsreel *Welt im Film* (*World in Film*), explicitly pro-pagandistic programs. But he was certain that the novelty of these offerings would soon wear off. Furthermore, he doubted that Germans would "come in week after week to play the guilty pupil."[26] Even when American feature films were added to the programs as planned, Wilder predicted, moviegoers would doze apathetically through the educational part and wake up only for the entertaining, glamorous, and escapist feature films, such as *Cover Girl* (1944) with Rita Hayworth. But, he pointed out, a film like this, however well made, "does not particularly help us in our program of re-educating the German people." He continued:

> Now *if* there was an entertainment film with Rita Hayworth or Ingrid Bergman or Gary Cooper, in Technicolor if you wish, and with a love story—only with a very special love story, cleverly devised to help us sell a few ideological items—such a film would provide us with a superior piece of propaganda: they would stand in long lines to buy and once they bought it, it would stick. Unfortunately, no such film exists yet. It must be made. I want to make it.[27]

Wilder then outlined the story he already had in mind, the idea for which allegedly stemmed from a random conversation he had had with a woman clearing rubble on Kurfürstendamm. His film was to be a love story about a GI who at first does not understand what the war had been all about and the widow of a German fighter pilot who feels Germans no longer have anything to live for. In their first encounter, she tells the GI that she is desperately waiting for the Americans to repair the gas pipe not, as he sympathetically presumes, because she wants to cook but because she wants to commit suicide. In the end, Wilder explained, the boy would *not* get the girl. Instead, the woman would strike a match, light the gas, and prepare dinner, having found "something new to live for," while the soldier, never a "theorizing apostle of democracy," would return home with a new understanding of the significance of democratic values. Wilder added that during his last two weeks in Berlin he had talked to numerous people, studied GIs' lingo, "fraternized" with all kinds of Germans, and almost sold his wristwatch on the black market, and now he would return to Hollywood with a notebook full of his impressions as well as photographs of "every corner" which he would need to get the atmosphere right.[28]

A Foreign Affair (1948)

Wilder did end up making his movie about a German-American love affair in Berlin during the occupation, but that was two years later, and it turned out quite differently from the way he had first conceived it. Instead of a *Trümmerfrau* (literally, rubble woman) and war widow, weary of life, who through her love for an American GI and the new democracy rediscovers something to live for, the story now centered around a worldly-wise nightclub singer with a Nazi past who seduces a naive American captain in order to avoid being arrested and sent to an internment camp.

Not all of the reasons for the postponement and changes are known.[29] In discussions of Wilder's memo, ICD members had pointed out that conditions in Germany were constantly changing, so that a film set in the present risked quickly becoming outdated.[30] A *Trümmerfrau* contemplating suicide might have had a dramatic attraction in the summer of 1945 but a year later would no longer represent the situation in Germany.[31] Moreover, because of high production costs, the film had to appeal to both German and American audiences. Finally, it should convince Americans of the need for a prolonged occupation and teach Germans that "the essence of democracy lies in respect for human personality."[32] So Wilder abandoned his original idea, which sounded like an educational melodrama, and instead came up with a jaunty romantic comedy, which OMGUS would consider politically irresponsible upon its completion in 1948.[33]

Rather than Rita Hayworth or Ingrid Bergman, Wilder cast Marlene Dietrich in the starring role. She plays the alluring nightclub singer Erika von Schlütow—whose name with its noble "von" is unfamiliar enough to Americans to delay them in locating her denazification file and whose umlaut they consistently drop, thereby unintentionally pronouncing a name (von Shluttow) that suggests that this woman does not hesitate to make use of her skills as a seductress. As the audience learns later in the movie, Erika had been the mistress of a high-ranking Nazi, the head of the secret police. Old newsreels show them together at the opera with Hitler confidentially whispering something in her ear. At this point, viewers realize how strategically Erika has chosen Captain Pringle (John Lund) as her lover. In the beginning, it seemed that she was interested in this not particularly impressive member of the occupation forces because of his aptitude for getting her whatever she wants from the black market (in one of the first scenes, even a mattress!). But Pringle also works in the denazification office, which determines the treatment of individuals deemed to have been Nazis. For obvious reasons, he has forged a reversal of the decision in Erika's case, changing her fate from "labor camp" to "clearance."

Their mutually profitable liaison comes under threat when a congressional delegation, alarmed by reports of fraternization, arrives to investigate the morale (and morality) of the troops. The experienced commander in Berlin, the jovial and witty Colonel Plummer, easily convinces the delegation's five male members that it is a tough job to turn this "country of open graves and closed hearts" into a civilized state, but he and his men are trying "to lick it" as well as they can.[34] On their introductory tour of the city, however, the one female delegate, a prudish and moralistic congresswoman from Iowa with the telling name Phoebe Frost (Jean Arthur), alone has noticed happy erotic fraternization everywhere. When Plummer concedes that some soldiers occasionally get out of line, Frost calls this a flagrant understatement. She had overheard that von Schlütow, whose lascivious performance she had witnessed on an undercover investigation at the nightclub Lorelei,[35] was once "Göring's girl or Goebbels's girl," but she has gotten away with it because "some big brass" in the American occupation force protects her. In an error typical of comedies, Frost chooses Pringle, of all people, as her assistant on her mission to hunt the culprit down. By the time she learns that it is he who fell for Erika, she herself has already fallen for Pringle, while he now starts to feel attraction for the "defrosting" congresswoman, who is about to give up her moralizing and even trades her typewriter for a backless evening gown in order to look nice for him. Finally, to lure the jealous ex-Gestapo head out of hiding and into a shootout, and so make up for his interference in the denazification effort, Pringle has to pose publicly as Erika's lover one last time, thereby risking his life and his nascent relationship with the congresswoman. But, as can be predicted in a comedy, when the shooting is over, it is not Pringle who lies dead on the floor of the Lorelei but the Nazi, killed by American soldiers. Yet the film does not end here; in a final joke, the script hints that Pringle is not so eager to follow the all-forgiving Phoebe home to Iowa and that Erika might not end up in a labor camp after all, given the enthusiasm with which a number of military policemen accept the assignment to escort her.

In contrast to Wilder's initial idea for a reeducational storyline in an entertaining movie aimed primarily at German audiences, the eventual version of *A Foreign Affair* addresses Americans just as much. Indeed, it holds more, and more critical, lessons for them than for the postwar Germans. Nevertheless, postwar Germans could have learned some things from the movie, had they been able to watch it. First of all, there is the opening scene that spoofs the opening of Leni Riefenstahl's famous propaganda film *Triumph des Willens* (*Triumph of the Will*, 1935) and indicates some significant differences between Nazi dictatorship and democracy.[36] Riefenstahl portrays Hitler's flying into Nuremberg for the 1934 party rally as a majestic, godlike descent to his faithful followers. To a Wagnerian soundtrack, the camera pans through the cockpit window over dramatic cumulus clouds. As the medieval town of Nuremberg comes into view, the music incorporates the Nazi Party anthem *Horst-Wessel-Lied*, while the plane casts a cruciform shadow onto the houses and streets along which marching columns now can be detected. On the airfield below, a crowd of mostly women and youngsters enthusiastically awaits the incoming plane, and they burst into loud shouts of "Heil" and raise their right arms when, several minutes into the film, Hitler finally emerges. *A Foreign Affair* also starts aboard an incoming flight, but everything else is different. The little plane is seen from some distance, rocking up and down, while cheerful music plays. Viewers quickly see who is coming: on the plane, an officer, awakening the sleeping congressmen, points out that Berlin has just come into view. While Representative Frost is busily studying her reports, the five male delegates, from different states and of different political convictions, immediately start to argue over what Americans should do about the utterly destroyed city. Plant grass and graze longhorns? Rebuild industry? With or without organized labor? Send food, but also make sure the Germans know where it comes from? At this point, the Democrat from the Bronx emphatically declares, "If you give a man a loaf of bread, it's democracy; if you leave the wrapper on, it's imperialism," and the congresswoman has to remind her colleagues that they have been sent to Berlin for quite a different reason than deciding such big questions. In contrast to Nazi dictatorship with its one unquestioned male leader and an uncritical mass envisioned as female, democracy, viewers are invited to discover, gives power to the people, both men and women; it is all about the exchange of ideas and arguments—and it can even be fun to watch. Down on the airfield, however, the detail of soldiers assigned to welcome the delegation is not very happy about the visitors coming to investigate their morale. Colonel Plummer assures the waiting GIs that, although he suspects that some of them "are working too hard to enlighten the civilian population," he is aware that "after all, this isn't a boy scout camp." Even for democrats like the Americans, German viewers could have learned, democratic procedures can be annoying at times.

In the film itself, however, the German characters do not learn anything. A man with a Hitler moustache is called into the denazification office because his son has been drawing swastikas all over the neighborhood. Since little Gerhard is at this moment drawing a swastika on Pringle's desk, the father threatens to break his arm and promises Pringle that he will lock the boy up in a dark room without food. Taking Pringle's ironic question about why he does not shove the boy into a gas chamber as an order, he answers, "Yes, Herr Kapitän!" Pringle has to clarify that the Allies have done away with concentration camps, and he prescribes that the boy join one of the American-run German Youth clubs: "Some baseball and a little less heel clicking is what he needs." Father and son click their heels as they leave the room, the father with a swastika drawn on the back of his jacket. Another character who seems not to have learned anything is the waiter at the Lorelei, who bows deeply when the former chief of the Gestapo reappears to find Erika and her American lover.

Erika, for her part, does not have anything to learn, since she understands the world only too well. The audience does not find out whether she was ever a convinced Nazi. There are some hints that she does not care about politics but is simply intent upon manipulating the powerful men of the moment to serve her private interests. Toward Pringle she presents herself as an opportunist. When, after having seen her together with Hitler in the newsreel, he asks her "how much of a Nazi" she was, she downplays the question by invoking the cliché of women as unpolitical and superficial: "Oh, Johnny! What does it matter, women's politics? Women pick out whatever is in fashion and change it like a spring hat." Erika seems to be well aware that Pringle is not only really worried about her possible political involvement with Nazism but, if anything, gets a certain thrill from her forthright amorality and the fact that she is a former enemy. (In an earlier treatment of the film, he lovingly calls her the "Beast of Belsen"; in the film itself, this becomes "blonde witch" and "you gorgeous booby trap."[37]) Hence, Erika sees no reason to take seriously Pringle's occasional, half-hearted references to reeducation. When, for example, he tries to lecture her—"What you Germans need is a better conscience"—Erika makes fun of both his overbearing manner and her own readiness to submit herself to dictatorship. "I have a good conscience," she answers, "I have a new *Führer* now. You." And she raises her right arm: "Heil Johnny." His reply confirms that he gets a kick out of this ironic play: "You heil me once more and I'll knock your teeth in," he says, embracing her passionately.

Erika von Schlütow is by far the most ambiguous, complex character in *A Foreign Affair*. The role was played by the German-born Hollywood star Marlene Dietrich, who was famous at the time for her anti-Nazi attitude and had recently received the US government's Medal of Freedom for her patriotic dedication in entertaining US troops during the war. For Erika's performances at the Lorelei, Dietrich wore her own dress from those USO shows.[38] Much of contemporary viewers' evaluations of the von Schlütow character, their predisposition either to like Erika and believe her self-portrayal or resent and mistrust her character, would have depended on their feelings for Marlene Dietrich. For American audiences, the presence of Dietrich, who was beyond political suspicion, made it harder to condemn both political opportunists in Nazi Germany and postwar German *Fräuleins* seducing American soldiers without considering their motivations. For German audiences, who were dropped as a target group only after the movie's completion, the film would have offered the challenging combination of an emigrant who had actively supported the war against Nazi Germany (and whom nationalists regarded as a traitor), playing a woman who had curried favor with Nazi leaders and then presented herself to Americans—in both the movie and the audience—as a victim of Allied bombing and the Soviet conquest of Berlin.[39]

In contrast to the unrepentant German nightclub singer, the American congresswoman changes significantly over the course of the plot. While still on the plane, Frost declares that if the delegation finds that reports about "some kind of moral malaria" among the occupation troops are true, it will have to "fumigate that place with all the insecticides at [its] disposal." With her equally naive and absolutist views about good and evil, she is a caricature of those Americans who still have to learn that, as Colonel Plummer on the airfield below simultaneously puts it, "You cannot pin sergeant's stripes on an archangel." By falling in love with Pringle, Phoebe soon learns that romance can compromise both personal and political integrity. Her interest in Pringle is tempered neither by her knowledge that he is engaged (upon arriving, she delivered a birthday cake to him from his fiancée in Iowa) nor by her discovery that he has protected Erika from being sent to a work camp because of her Nazi past.[40] Eventually, she disqualifies herself as "an objective observer," though the movie presents Frost's suspension of black-and-white moral judgments as a gain in understanding human needs and desires.

The makers of *A Foreign Affair* used the popularity of comedies, especially with female audiences in the United States, to plead for more tolerance of erotic fraternization. In addition, by asking within an eroticized setting of gender relations questions about how to reeducate Germans and to what ends, the film rejects simplistic ideals. At a point when Frost is still "after the head" of von Schlütow's protector, Pringle (self-servingly) points out how unrealistic her expectations are: "You expect [the occupation soldier] to be an ambassador, a salesman of goodwill. You want him to stand there on the blackened rubble of what used to be the corner of what used to be a street with an open sample case of assorted freedoms waving the flag and giving out with the Bill of Rights. Well, that's not the way it works." The ICD also conceived of the occupation soldier as an "ambassador for our country and her ideals." But *A Foreign Affair* emphasizes that these soldiers are human, able and willing to fall in love, even with (former) enemies, and it portrays Americans' lack of political prejudices—their openness in their choice of erotic partners—if not as one of the ideals of their country, then at least as a charming trait of their national character.

The Big Lift (1950)

Immediately after the Soviets had ended their blockade of Berlin in May of 1949, George Seaton started to shoot his feature film about the successful Western Allied airlift. *The Big Lift* combines extended depictions of skillful cooperation between pilots and ground control, the intrepidness of air crews, airmen's rough but warm comradeship, and America's impressive technical resources with two very different stories about American sergeants and their relationships with German girlfriends.[41] The two buddies—boyishly charming flight engineer Danny MacCullough (Montgomery Clift) and middle-aged, heavily built air-traffic controller Hank Kowalski (Paul Douglas)—embark on their mission with very different attitudes toward the Germans. Aware of his own deep anti-German sentiments, Hank predicts he may not do "a very good job" and asks to be replaced, but without avail. When, on their flight into Frankfurt, another GI comments on the massive destruction, Hank remarks, "Not enough. This is where they should have used the A-bomb." The audience later learns that he was badly mistreated in a German prisoner-of-war camp. In contrast, Danny, who has never been to Germany, is eager to get out of the airport, soon learns some basic German, and wants to get involved with the "Krauts" they have been sent to supply.

Danny finds his chance to get involved when, as a crew member on the 100,000th flight into Berlin, he is selected to receive a gift of gratitude from "all the women of Berlin" presented to him by young, ladylike Frederica Burkhard (Cornell Borchers) in a ceremony on the Tempelhof airfield. Press photographers demand a kiss from the handsome couple, and a journalist's human interest reportage later earns Danny a 24-hour pass to the city of Berlin. In the course of that day, he becomes romantically interested in Frederica and with great empathy observes the postwar scarcity: women's hard labor in the rubble fields; Soviet soldiers' harassment of locals; and other oddities of the blockaded, divided, and multiply governed city.

Frederica claims that she feels drawn to Danny after years of fear and loneliness as a war widow, and soon Danny applies for permission to marry her before returning to the United States. Hank warns him against this. He mistrusts Frederica's self-presentation as a victim and, in fact, finds out that her husband was in the SS (which she had earlier denied) and that her father was not, as she had stated, a Nazi opponent who had disappeared after protesting the burning of books but had divorced her mother because she was Polish. When Danny confronts Frederica, she admits to having lied to him but explains that she had wanted to appear pitiful and brave. "When you live in the sewer, you soon discover that the sewer rat is best equipped to survive," she adds. After a thoughtful stroll alone through the rubble, where he again notices much poverty, Danny returns and wordlessly accepts Frederica's apology.

The viewers, however, know more than he does. They have already witnessed Frederica's quickly hidden offense when Danny jokingly remarked that the damaged statues of Prussian heroes from the former *Siegesallee* (Victory Avenue) "do not look so *Sieges* anymore."[42] And later they see Frederica smiling shiftily after Danny has managed to accelerate the process of getting permission to marry her. At both moments, the usually soft music becomes ominous. The audience's misgivings find confirmation when Frederica's observant neighbor discovers that she plans to use Danny only to enter the United States, where she will divorce him as soon as possible and reunite with her husband, who has escaped denazification and, under a false identity, started a little shop in St. Louis. Just in time, Danny learns about Frederica's fraud and returns home alone and disillusioned.

Hank, by contrast, misses no opportunity to order Germans around, in English. He demonstratively refuses to shake hands with them and makes them give way to him on the sidewalk by stepping down into the gutter. Yet he, too, finds himself a "Schatzi" in Berlin, Gerda (Bruni Löbel). Danny is astonished to hear it; he would have thought that his buddy, with all his disdain for the German people, would date some American secretary at OMGUS. Hank explains to him that American women complicate relationships by insisting on their independence. "With Gertie it is different. When I want to see her, I see her; if I feel like talking, she talks, and if I don't feel like it, she keeps her mouth shut," he announces with self-satisfaction. "Anyway," he adds, revealing that his interest is not so much erotic as one of convenience, "she gives me a one-day service on my laundry. The PX takes a week."[43] While the two couples are having drinks together, Hank continuously belittles "Gertie," whose real German name he refuses to use.[44]

In contrast to the bourgeois Frederica, Gerda comes from a proletarian family. Her skills in foreign languages and views of the current political situation are the result not of higher education but of her contacts with soldiers of the different occupation forces. Gerda's shame over her father's believing "in the wrong things" (in contrast to Frederica's allegedly anti-Nazi father) leads Hank to lecture her, Frederica, and Danny on the reasons why the Germans "got sucked in by Hitler." German "papas" had always told their kids "what to say, when to shut up, what to do, what to think," and since even "jerks" were permitted this authority, "another jerk like Hitler" was able to become "the papa for all." When Danny and Frederica point out that Hank treats Gerda in exactly the same way, he pauses, dumbfounded. Admitting that they are right, he patronizingly gives his girlfriend permission to disagree with him and ask him questions from now on. Several film critics have found the conversation among the four in this scene contrived and the weakest part of the movie. Yet it demonstrates the contradiction of teaching democracy in authoritarian ways while explicitly expanding the question of equality into romantic relationships between men and women.

Gerda, happily surprised by Hank's permission, starts by asking what democracy is. Hank finds that he does not really know how to answer this question and dismisses it as stupid. "Democracy is democracy"; how, he wonders, can one not understand this? But Gerda, who has been reading both American- and Russian-licensed German newspapers, is seriously interested and wants to find out what democracy is so that she can decide whether or not she likes it. Hank tells her to take his word that she would like it. But this is not enough for her, for she realizes that it was a mistake to take her father's word that Nazism was a good idea. She wants more information, and she does not stop reading. Her selections are guided by the fact that she is considering following Hank to the United States. Viewers see her studying a brochure entitled *Things You Should Know about the United States*, and she tells Hank that she has also read "your Constitution, the Bill of Rights, what Lincoln said and Wilson and Roosevelt." When Hank comes to her place and orders her around, Gerda refuses to obey, calling Hank, with his authoritarian, patriarchal attitudes, a "disgrace to America." She cites the Bill of Rights to him and when he gets angry and threatens to hit her, calls him a "storm trooper"; demands that he leave her apartment (again quoting her right to do so); and, after Hank mentions all the cigarettes, candy, and stockings he has given her, throws cans of Spam at him. Suddenly, Hank's face lights up: "Baby, now you have got it. This is what I have been trying to tell you. Don't let anybody push you around, not even me. That's democracy. . . . You are a citizen, honey!" In the end, Gerda decides to remain in Germany because "one day" she wants to see "the right kind of Germany" and help it, though she is unsure about how much help she can be. And Hank, who has now started to shake hands with Germans and talk to them in a friendly manner—and in German—finds a pretext to stay longer despite the Berlin blockade's having been lifted.

While it is true that *The Big Lift* spells out its political message, it is less simplistic than it may seem at first sight. The film's two "case studies" of gender relations open critical debate about how to teach, and live, democracy. Danny and Frederica appear to be on equal terms with each other. And since Frederica skillfully criticizes undemocratic behavior, whether exemplified by the Third Reich or Hank's paternalism toward Gerda, Danny finds no need to reeducate her. However, the exposure of her scheming shows her to be one of those incorrigible Germans who do not deserve Americans' new sympathy and trust. From the vantage of her new understanding, Gerda tries to explain that Frederica has not yet "unlearned" certain things, such as the belief that the ends justify the means, or that it is acceptable to lie and betray one's friends for one's own advantage. Nevertheless, contemporary viewers might have wondered whether someone who strategically employs talk of democratic ideals and uses other people's empathy for utterly selfish ends can really be reeducated. Some might even have felt confirmed in their uneasiness with self-confident, independent women like Frederica.

Hank is just the sort of man who feels uncomfortable with the independence that women gained during the war. Although his anti-German sentiments should lead him to prefer American women, he chooses Gerda—albeit Americanizing her name—mainly because she is submissive. The two, however, undergo a learning process together. By studying American democracy, Gerda learns to stand up to Hank's authoritarian behavior. And Hank realizes that he cannot claim the superiority of American democracy over the "people's democracy" advocated by the Soviet soldiers, with whom Gerda is friendly, on the basis of Americans' right to disagree with their political leaders while at the same time forbidding Gerda to disagree with him. Although granting her this right is at first patronizing, in the end he learns to enjoy her emancipation.

Conclusion

At first glance, the blending of the political and the private, of reeducation and romance, in *A Foreign Affair* and *The Big Lift* is not surprising. Like many entertainment films, both deal with romantic turbulence, and, as more or less realistic portrayals of postwar Germany, both mirror the historical situation in which American male occupiers sought affairs and romances with German women who, in turn, made themselves easily available to the American soldiers, who could offer them consumer goods and were in better physical shape and better-humored than most of Germany's defeated veterans. Yet, *A Foreign Affair* and *The Big Lift* do not simply provide realistic stories that, because they were shot on location, offer historians an accurate sense of the postwar zeitgeist. Viewing them only as such misses the elements of their construction that, perhaps, do make them surprisingly informative in more complex ways.

Reeducators had to decide which Germans could probably be reeducated and which were not worth the effort. Both movies combine the topic of reeducation with the phenomenon of "erotic fraternization" in that the search for worthwhile candidates for reeducation is played out as a search for worthwhile lovers. Heterosexual romance with German women thus becomes a metaphor for the pitfalls and promises of reeducation. *A Foreign Affair*, for instance, presents an ambivalent German female character who keeps viewers wondering whether she can be turned into a democrat. Though they learn in the course of the movie to mistrust her, they are still invited to continue their sympathy for her. *The Big Lift* develops two contrasting cases. Frederica, with her good education and insightful comments, at first appears hardly to need reeducation and, yet, turns out to be a hopeless case. Gerda, by contrast, might be simpler and less cultured, but she quickly learns to value democracy and actively puts it into practice. Therefore, and instructively, sweet and credulous Danny's relationship with Frederica nearly ends in catastrophe and certainly in disappointment, while grumpy, mistrustful Hank has better luck with Gerda. Ironically, the moral of this contrast was turned upside down in the mutilated version of the film distributed in Germany three years later. Because it cut out Frederica's exposure as an incorrigible Nazi and suggested that her romance with Danny led to a happy married life in the United States, some German critics perceived their now-trusting relationship as ideal, and Hank's and Gerda's—burdened as it seemed with fighting and political arguments—as flawed.[45] A review in the *Spandauer Volksblatt* that revealed the movie's original ending suggests that the problem of hopeless reeducation

111

cases might have been rejected by German audiences in the early 1950s, for the critic took the movie as evidence of strong American resentment against Germans in the immediate postwar period, and he indignantly blamed the German actress Cornell Borchers, who played Frederica, for having accepted such a "defamatory role."[46]

A second surprising aspect of the two films is the self-criticism of the United States that they include. In the case of *A Foreign Affair*, the supposedly disrespectful depiction of the American occupying forces resulted in a ban on showing the film in postwar Germany. The few German film critics who attended a special screening of the film in 1948, before OMGUS stopped its release, were, however, particularly impressed by the fact that the American characters were not presented as flawless. From such a liberal and courageous film, one of them thought, those Germans who mocked reeducation could learn what the American victors meant by "democracy."[47] Yet, at least for a part of the movie's American audience of the time, Erika's joke of hailing Captain Pringle as her new *Führer*—"Heil Johnny"—teetered on the edge of what they could tolerate. The criticism of American characters in *The Big Lift* was answered by those characters' learning processes. Danny learns to be less naïve, while Hank sees the paradox in advocating American democracy and, at the same time, ordering his girlfriend around. He finally welcomes her emancipation, not least from him, because it shows her successful reeducation.

This leads to the movies' third surprise. As they both use gender relations to address the predicaments of reeducation, their characters' little projects of personal reeducation can also be read as critiques of conventional gender relations. Reeducation, or at least reorientation, is also needed in romantic relationships—for men and women, Germans and Americans. Democracy appears to be not just a political project on a large scale but a personal enterprise in human relations. This message, however, is perhaps a very contemporary reading, which may have gone unnoticed by many viewers of the time.

Notes

1. See, for example, Konrad Jarausch, *After Hitler: Recivilizing Germans, 1945–1995* (New York: Oxford University Press, 2006); and Edgar Wolfrum, *Die geglückte Demokratie: Geschichte der Bundesrepublik Deutschland von den Anfängen bis zur Gegenwart* (Stuttgart: Klett-Cotta, 2006).

2. See, for example, Franz Neumann, "Reeducating the Germans: The Dilemma of Reconstruction," *Commentary* 6 (1947): 517–25; Henry Kellermann, "Von Reeducation zu

Reorientation: Das amerikanische Reorientierungsprogramm im Nachkriegsdeutschland," *Umerziehung und Wiederaufbau: Die Bildungspolitik der Besatzungsmächte in Deutschland und Österreich,* ed. Manfred Heinemann (Stuttgart: Klett-Cotta, 1981), 86–102; *The Political Re-education of Germany and Her Allies after World War II,* ed. Nicholas Pronay and Keith Wilson (London: Croom Helm, 1985); Thomas Alan Schwartz, "Reeducation and Democracy: The Policies of the United States High Commission in Germany," in *America and the Shaping of German Society, 1945–1949,* ed. Michael Ermarth (Providence, RI, and Oxford: Berg, 1993), 35–46.

3. Brigitte J. Hahn, *Umerziehung durch Dokumentarfilm? Ein Instrument amerikanischer Kulturpolitik im Nachkriegsdeutschland (1945–1953)* (Münster: LIT, 1997).

4. Another example is Samuel Fuller's *Verboten!* (1955), which tells the story of a young German woman who plans to exploit an American GI's love for her and marries him but finally ends up falling in love herself and gives up her Nazi convictions. This movie is not included here, since it does not show the process of her political conversion but only the lesson she teaches her younger brother (who is a member of Werwolf, a pro-Nazi resistance group) by taking him to the Nuremberg trial. Jennifer Fay's book *Theaters of Occupation: Hollywood and the Reeducation of Postwar Germany* (Minneapolis: University of Minnesota Press, 2008) deals almost exclusively with Americans films produced before and during the war.

5. For the most detailed study, "Women in Nazi Germany," July 1944, by Ruth and Robert Kempner, see Felicitas Hentschke, *Demokratisierung als Ziel der amerikanischen Besatzungspolitik in Deutschland und Japan: 1943–1947* (Münster: LIT, 2001), 170–74.

6. Morris Janowitz, "German Reactions to Nazi Atrocities," *American Journal of Sociology* 52, no. 2 (1946): 141–46, 144–45.

7. The American military government did not open a Women's Affairs Section until March 1, 1948. See Hermann-Josef Rupieper, "Bringing Democracy to the Frauleins. Frauen als Zielgruppe der amerikanischen Demokratisierungspolitik in Deutschland 1945–1952," *Geschichte und Gesellschaft* 17 (1991): 61–91; Pia Grundhöfer, *'Frauen reichen die Hand' – britische und amerikanische Frauenpolitik in Deutschland im Rahmen der demokratischen re-education nach 1945* (Egelsbach: Hänsel-Hohenhausen Mikroedition, 1999); and Marianne Zepp, *Redefining Germany: Reeducation, Staatsbürgerschaft und Frauenpolitik im US-amerikanisch besetzen Nachkriegsdeutschland* (Göttingen: V & R Unipress, 2007).

8. That is, men of the civilian German population. Several soldiers were court-martialed, however, for having "engaged in social contact" with famous German prisoners of war. See Earl F. Ziemke, *The U.S. Army in the Occupation of Germany 1944–1946* (Washington, DC: Center for Military History, 1975), 321–22.

9. Percy Knauth, "Fraternization: The Word Takes on a Brand-New Meaning in Germany," *Life,* 2 July 1945, 26; and Julian Bach, *America's Germany: An Account of the Occupation* (New York: Random House, 1946), 76. On American-German "erotic fraternization," see John Willoughby, "The Sexual Behaviour of American GIs during the Early Years of Occupation in Germany," *Journal of Military History* 62, no. 1 (1998): 155–75; Susanne zur Nieden, "'Erotic Fraternization:' The Legend of German Women's Quick Surrender," in *Home/Front: The Military, War, and Gender in Twentieth Century German,* ed. Karen Hagemann and Stefanie Schüler-Springorum (New York: Berg,

2002), 297–310; Petra Goedde, *GIs and Germans: Culture, Gender, and Foreign Relations, 1945–1949* (New Haven, CT: Yale University Press, 2003); and Annette Brauerhoch, *"Fräuleins" und GIs: Geschichte und Filmgeschichte*, (Frankfurt/M.: Stroemfeld, 2006). For a comparison with the other western zones of occupation, see: *Es begann mit einem Kuss: Deutsch-Alliierte Beziehungen nach 1945/It Started with a Kiss: German-Allied Relations After 1945*, ed. Florian Weiss (Berlin: Jaron, 2005).

10. The campaign rather seems to have caused some amusement on both sides. Many examples of humorous attitudes toward the prohibitions are reported, such as provocations by young women, swinging and tapping their hips when passing soldiers, whispering "verboten!" See Knauth, "Fraternization," 35.

11. Quoted by Ziemke, *The U.S. Army*, 324.

12. "German Girls: U.S. Army Boycott Fails to Stop GIs from Fraternizing with Them," *Life*, July 23, 1945, 36.

13. Ziemke, *U.S. Army*, 325, 327. Germans were included in the American War Brides Act of December 1945, but not until January 1947. The legitimization of liaisons through marriage led to a change in German women's representations from prostitutes and seductresses to loving (post)war wives and symbols of German-American friendship. See Raingard Esser, "'Language No Obstacle': War Brides in the German Press, 1945–49," *Women's History Review* 12, no. 4 (2003): 577–603.

14. On June 4, 1945, the Military Government of the United States published a memo illogically stating: "Contraction of venereal disease or the facts concerning prophylactic treatment will not be used directly or indirectly as evidence of fraternization"; quoted in Ziemke, *U.S. Army*, 325; on the treatment of the venereal disease problem by the US Army, see Willoughby, "Sexual Behaviour," 160–66.

15. Quoted in Ziemke, *U.S. Army*, 325.

16. Douglas Schneider to Robert McClure, memorandum, May 30, 1945, partly quoted in Goedde, *GIs and Germans*, 74.

17. Knauth, "Fraternization," 26.

18. Maurice Zolotow, *Billy Wilder in Hollywood* (New York: G.P. Putnam's Sons, 1977), 155.

19. Brauerhoch, *"Fräuleins" und GIs*, 369–89.

20. Ibid., 337–67.

21. Amy Lawrence, *The Passion of Montgomery Clift* (Berkeley: University of California Press, 2010), 61; see, for example, the contemporary review by Bosley Crowther in *The New York Times*, April 27, 1950.

22. Rainer Rother, "Eine Luftbrücke zur Hochzeit: *The Big Lift* vs. *Es begann mit einem Kuß*," in *Kuss*, 75–80.

23. See the detailed reconstruction of the production process of this film, which came to be known as *Die Todesmühlen* ("The Death Mills"), in my book *Beschämende Bilder: Deutsche Reaktionen auf alliierte Dokumentarfilme über befreite Konzentrationslager* (Stuttgart: Steiner, 2012), 149–170. On its screenings in Germany, see also my articles "Disappointed Hopes for Spontaneous Mass Conversions: German Responses to Allied Atrocity Film Screenings, 1945–46," *Bulletin of the German Historical Institute* 51 (2012): 39–53; and "22 March 1946: Screenings of *Die Todesmühlen* Spark Controversy over German Readiness to Confront Nazi Crimes," in *A New History of German Cinema*,

ed. Jennifer Kapczynski and Michael Richardson (Rochester, NY: Camden House, 2012), 321–27.

24. The rumor was planted by filmmaker Hanus Burger, who saw himself as the actual director of the atrocity film. Sounding spectacular, this dark insinuation has been taken up by several commentators on *Die Todesmühlen*, especially in the press, often presented in the tone of investigative journalism. See Hanus Burger, *1212 sendet: Tatsachenroman* (East Berlin: Deutscher Militärverlag, 1965), 382; and Burger, *Der Frühling war es wert: Erinnerungen* (Munich: Bertelsmann, 1977), 257.

25. An atrocity film was, contrary to claims in the literature, not part of these programs.

26. Billy Wilder, Propaganda through Entertainment, August 16, 1945, NARA: RG 260/OMGUS, ICD, MPB, Box 280, Folder: Film Production (printed as an appendix to Ralph Willett, "Billy Wilder's *A Foreign Affair* (1945–1948): 'the trials and tribulations of Berlin'," *Historical Journal of Film, Radio and Television* 7, no. 1 (1987): 3–14.

27. Ibid., emphasis in the original.

28. Ibid. Also see David Culbert, "Hollywood in Berlin, 1945: A Note on Billy Wilder and the Origins of *A Foreign Affair*," *Historical Journal of Film, Radio and Television* 8, no. 3 (1988): 311–16.

29. For some details see Ed Sikov, *On Sunset Boulevard: The Life and Times of Billy Wilder* (New York: Hyperion, 1998), 233–82; and Tracy Oliver, who had access to production files and different versions of the filmscript: "Marlenes und Wilders 'Foreign Affair' (1945–1948)," in *Friedrich Hollaender*, ed. Viktor Rotthaler (Hambergen: Bear Family Records, 1996), 61–7.

30. Outline of discussion requested by General McClure concerning Wilder proposed film, 15 February 1946, NARA: RG 260/OMGUS, ICD, MPB, Box 280, Folder: Film Production.

31. James A. Clark to General McClure, Proposed Movie of Billy Wilder, 13 March 1946, NARA: RG 260/OMGUS, ICD, MPB, Box 280, Folder: Film Production.

32. Outline of discussion, February 15, 1946.

33. Stuart Schulberg, "A Communication: A Letter about Billy Wilder," *Quarterly of Film, Radio and Television* 7, no. 4 (Summer 1953): 434–36, here 435.

34. In one of Plummer's speeches, Wilder's original story of a "woman of the rubble" who finally uses gas for cooking a humble meal rather than committing suicide comes up.

35. Lorelei is the name of both a rock on the River Rhine and the legendary mermaid who distracted sailors and capsized their boats when she combed her blonde hair on this rock.

36. Gerd Gemünden has pointed this out in his inspiring interpretation of the film "In the Ruins of Berlins: *A Foreign Affair* (1948)" in his book *A Foreign Affair: Billy Wilder's American Films* (New York: Berghahn Books, 2008), 54–75; here 62–3.

37. Quoted in Sikov, *Sunset Boulevard*, 233.

38. Gemünden, "In the Ruins," 71; see more generally Gemünden's interpretation of Wilder's use of Dietrich and Arthur as "gendered allegories of nation," 66–71.

39. On the reception of Dietrich and her Hollywood films in Nazi Germany, see Erica Carter, "Marlene Dietrich: The Prodigal Daughter," in *Dietrich Icon*, ed. Gerd Gemünden and Mary R. Desjardins (Durham, NC: Duke University Press, 2007), 186–207; for examples of hostile anonymous letters to Dietrich during her tour to Germany in May

1960, see *Marlene Dietrich: Dokumente, Essays, Filme*, ed. Werner Sudendorf, vol. 1 (Munich: Hanser, 1977), 20–4.

40. In this respect, though, the film offers the interpretation that Frost believes Plummer's willful fable, according to which Pringle was assigned to become involved with von Schlütow in order to serve as the bait that would make the head of the Gestapo come out of his hiding.

41. Except for the two protagonists, all military personnel appearing in the film were actual members of the US Armed Forces on duty in Germany, as the opening credits announce.

42. Rainer Rother points out that Danny, at this moment, looks at a statue of Prussian King Frederick II, after whom Frederica might be named, and he reminds us of the Allied attempt to explain Germans' submission to Nazi dictatorship with reference to their long history of authoritarian rule from Frederick II to Bismarck to Hitler. Rother, "Der Film *The Big Lift* und die Umorientierung eines Feindbildes," in *Der Film in der Geschichte*, ed. Knut Hickethier, Eggo Müller, and Rainer Rother (Berlin: Sigma, 1997), 211–19; here 216.

43. This practical motivation to pursue relationships with German women was not uncommon. Among the things that constituted the "good deal" GIs were most interested in, as one of them confessed in a letter to the editor of the *New York Times*, was "a woman to do laundry and pressing for cigarettes or candy." Another GI quoted the soldiers' saying, "Fraternization is the best solution to the laundry problem"; Theodore Singer, "Letter to the Editor," *New York Times*, November 30, 1945; Davis, *Conqueror*, 144.

44. When she introduces herself to Frederica and Danny as "Gerda," Hank brutally interrupts her: "Gertie is good enough." The film does not provide her with a family name.

45. See *Evangelischer Filmbeoachter* 18 (1953): 161; and, critical of the supposedly simplistic confrontation of right and wrong, Helene Rahms, "Zu *Es begann mit einem Kuß*," *Frankfurter Allgemeine Zeitung*, April 30, 1953.

46. "Es endete ganz anders . . . ," *Spandauer Volksblatt*, May 29, 1953. The critic labeled the cut version, with which the American production company now wanted to earn money in Germany, a "Trojan horse" and appealed to his readers' national pride not to see it.

47. See the quotations in Brauerhoch, *"Fräuleins" und GIs*, 386n21.

Part II

The Military, Politics, and Changing Masculinities

Chapter 5

Banning the Soldier Hero: American Regulations, German Youth, and Changing Ideals of Manhood in Occupied Württemberg-Baden, 1945–1949

Kathleen J. Nawyn

In planning for the occupation of Germany during World War II, American officials were acutely aware that neither a costly defeat in World War I nor the restrictive peace treaty that followed had stopped the Germans from instigating a new conflict just twenty years later. The Americans believed that even if Germany lost the current war, it would eventually rearm and start another.[1] The trouble, they concluded, was a German militarism characterized by both a belief in the use of force in international relations and the strong influence of martial ideals and the military itself on state and society. US officials saw this militarism embodied in an aggressive armed forces and an industrial system customized for war production, as well as in a culture marked by military aesthetics and shaped by values that celebrated Germany's military tradition and espoused the glories of war.[2] The Americans were also convinced that many forces in Germany had contributed to the problem. As one State Department analysis determined, "the militaristic spirit" had "become deeply embedded in the psychology and social institutions of the whole people," and the problem could therefore only be redressed "by prolonged disarmament and by fundamental reforms in German economic and social relationships and in German education."[3] In keeping with their convictions, US officials developed an array

119

of occupation policies designed to eliminate all symptoms and sources of German militarism, hoping thereby to help prevent another war.

Because eradicating militarism meant, in part, eradicating a German proclivity for idolizing soldiers and glorifying war, these American demilitarization efforts can be viewed as part of a broader narrative of changing conceptions of masculinity in Germany. Scholars have explored the close ties between military service and masculinity in Germany and identified important changes in the country's historical development after World War II.[4] During the anti-Napoleonic wars of 1813–15, a model of martial masculinity emerged that remained influential for more than a century, even as it evolved over time and sometimes fragmented.[5] Integral to this model were notions of courage, strength, and patriotism. Above all, as Karen Hagemann writes, "when their country needed to be defended, 'real' men had to display a 'heroic spirit' and to fight and die willingly for the 'honor' and 'liberty' of the 'fatherland.'"[6] Challenged in the wake of World War I, this masculine ideal nevertheless gained strength during the Weimar Republic, reaching its ascendancy during the Third Reich when National Socialist ideology called for all men and boys to emulate the hardened soldier who willingly sacrificed his life for the fatherland.[7] One consequence of World War II, however, was a "crisis of masculinity."[8] German soldiers had learned that war was hardly a heroic enterprise, they had failed as defenders of their families and fatherland, millions were dead or captive, and many who did return home were physically or psychologically broken and incapable of caring for their loved ones. By the mid-1950s, moreover, both the militarized masculinities of the prewar era and the damaged masculinities of the immediate postwar period had been replaced in West Germany by more benign conceptions of masculinity, including new prescriptive ideals that presented men as morally strong, devoted fathers.[9] German conceptions of masculinity continued to evolve in the decades that followed, due in part to the protest movements of the 1960s, but broad support for the martial ideals of the early twentieth century has not returned.

In this narrative of change, the Americans' deliberate attempt to demilitarize German culture has so far received little attention.[10] Scholars have investigated the geopolitical, economic, and military aspects of demilitarization and analyzed cultural change in Germany through the lens of American denazification and democratization efforts.[11] But few have probed the impact of cultural demilitarization initiatives at the grassroots level or their influence on gender relations.[12] Although American directives targeted seemingly mundane features of German life—for instance, banning the wearing of military

120

uniforms and requiring that library books venerating soldiers be confiscated—their ramifications were significant. In effect, the US military government took away a box of tools the Germans had long used to teach boys and men their masculine duties—uniforms, parades, textbooks, lesson plans, paramilitary training, and even the German army itself. If German wartime and postwar experiences discredited old ideals of martial masculinity, American initiatives actually made the propagation of these ideals illegal. US policy also encouraged the Germans to change their objectives, supported those who did so on their own, and, through these actions, served to promote new ideas. American intervention during the occupation years thus facilitated the development of more benign models of masculinity and assisted in ensuring their durability.

This chapter examines the impact of American intervention by focusing on German-run youth groups in Württemberg-Baden, one of three states in the US occupation zone, from late March 1945 until the end of the occupation on September 1, 1949. Encompassing much of the southern half of Germany, the US zone also included the states of Hesse and Bavaria, with Württemberg-Baden comprising a pocket in the west bordering the French zone. The Americans created the state in 1945 after the Allies divided the German states of Baden and Württemberg between the US and French zones, producing a hybrid state with two histories and a unique set of official records, both of which enhance its value as a case study.[13] Here, as elsewhere in their zone, the Americans explicitly sought to keep German youth programs free of militaristic leaders, military trappings, and paramilitary activities. Significantly, they encountered substantial support for this effort from the Germans themselves, as many Germans, especially those with a Christian, liberal, social democratic, or communist worldview (*Weltanschauung*), were also determined to refocus organized programs for their nation's young people. Thus, already during the late 1940s, Americans and Germans became partners in nurturing an ideal of manhood that had little to do with the military.

Implementing American Policies

"Although this was always denied by Hitler Youth leaders after 1945, the hallmark of [Hitler Youth] socialization was militarization, with a view to a war of territorial expansion and, as its predetermined goal, the neutralization of Europe's Jews," historian Michael Kater observes in his 2004 study of the Nazi youth organization. For German boys, uniforms and marching were ubiquitous. Their camping trips included rifle practice, flag ceremonies, and war games played out under a hierarchically organized command structure. When drilling, they chanted songs that were "clearly martial in character, related to Fatherland, duty, honor, blood and soil, and above all fighting and death."[14] Nazi leaders also armed the boys with goals, urging them to emulate Germany's military heroes and inviting soldiers to share their inspirational stories at youth gatherings.[15] National Socialist ideology called both boys and girls to serve the German *Volksgemeinschaft* (national community), yet their assigned roles were different. As strong and courageous comrades of Nazi males, females were to marry, bear children, impart Nazi values, and raise future soldiers, as well as support Germany's fighting men emotionally, economically, and in some cases—before marrying—militarily as Wehrmacht auxiliaries. But there were limitations on their service: they were always to be protected by men.[16] As one girl later remembered, "I felt it was a terrible fate to have been born a girl. You see, it meant I could not place my life at the disposal of the Fatherland."[17]

Militarizing activities like those of the Hitler Youth had not drawn questions or criticism in most of German society for decades. Since the nineteenth century, the state and the military, as well as youth organizations, had tried to encourage boys to admire soldiers and view war as a venue in which to prove their manhood, even to the point of dying for the fatherland. Schoolbooks, novels, songs, poems, ceremonies, and youth programs had propagated these ideas. The Nazis had only magnified, expanded, and further institutionalized these efforts.[18] Long before World War II began, German youngsters were told by National Socialist Party officials, Hitler Youth leaders, and schoolteachers that their country was preparing for a war that was inevitable.[19]

While not aware of all of the details, America's wartime planners knew that the Nazis were providing paramilitary training and aggressively indoctrinating Germany's youth. Concerned that disillusioned male youngsters with military skills might endanger American occupation forces, they also viewed Germany's youth as a major long-term problem. The most deeply indoctrinated Germans were those belonging to the generation of young people who had joined the Hitler Youth and its female counterpart, the League of German Girls (Bund Deutscher Mädel, or BDM), but this generation was also the future of the nation.[20] Recounting his recent experiences in occupied Germany in 1946, journalist Julian Bach captured American thinking regarding German children in its most basic form, writing, "You watch a youngster, perhaps aged six, goose-stepping back and forth by the road every time an Allied truck passes. He thinks he is being cute . . . . You think so too . . . . Until you remember that unless he is taught to stop goose-stepping, your son may be doing close-order drill."[21]

In keeping with these concerns, American policies at the start of the occupation disbanded the Hitler Youth and the BDM and required that Allied officers approve all new youth groups, though their formation was left to German initiative.[22] Later, the Americans modified their approach. Reflecting the belief that German children were, as one officer put it, "probably the most important raw material out of which a regenerated Germany can be built," an October 1945 directive established new objectives for youth programs even as it specifically banned certain traditional practices. American officials were now to encourage the creation of new youth groups and sections of "well-established international youth organizations" that they knew from home, such as the Boy Scouts, Girl Scouts, Young Men's Christian Association (YMCA), and Young Men's Hebrew Association (YMHA). All groups, the directive explained, should exist for cultural, religious, or recreational purposes and should help to develop democratic ideas and qualities such as independent thinking and tolerance. Political groups were not allowed, and military government officers had to prevent the revival of military, paramilitary, or Hitler Youth–type activities. German officials were to inform all those involved with youth programs that they would be severely punished not only if they tried to spread or defend National Socialist ideas, but also if their efforts included anything that glorified militarism or nationalism or explained how to prepare for or fight a war. Parades, drilling, and marching were prohibited, and US officials had to approve all uniforms and emblems. The directive also stated that the Germans should establish district youth committees to oversee local groups, but that American authorities still had to authorize all groups.[23] During the years that followed, the Americans made some changes to the regulations—political restrictions were relaxed, for example—but the directive's basic goals and constraints remained in place until the occupation ended.

In general, the Americans ceded responsibility for youth programs to the Germans. The role of military government youth officials was limited. Philosophically disinclined to issue demands concerning youth activities, they also faced staffing and resource constraints. Over time, aside from exercising oversight, their attention centered especially on helping to develop competent leaders. In areas where US Army tactical units were stationed, German youth groups received additional American aid. In April 1946, the Army formalized soldier outreach efforts to German youngsters in its Army Assistance Program to German Youth Activities (GYA), which provided badly needed equipment, facilities, transportation, and other aid to German groups and sponsored activities and youth centers for both organized and unorganized youth in an effort to prevent juvenile delinquency and foster democratic development.[24] In the late 1940s, however, far more Germans participated in German youth groups than in the GYA program.[25]

Membership policies for the new German youth organizations were lenient. In fact, military government officers advised German officials to welcome former Hitler Youth members and the children of SA men (Brownshirts) and Nazi Party members; they were especially interested in reeducating Nazi youth.[26] But the Americans were more careful in monitoring the leadership and character of German youth activities. In accordance with broader personnel policies, military government officers had to approve all German officials appointed to state and municipal posts responsible for youth activities. They also evaluated all members of the district committees and all proposed leaders of new groups, rejecting as unacceptable any individuals judged to have been active Nazis or militarists during the Third Reich.[27] By mid-1947, they had granted the district committees the authority to approve all youth leaders and groups, but these bodies had to inform US officials of their decisions and the latter could still intervene, if necessary.[28]

Youth officials heard the American message. Responding to US requests for information on their plans, hopeful youth organizations submitted applications proposing to offer German youngsters religious and musical instruction, healthy sporting activities, and opportunities for hiking. Some also addressed the issue of militarism directly in their submissions or official documents, either explicitly eschewing militaristic activities or promising to fight against militarism itself. Thus, the March 1946 statutes of the German Boys' Club (Deutsche Jungenschaft), whose members had a variety of ideological leanings, stated that "in sport and game" they would reject "every militaristic activity."[29] The successor organization of the Weimar Republic's Socialist Workers' Youth, the Socialist Youth of Germany—Falcons (Sozialistische Jugend Deutschlands—Die Falken), listed among its aims the eradication of Nazi and militaristic thought from home and school,[30] while the communist-leaning Swabian People's Youth (Schwäbische Volksjugend) included among their goals the overcoming of "the spiritual and practical causes and effects of fascism and militarism."[31]

Under the circumstances, youth groups were unlikely to propose sponsoring paramilitary exercises or preparing boys for war, and American officials could not be sure that all approved organizations were genuinely committed to their stated agendas. Initially, however, even authorized groups had to notify the local military government in advance of all meetings and allow US personnel to attend.[32] American policy also required youth groups to submit regular reports on their gatherings, and military government observers occasionally reported on them as well.

Skepticism and Violations

There were certainly Germans who disagreed with specific elements of the regulations. Some adolescents and their leaders clearly missed the flags, uniforms, and marching that had been a part of so many youth programs since before the Nazi era.[33] Even the communist and socialist youth organizations of the Weimar Republic had worn distinctive outfits during meetings and carried organizational banners and flags during demonstrations and outings. After 1945, youth gatherings sometimes still included diluted versions of these activities, although only when sanctioned by the Americans. In mid-1947, for instance, military government officials reported receiving a growing number of requests from groups that wanted to "march and carry banners." The Germans described the marches "as 'parades without commands,'" the Americans noted, and typically wanted permission "to do this in their sports uniforms with some form of flag or pennant being carried by their leaders."[34]

The Americans apparently had few objections, but they also kept an eye on the rules. As of September 1947, they were permitting sports uniforms to be worn without specific authorization and interpreting current regulations to mean that organizations could freely "wear distinctive garb or emblems and display distinctive banners or flags known to be part of their established paraphernalia" when they were licensed. But the organizations still had to secure approval for any banners, uniforms, or comparable items introduced later. The point was to keep these things under military government control, a US official explained, but not to interfere with group activities other than to accomplish the objective of the regulations, "namely, the prevention of a return to Nazism and militarism."[35] Similar reasoning was evident in a reply to a sports group in the town of Geradstetten in mid-1948 when it asked that some 150 athletes be allowed to march several blocks from a schoolyard to a nearby athletic field in connection with a sports competition. The aim of the procession, the petition assured, was solely to attract notice and encourage attendance—thus ensuring the financial success of the contest.[36] Granting conditional approval, a US official reminded the organization that directives against marching were still valid. Therefore, the athletes might "walk through the streets as a group" if they wished, but they might not walk in step, in formation, or to music.[37]

Occasionally, Germans violated the rules. In August 1946, American officials in Heidelberg suspended Boy Scout activities for a time and removed the leader of a group of 200 scouts because the man "wore an unauthorized uniform, printed posters without Military Government permission, and gave militaristic titles to specific groups under him."[38] While these were relatively minor infractions, prior events elsewhere in the US zone made the rather severe American response more understandable. Earlier, twelve Bavarian youths had been convicted of possessing explosives and using the cover of an unauthorized youth organization to create a new Nazi movement. The group had adopted symbols and methods used by the Hitler Youth and SA and "engaged in semi-military drill, sang military songs, informed on civic officials, and blacklisted, defamed, and attacked girls who associated with American soldiers." US officials had likewise determined that a scout group in Wiesbaden was planning subversive activities.[39]

In at least one case, US military police apprehended some Boy Scouts for wearing uniforms. This prompted a military government official to remind all of the state's youth authorities that uniforms must not be worn unless the Americans had specifically approved them. He also alluded to larger issues at stake, pointing out that the German Scouts—whose history was widely regarded as militaristic—were essentially on probation with the international movement. Foreign Boy Scout leaders would be watching them carefully, he noted, adding, "they will want to know whether character-building will be emphasized or uniforms, marching, and other external characteristics." [40]

Perhaps more worrisome were the attitudes of young German veterans who appeared unwilling or unable to adapt to new circumstances—and who even into their early twenties were eligible to join youth organizations. Some had a hard time letting go of their previous values, or their status. Others, rightly or wrongly, felt unfairly disdained, ignored, or blamed. Many had proven their merits as soldiers only to find that their skills were no longer valued or were condemned. Some interpreted criticism of the war, militarism, and Nazi ideals as disparagement of their own experiences or devaluation of their contributions. These complaints could translate into skeptical, contemptuous, or defiant attitudes toward official reeducation initiatives.[41]

Such was the case in January 1946 when a speaker participating in the Württemberg-Baden Interior Ministry's "Reflection" (*Besinnung*) lecture series addressed the topic "Who is helping the youth?" After the man offered his views on the state of Germany's young people and what the goals, functions, and structure of a reconceived youth program should be, there was a brief discussion period. Several attendees later sent the ministry accounts of the event which noted that the liveliest response from the relatively large number of young men in the audience had come during a short speech by a local pastor who had himself served in the war.[42] One correspondent described the episode succinctly, starting with a summary of the pastor's comments: "Must state: It is not permissible to throw into the dirt all of the values for which many died. (Unrest in the auditorium.)"[43] Another writer, whose report hinted at socialist sympathies, offered a microcosmic picture of the evening, stating that he had closely watched four young veterans who were probably only nineteen or twenty years old. "They sat there with completely hostile faces, a superior, contemptuous smile on their faces. I had the impression the four young men . . . cannot be shaken by anything any more. They made biting comments continuously." Only when the pastor spoke did they suddenly come alive, shouting approval.[44]

The author of a July 1946 letter to the youth magazine *Das junge Wort*, which was produced in conjunction with the state's Culture Ministry, similarly suggested that some young people were developing dangerous attitudes toward the past. It often seemed as if memories of the horrors of the war years were beginning to fade, he wrote, with many talking about the time when Germany was still the victor. "It is part of human nature to quickly forget the unpleasantness of the past," he observed, but idealizing the war and whitewashing wartime events posed a serious danger. This had occurred after the last war, with a militarized society, another war, millions of victims, cities in ruins, and the loss of political autonomy as the results. Germany's youth could not be held accountable for these developments, he conceded, but they would be guilty in the future if they did not draw the right lessons from the past. Among other things, this meant recognizing that Germany's current situation had been caused by "our former Führer and the people who made his rule possible," not by Jews, Communists, German generals, or "malevolent fate." They should, further, not try to extract some meaning from the "obvious nonsense" of the last war. Yes, most young men had believed they were defending their homeland and therefore should not be reproached for their behavior. But they should also not hold up their service as something meritorious, however long and brave. In the end, it was all for a "small criminal clique" and hurtful to the German people.[45]

Reconceptualizing German Youth Activities

As the letter to *Das junge Wort* hints, despite occasional protests and violations, and despite disquieting attitudes in some quarters, the Americans ultimately found many allies in their demilitarizing efforts. There were a large number of Germans who, like their occupiers, believed changes were needed. German perspectives had thus clearly evolved since the Weimar years, when those challenging the status quo had been limited in both quantity and influence. After World War I, the German left—in particular the peace movement, trade unions, and social democratic and communist organizations—had condemned German militarism, its glorification of war, its emphasis on the soldier as a masculine ideal, and educational practices that perpetuated these failings. But these critics of German militarism had comprised only a large and splintered minority whose voices were increasingly drowned out.[46] Another war had expanded their numbers, however, and American regulations now assisted them, by both requiring some of the very changes they had demanded in the past and keeping the public sphere largely free of competing views.

In Württemberg-Baden, state and local officials repeatedly called for cleansing youth programs of harmful practices and using them to prevent rather than prepare for war. In April 1946, the liberal Deputy Culture Minister Theodor Bäuerle, who had belonged to the German Democratic Party (Deutsche Demokratische Partei or DDP) during the Weimar Republic, told members of a new state youth committee that introducing young people to the spirit of democracy was their most important task. He named as the goal "actions based on freedom and responsibility," adding that commitment and freedom were interdependent. *Gemeinschaft* (community), he maintained, was not about uniforms and training, but rather about the cooperation of self-reliant people and groups.[47] Bäuerle's colleague Heinrich Hassinger, a former DDP member who handled youth affairs for the Culture Ministry, spoke regularly about the importance of redirecting youth activities. In January 1946, he insisted to the young veterans and others assembled at the Interior Ministry's lecture on youth issues that there should be "respect for the *Heldentod* [heroic death on the battlefield]," but that Germany's youth should not let themselves be misused again, and they should now be educated with this in mind.[48] Five months later, he similarly told several hundred young Germans gathered in Stuttgart for State Youth Day that Germany's young people would never again be allowed to be "misused for any egoistic or martial purpose."[49] Hassinger believed that the "physical toughening" of youngsters during the Third Reich, the fact that the "souls of the youth had been uniformed," and other evils of the Nazi system had contributed directly to the wretched physical, spiritual, and intellectual condition of young Germans at the end of the war. His own work and the efforts of youth leaders throughout the state, he suggested at a January 1947 conference, were now aimed at helping these young people and rescuing them "for civilization, culture, and, with that, for the future."[50]

Other officials saw youth work as a means to foster peace. In June 1946, Ulm's top youth official, the Social Democrat Hugo Roller, assured a member of a German peace group that the motto "Never Again War" guided all of his efforts. As a fourteen-year-old, Roller had been a founding member of the local Socialist Workers' Youth organization and during the 1932 election campaign had helped to put up Social Democratic Party (Sozialdemokratische Partei Deutschlands, or SPD) posters proclaiming, "Who Votes for Hitler, Votes for War." "Already before the Third Reich, I promoted pacifism in youth education," he now explained, "and will, of course, after this murderous war, more than ever exert all of my energy for peace."[51] Social Democratic Interior Minister Fritz Ulrich revealed similar goals in the summer of 1947 in addressing some 9,000–15,000 *Falken* from all over western Germany at a Stuttgart rally. According to a military government report describing the event, Ulrich reminded the young people that "for 80 years the German SPD had been fighting against militarism and hate among the nations and for peace and understanding." He then "spoke of the determination to educate the youth in this spirit of peace and harmony among the nations" and exhorted his audience to look for new heroes. "The nationalists," he argued, "used to say that he who wages war, destroys cities and sows discord among the people is a hero." But now "a new and different hero worship must be introduced. He shall be a hero who builds cities, safeguards the peace and makes people happier, richer and more harmonious in their community life."[52]

In calling for change, German officials did not necessarily distinguish between boys and girls. Both were to serve the German people by seeking peace, fostering international understanding, and helping to rebuild Germany socially, politically, and spiritually. In the immediate postwar years, females might even assist with physical reconstruction, as the iconic *Trümmerfrauen* (literally "rubble women") demonstrated in clearing urban streets. Moreover,

promoting peace and reconstruction, rather than glorifying war and soldiers, represented a significant shift in values for both genders, as the Nazis
had also assigned girls vital tasks in sustaining the Third Reich's militarized
Volksgemeinschaft. Still, as Ulrich intimated in contrasting military heroism
with the achievements of builders and peacemakers, the implications for each
were different. The Americans' insistence on cultural demilitarization, combined with their dissolution of Germany's armed forces, made a masculine ideal
toward which German boys had long aspired both unattainable and taboo.
These developments also eliminated a fundamental source of male authority
in Germany—military service—and effectively required the reconstitution of
this authority on a different basis at a time when the wartime shortcomings
of German men had already undermined their standing.[53] Girls, meanwhile,
continued to face a future in subordinate roles as wives and mothers.[54] But their
responsibilities were now transformed. And how they supported Germany's
boys and men and the values they imparted to their sons had to change.

In their efforts to reform youth programs, state and local leaders received
support from other German groups and initiatives. Especially active was the
small Württemberg section of the Women's International League for Peace
and Freedom (Internationale Frauenliga für Frieden und Freiheit, or IFFF),
founded in 1915 and the oldest international women's peace organization,
which advocated a new approach to raising and educating German children.
Its members periodically sponsored meetings, issued pamphlets, and penned
articles for area newspapers that called for women to work to prevent future
wars, encouraging them to promote international understanding and to
ensure that children were educated in a "new spirit."[55] The IFFF section also
printed flyers aimed at "Mothers, Educators, [and] Friends of Children" that
repeated pleas the organization had already voiced in the decade after World
War I, urging German women to refuse to let children play with toy soldiers
and weapons, to give books about animals and plants as gifts rather than those
glorifying war and military achievements, and to present scientists rather than
soldiers to children as heroes and role models.[56]

For some Germans, concerns about the future character of German youth
activities were manifested in doubts expressed regarding the reconstitution
of the Boy Scouts. There were those who saw the organization as harmless—
North Württemberg Christian Democratic Union (Christlich Demokratische
Partei, or CDU) party secretary Arthur Ketterer, for example, told a military government official in May 1946 "that it should be the only uniformed
group allowed in Germany," asserting that "until 1933 it maintained a truly

democratic character."[57] But earlier that year, about the time a Stuttgart pastor was attempting to form a small troop, representatives of the Communist Party (Kommunistische Partei Deutschlands, or KPD), the German Peace Society, the SPD women's organization, and the IFFF had voiced strong reservations about reestablishing the Boy Scouts. They argued that in Germany they could expect a "militant organization" to emerge—after all, its incarnation during the Weimar Republic had cooperated with the extreme right-wing League of Frontline Soldiers (Stahlhelm – Bund der Frontsoldaten), founded in 1918.[58] A KPD politician later informed an American official that he thought the Boy Scout movement was very dangerous. Unlike in the United States, he contended, in Germany it had been a paramilitary organization. The secretary of Stuttgart's SPD agreed, calling the group "the militarists' spiritual preschool."[59] As late as November 1948, Leon Shelnutt, the US official responsible for youth programs in Württemberg-Baden, was still commenting that many Germans considered scouting militaristic. Scout organizations were having trouble raising money because of this, he observed, and it was one reason the Americans had not permitted them to wear uniforms. Giving the boys uniforms would help to strengthen this notion, he explained.[60]

If Germans on the left were apprehensive about the Boy Scouts, the socialist *Falken* also came in for criticism for their clothing and activities during their 1947 rally in Stuttgart. Some observers, noted the left-leaning *Stuttgarter Zeitung* newspaper, "saw a danger in the uniforms, the emblems, [and] the marching songs, given the mentality of our nation."[61] An American report also acknowledged complaints received about parades and uniforms, but sounded less worried, citing ambiguous evidence. Defining what constituted a parade was difficult, it suggested, "as the visitors had to cover many distances by foot and, therefore, naturally went in a group." Similarly, while a few youngsters had worn navy blue shirts, the chairman of the Württemberg *Falken* had indicated that the group's leaders had not requested or even desired this and that many young people "simply had these shirts from former years."[62] Indeed, both the male and female members of the Weimar Socialist Workers' Youth had worn navy blue shirts as a major piece of their uniforms. Whatever the real story may have been, it was clear some Germans were concerned. In this case, the criticism may have originated from political conservatives keeping an eye on the socialist youth.

In local newspapers, which operated under licenses from the military government, journalists and other observers also discussed the problem of German young people more generally, calling for a transformation in youth values to focus on constructive goals.[63] One writer, for instance, contended that Germany's young people were living in an age where their recent experiences were of no use. "No one needs soldiers, marchers, destroyers, followers, and the exaggerated emotionalism of martial instinct," he argued. What was needed now was "commitment to the rebuilding of our homeland, to mutual help between individuals, to the preservation of peace and the regaining of freedom of thinking and acting, to life values, therefore, for which one indeed does not receive medals and decorations, but for which one arguably receives the only desirable human prize, namely, inner human dignity."[64]

Young Germans responded to such proposals with skepticism. They resented being lectured by their elders, who they felt had lost their political credibility during the Third Reich. Many young people believed, too, that they already had learned their lesson. When in February 1946 Ulm's *Schwäbische Donau-Zeitung* newspaper asked its young readers what they expected from organized youth groups, one responded that they should no longer feed adolescents with plans for world conquest and teachings of hate, but instead encourage love for other people and teach the laws of humanity.[65] A month later, another youth told North Baden officials that Germany's young people did not want to again be raised to be soldiers and to die. Instead, they wanted to acquire practical skills, learn about a variety of subjects, and have a chance to just have fun.[66] A twenty-four-year-old dentistry student who had co-founded a youth club in Buchen likewise told a military government interviewer that the goal of such organizations "should be to lead youth away from militarism and marching, to a more human attitude."[67]

Ultimately, most youth group activities were harmless in form, if not always in intellectual content. American observers occasionally remarked on the lingering nationalistic and National Socialist attitudes of young Germans.[68] And German youth leaders themselves sometimes expressed nationalistic or chauvinistic ideas without really perceiving—or admitting—the close tie between their thinking and the spiritual universe of Nazism.[69] But these ideas did not normally lead to militaristic teachings or paramilitary drill. Instead, organizations devoted weekends to hiking and camping and evenings to singing, Bible study, crafts, theater, lectures, and discussions, their specific activities dependent upon their *Weltanschauung.*[70] Boy Scout troops seemed to encounter trouble more often than other groups. Yet in June 1949, the military government's Leon Shelnutt also attended a rally where youngsters from Stuttgart were being sworn into the Boy Scouts and later reported that it seemed very much like ceremonies he had witnessed in the United States. In fact, he added, it was "certainly less militaristic (perhaps because I was there)."[71]

In some cases, youth groups spent time explicitly considering the issues of war and military service. In April 1946, some 75 members of an Ulm youth organization attended a lecture on Rudolf Thiel's 1931 book *Männer gegen Tod und Teufel: Aus dem Leben grosser Ärzte* (*Men Against Death and the Devil: The Lives of Great Doctors*), in which the speaker presented doctors and scientists as role models. "It was not the hypocritical heroism of the glory- and blood-covered battlefield that captivated us, but the quiet valor of researchers and doctors who devoted their lives to the good of humanity," explained a girl reporting on the talk. "On this evening, we left the small auditorium deeply impressed."[72] Several months later, a former major and holder of the Knight's Cross of the Iron Cross, a military award that recognized exceptional bravery or military leadership in combat, spoke to a gathering of the communist Schwäbische Volksjugend about the horrors of war and warned them not to listen to those who were once again trying to portray war as something uplifting. From their childhood, through books and games, youngsters were taught "the myth of the 'heroic front soldier,'" he said. But no person was a hero or was born to be a hero, and the driving force of the front soldier was most often not heroism but simply the instinct of self-preservation. The former officer contended that the front soldiers from World War I had failed in not teaching Germany's youth to abhor war. The current generation needed to do better.[73]

There were larger events, too. In August 1946, an antiwar rally in Stuttgart organized by the *Falken* drew about 2,000 young people.[74] That September, some 100 *Falken* and their followers attended a similar event in Heidelberg where, according to a military government report, the keynote speaker argued that the duty of Germany's youth should be to work for their country's welfare, not to die for it. Using militant language reminiscent of international socialism's past, he urged the youth to be "fighters for the brotherhood of the world" and to do everything they could "for the re-entry of Germany into the family of nations."[75]

In the later years of the occupation, evolving political conditions led some German youth groups to engage with the increasingly consequential issues of conscription and rearmament. By the fall of 1947, relations between the Western Allies and the Soviet Union had soured nearly to the point of unworkability in Germany, the Cold War's fault lines were rapidly emerging, and low-level military planners in the Pentagon were starting to speculate on what role German forces might play in defending western Europe in some distant future.[76] Changes in US occupation policies reflected these shifting realities—among them, improved financial and personnel support for educational initiatives that encouraged democratic development in Germany— but the United States also remained committed to its cultural demilitarization program.[77] In September 1948, the military government's *Information Bulletin* again described "preventing the recurrence of any totalitarian or militaristic tendencies among youth organizations" as one of the guiding principles of its youth work.[78]

The possible implications of the growing East-West divide nevertheless worried the Germans, and some youth groups acted on their concerns. Most impressively, Stuttgart's youth parliament caused a stir when it took on Württemberg-Baden's legislature (Landtag) in October 1947. The youth parliament, a roughly 100-member group representing some 37,000 organized young people, officially asked the legislators to amend the state constitution to declare that no person could be forced by law into military service, either bearing arms or in an auxiliary capacity. Although the widespread criticism of the misuse of Germany's youth during the Third Reich might have made the prompt approval of this change a reasonable expectation, the Landtag reacted sluggishly, in part because they recognized Germany's insecure position trapped between East and West. After a contentious meeting involving the youth parliament, Landtag representatives, public officials, and journalists, followed by the parliament's threat of a public demonstration, the Landtag eventually passed a free-standing law that stated that "no one may be forced into war service with a weapon." That the state's lawmakers felt compelled to act, even against their own preferences, was suggested by the fact that just 46 of 100 Landtag delegates were present for the vote, 3 of whom abstained.[79]

A front-page editorial in the *Stuttgarter Zeitung* subsequently condemned the law as a weak and easily revocable substitute for an amendment, but other Germans were more optimistic.[80] One SPD Landtag delegate, who had lobbied for the provision's adoption, conceded in a letter to the editor that she would have preferred a change in the constitution, but she also defended the law's inspirational value, its historical significance, and the importance of making incremental progress toward a more substantial goal.[81] Another letter writer suggested that the law's significance lay in showing clearly that Germany's youth had never had, or at least had renounced, "that condemnable spirit," that is, militarism.[82]

Some young people offered additional support for this claim when they joined an intensifying public debate regarding the possibility of rearmament.[83]

In late 1948, Stuttgart's youth committee, which included representatives of nineteen youth groups, took a strong stance in a resolution addressed to the Landtag that rejected a local politician's proposal for contributing German troops to the defense of western Europe. The youth organizations, the committee asserted, worked hard to give young people "more attractive and better ideals than those of war and the annihilation of people," which had "always brought us and all of humanity only hardship and misery." They therefore refused to assume the role of cannon fodder, for anyone. "If the deaths of millions of people, the distress of war invalids and surviving dependents, our destroyed cities—if that can all have some meaning," it concluded, "then only this, to derive from it the realization that there must be <u>no more war</u>."[84]

Both the debate and the active participation of youth groups would continue after the founding of the Federal Republic of Germany in 1949. Following the start of the Korean War in mid-1950, American policymakers officially endorsed the rearming of the Federal Republic and, with their allies, subsequently sought a way to secure West German help in defending western Europe while also safeguarding western Europe from the Germans themselves. Eventually resulting in the creation in 1955 of a Bundeswehr safely tethered within the North Atlantic Treaty Organization, these developments provoked a jumble of West German reactions, among them pragmatic support for integration with the West, worries that a powerful military might imperil the fledgling democratic state, fears that arming the Federal Republic would end any chance for reunification with East Germany, and denunciations of the very idea of fighting for allies who still held German generals behind bars as war criminals.[85] Often deeply involved in the discussions, as well as those that followed regarding the reintroduction of conscription, West Germany's youth organizations adopted positions along a spectrum from enthusiastic support of rearmament to adamant resistance rooted in pacifism. It is worth noting, however, that even groups that favored a new army advocated changes in its character. The statutes of the Federal Youth Council (Bundesjugendring), whose members included most of the country's major youth organizations, called for energetic efforts to combat a revival of militarism and nationalism, and in 1956 the council approved a resolution on the establishment of the Bundeswehr that called for a civilian-controlled, more humane military and warned that it would fight every attempt to "surround the life and duties of a soldier with an outdated national nimbus or an unnecessary pathos."[86] Even as it became clear that some of West Germany's sons would again become soldiers, it seemed unlikely the nation's youth organizations would be actively equipping them for war.

Conclusion

In assessing the changes in Württemberg-Baden's youth culture during the occupation years, it is essential to remember that only a portion—although a rather large portion—of the state's several million youth belonged to organized groups. In January 1949, for example, twenty-two Stuttgart youth organizations had more than 40,000 members combined, but 70,000 young people in the city had not joined any groups.[87] Skeptics could also point to the past as a check on excessive optimism, noting that pacifist activism after World War I had eventually been trampled underfoot by the jackboots of stronger nationalist and militaristic movements.

Still, there had been concrete changes. American military government regulations had demanded the demilitarization of youth activities and prevented individuals who disagreed with their plans and objectives from exercising public influence. At the same time, many Germans genuinely supported these actions—Germans who had promoted similar ideas during the interwar years and others who had drawn their own lessons from the suffering experienced by their nation during World War II. By 1949, military-style uniforms, soldier songs, and drill instruction were no longer key components of youth programs. Additionally, many groups had declared their opposition to militarism and war, and youth organizations would continue to reject militarism and advocate peace in the years that followed.[88] Equally important for Germany's future were two deeper currents. On the one hand, these changes were sustained in part by a widely shared conviction that Germany's boys should no longer be raised to be soldiers. On the other, influential voices were offering German youth an alternative masculine ideal: the hero who sought to rebuild Germany, promoted peace, and worked for the good of his neighbors and all of humanity—and for whom fighting and dying for the fatherland were neither sublimely glorious nor a desirable goal.

Notes

1. See, for example, Memorandum, Meeting on the German Problem, August 31, 1944, U.S. National Archives [NA], Record Group [RG] 56, Entry 360P, Box 21, F: Conferences—Mr. White's Office 1944; T.N. Grazebrook to Commander Owen et al., September 16, 1944, NA, RG 331, Supreme Headquarters, Allied Expeditionary Force [SHAEF], Entry 26, Box 92, F: 388.4-1 Disposal of the German Military Staff.

2. Kathleen J. Nawyn, "'Striking at the Roots of German Militarism': Efforts to Demilitarize German Society and Culture in American-Occupied Württemberg-Baden, 1945–1949" (Ph.D. diss., University of North Carolina at Chapel Hill, 2008), chap. 2.

3. "Comment on the Proposals Advanced by the Hon. Gerard Swope on the Treatment of Germany," n.d., attached to F.D.R. Memorandum for Hon. Cordell Hull, September 7, 1943, NA, RG 59, Decimal File 1940–1944, Box 2941.

4. Ute Frevert, "Gesellschaft und Militär im 19. und 20. Jahrhundert: Sozial-, kultur- und geschlechtergeschichtliche Annäherungen," in *Militär und Gesellschaft im 19. und 20. Jahrhundert*, ed. Ute Frevert (Stuttgart: Klett-Cotta, 1997), 12–14; Richard Bessel, "Was bleibt vom Krieg? Deutsche Nachkriegsgeschichte(n) aus geschlechtergeschichtlicher Perspektive—Eine Einführung," *Militärgeschichtliche Zeitschrift* 60 (2001): 297–305.

5. Karen Hagemann, "German Heroes: The Cult of Death for the Fatherland in Nineteenth-century Germany," in *Masculinities in Politics and War: Gendering Modern History*, ed. Stefan Dudink, Karen Hagemann, and John Tosh (Manchester, UK: Manchester University Press, 2004), 116–134; Karen Hagemann, "Of 'Manly Valor' and 'German Honor': Nation, War, and Masculinity in the Age of the Prussian Uprising Against Napoleon," *Central European History* 30, no. 2 (2001): 187–220; Marcus Funck, "Ready for War? Conceptions of Military Manliness in the Prusso–German Officer Corps before the First World War," in *Home/Front: The Military, War and Gender in Twentieth-Century Germany*, ed. Karen Hagemann and Stefanie Schüler-Springorum (Oxford: Berg, 2002), 43–67; and Stefanie Schüler-Springorum, "Flying and Killing: Military Masculinity in German Pilot Literature, 1914–1939," in Hagemann and Schüler-Springorum, *Home/Front*, 205–232.

6. Hagemann, "German Heroes," 131.

7. Elisabeth Domansky, "Militarization and Reproduction in World War I Germany," in *Society, Culture, and the State in Germany, 1870–1930*, ed. Geoff Eley (Ann Arbor: University of Michigan Press, 1996), 427–463; George Mosse, *Fallen Soldiers: Reshaping the Memory of the World Wars* (New York: Oxford University Press, 1990), chap. 5; Karen Hagemann, "Home/Front: The Military, Violence and Gender Relations in the Age of the World Wars," in Hagemann and Schüler-Springorum, *Home/Front*, 1–41; Rene Schilling, "Die 'Helden der Wehrmacht'—Konstruktion und Rezeption," in *Die Wehrmacht: Mythos oder Realität*, ed. Klaus-Jürgen Müller and Hans-Erich Volkmann (Munich: R. Oldenbourg Verlag, 1999), 550–572; Ute Frevert, *A Nation in Barracks: Modern Germany, Military Conscription and Civil Society* (Oxford: Berg, 2004).

8. Heide Fehrenbach, *Cinema in Democratizing Germany: Reconstructing National Identity after Hitler* (Chapel Hill: University of North Carolina Press, 1995), 95.

9. Fehrenbach, *Cinema*, 95–97; Robert G. Moeller, "The 'Remasculinization' of Germany in the 1950s: Introduction," *Signs* 24, no. 1 (1998): 101–106; Heide Fehrenbach, "Rehabilitating the Fatherland: Race and German Remasculinization," *Signs* 24, no. 1 (1998): 107–27; Robert G. Moeller, "'The Last Soldiers of the Great War' and Tales of Family Reunions in the Federal Republic of Germany," *Signs* 24, no 1 (1998): 129–45; Frank Biess, "Survivors of Totalitarianism: Returning POWs and the Reconstruction of Masculine Citizenship in West Germany, 1945–1955," in *The Miracle Years: A Cultural History of West Germany, 1949–1968*, ed. Hanna Schissler (Princeton, NJ: Princeton University Pres, 2001), 57–82; and Frank Biess, "Men of Reconstruction—The Reconstruction of Men: Returning POWs in East and West Germany, 1945–1955," in

Hagemann and Schüler-Springorum, *Home/Front*, 344–45. Regarding new conceptions of masculinity, see also Uta G. Poiger, "A New, 'Western' Hero? Reconstructing German Masculinity in the 1950s," *Signs* 24, no. 1 (1998): 147–162; and Clayton J. Whisnant, "Styles of Masculinity in the West German Gay Scene, 1950–1965," *Central European History* 39, no. 3 (2006): 359–93.

10. In referring to "culture," this chapter draws on a definition articulated by historian Akira Iriye, that of "culture as 'structures of meaning,' including 'memory, ideology, emotions, life styles, scholarly and artistic works, and other symbols.'" Akira Iriye, *Cultural Internationalism and World Order* (Baltimore: Johns Hopkins University Press, 1997), 3.

11. The former include, among many others: John Gimbel, *The American Occupation of Germany: Politics and the Military, 1945–1949* (Stanford, CA: Stanford University Press, 1968), Raymond G. Stokes, *Divide and Prosper: The Heirs of I. G. Farben under Allied Authority, 1945–1951* (Berkeley: University of California Press, 1988), Gerhard Wettig, *Entmilitarisierung und Wiederbewaffnung in Deutschland, 1943–1955* (Munich: R. Oldenbourg Verlag, 1967), and David Clay Large, *Germans to the Front: West German Rearmament in the Adenauer Era* (Chapel Hill: The University of North Carolina Press, 1996). Works on efforts to reorient German culture, which typically only touch on cultural demilitarization initiatives, range from James F. Tent's important early analysis *Mission on the Rhine: Reeducation in American-Occupied Germany* (Chicago: University of Chicago Press, 1982) to local studies such as Ulrich M. Bausch's *Die Kulturpolitik der US-Amerikanischen Information Control Division in Württemberg-Baden von 1945 bis 1949: Zwischen militärischem Funktionalismus und schwäbischem Obrigkeitsdenken* (Stuttgart: Klett-Cotta, 1992) and Steven P. Remy's *The Heidelberg Myth: The Nazification and Denazification of a German University* (Cambridge, MA: Harvard University Press, 2002). Recently several scholars have reflected on the long trajectory of the twentieth century and offered bird's-eye analyses of the clear shift in values and priorities after World War II in Europe, with Germany at its core. Key among these studies are Volker R. Berghahn's *Europe in the Era of Two World Wars: From Militarism and Genocide to Civil Society, 1900–1950* (Princeton, NJ: Princeton University Press, 2006) and James J. Sheehan's *Where Have All the Soldiers Gone? The Transformation of Modern Europe* (Boston: Houghton Mifflin, 2008).

12. Scholars interested in the experiences of veterans in postwar Germany have explored aspects of these issues. See, for example, Jay Lockenour, *Soldiers as Citizens: Former Wehrmacht Officers in the Federal Republic of Germany, 1945–1955* (Lincoln: University of Nebraska Press, 2001), Bert-Oliver Manig, *Die Politik der Ehre: Die Rehabilitierung der Berufssoldaten in der frühen Bundesrepublik* (Göttingen: Wallstein Verlag, 2004), and Frank Biess, *Homecomings: Returning POWs and the Legacies of Defeat in Postwar Germany* (Princeton, NJ: Princeton University Press, 2006).

13. The Allies divided the two states for reasons of operational expediency (including the Americans' desire to control Mannheim's Rhine River port and the autobahn and railroad line running from Karlsruhe to Ulm), but the resulting conglomerate was challenging to govern, as the Germans resented the division and two state administrations had to be integrated. As it was, the two states had been part of a united Germany only since 1871, with rich histories as the Kingdom of Württemberg and Grand Duchy of Baden. For research purposes, however, this hybrid quality has advantages. It offers a chance to assess the impact of US zonal policies on what remained essentially two states with similar, but

distinct, histories and traditions. Also, because North Baden retained an administrative identity under, but separate from, the state ministries located in North Württemberg, there are two rich, interconnected sets of state-level records available that document the occupation years.

14. Michael H. Kater, *Hitler Youth* (Cambridge, MA: Harvard University Press, 2004), 28–37.

15. Schilling, "Die 'Helden der Wehrmacht,'" 570.

16. Kater, *Hitler Youth*, chap. 3; Guido Knopp, *Hitler's Children*, trans. Angus McGeoch (Stroud: Sutton, 2004), chap. 2; Karen Hagemann, "Mobilizing Women for War: The History, Historiography, and Memory of German Women's War Service in the Two World Wars," *Journal of Military History* 75 (2011): 1073–91.

17. Quoted in Knopp, *Hitler's Children*, 64.

18. Hagemann, "German Heroes," 128–31; Andrew Donson, "Models for Young Nationalists and Militarists: German Youth Literature in the First World War," *German Studies Review* 27, no. 3 (2004): 579–598; Frevert, *Nation in Barracks*, 213–18, 247–49.

19. Kater, *Hitler Youth*, 29.

20. H-127, March 8, 1944, attached to note from D[avid] H[arris], March 11, 1944, NA, RG 59, Notter File, Entry 500, Box 154, F: H-Policy Summaries 126–49; Sumner Welles, *The Time for Decision* (New York: Harper & Brothers, 1944), 357–58. Regarding American views, see also Karl-Heinz Füssl, *Die Umerziehung der Deutschen: Jugend und Schule unter den Siegermächten des Zweiten Weltkriegs, 1945–1955* (Paderborn: Schöningh, 1994), chap. 2.

21. Julian Bach Jr., *America's Germany: An Account of the Occupation* (New York: Random House, 1946), 25.

22. SHAEF, *Handbook for Military Government in Germany*, December 1944, NA, RG 331, SHAEF, Entry 47, Box 7; SHAEF, *Technical Manual for Education and Religious Affairs*, February 1945, ibid.

23. M.C. Stayer to the Chief of Staff, September 26, 1945, and attachments, NA, RG 260, Records of the U.S. Group Control Council, Box 16, F: AG 353.9 German Youth (Reeducation & Rehabilitation; German Youth Activities Program); Richard Griffin Banks, "The Development of Education in Württemberg-Baden Under United States Military Government" (M.A. Thesis, University of Virginia, 1949), 99–100.

24. Marshall Knappen, *And Call It Peace* (Chicago: University of Chicago, 1947), 47–48, 138–141; "History of Youth Activities," n.d. [ca. mid 1946], NA, RG 260, Office of Military Government, US [OMGUS], Office of Military Government Württemberg-Baden [OMGWB], Box 514, F: Civil Censorship; Banks, "Development," 97–100; "Another Chance for German Youth," *Military Government Weekly Information Bulletin*, April 11, 1946, 5–9, Wisconsin Digital Collections, The History Collection, Germany Under Reconstruction [WDC], http://digital.library.wisc.edu/1711.dl/History .omg1946n038; Headquarters, U.S. Army, Europe, Historical Division, "The U.S. Armed Forces German Youth Activities Program, 1945–1955," August 1956, WDC, http://digital.library.wisc.edu/1711.dl/History.GerYouth.

25. In March 1948, German youth groups in the US zone reported 1,256,712 members, with 386,933 in Württemberg-Baden alone. In February 1948, the GYA program recorded 366,496 participants in the whole zone. In both cases, the actual

number of young people involved was lower, as some joined multiple groups. Office of Military Government for Germany (U.S.), Education and Cultural Relations Division, "German Youth Between Yesterday and Tomorrow, 1 April 1947–30 April 1948," April 30, 1948, 39, 44, WDC, http://digital.library.wisc.edu/1711.dl /History.YouthYesTom.

26. 1. Sitzung des Jugendring–Ausschusses, December 19, 1945, Stadtarchiv Ulm [StAU] E320 SJR Geschichte; "Jugendbetätigung," n.d., Generallandesarchiv Karlsruhe [GLA] 356 Zug. 1969-10 No. 2.433.

27. Stayer to the Chief of Staff, September 26, 1946, and attachments, NA, RG 260.

28. Jugend und Freizeitbetätigung Allgemeine Richtlinien für Württemberg-Baden, July 1947, GLA 356 Zug. 1977–31 No. 799.

29. Leon A. Shelnutt to Inform. Serv. Div. Press Branch, September 28, 1948, NA, RG 260, OMGUS, OMGWB, Box 963, F: C-12 Deutsche Jungenschaft; *Deutsche Jungenschaft* (Aalen: W.A. Stierlin Buchdruckerei, 1946), 8, ibid. Unless otherwise noted, all translations are my own.

30. Daily Report, Education and Religious Affairs, 23 April 1946, April 24, 1946, NA, RG 260, OMGUS, OMGWB, Box 888, F: Weekly Reports E&CR [2].

31. Satzungen der Schwäbischen Volksjugend (SVJ), April 14, 1946, Hauptstaatsarchiv Stuttgart [HStA] EA 1/013 Bü 50.

32. "An die Sportvereine!" *Amtsblatt der Stadt Ulm und des Landkreises Ulm*, January 3, 1946, 198; William J. Truxal to Herr Karl R., December 18, 1946, GLA 356 Zug. 1977–31 No. 800; William J. Truxhal to Herr Erwin O., December 18, 1946, ibid.

33. Mark Edward Ruff, *The Wayward Flock: Catholic Youth in Postwar Germany, 1945–1965* (Chapel Hill: University of North Carolina Press, 2005), 59–60; H. P. van der Berg to Chief, Information Control Division, June 18, 1946, NA, RG 260, OMGUS, OMGWB, Box 89, F: 350.2 Political Movements, Organizations, and Activities Ulm 1946 [2]; Semi-Monthly Progress Report, August 15, 1947, NA, RG 260, OMGUS, OMGWB, Box 887, F: Semi-Monthly Progress Report (1947).

34. Education and Religious Affairs Division Weekly Report, June 27, 1947, NA, RG 260, OMGUS, OMGWB, Box 888, F: Weekly Reports E&CR 1947.

35. L. D. Gresh to Director, Office of Military Government for Hesse, September 9, 1947, NA, RG 260, OMGUS, Education and Cultural Relations [E&CR] Division, Box 128, F: Youth Activities 1946 & 1947.

36. Sportfreunde Geradstetten to Militärregierung in Stuttgart, July 28, 1948, NA, RG 260, OMGUS, OMGWB, Box 970, F: Equipment & Supplies—German Youth.

37. Aksel G. Nielsen to Sportfreunde Geradstetten, August 3, 1948, ibid.

38. OMGUS, Internal Affairs and Communications Division, Education and Religious Affairs Branch, "Youth Activities. Report on German Youth, Second Year of the Occupation, 1 April 1946 – 31 March 1947," March 31, 1947, 14 NA, RG 260, OMGUS, E&CR Division, Box 128, F: Youth Activities 1946 & 1947.

39. Henry J. Kellermann, "The Present Status of German Youth," Part II, *Department of State Bulletin*, July 21, 1946, 84.

40. Württembergischer Landesjugendausschuss to Städt. Wohlfahrts- u. Jugendamt, Abt. Jugendreferat, September 25, 1948, StAU E320 Band 16; Leon A. Shelnutt to Dep. Director, November 8, 1948, NA, RG 260, OMGUS, OMGWB, Box 973, F: Youth

Activities [4]; John P. Steiner to Land-, Kreis- und Stadt-Jugendausschüsse in Württemberg-Baden, September 9, 1948, Stadtarchiv Stuttgart [StAS] HA Gruppe 4 Abl. 29.1.1974 No. 4651-9 Ring deutscher Pfadfinder.

41. Stephen G. Fritz, *Frontsoldaten: The German Soldier in World War II* (Lexington: University of Kentucky Press, 1995), 220–24; Henry J. Kellermann, "The Present Status of German Youth," Part I, *Department of State Bulletin*, July 14, 1946, 49–52.

42. "Betr.: Vortrag vom 24.1.1946 'Wer hilft der Jugend?' " January 29, 1946, HStA EA 1/013 Bü 12; Protokoll über den Vortrag Paul Schempp in der Vortragsreihe BESINNUNG des Innenministeriums, January 25, 1946, ibid.

43. "Diskussion über den Vortrag 'Wer hilft der Jugend?' des Herrn Paul Schempp am 24. Januar 1946," n.d., ibid.

44. "'Wer hilft der Jugend?' (Grundsätzliche Betrachtung zum Referat Paul Schempp 24. Januar 1946 im Festsaal des Furtbachhauses)," n.d., ibid.

45. Briefkasten, *Das junge Wort* [*DJW*], August 1, 1946, 10.

46. See Karl Holl and Wolfram Wette, ed., *Pazifismus in der Weimarer Republik. Beiträge zur historischen Friedensforschung* (Paderborn: Schöningh, 1981); also Jennifer A. Davy, "'Manly' and 'Feminine' Antimilitarism: Perceptions of Gender in the Antimilitarist Wing of the Weimar Peace Movement," in *Frieden—Gewalt—Geschlecht: Friedens- und Konfliktforschung als Geschlechterforschung*, ed. Jennifer A. Davy, Karen Hagemann, and Ute Kätzel (Essen: Klartext Verlag, 2005), 144–165; Wolfram Wette, *Militarismus in Deutschland: Geschichte einer kriegerischen Kultur* (Darmstadt: Primus, 2008), 133–63.

47. Landesausschuss für Jugendpflege und Jugendbewegung, Niederschrift über die erste (konstituierende) Sitzung, April 29, 1946, StAU E320 SJR Geschichte. Bäuerle was an "adult education leader" whom military government education officer Richard Banks described as a "strongly anti-Nazi," apolitical "professional educator." Banks, "Development," 110. See also Theodor Bäuerle, "Life," August 14, 1946, NA, RG 260, OMGUS, OMGWB, Box 883, F: 302.12.

48. "Diskussion über den Vortrag 'Wer hilft der Jugend?' des Herrn Paul Schempp am 24. Januar 1946," n.d., HStA EA 1/013 Bü 12. Heinrich Hassinger had been a teacher before becoming actively involved in youth affairs in Hesse in 1919. When the Nazis took power, he was released from his position as "politically unreliable." "Heinrich Hassinger ein Sechziger," *Stuttgarter Zeitung* [*SZ*], April 14, 1948.

49. "Der Landesjugendtag 1946," *SZ*, June 25, 1946; "Landesjugendtag in Württemberg," *Schwäbische Donau-Zeitung* [*SDZ*], June 29, 1946.

50. Heinrich Hassinger, "Gebt der Deutschen Jugend eine Chance!" *DJW*, March 15, 1947, insert.

51. Hugo Roller to Herr W. H., June 14, 1946, StAU E320 Stadtjugendring Schriftwechsel an 1945–1949; "Sozialdemokrat mit dem Herzen" *Schwäbische Zeitung*, May 13, 1987, StAU G2 Roller, Hugo; "Die Macht stand auf der anderen Seite," *Schwäbische Zeitung*, January 22, 1984, ibid. For more on Roller's views, see 1.Sitzung des Jugendring-Ausschusses, December 19, 1945, StAU E320 SJR Geschichte.

52. "Socialist Youth Meeting of the 'Falcons' in Stuttgart," September 1, 1947, NA, RG 260, OMGUS, OMGWB, Box 972, F: Reference Material Youth Activities Section ECR Div [1]. Although this document cites 15,000 attendees, a later report puts the figure at 9,000. See note 62.

53. On the reconstitution of male authority in the 1950s, see Moeller, "Remasculinization" and "Last Soldiers"; Fehrenbach, "Rehabilitating"; and Biess, "Survivors."

54. Robert G. Moeller, *Protecting Motherhood: Women and the Family in the Politics of Postwar West Germany* (Berkeley: University of California Press, 1993); Ruff, *Wayward Flock*, chap. 3; Annemarie Meister, "Musterkinder, Heldenjungen und Muttermädchen. Von der Kontinuität der Kindheitsbilder vor und nach 1945," *Von Trümmerkind zum Teenager: Kindheit und Jugend in der Nachkriegszeit*, ed. Doris Foitzik (Bremen: Edition Temmen, 1992), 68–70.

55. Internationale Frauenliga für Frieden und Freiheit, Satzungen, n.d. [ca. early 1946], StAS HA Gruppe 0 Abl. 27.4.1972 No. 0143; "'Ohne Liebe kein Friede,'" *Badische Neueste Nachrichten*, May 3, 1947; Intelligence Report, July 7, 1949, NA, RG 260, OMGUS, OMGWB, Box 459, F: Weekly Intelligence Reports. 5 May 49 to 25 Aug 49, vol. VI; Betty Binder-Asch, "Zur Friedensarbeit der Frauen," *SZ*, February 2, 1946; Anna Haag, " . . . Und wir Frauen?" n.d. [ca. April 1946], StAS HA Gruppe 0 Abl. 27.4.1972 No. 0143. For an introduction to the (limited) political work of women in postwar Stuttgart, see Andrea Hauser, "Frauenöffentlichkeit in Stuttgart nach 1945—Gegenpol oder hilflos im Abseits?" in *"Das Schicksal Deutschlands liegt in der Hand seiner Frauen"—Frauen in der deutschen Nachkriegsgeschichte*, ed. Anna-Elisabeth Freier and Annette Kuhn (Düsseldorf: Schwann, 1984), 51–89.

56. Internationale Frauenliga für Frieden und Freiheit, Gruppe Württemberg, to Kultministerium, February 15, 1949, and enclosure, HStA EA 3/101 Bü 204. On the Weimar period, see Davy, "'Manly' and 'Feminine' Antimilitarism," 160–61.

57. Daniel Lee McCarthy to Chief, Information Control Division, May 7, 1946, NA, RG 260, OMGUS, OMGWB, Box 88, F: 350.2 Political Movements, Organizations, and Activities Stuttgart 1946 [2]. See also Ludwig Lefebre to Chief, Information Control Division, April 29, 1946, NA, RG 260, OMGUS, OMGWB, Box 86, F: 350.2 Political Movements, Organizations, and Activities Heidelberg 1946 [2].

58. To Herr Dr. Steinbach, February 26, 1946, HStA EA 1/013 Bü 49.

59. Daniel Lee McCarthy to Chief, Information Control Division, April 24, 1946, NA, RG 260, OMGUS, OMGWB, Box 88, F: 350.2 Political Movements, Organizations, and Activities Stuttgart 1946 [2].

60. Leon A. Shelnutt to Dep. Director, November 8, 1948, NA, RG 260.

61. "Die Falken-Tage in Stuttgart," *SZ*, September 3, 1947.

62. Semi-Monthly Progress Report, September 15, 1947, NA, RG 260, OMGUS, OMGWB, Box 887, F: Semi-Monthly Progress Report (1947).

63. Kurt Fried, "Was ist mit der Jugend?" *SDZ*, December 1, 1945; Olaf Saile, "Ein Wort an die deutsche Jugend," *SZ*, July 10, 1946; Robert Widéra, "Rumorende Jugend," *SZ*, February 15, 1947.

64. "Begeisterung nicht Pathos," *SZ*, April 25, 1946.

65. Kurt Fried, "Die Jugend antwortet," *SDZ*, February 16, 1946.

66. Protokoll der Sitzung des Jugendrates von Nordbaden, March 25, 1946, Stadtarchiv Heidelberg AA 3 No. 3b.

67. Ludwig Lefebre to Chief, Information Control Division, 29 April 1946, NA, RG 260.

68. Kellermann, "The Present Status of German Youth," Part I, 49–52; "Youth Activities. Report on German Youth, Second Year of the Occupation," March 31, 1947, NA, 6 RG

260; "Heidelberg Youth Organizations," June 4, 1948, NA, RG 260, OMGUS, OMGWB, Box 457, F: Weekly Intelligence Reports, 11 Aug 47–4 June 48, Vol. II.

69. Arno Klönne, "'Kulturkampf': Bemerkungen zur Schul- und Jugendpolitik der Besatzungsmächte in Deutschland nach 1945," in *Jahrbuch für zeitgeschichtliche Jugendforschung 1994/95* (1995): 36–8.

70. See, for example, Evang. Jungmännerwerk, Bezirk Blaubeuren, to Herr Roller, March 23, 1946, StAU E320 Stadt-Jugendring Schriftwechsel an 1945–1949; Naturfreunde-Jugend Karlsruhe, *Tätigkeitsbericht über das Jahr 1946*, Stadtarchiv Karlsruhe 8/StS 20 No. 662.

71. Daily Journal, June 24, 1949, NA, RG 260, OMGUS, OMGWB, Box 890, F: Daily Report of Activities E&CR Div from 26 May 1949 to 12 July 1949.

72. Schwäbischer Jugendbund, Ulm/Donau, Wochenbericht vom 8.4.1946 bis 14.4.1946, n.d., HStA EA 3/301 Bü 1218.

73. "Gegen den Militarismus," *DJW*, August 1, 1946, 13.

74. Weekly Political Intelligence Report, August 28, 1946, NA, RG 260, OMGUS, OMGWB, Box 88, F: 350.2 Political Movements, Organizations, and Activities Stuttgart 1946 [3].

75. Intelligence Report No. 338, October 8, 1946, NA, RG 260, OMGUS, OMGWB, Box 85, F: 350.2 Political Movements, Organizations, and Activities Heidelberg 1946 [2].

76. Laurence W. Martin, "The American Decision to Rearm Germany," in *American Civil-Military Decisions: A Book of Case Studies*, ed. Harold Stein (Birmingham: University of Alabama Press, 1963), 646. On the earliest Allied discussions regarding a possible German military contribution, see Large, *Germans to the Front*, 35–8.

77. Directive to Commander-in-Chief of U.S. Forces of Occupation, Regarding the Military Government of Germany, July 11, 1947, in *American Experiences in Military Government in World War II*, ed. Carl J. Friedrich and Associates (New York: Rinehart & Company, 1948), 402–415; "German Youth Between Yesterday and Tomorrow," 2. On the impact of shifting US priorities on military government efforts relating to Germany's education system, see Tent, *Mission on the Rhine*, chap. 6.

78. "Military Government and Germany's Youth," *Information Bulletin*, September 21, 1948, 12, WDC, http://digital.library.wisc.edu/1711.dl/History.omg1948n144.

79. "Kriegsgegner wollen am 8. Mai demonstrieren," *SDZ*, April 8, 1948; To Leon A. Shelnutt, April 8, 1948, NA, RG 260, OMGUS, OMGWB, Box 964, F: C-22 Jugendparlament; Intelligence Report, April 7, 1948, NA, RG 260, OMGUS, OMGWB, Box 816, F: Intelligence Reports 1948; "Jugend will Kriegsdienst verweigern," *Rhein-Neckar-Zeitung*, 8 April 1948; "Landtag nimmt Gesetz über Kriegsdienstverweigerung an," *SZ*, April 24, 1948.

80. "Ein kraftloses Gesetz," *SZ*, April 28, 1948.

81. Briefe an die Herausgeber, *SZ*, April 30, 1948.

82. Briefe an die Herausgeber, *SZ*, May 15, 1948.

83. Intelligence Report, December 9, 1948, NA, RG 260, OMGUS, OMGWB, Box 458, F: Weekly Intelligence Reports, 4 Nov 48, to 27 Jan 49, Vol. IV; "Aufruf der Jugend!" December 19, 1949, StAU E320 Stadtjugendring Schriftwechsel an 1945–1949. For more, see the chapter by Friederike Brühöfener in this volume.

84. Intelligence Report, December 22, 1948, NA, RG 260, OMGUS, OMGWB, Box 818, F: Intelligence Reports 1948–1949 (emphasis in original).

85. Large, *Germans to the Front*; Michael Geyer, "Cold War Angst: The Case of West-German Opposition to Rearmament and Nuclear Weapons," in Schissler, *Miracle Years*, 376–408.

86. Hans Ehlert, "Innenpolitische Auseinandersetzungen um die Pariser Verträge und die Wehrverfassung 1954 bis 1956," in *Die NATO-Option*, vol. 3: *Anfänge westdeutscher Sicherheitspolitik, 1945–1956*, ed. Militärgeschichtliches Forschungsamt (Munich: R. Oldenbourg Verlag, 1993), 395–404. Among others, the council's members included the Boy Scouts, *Falken*, and Catholic and Protestant youth organizations.

87. Intelligence Report, January 19, 1949, NA, RG 260, OMGUS, OMGWB, Box 818, F: Intelligence Reports 1948–1949.

88. On youth organization goals in later years, see, for example, Satzung des Stadtjugendringes Stuttgart, September 13, 1954, StAS HA Gruppe 4 Abl. 29.1.1974 No. 4651–5 Akten betr. Satzung; Stadtjugendring Stuttgart, Satzung, July 2, 1962, ibid.; Bund Junger Genossenschafter, Jugendgruppe Ulm, to Stadtjugendring, January 29, 1954, and attachments, StAU E320 Band 1; Helmut M. to Leiter des Stadtjugendrings, August 13, 1954, and attachment, ibid.; "Empfehlungen des Landesjugendrings Baden-Württemberg," November 25, 1964, ibid.

Chapter 6
Sending Young Men to the Barracks: West Germany's Struggle over the Establishment of New Armed Forces in the 1950s

Friederike Brühöfener

Following the collapse of the Nazi regime on May 8, 1945, the Allies established their authority in four occupation zones. Signs of defeat were visible all over Germany as the occupation forces maneuvered their vehicles through cities that Allied bombing had reduced to rubble. Amid the ruins, returning prisoners of war (POWs) represented one of the most "powerful symbols" of Germany's abject status.[1] Over the next decade, millions of veterans found their way back, first into the various occupation zones and then, after they were established, into the two Germanys.

The POWs who returned to West Germany not only arrived in a society that was going through an intense process of denazification and demilitarization,[2] but also found themselves in a society that had largely given up the practice of cherishing the military as a symbol of national prowess.[3] Typical of the postwar rhetoric was a statement by Carlo Schmid, a leading politician of the reestablished Social Democratic Party (Sozialdemokratische Partei Deutschlands, or SPD), who proclaimed in 1946, "We never want to send our sons into the barracks again!"[4] This attitude informed the ways that society welcomed back its men. With the support of the churches, West German officials were eager to integrate the returning soldiers into society. This meant reintegrating the POWs into the civilian workforce and into families that contemporaries judged to be "incomplete" due to the missing male head of the household.[5] As the postwar years wore on, POWs were increasingly presented as gentle, loving family men. This ideal of civilian masculinity represented a sharp contrast to the model of militarized and aggressive masculinity that had dominated the public during the Nazi era. In the context of West Germany's postwar reconstruction, the ideal place where men gained their status was the family circle, not the battlefield.[6]

The growing tensions of the Cold War, however, soon called this trend into question. The Berlin Blockade in 1948–49 and the outbreak of the Korean War in June 1950 caused the former Western Allies to review their agenda. The US government, in particular, pondered whether West German forces could function as a bulwark against potential threats from the east. Although British and French leaders (especially the latter) were less enthusiastic, the United States found an avid ally in Konrad Adenauer, the first chancellor of the Federal Republic of Germany (FRG). Adenauer led a conservative government composed of the Christian Democratic Party (Christlich Demokratische Union, or CDU), the Christian Social Party (Christlich Soziale Union, or CSU), the liberal Free Democratic Party (Freie Demokratische Partei, or FDP) and the German Party (Deutsche Partei, or DP), and he had already begun to discuss West Germany's security policy with former Wehrmacht officers in 1948. In an interview with the *Cleveland Plain Dealer* in December 1949, only eight months after the creation of the Federal Republic, he expressed his willingness to contribute to a Western defense effort. After cumbersome negotiations, the chancellor's hopes were answered in December 1950 when the Western Allies formally agreed to foster the FRG's rearmament. In 1952, Italy, the Benelux nations, France, and the Federal Republic signed a treaty that would allow West Germany to establish armed forces as part of a pan-European military force called the European Defense Committee (EDC).[7]

The international decision represented not only an extraordinary turn in international geopolitics, but also a challenge to West German society. While German POWs were still returning, mainly from Soviet POW camps, the prospect of national armed troops made it likely that West German men would soon return to the barracks. This possibility stirred immediate discussions among the opposing political parties, most notably between Adenauer's government, the SPD, and the Communist Party (Kommunistische Partei Deutschlands, or KPD). Outside the parliamentary halls, the churches and factions of the labor unions joined women's, peace, and youth groups that objected to Adenauer's political course. Citizens wrote letters to government officials pointing out the advantages and disadvantages of military service, while the media reported and commented extensively on the rearmament debates. In this way, the plan to field West German troops would occupy all parts of society and divide the young Federal Republic.[8]

Scholars seeking to explain this uproar emphasize the changing attitudes toward war and military service in postwar West Germany.[9] Focusing on the cultural dimension of the debate, recent studies stress among other things competing opinions on two related issues: Pondering how military life and service would influence the behavior of young men who joined the army, contemporaries also debated the question of whether the army could and should once again function as a "school of the nation."[10] According to these studies, the debate about rearmament was also a debate about the military as a social institution. Building on this research, this chapter shows that, because contemporaries defined military service as a man's duty, the rearmament debate was also a debate about conflicting ideals of masculinity and their influence on society and culture. The legacy of World War II required a reformulation of masculine traits that would be acceptable for young men serving in the new armed forces. This search for adequate masculine traits helped West Germans come to terms with the prospect of sending large numbers of young men to the barracks again and thus enabled the government to pursue rearmament and establish the Bundeswehr as a conscript army. In the wake of World War II, the quest for socially acceptable concepts of military masculinity also functioned as a vehicle to define—if not reassert—a gender system that, according to contemporary judgment, would be suitable for the newly established West German society.

Seeking to trace how various members of West German society sought to define and negotiate military masculinity, this chapter analyzes parliamentary debates, negotiations within the Ministry of Defense, and statements of church, social, and protest groups as well as press comments. It first examines the early rearmament debates that defined military service as a man's duty and then explores the discussions that developed in the mid-1950s, during which Germans increasingly deliberated the social implications of military service.

Paving the Way to the Barracks: The Prospect of a West German Army

Chancellor Adenauer's performance on the international stage and the multilateral agreements of 1950 and 1952 attracted a great deal of national attention, compelling Adenauer to address his audience back home. In lengthy speeches in front of the Bundestag, the West German parliament, the chancellor and his supporters articulated the government's reasons for establishing armed forces. On November 8, 1950, Adenauer asserted that he viewed the establishment of armed forces as a natural right that every state possessed, including the FRG, and he stated that it was imperative for the FRG to make use of this right in order to protect itself. If West Germans did not want to surrender their lives and freedom to the yoke of the Soviet Union, Adenauer argued, they had to establish armed forces.[11] Adenauer's speech revealed the government's assumptions about who would have to bear the main responsibility for taking up arms. Noting the brutal behavior of Soviet soldiers toward "men, women and girls" at the end of World War II, Adenauer stated that it was the duty of every male "citizen with common sense" (*Bürger mit gesundem Empfinden*) to defend West Germany and all its inhabitants against any threat from the east.[12] This understanding was shared and further specified by Richard Jaeger, who led the state executive committee of the CDU's Bavarian sister party, the CSU. In early February 1952, Jaeger argued that every male citizen had the duty of self-defense (*Notwehrpflicht*). In his view, the "duty of a paterfamilias to defend his wife and children" meant that the "younger generation" had a duty to accept military conscription in order to defend "their mothers, their sisters, their brides."[13] While assigning women to the domestic sphere of housekeeping and childrearing, the conservative government thus conferred on men the duty of protecting this sphere and the entire country.[14]

Adenauer's and Jaeger's speeches were highly energetic and aggressive, for they responded to the fierce criticism of the opposing parties, above all the Social Democrats and Communists, as well as to the opposition within the ranks of their own coalition. Interpreting Germany's disarmament after World War II as God's righteous punishment for the sins of the German people, the CDU politician and Minister of Interior, Gustav Heinemann, for instance, openly rejected rearmament and resigned in October 1950.[15] During his struggle with Heinemann, however, Adenauer could rely on both the majority of his party members and the support of the coalition parties. Individual party factions disagreed deeply on the details of rearmament, but the FDP endorsed the overall plan to establish national armed forces, agreeing that it was Germany's right to do so. The FDP also agreed that it was every man's duty to defend the FRG and all its inhabitants. FDP leaders further hoped that the military would have social value beyond being a defensive force. An internal report distributed in January 1953 acknowledged the educational value of military service and argued that young men could gain "technical skills" and simultaneously form a "strong personality" during their military training.[16] They hoped young men would leave the Bundeswehr as "masters of the machine" who would become valuable in the labor market.[17]

While Adenauer could control his own party (the CDU/CSU) and its coalition members, he was not able to win over the opposition. The Social Democrats expressed especially fierce criticism. In light of the apparent divide between East and West Germany, the party argued that this rift could not be bridged but would become even bigger if the government were to establish armed forces. In addition, the party feared that the establishment of a new military and conscription would eventually lead to the remilitarization of the entire state and society.[18] In 1952, the SPD even appealed to the Federal Constitutional Court to curtail the rearmament, arguing that the FRG's constitution of 1949, the Basic Law (Grundgesetz), did not provide for an army, let alone conscription.[19] In fact, the Basic Law neither explicitly allowed nor prohibited the establishment of armed forces. The only statement that referred to military service stipulated that no one should be compelled "against his conscience to render military service."[20] This legal situation, the Social Democrats argued, meant that the Basic Law would have to be amended if a national army was to be established. From the SPD's perspective, the appeal was a smart move, because amendments to the Basic Law required a two-thirds majority in the Bundestag, a number that the government could not achieve at that point.

In light of the parliamentary opposition and the strong antimilitarization protests outside the Bundestag, it seemed unlikely that the chancellor would be able to achieve his goal. The elections of 1953, however, disabused Adenauer's severest critics of any notions of blocking his agenda. Receiving even more votes than in the first elections in 1949, the CDU celebrated a stunning victory. Adenauer's new center-right coalition enjoyed a two-thirds majority and pursued its plans, including amendment of the Basic Law. The amendment, approved in May 1954, gave the federal government the power to legislate on foreign affairs and defense, including the conscription of men who had reached the age of eighteen.

Even though continued Social Democratic opposition to Adenauer's policies had made ratification of the amendment cumbersome, the parliamentarians quickly agreed that compulsory military service was a duty that rested solely with the Federal Republic's male citizens. Military service, CDU politician Karl Weber declared during a meeting of the Federal Law Committee

(Ausschuss für Rechtswesen und Verfassungsrecht) in February 1954, "traditionally never referred to women," but was always limited to men.[21] He justified this reading of history by referring to women's and men's "fundamentally different nature." Endorsing this idea, FDP politician Elisabeth Maria Lüders argued that limiting military service to men was necessary, because women "could not handle weapons," and men "could not handle babies."[22] The National Socialist past functioned as another important disincentive. The Third Reich had mobilized more than 500,000 women for auxiliary service in the Wehrmacht between 1939 and 1945, and West German politicians did not want to follow in Hitler's footsteps.[23] As a result, the amendment of the Basic Law referred to the recruitment of men only.

While Adenauer secured support for rearmament in the Bundestag, the conservative government still faced intense opposition outside of the parliamentary halls. Many West Germans rejected both rearmament and the introduction of conscription. This extraparliamentary resistance began to take shape as soon as the international debates suggested that West Germany might participate in a Western defense force. The opposition to rearmament and warfare also became apparent in opinion polls that numerous research institutes conducted between 1949 and 1952. For instance, a survey conducted by one of the leading market research institutes, EMNID, in December 1949 and January 1950 showed that "75 percent of West Germans" refused the idea of "becoming a soldier" or seeing "their sons, or their husbands" becoming soldiers, and 63 percent opposed conscription.[24] The latter was still a high number, but the pollsters emphasized that interviewees wanted to see the "the educational value of having a military preserved" and thus fewer people objected to compulsory military service.[25] As historian Michael Geyer stresses, this overwhelming rejection of rearmament and conscription declined relatively slowly; only in late 1956 did a majority of the public come to support rearmament. But this did not mean that they approved of compulsory military service. It was not until 1963 that 50 percent of Germans came to support conscription.[26]

In addition to counting the numbers, pollsters recorded answers of interviewees verbatim. These answers provide further insight into the various reasons why Germans voted for or against rearmament and conscription. While in October 1951 some interviewees who seemed in favor of rearmament maintained that national forces were a necessary instrument for West Germany's defense, others argued that military service was one way for young men to avoid unemployment and make a living. The latter observation was most likely influenced by the meager living standards that shaped the early postwar years.[27] Given the unsettled and rough living conditions that persisted in the FRG, joining the army represented a better option than being unemployed and "loitering" in the streets. Arguing, moreover, that military service "won't hurt" (*"Militär hat noch keinem geschadet"*), some interviewees asserted the educational value of military service, and both men and women stated that young men would learn discipline and orderliness while serving.[28]

The reasons for which interviewees rejected rearmament and conscription were also diverse. Some argued that no man should be forced to fight alongside the former Western Allies as long as former Wehrmacht soldiers were still "vilified" and in captivity as POWs.[29] This comment reflects the fact that, even though most German POWs had been released from the Soviet Union by the late 1940s, a significant number of POWs and civilians who had been convicted as "war criminals" by Soviet courts still remained in captivity. Others, especially older men and women who had experienced the First and the Second World War, as well as supporters of the left parties, argued that the military was a breeding ground for brutality and that nobody should be forced to undergo that ordeal again.[30]

Even if the attitudes expressed in these opinion polls were not reflected in the 1953 elections, the overall results of the early opinion polls were certainly not the outcome that the Adenauer administration had hoped for. Yet, while polls could have disappeared into any drawer, the same was not true for the opposition that became manifest in the streets of West German cities. The *Ohne-Mich* ("Without Me") movement, which encompassed all strata of society and a broad political spectrum, had been gaining increasing influence since the early 1950s.[31] Protesters took to the streets with gatherings, rallies, and demonstrations. Their manifold motives greatly resembled the answers that interviewees had given in opinion polls. Some protesters objected to rearmament because of an offended sense of honor or because they distrusted the victorious Allies, while others opposed it on moral and ethical grounds. Young men between their teens and late twenties were especially avid, declaring that they did not intend to enlist for military service. Their opposition to rearmament was most likely because they would be the first ones sent to the barracks in case of conscription.[32] Moreover, numerous women's groups supported these young men, objecting to their sons and husbands leaving home and family again in order to join the army and defend home and country.[33]

Introducing Conscription: The Benefits and Perils of Military Service

The conservative government and former Wehrmacht officers whom Adenauer had employed to deliberate about the potential rearmament rebutted these protests as male "reluctance to endure military service" (*Wehrunwille*).[34] Depicting the protesters as "unpatriotic," they sought to convince the public that "protection of home and country" was necessary, given rising Cold War tensions. The antirearmament protests were, however, not the only hurdle that Adenauer had to overcome. In late 1954, he also faced trouble on the international stage. In August of that year, the French assembly refused to ratify the 1952 treaty that had envisioned West German troops as part of the EDC. While this could have ended the prospect of West German rearmament, the US government was able to convince the French government in October 1954 to join the three Benelux states, Canada, the FRG, Italy, the United Kingdom, and the United States in signing the Paris Accords. This treaty granted West Germany's sovereignty and its right to establish armed forces that would be put under the command of the North Atlantic Treaty Organization (NATO). Following the agreement, which the Bundestag ratified in early 1955, the Adenauer administration lost no time in pursuing rearmament, passing a series of corresponding laws, including the Volunteer Law (Freiwilligengesetz) in July 1955 and, eventually, a Compulsory Military Service Act (Wehrpflichtgesetz) in July 1956.[35] Under the international treaty, the government planned to establish a military force of up to 500,000 men. The need for soldiers was immense, and the government eagerly pushed for compulsory military service.

As the pace of rearmament accelerated, West Germans were increasingly forced to come to terms not only with professional national armed forces, but also with the introduction of universal conscription. This aggravated the ongoing national debates. Since the establishment of a conscript army entailed drafting large numbers of young men, Germans increasingly focused on the social implications of armed forces. One place for an intensive discussion of the issue was the mainstream press, which paid careful attention to these developments. The liberal magazine *Der Spiegel*, which used every opportunity to criticize Adenauer's government, published an opinion survey titled "What is the Bundeswehr's function?" ("*Wozu dient die Bundeswehr?*"). According to this poll, 44 percent of the interviewees preferred a conscription army, while 37 percent favored a professional volunteer army, and 19 percent remained undecided. Eager to gauge why West

Germans supported rearmament, *Der Spiegel* pointed out that it was not international prestige that caused West Germans to support rearmament. To the contrary, said the magazine, a great majority of interviewees emphasized domestic reasons. They believed that the military was a valuable "educational institution" (*Erziehungsanstalt*) that could inculcate "internal, domestic" (*häusliche*) qualities. Like some interviewees in the early 1950s, 60 percent of those surveyed agreed that young men could learn "proper manners" and "orderliness" while serving in the military.[36]

This thinking was most likely influenced by the educational principles that West Germans tended to value in the 1950s. Many parents believed that orderliness and assiduousness were important educational goals.[37] The assumption that military service would teach young men these qualities was widespread. In accordance with this thinking, public commentators and parliamentarians even recommended military service as a solution to larger social issues, such as the *Halbstarken* (literally: half-strong) problem. Contemporaries used this term for the groups of "unruly" youngsters who gathered in the streets of West German towns and cities in the mid-1950s and unsettled many "orderly" citizens. These young men and women followed the fashion of American movie idols such as James Dean. Their rebellious public conduct challenged the dominant understanding of how young men and women should behave and look.[38] In particular, contemporary moralists judged their behavior unsuitable. Eager to influence and change the behavior of the *Halbstarken*, some critics highlighted the positive pedagogical influence of military life and insisted that unruly youngsters should be recruited into the Bundeswehr. They argued that if the adolescents who lacked discipline and orderliness went through basic military service, they would learn proper male behavior and become more acceptable to society.[39] The debate about the *Halbstarken* and Bundeswehr recruits thus became a struggle over competing notions of masculinity, for contemporaries disputed how young West German men—especially those who entered the barracks—should behave.

This struggle becomes especially apparent in arguments that the military was not a valuable educational place for young men. Members of the Ministry of Defense who did not embrace the "domestic" notion of military education and training voiced strident criticism. One of the severest critics was former Wehrmacht officer Wolf Graf von Baudissin, who had joined the Amt Blank, the predecessor of the Ministry of Defense, in 1951 and would soon become one of the leading theorists of the Bundeswehr. As head of the division's Department of Inner Structure (Abteilung für Inneres Gefüge),

Baudissin and his supporters developed the foundational concept for the military's internal structure, which promoted a new type of soldier: the "citizen in uniform" (*Bürger in Uniform*).[40] Seeking to conflate citizens' rights with military demands, Baudissin argued that the new West German soldier should enjoy all the basic rights of citizenship, such as the right to vote and freedom of speech.[41] In fact, this new concept of Inner Command (*Innere Führung*) also implied a notion of social education that aimed to improve the soldier's attitude and his personality. In contrast to those who advocated the inculcation of "domestic skills," his supporters believed that the military's educational mission lay, first of all, in strengthening the soldiers' obedience to the Basic Law and invoking a sense of responsibility to the democratic society.

Yet Baudissin did not support the idea that the Bundeswehr should be the prime place for turning young men into full-fledged, responsible citizens with superior manly qualities.[42] Rather, he stated that the idea of the military as the prime institution for training young citizens would represent an obstacle to the democratic lifestyle of the FRG. In his view, the educational responsibility for young men rested with their parents, schools, and churches.[43] Moreover, he argued, the capacities of the Bundeswehr would be overburdened if it alone were put in charge of turning young soldiers into responsible citizens. This education should have occurred long before they joined the armed forces.[44] Baudissin proved to be an outspoken opponent of the idea that the Bundeswehr should become a "school of the nation." He argued vehemently against the image of the Bundeswehr as an institution that parents could use to reform their ill-behaved sons and teach them socially acceptable manners.[45]

Even though his concept became the official policy of the Bundeswehr and was embraced by many parliamentarians and figures outside parliament, Baudissin faced intense opposition and criticism within the Ministry of Defense and from conservative parliamentary forces. Some conservative generals in the Bundeswehr who had already served in the Wehrmacht and conservative politicians argued that his approach was not "soldierly" enough and would eventually jeopardize the Bundeswehr's prowess.[46] Apart from this internal reproach, Baudissin's concept did not entirely resonate with the government. In August 1956, he noted in his official diary that Chancellor Adenauer and members of his cabinet had not entirely bid farewell to the image of the military as a valuable educational institution for young men. Baudissin observed that Adenauer was happy to hear about a "working woman who hoped that the Bundeswehr would educate (*erziehen*) her ill-bred son."[47]

Another indication that this position was favored within the government was a memorandum published by the Adenauer administration in July 1956 to promote the introduction of compulsory military service. The document first and foremost emphasized that conscription was necessary due to the tensions of the Cold War, which endangered peace in central Europe in general and West Germany's security in particular. But the memorandum also argued that military service was a valuable "training for life" and would be beneficial to the "people's health" (*Volksgesundheit*) as it fostered comradeship and physical fitness. The memorandum can be read as an official reaction to the national discussion that centered on the military as a valuable educational institution.[48] The fact that the Adenauer government distributed a brochure legitimating the founding of the Bundeswehr in this way can also be read as a response to continuing public concern about the introduction of universal conscription that the government faced in the mid-1950s. The prospect of compulsory military service caused Christian groups and youth welfare professionals in particular to question the salutary function of military service. Instead of perceiving the army as a valuable institution that would foster young men's proper behavior, public discussion began to suggest exactly the opposite: that the Bundeswehr was a breeding ground for socially unacceptable male behavior. One of the groups expressing such concerns was the League of German Catholic Youth. Even though this group supported the rearmament, it worried that a conscript army would promote behavior that would eventually endanger the value system of the Federal Republic.[49] Without being overtly explicit, the youth group pictured the military as an institution in which men could fall victim to a lifestyle that would not foster "decency," but "debauchery."[50]

While church groups were the most vocal critics of a "decay of the manners" of young recruits, concerns about their "improper behavior" were not limited to the Christian milieu.[51] In 1955 the Working Group for Youth Care and Welfare (Arbeitsgemeinschaft Jugendpflege und Jugendfürsorge), which operated on a federal level, met in Cologne to discuss the issue of "Youth Protection and Wehrmacht" (*Jugendschutz und Wehrmacht*).[52] In a lengthy report, the working group detailed various perils that its members associated with military service. One of their major concerns was the excessive consumption of alcohol and tobacco. The working group criticized "soldierly" drinking and smoking habits, which they perceived as typical "attributes of comradely etiquette."[53] While excessive drinking represented for them an obstacle to the soldier's safety as well as the army's effective functioning, the working group, reflecting the increasing political tensions during the Cold War, also worried

155

about the threat of espionage After all, they argued, the "enemy" could deposit alcohol (*Beutealkohol*) somewhere to trap soldiers.[54] The working group was further troubled by possible "sexual dangers" such as prostitution and homosexuality. Fearing the recurrence of Wehrmacht brothels (*Wehrmachtsbordelle*), they judged both prostitution and homosexuality as improper and unsuitable for future West German soldiers.[55]

The working groups' concerns about the soldiers' alcoholic and sexual excesses resounded with citizens who lived in prospective garrison cities.[56] For them, "sexual vices" and "immoral behavior" represented a threat to their communities. Whereas discussions of soldierly homosexuality hardly ever surfaced in public debates, remarks about other "sex crimes" (*Sittlichkeitsverbrechen*) were quite common. Reporting about the town of Fürstenau in Lower Saxony, *Der Spiegel* noted in 1956 that the townspeople were not entirely happy about the prospect of becoming a garrison city.[57] Aldermen were quoted as saying that many of the young men who would be drafted for the Bundeswehr did not exhibit the "steadiness" that would conform to the "aspired soldierly representation in public."[58] In particular they feared that the city would soon face prostitution.[59] Like the council members of Fürstenau, inhabitants of other garrison cities and some women's groups also expressed concerns about mixing Bundeswehr soldiers with the female population. In contrast to the League of German Catholic Youth, which suggested that "proper" young women could positively influence soldiers' behavior, citizens living in garrison cities feared the young men in military uniform would pose a moral threat to proper young women.[60]

Much of the concern of youth welfare professionals, Christian youth groups, and anxious citizens who associated specific perils with the establishment of armed forces was rooted in the homosocial living conditions of young conscripts. They perceived the Bundeswehr as a "men's society" (*Männergesellschaft*) and feared the social dangers of such an institution.[61] They believed that young male recruits were especially susceptible to the perils of military life. Since military regulations envisioned that all men who had reached the age of eighteen would be eligible for military service and most would begin their basic training at about twenty, welfare professionals concluded that conscripts would enter the army at their "sexually most active age."[62] This was especially troubling to some Germans, since the young men would live together in barracks where groups of at least four soldiers shared one bedroom, the so-called *Stube*, where each one would have no more than his own bed and locker. Because the garrisons were also located in rather remote areas or at the peripheries of cities and towns, soldiers would have limited contact with the "normal population"—male and female civilians—even in their leisure time.[63] According to the Working Group on Youth Protection, quartering sexually active men in this way and detaching them from their friends, family, and loved ones would soon lead to "improper behavior"—by which they seem to have meant homosexuality and prostitution.

Although it is not possible at this point to say anything about the behavior of the first young soldiers who served in the Bundeswehr, sources indicate that the moral vices of military service not only alarmed part of the public but also concerned military leaders. Soon after the first draftees moved into barracks scattered all over West Germany in the spring of 1957, the recruits' questionable behavior unsettled commanding officers. Internal correspondence between the leading generals and the legal advisor of the 6th Military District in Bavaria shows that the command was concerned about how to deal with soldiers who visited "louche streets and bars."[64] Working together with vice squads in Munich, the military police found soldiers visiting places that normally would be avoided by "proper citizens," because they were frequented by "prostitutes," "*souteneurs*" (pimps), "homosexuals," and "other asocial elements."[65] The commanders, who sought legal advice on how to deal with these issues, found the soldiers' behavior unacceptable. By visiting such questionable places and exhibiting improper behavior, soldiers not only endangered their own health and, thus, their ability to serve, but also damaged the "reputation of the Bundeswehr in public." The commanding officers made it clear that conscripts who behaved improperly would jeopardize the "trust of the population."[66]

Casting a positive light on the Bundeswehr and gaining the "trust of the population" were clearly of the utmost importance to the government and military leadership. The Bundeswehr and its soldiers could only be integrated into society and function successfully if it enjoyed popular trust and support. The question of the soldier lifestyle led military experts and politicians on the Bundestag Committee of Defense to discuss various ways in which recruits' behavior could be channeled. One option favored by committee members was restricting soldiers' free time. By 1954, they were having discussions on limiting soldiers' nightly leisure time, which they proposed to enforce by setting a curfew (*Zapfenstreich*) for return to the barracks.[67] CDU politician Georg Kliesing, for example, criticized the fact that after entering the military, young recruits were often told that they were "whole men" and, as a consequence, granted "generous nightly free time."[68] According to Kliesing, this argument and the freedom granted to young conscripts could be good neither for their health nor their morale. Not all members of the committee shared Kliesing's view; others feared that the restricting soldiers' free time would represent an exaggerated military paternalism and violate the soldiers' rights as free citizens.[69] The question of restricting nightly free time to protect recruits' morale was, however, revisited again in the late 1950s.[70]

Some parliamentarians and military representatives looked to the recruits' direct superiors to influence their behavior. Even though the image of the "citizen in uniform" was intended to replace the much older concept of the military commander acting like a "father figure" with the notion that recruits and superiors were "partners," the image of older officers displaying irreproachable manners and behavior in order to influence younger soldiers was still influential in the 1950s.[71] Franz-Joseph Strauß, who was appointed Minister of Defense in 1956, agreed, for instance, that the behavior of superior officers toward women needed to be especially exemplary.[72]

In addition to public statements, the Ministry of Defense released a number of publications that focused on the education, in particular the moral education, of soldiers. In 1959, for instance, chief of staff General Adolf Heusinger[73] released guidelines devised for commanders and official use only. These pieces of advice included a small but explicit section regarding the soldiers' virtuous and proper behavior.[74] Tackling the issue of alcohol, the document noted that some soldiers mistakenly thought that excessive consumption was a manly act. While accepting occasional drinking in informal settings, the guidelines stated that excessive drinking was anything but an acceptable practice for a man.[75] Arguing, in addition, that a process of "sexualization" had begun to take place in the army, Heusinger criticized the use of what he saw as overly aggressive language and "dirty jokes." He found such behavior unacceptable, an indication of soldiers' verbal "immaturity and squalidness" (*Unreife und Unsauberkeit*).[76] In addressing these problems candidly, the guidelines show how seriously the military took the issue of soldiers' moral behavior.

Conclusion

Once the issue of whether and how the Federal Republic should rearm was discussed on the international and national stages, the West German press, parliamentarians, concerned citizens, and welfare workers began debating how life in the barracks would influence the manners and behavior of young recruits. Since military service was defined as a man's duty and the Bundeswehr

was designed as a homosocial men's society, these debates entailed the negotiation and redefinition of competing notions of masculinity. While many
Germans still believed that military service would foster socially acceptable
male behavior, others saw it as a breeding ground for socially unacceptable,
if not illegal, activity. They feared that recruits would frequent prostitutes,
engage in homosexual conduct, or behave inappropriately toward "proper"
women and girls. Their concerns were, on the one hand, influenced by memories of the Wehrmacht's often brutal conduct toward civilians during World
War II, while on the other, they reflected the belief that military life would
influence and foster young men's natural sex drive in a negative way. Leading
figures in the Bundeswehr and the Ministry of Defense responded to these
concerns, because they were eager to fashion a military that was distinct from
the Wehrmacht and that could be integrated into the social structures of the
newly founded Federal Republic. They viewed the perceived improper and
illicit male behavior of recruits as a threat to the success of the armed forces
and to society's acceptance of the Bundeswehr, which they considered indispensable. The debates surrounding the social behavior and moral standards of
Bundeswehr soldiers can be interpreted as part of the overall attempt to fashion military forces that could be integrated into the new West German society.

Notes

1. See Robert G. Moeller, "'The Last Soldiers of the Great War' and Tales of Family
Reunions in the Federal Republic of Germany," *Signs* 24 (1998): 129–45, 129; and
Frank Biess, *Homecomings: Returning POWs and the Legacies of Defeat in Postwar Germany*
(Princeton, NJ: Princeton University Press, 2006), 43.
2. On the process of denazification and demilitarization in the American zone, see,
for example, Kathleen J. Nawyn, "'Striking at the Roots of German Militarism': Efforts to
Demilitarize German Society and Culture in American-Occupied Wurttemberg-Baden,
1945–1949" (PhD diss., University of North Carolina, Chapel Hill, 2008).
3. For this argument, see Konrad H. Jarausch, *After Hitler: Recivilizing Germans, 1945–
1995* (Oxford: Oxford University Press, 2006), 43–5.
4. Quoted in Dieter Gebhardt, "Militär und Krieg im Geschichtsunterricht nach 1945:
Eine Skizze zur Historischen Bildungsforschung," *Geschichte in Wissenschaft und Unterricht*
2 (1990): 81–100.
5. Robert G. Moeller, *War Stories: The Search for a Usable Past in the Federal
Republic of Germany* (Berkeley: University of California Press, 2001), 121; and Biess,
Homecomings, 120–125. See also Jörg Echternkamp, "Wut auf die Wehrmacht? Vom
Bild der deutschen Soldaten in der unmittelbaren Nachkriegszeit," in *Die Wehrmacht:*

Mythos und Realität, ed. Rolf-Dieter Müller and Hand-Erich Volkmann (Munich: Oldenbourg, 1999), 1058–80.

6. Moeller, "Last Soldiers," 145; and Richard Bessel, "Was bleibt vom Krieg? Deutsche Nachkriegsgeschichte(n) aus geschlechtlicher Perspektive—Eine Einführung," *Militärgeschichtliche Zeitung* 60 (2001): 297–305.

7. Norbert Wiggershaus, "Die Entscheidung für einen westdeutschen Verteidigungsbeitrag 1950," in *Anfänge westdeutscher Sicherheitspolitik*, ed. Militärgeschichtliches Forschungsinstitut, vol. 1: *Von der Kapitulation bis zum Plevenplan* (Munich: Oldenbourg, 1982), 327–402. See also Gerhard Wettig, *Entmilitarisierung und Wiederbewaffnung in Deutschland, 1943–1955: Internationale Auseinandersetzungen um die Rolle der Deutschen in Europa* (Munich: Oldenbourg, 1967).

8. For a recent discussion of the movement, see Michael Werner, *Die "Ohne mich"-Bewegung: Die bundesdeutsche Friedensbewegung im deutsch-deutschen Kalten Krieg 1949–1955* (Münster: Monsenstein und Vannerdat, 2006).

9. Michael Geyer, "'Cold War Angst': The Case of West-German Opposition to Rearmament and Nuclear Weapons," in *Miracle Years: A Cultural History of West Germany, 1949–1968*, ed. Hannah Schissler (Princeton, NJ: Princeton University Press, 2001), 376–408; Klaus-Jürgen Bremm, "Wehrhaft wider Willen? Die Debatte um die Bewaffnung Westdeutschlands in den fünfziger Jahren," in *Entschieden für den Frieden: 50 Jahre Bundeswehr 1955–2005*, ed. Klaus-Jürgen Bremm (Freiburg: Rombach, 2005), 28397.

10. Kai Uwe Bormann, "Als 'Schule der Nation' überfordert: Konzeptionelle Überlegungen zur Erziehung der Soldaten in der Aufbauphase der Bundeswehr," in *Reform, Reorganisation, Transformation: Zum Wandel in deutschen Streitkräften von den preußischen Heeresreformen bis zur Transformation der Bundeswehr*, ed. Karl-Heinz Lutz et al. (Munich: Oldenbourg, 2010), 345–368. See also Ute Frevert, *Nation in Barracks: Modern Germany, Military Conscription and Civil Society* (Oxford and New York: Berg Publisher, 2004), 275; and Frevert, "Das Militär als Schule der Männlichkeiten," in *Männlichkeiten und Moderne: Geschlecht in den Wissenskulturen um 1900*, ed. Ulrike Brunotte (Bielefeld: Transcript-Verlag, 2008), 57–75.

11. Verhandlung des Deutschen Bundestags, 98. Sitzung, 8. November 1950, in *Verhandlungen des Deutschen Bundestages* (Bonn: Bonner Universitäts-Buchdruckerei), 3566. See also David Clay Large, *Germans to the Front: West German Rearmament in the Adenauer Era* (Chapel Hill, University of North Carolina Press, 1996), 156.

12. Verhandlung des Deutschen Bundestags, 98. Sitzung, 8. November 1950, *Verhandlungen des Deutschen Bundestages*, 3566. See also Uta Poiger, "Krise der Männlichkeit. Remasculinisation in beiden deutschen Nachkriegsgesellschaften," in *Nachkrieg in Deutschland*, ed. Klaus Naumann (Hamburg: Hamburger Edition HIS, 2001), 227–63.

13. Verhandlungen des Deutschen Bundestages, 191. Sitzung, 8. Februar 1952, 8178.

14. For a discussion of West German family policies, see Elizabeth Heinemann, *What Difference Does a Husband Make? Women and Marital Status in Nazi and Postwar Germany* (Berkeley: University of California Press, 1999), 137–75.

15. Large, *Germans to the Front*, 74–7.

16. Rundschreiben der Freie Demokratische Partei (10. Januar 1953), in Archiv des Liberalismus, Bundespartei, Fachausschuss Verteidigung 904: Protokolle.

17. Ibid. See also Thorsten Loch, *Das Gesicht der Bundeswehr: Kommunikationsstrategien in der Freiwilligenwerbung der Bundeswehr 1956 bis 1989* (Munich: Oldenbourg, 2008), 175.

18. For a discussion of SPD politics, see, for example, Frevert, *Nation in Barracks*, 262–67.

19. Large, *Germans to the Front*, 155.

20. Marc Cioc, "Reforging the Basic Law: Wehrhoheit, Wehrgewalt and the Question of German Rearmament, 1950–1956," in *Germany and America: Essays in Honor of Gerald R. Kleinfeld*, ed. Wolfang-Uwe Friedrich (New York: Berghahn Books, 2001), 59–75.

21. 6. Sitzung des Ausschusses für Rechtswesen und Verfassungsrecht, February 9, 1954, 64–5. For this debate, see also Swantje Kraake, *Frauen zur Bundeswehr—Analyse und Verlauf einer Diskussion* (Frankfurt/M.: P. Lang, 1992), 52.

22. 6. Sitzung des Ausschusses für Rechtswesen und Verfassungsrecht, Februrary 9, 1954, 64–65. See also Karen Hagemann, "Mobilizing Women for War: The History, Historiography, and Memory of German Women's War Service in the Two World Wars," *Journal for Military History* 75 (2011): 1055–93.

23. See 7. Sitzung des Ausschusses für Fragen der Europäischen Sicherheit, February 22, 1954, 24.

24. See Geyer, "Cold War Angst," 376–408; and "75 percent of West Germans refuse to become soldiers," opinion survey conducted by EMNID, Institut für Markforschung und Markbeobachtung Bielefeld, December 1949/January 1950, in Bundesarchiv Koblenz, Presse und Informationsamt der Bundesregierung B 145/1568. The findings of this survey correspond with the results of an opinion poll conducted in December 1949 by the United States Information Service Division of the High Commission for Occupied Germany (HICOG) Public Affairs Office. See Opinion Poll, "German Attitude Toward an Army and Military Training," in National Archives, College Park, Maryland (NARA), RG 306 – al 1005, fol. HICOG 9. For less radical results of the Allensbach surveys, see Geyer, "Cold War Angst," 379.

25. "75 percent of West Germans."

26. Geyer, "Cold War Angst," 387.

27. Frank Nägler, *Der gewollte Soldat und sein Wandel: personelle Rüstung und innere Führung in den Aufbaujahren der Bundeswehr 1956 bis 1964/65* (Munich: Oldenbourg Verlag, 2010).

28. "Die Stimmung im Bundesgebiet," October 1951, in Bundesarchiv Koblenz, B 145/4221.

29. Ibid.

30. Michael Geyer has termed this opposition "injured citizenship," which indicated a "rejection of a personal commitment toward the state." See Geyer, "Cold War Angst," 386.

31. Nick Thomas, *Protest Movements in 1960s West Germany: A Social History of Dissent and Democracy* (Oxford and New York: Berg Publisher, 2003), 31. See further, Hans-Erich Volkmann, "Die Innenpolitische Dimension Adenauerscher Sicherheitspolitik in der EVG-Phase," in *Anfänge westdeutscher Sicherheitspolitik 1945–1956*, ed. Militärgeschichtliches Forschungsamt, vol. 2: *Die EVG Phase* (Munich: Oldenbourg, 1990), 493–95.

32. Thomas, *Protest Movements*, 31.

33. See Irene Stoehr, "Phalanx der Frauen? Wiederaufrüstng und Weiblichkeit in Westdeutschland 1950–1970, in *Soziale Konstruktionen – Militär und Geschlechterverhältnisse* (Münster: Verlag Westfälisches Dampfboot, 1999), 187–204.

34. See Frevert, *Nation in Barracks*, 260. The perceived *Wehrunwille* continued to inform the military's debates far into the 1950s; see the protocols of the Sachverständigentagung

in Siegburg in 1953, Bundesarchiv-Militärarchiv (BA-MA) Freiburg, N 717 Nachlass Wolf Graf von Baudissin, diary, fol. 1.

35. Roland G. Foester, "Innenpolitische Aspekte der Sicherheit Westdeutschlands, 1947–1950," in *Anfänge westdeutscher Sicherheitspolitik 1945–1956*, vol. 3: *Die Nato Option* (Munich: Oldenbourg, 1993), 514–38.

36. "Wozu dient eine Bundeswehr?," *Der Spiegel*, July 18, 1956, 29–31. For a discussion of this survey, see also Frevert, *Nation in Barracks*, 274; Bormann, "Als 'Schule der Nation' überfordert," 345. See further Nägler, *Der gewollte Soldat und sein Wandel*, 341–47.

37. Annemarie Meister, "Musterkinder, Heldenjungen und Muttermädchen: Von der Kontinuität der Kindheitsbilder vor und nach 1945," in *Vom Trümmerkind zum Teenager*, ed. Doris Foitzik (Bremen: Edition Temme, 1992), 58–72. See also Nägler, *Der gewollte Soldat*, 341–43.

38. Uta Poiger, *Jazz, Rock, and Rebels: Cold War Politics and American Culture in a Divided Germany* (Berkeley: University of California Press, 2000), 80–1, 96–8.

39. Ibid., 73–4.

40. Dieter Krüger and Kerstin Wiese, "Zwischen Militärreform und Wehrpropaganda. Wolf Graf von Baudissin im Amt Blank," in *Wolf Graf von Baudissin 1907 bis 1993*, ed. Rudolf Schlaffer and Wolfgang Schmidt (Munich: Oldenbourg, 2007), 99–110.

41. This idea stood in sharp contrast to the command of the German Reichswehr, which had considered itself apolitical and above party lines.

42. Robert G. Moeller, "Heimkehr ins Vaterland: Die Remaskulinisierung Westdeutschlands in den fünfziger Jahren," *Militärgeschichtliche Zeitung* 60 (2001): 403–36. See also Kai Uwe Bormann, "Erziehung des Soldaten: Herzstück der Inneren Führung," in *Wolf Graf von Baudissin 1907 bis 1993*, 111–26.

43. Moeller, "Heimkehr ins Vaterland." For this argument, see also "Um die Kontrolle der Bundeswehr," *Süddeutsche Zeitung*, January 26, 1956, 3. "Liebe Leser,"*Deutsche Volkszeitung*, August 25, 1956, 2.

44. Protokoll der Sachverständigentagung in Siegburg (September 25/26, 1953), in BA-MA, Nachlass 717 Baudissin, fol. 1. See also Nägler, *Der gewollte Soldat und sein Wandel*, 66.

45. See Baudissin's remarks on a meeting with the Catholic Women's League on October 3, 1956, in BA-MA, Nachlass Baudissin 717, fol. 3. For a critical discussion of Baudissin's concepts and the disputes that accompanied its inception, see also Klaus Naumann, "The Battle over 'Innere Führung'," in *Rearming Germany*, ed. James S. Corum (Leiden: Brill, 2011), 205–20.

46. "Gelobt sei, was hart macht!' Das 'innere Gefüge' der Bundeswehr," *Deutsche Volkszeitung* September 1, 1956, 4. See also Frevert, *Nation in Barracks*, 265.

47. Baudissin Diary entry in BA-MA N 717, fol. 2 diary

48. For this argument, see also Frevert, *Nation in Barracks*, 274.

49. Der Bund der Deutschen Katholischen Jugend, "Aktionsplan für die Vorbereitung und Betreuung junger Katholiken in den deutschen Verteidigungsstreitkräften," in BA-MA BW II / 1327. See also Institut für Staatslehre und Politik e.V. Mainz, ed., *Der Deutsche Soldat in der Armee von morgen: Wehrverfassung, Wehrsystem, Inneres Gefüge* (Munich: Isar Verlag, 1954), 129–44. For a discussion of the Deutsche Katholische Jugend, see Volkmann, "Die Innenpolitsche Dimension," 574–75

50. Ibid.

51. Dagmar Herzog, "Desperately Seeking Normality: Sex and Marriage in the Wake of War," in *Life after Death: Approaches to a Cultural and Social History of Europe during the 1940s and 1950s*, ed. Richard Bessel and Richard Schumann (New York: Cambridge University Press, 2003), 161–92, 176.

52. The official name Bundeswehr was only introduced in the spring of 1956. Previously, contemporaries used the term Wehrmacht or Streitkräfte (armed forces) to refer to the new West German military. See Sitzung der Arbeitsgemeinschaft Jugendpflege und Jugendfürsorge – Aktion Jugendschutz, April 18 and 19, 1955, in DGB-Archiv, Archiv der Sozialen Demokratie (AdsD), DGB-Bundesvorstand, Abteilung Jugend, 5/DGAU000447.

53. Ibid.

54. Ibid.

55. Ibid.

56. For the contested establishment of garrison towns, see Wolfgang Schmidt, *Integration und Wandel: Die Infrastruktur der Streitkräfte als Faktor sozioökonomischer Modernisierung in der Bundesrepublik 1955 bis 1975* (Munich: Oldenbourg, 2006), 205, 364–65.

57. "Garnisionspläne: Umfrage am Biertisch," *Der Spiegel*, November 26, 1956, 22.

58. Ibid.

59. Ibid. See also "Invasion der leichten Mädchen: 100.000 Prostituierte überschwemmen Westdeutschland," *Deutsche Volkszeitung*, August 1, 1959, 16.

60. See, for example, the official diary entry about the preparation for a meeting between defense minister Theodor Blank and a women's group in BA-MA, N 717 Nachlass Baudissin, Tagebuch, fol. 3.

61. Sitzung der Arbeitsgemeinschaft Jugendpflege und Jugendfürsorge—Aktion Jugendschutz.

62. Ibid. For the military regulations, see H.W. Napp, ed., *Wehrpflichtgesetz: Textausgabe mit Erläuterungen* (Lübeck and Hamburg: Matthiesen, 1956), 9 and 13.

63. "Aufbau der Bundeswehr wird zu einer Tragikkomödie," *NRZ*, September 13, 1956. See further, Annual Report 1958 by military bishop Mundt, in Evangelisches Zentralarchiv in Berlin (EBZ), Bestand 2 Kirchenamt, fol 41 26. These concerns increased especially among military experts due to the Adenauer government's eager plans to quickly establish the Bundeswehr as a 500,000-man-strong army. See Deutscher Bundestag, 3. Wahlperiode, *Bericht des Wehrbeauftragten des Deutschen Bundestages für das Berichtsjahr 1959* (Drucksache 1796), April 8, 1960.

64. Writing by a legal adviser to a commander on March 17, 1958, in BA-MA, BW 1, fol. 316384. See also the internal correspondence about the possible legal and disciplinary dealing with prostitution, in BA-MA, BW II/20 222.

65. Ibid.

66. Ibid.

67. Protokoll der 22. Sitzung des Ausschusses für Fragen der Europäischen Sicherheit, November 30, 1954.

68. Ibid.

69. Ibid.

70. 61. Sitzung: Ausschusses für Verteidigung, Oktober 14, 1959.

71. See, for example, letter by B. Bellersen (June 8, 1956), Nachlass Baudissin 717/19.

72. "Bundesverteidigungsminister Franz-Joseph Strauss im Rahmen des 3. Teils der Sendereihe 'Richt' Euch – Wonach?'," WDR January 1, 1958, 7:20pm, in: Archiv der Sozialen Demokratie, SPD Bundestagsfraktion Parlamentarische Geschäftführung Adolf Arndt, 2/BTFA0000447.

73. Born in 1897, Heusinger moved in the highest ranks of German Army High Command during World War II, and in 1944 he briefly assumed the position of chief of the army general staff.

74. Richtlinien für die Erziehung 1959/60, in BA-MA BW 1, fol. 66477.

75. Ibid.

76. Ibid. See also letter by G. O., 7. July 1955, in BA-MA, BW 2, fol. 1246.

Chapter 7
Service by Other Means: Changing Perceptions of Military Service and Masculinity in the United States, 1940–1973

Amy Rutenberg

In 1973, the US military completed its move from a force based on conscription to an All-Volunteer Force (AVF). At the time, one Democratic senator explained that the shift was "a clear result of the Vietnam War, which, because of its unpopularity . . . caused the President and Congress to yield to the tremendous pressure to end the draft at almost any price."[1] Scholars have largely agreed. They point to the poor morale, perception of national dishonor, and sense of crisis caused by the Vietnam War as reasons for Americans' shift in attitude toward military service.[2] Antiwar organizations with nationwide followings, such as Students for a Democratic Society (SDS), along with hundreds of smaller, local antiwar groups and organizations that supported conscientious objectors (COs), like the Central Committee for Conscientious Objectors (CCCO), helped foment what historian John Whiteclay Chambers II termed "a massive campaign of public disobedience" against the war in general and specifically against military service.[3] The US military had no choice but to end conscription.

Although it is true that the Vietnam War precipitated the move to the AVF, I argue that dissent against the war also focused men's preexisting ambivalence toward military service, an ambivalence that grew as a result of the political and social circumstances of the long postwar. Three major factors contributed the growth of this ambivalence. First, an evolving popular

165

culture deemphasized the importance of military service for masculine identity. Second, military manpower policy expanded the number of mechanisms through which men could evade military service in the late 1960s and early 1970s. The patterns of draft avoidance used by many men during the war—early marriage and fatherhood, particular occupational choices, and expanded college enrollment—were the result of manpower policies that defined a wide range of civilian roles as the equivalent of military service. Third, various pacifist, New Left, and civil rights organizations began to equate masculinity with the avoidance of military service. Together, these factors eroded the connection between military service and masculine citizenship in the United States.[4]

The Popular Image of Military Masculinity

Ambivalence toward military service was increasingly reflected in cultural productions during the 1950s and early 1960s, in stark contrast to the heroic representations of soldiers that were common during the 1940s. During World War II, producers of popular culture created what historian Christian G. Appy has termed "sentimental militarism"—imagery that constructed the enlisted man as a peace-loving citizen reluctantly fighting to protect his loved ones and proving his patriotism and manhood in the process.[5] Reporters glorified the everyday bravery of the average GI, whom they portrayed as anything but average. It was a world in which, according to *New Yorker* staff writer and infantry soldier E. J. Kahn Jr., "the jungle was tough and the Japs were tougher, but the Yanks were the toughest of all."[6] Although life in the mosquito-infested jungles of the South Pacific or the freezing mud of Europe was miserable, the perseverance of the American soldier made him special.

Despite war propaganda designed to remind the public that men in essential war industries could also fulfill the masculine role of protector, songs like "4-F Charlie" (1943), which depicted a man deferred for physical reasons as "a complete physical wreck" who could "never be a father," implied that a man who did not enter the armed forces could never be useful or worthy of love. Women would not "praise [the] martial daring" of a man who never wore a uniform.[7] The movie *Since You Went Away*, David O. Selznick's 1944 homage to "that unconquerable fortress, the American Home," depicted nonmilitary men of fighting age as hoarders and naysayers. The heroines, a household of women left behind, loved their men because they were willing to fight, despite the financial and emotional strain their absence caused their families.[8] Positive images of patriotic, manly soldiers willing to sacrifice themselves in the name of their country and loved ones appeared in movies like *Eagle Squadron* (1942), *So Proudly We Hail!* (1943), *Bataan!* (1943), and *The Purple Heart* (1944).

The dominant form of "sentimental militarism" shifted, however, in the years of the early Cold War. Hollywood adapted to the ambiguities of the Cold War, a conflict without an enemy that the United States could directly engage, by creating "strained and defensive" images of the military.[9] For every holdover like *The Sands of Iwo Jima* (1949), a heroic tale of the American assault on the Japanese island stronghold starring John Wayne, Hollywood produced a film like *Pork Chop Hill* (1959). This movie, which focused on American GIs in Korea who have been ordered to retake a barren hill overrun by Chinese troops, criticized military bureaucracy and the futility of combat against an undefined enemy. War, according to *Pork Chop Hill*, was not glorious, and battle did not pave the way toward manhood.

Historian Andrew J. Huebner outlines a concurrent shift in what he terms the "warrior image" during the 1950s and early 1960s. War stories published in this period like Norman Mailer's *The Naked and the Dead* (1948), James Michener's *The Bridges of Toko-Ri* (1953), Joseph Heller's *Catch-22* (1961), and James Jones's *The Thin Red Line* (1962), as well as press coverage of the Korean War, showcased the fear, pain, and discouragement of American soldiers and helped widen the "definition of the masculine, American fighter."[10] On the whole, the popular culture of this period presented a far different image from the heroes of a decade before, attributing more vulnerability and uncertainty to American soldiers.

Such equivocal war stories were complemented by the images of domestic masculinity that became common during the same decades. A growing economy combined with the GI Bill, which offered low-interest home and business loans, money for education, and additional severance pay to demobilized veterans, helped propel Americans into middle-class home ownership. Tax codes, credit laws, and mortgage-lending practices favored families that met the suburban ideal of the wage-earning father and stay-at-home mother. Men engaged with the mass market on an ever-greater scale, as consumer durables like cars, houses, and appliances took on new importance.[11] Popular advice books and magazines encouraged fathers to play a greater role in rearing their children.[12] Family television shows like *The Donna Reed Show*, *Leave It to Beaver*, and *Father Knows Best*, along with novels like Sloan Wilson's *The Man in the Gray Flannel Suit* (1955), which chronicled a World War II veteran's difficulties in adjusting to suburban living and corporate culture, conveyed the importance of home and family to suburban men.[13] Regardless of race or class differences and the diverse realities of men's lives, popular imagery in the 1950s validated a masculinity that was firmly rooted in domesticity. Well before the Vietnam War, these images deemphasized the military as a route to honorable masculine citizenship.

Military Manpower Policies

Ironically, the second factor contributing to the thinning of the relationship between military service and manly citizenship was postwar military manpower policy itself. In a departure from its traditional mistrust of conscription and a large peacetime force, Congress maintained a continuous draft from 1948 until 1973 to meet the military's manpower needs. Along with the Department of Defense, it justified the decision to continue the draft during peacetime differently than during previous periods of conscription. In addition to procuring military manpower, the Cold War draft was designed to support a prolonged ideological, technological, and economic struggle against communism. There was no sense that this draft was only "for the duration," because there was no immediate military emergency through many of these years. Instead, during the 1950s and 1960s, the Selective Service System explicitly treated deferments as a form of social engineering. In World War I and World War II, deferments had been designed to maintain a functional war economy, but during the Cold War they were used as incentives to encourage men to matriculate, enter occupations defined as being in the national interest, marry, and have children. This policy of "manpower channeling" specifically defined such pursuits as service to the state, on a par with military service. At the same time, however, the policy resulted in a shrinking percentage of eligible men serving in the military. As more men gained legal deferments, it became easier to construe service as something that "other people" did. Thus, military service ceased being understood as a universal male citizenship obligation.

During World War II, the sheer number of men who served ensured a link between young American manhood and military service. Between the onset of the draft in 1940 and V-J Day in 1945, ten million men were inducted into the armed forces and an additional five million volunteered to bear arms for their country.[14] Social pressure—and the threat of imprisonment if they failed to answer the call of the Selective Service—ensured that even those with no personal inclination to fight joined the military when a draft notice arrived. Only 11,879 of more than 34 million draft-eligible men were convicted of violating the Selective Service Act between 1941 and 1947.[15] When men did fail to register, individuals or organizations like the American Legion often reported them to their local draft boards.[16] Moreover, the government approved no more than 138,000 men (and probably fewer) for CO status;[17] pressure to serve and legal barriers to conscientious objection were too high.

Toward the end of the war, the War Department, with support from President Franklin Roosevelt and later Harry Truman, began working on a Universal Military Training (UMT) bill in order to capitalize on Americans' widespread support for military service. The measure would have required all able-bodied American men between the ages of eighteen and twenty to undergo compulsory military training for a mandated period of time and brought them into a large, civilian reserve. Military planners claimed that training the entire male population would reduce the amount of time needed for mobilization should another war occur and would forestall the need for a substantial, expensive "force-in-being." Civilian advocates, meanwhile, contended that adopting UMT would act as a bargaining chip at peace negotiations, deter enemies from attacking American interests by holding out the threat of a quick US counterstrike, and strengthen the United Nations through a show of American commitment.[18]

Military planners never worked through the strategic details of how millions of American men with limited training would or could be deployed, but in the wake of World War II, the majority of Americans seemed to accept UMT as a military necessity.[19] Public opinion polls conducted between December 1945 and January 1956 showed that support for the idea ranged from 65 to 83 percent.[20] But such support was "soft"; most Americans may have approved of UMT in theory but they were unlikely to agitate for its passage into law, giving priority to other economic, political, and social concerns.[21]

Opposition to UMT, by contrast, was strong and well organized. A wide variety of interest groups, including labor, religious, educational, and pacifist organizations, from the American Federation of Labor to the National Educational Association to the American Civil Liberties Union, launched a coordinated campaign against UMT almost as soon as it was proposed. The War Department (and later the Department of Defense) was forced to respond to these critiques in its pro-UMT publicity, but the result was a campaign that addressed individual concerns without advancing a coherent justification for universal military training or a strong image of American citizenship based on military service.

Publicity supporting UMT came to focus on what training could offer young men as opposed to what young men owed to their country. Although literature discussed the democratizing effects of common training, the civic republican tradition of the citizen-soldier that had been so important in World War II propaganda virtually vanished. Proponents of UMT countered the opposition by asserting that UMT benefited the individual, not that manly citizenship required military service. For example, in his charge to the President's Advisory Commission on Universal Training, established in late 1946, President Truman admitted that he did not consider UMT to be a "military" program. "I want it to be a universal training program," he stated, "giving our young people a background in the disciplinary approach of getting along with one another, informing them of their physical makeup, and what it means to take care of this Temple which God gave us."[22] In 1947, the War Department produced a forty-two-page pamphlet that was clearly designed to calm any public fear about the possible evils of military service. Describing an experimental UMT unit that had been established at Ft. Knox, Kentucky, it portrayed the training facility more like a summer camp than an Army post. Captions under pictures of a park-like lawn framed by neat bungalows described "landscaped grounds" with "clean, airy barrack-dormitories" and "dayrooms with comfortable lounge chairs, record players, books and writing desks," while other photos showed classes full of engaged students being taught by Reserve Officers' Training Corps officers promising "open discussions" where "each man is made to feel that his ideas are important and original and individual thinking is encouraged." It is not until page 27 that the pamphlet mentions any military duty or portrays any form of military training, and even then it devotes relatively few pages to weapons, defense, or combat.[23]

Despite favorable public opinion, support from three sitting presidents, and the positive recommendations of several committees and commissions developed to examine the idea, Congress never passed a UMT bill. Instead, in 1951, the Department of Defense, Congress, and President Truman passed a new conscription law that recommitted the nation to a system of *selective* service. This law would ensure that military service would not be a universal obligation of American men for the foreseeable future.

Moreover, a significant portion of the American public believed that home was where men belonged, both as breadwinners and as defenders.[24] For example, in its programs to ensure preparedness against nuclear war, the Federal Civil Defense Administration emphasized family readiness over federal welfare programs. A privately funded, family-based model of defense became the center of President Eisenhower's National Shelter Policy in 1958. Emergency plans depended on the active leadership of a hands-on father who could protect his family in a nuclear attack. Civil defense publicity defined families as paramilitary units headed by fathers and called for timed evacuation drills and regular evaluation of familial emergency procedures.[25] A man's ability to protect his family as a civilian in his own backyard rather than as a soldier on a distant battlefield became a key element of national security. Accordingly, the Selective Service widened its deferment system throughout the 1950s in order to emphasize its changing priorities, offering deferments to both fathers and married men without children. The unintended consequence was to deemphasize military service for average male citizens and to domesticate defense.

Defense also became "civilianized" as government projections for the next war indicated that it would hinge on technology, not infantry. Students in the sciences and engineering were identified as important national security assets, not so much for what they could accomplish at the moment but for their future potential. After all, noted a 1950 report of the Selective Service's Scientific Advisory Committee, the relationship between basic knowledge and practical advancements in national defense was mercurial. Prior to World War II, nuclear physicists could have been "dismissed as a scientific luxury—a group of theoreticians not essential to the national defense,"[26] but by 1950, they had become indispensable. Accordingly, the Selective Service instituted a deferment program for all students during the Korean War. By the end of the 1952–53 school year, 20 percent of draft-eligible men had received student deferments.[27]

These numbers were significant enough to catch scholars' attention. In May 1952, three Cornell University sociologists initiated a study of male college students' attitudes toward military service, the draft, and deferments. Close to 3,000 students from eleven college campuses across the nation responded to their questionnaire, and of these, 83 percent reported negative opinions toward military service. College men did not want to be drafted, especially to fight in Korea—a conflict that only 46 percent of respondents supported. Moreover, they embraced their newly won deferments. Only one in ten of the students surveyed believed that the law granted special privileges to those eligible for deferments, while a full 96 percent claimed that they rarely or never felt guilty about not being in uniform, even with their country at war.[28]

Nevertheless, most men who were drafted entered the military. Even though the Korean War was not popular, an estimated 75 percent of the draft-age cohort during the war years served in the military; of the 25 percent who did not, two thirds were physically disqualified, while only one third sought deferments.[29] Moreover, between 1948 and 1950, only 204 cases of draft evasion appeared among approximately 10.8 million registrants. Once the Korean War began and draft calls increased, more cases of draft evasion were referred to the Justice Department—about 1,000 per month—but the majority of these were brought simply because men forgot to report address changes.[30] Finally, the numbers of men applying for CO status actually *declined* over the course of the war, from 12,000 in 1950 to 5,000 in 1952.[31]

After the Korean War, budgetary constraints and long-range strategic planning that relied heavily on air power led to a significant decrease in the demand for military personnel. As a result, the Army sought far fewer new recruits, inducting 471,806 men in 1953, but only 86,602 in 1960.[32] At the same time, the pool of available manpower was growing; approximately 200,000 more men turned eighteen in 1960 than in 1953.[33] As draft calls shrank, the Selective Service offered deferments to more draft-eligible men. By the end of the 1950s, most male college students were so certain that they would not be called that they did not bother to request an official student deferment. Also, in keeping with their higher physical and mental induction standards, the armed forces rejected more than half of the men to whom they sent draft notices.[34]

By the mid-1950s, the Selective Service was explicitly encouraging men to enter the vital fields of science and engineering and implicitly encouraging them to marry and become fathers through targeted draft exemptions, a tool it called "manpower channeling" or "pressurized guidance."[35] Occupational deferments alone increased almost 650 percent between 1955 and 1963, a rate of growth that far outpaced that of the cohort of draft-age men.[36] The agency began to define men who held occupational and dependency deferments *as* fulfilling their citizenship obligations. According to the Selective Service System's own publications, military service was not strictly necessary for American men so long as they performed some measure of national service that was sanctioned through the granting of a deferment. A memo included in a 1965 orientation kit for new members of local Selective Service boards acknowledged that "the threat of loss of deferment" would impel the registrant "to pursue his skill rather than embark on some less important enterprise," and encourage him "to apply his skill in an essential activity in the national interest."[37] Men who received such deferments had their draft eligibility extended from age 26 to 35, ensuring that trained men remained in crucial fields until an age when familial responsibilities would most likely keep them there. In other words, the Selective Service, supported by public opinion, actively discouraged military service among particular groups of men who could construct a form of masculinity that allowed them to fulfill their citizenship obligations precisely because they did *not* don a uniform.[38]

By 1965, the inequities that would characterize the Selective Service system during the Vietnam War had already become apparent. Economically privileged men with access to higher education learned how to "pyramid" deferments as they attended college, married, had children, and entered protected occupational fields. The poorest and least advantaged Americans failed induction exams at a rate higher than their representation in the population, thanks to their relative lack of health care and educational opportunities. Therefore, the burden of military service fell disproportionately on poor and working-class men, especially African Americans. Between 1967 and 1969, Congress and the Department of Defense tried to modify Selective Service regulations to spread the burden more evenly, but they refused to eliminate student deferments. Ultimately, federal policies had created a situation that divorced the rights of citizenship from the responsibilities of military service for a significant proportion of the American male population.

Peace Activism against Military Service and War

Growth in the size, scope, and visibility of activist organizations throughout the 1950s and 1960s was the third factor that helped separate military service from male citizenship obligations. Activists from varying backgrounds pioneered the tactics of direct action that would become so important to draft resisters during the Vietnam era; they made protest visible and, to some, desirable, and highlighted the dangers of conformity and consensus in American society. Ultimately, it was activism that paved the way for wider acceptance of COs, highlighted the inequities of the Selective Service system, and helped offer alternatives to men who did not wish to fight. Though most men who avoided military service were not activists and did not base their objections to serving on deeply held convictions, all draft avoiders benefited from the principled stand of pacifist, civil rights, and antimilitary activists.

Certification as a CO was difficult. Regulations in place during and after World War II stipulated that the status depended upon opposition to all wars

173

based on religious principle, specifically belief in a "supreme being."[39] As many as 93 percent of those accepted for CO status in wartime were members of historic peace churches, including Mennonites, Quakers, and Brethren. Most of the 6,000 men imprisoned for noncooperation with the draft fell outside of these denominations and thus could not meet the Selective Service's stringent guidelines.[40] The majority of certified COs served as noncombatants within the military structure, most often as medics.[41] A second group of approximately 12,000 men volunteered to work in Civilian Public Service (CPS) camps doing alternative service, frequently in the form of national preservation, forestry, and so on.[42]

Certification notwithstanding, the wartime public tended to look unfavorably on men who chose to avoid military service. COs were often feminized in the popular media, described as sissies, weaklings, cowards, and traitors. As historian Timothy Stewart-Winter argues, however, these men were aware that their choices regarding military service compromised their masculinity, especially since those who went to CPS camps or prison received neither pay for their service nor veterans' benefits upon discharge—deprivations that prevented them from fulfilling their masculine responsibilities as citizen-soldiers or as breadwinners. As a result, many COs at the time consciously sought the most dangerous jobs available or adopted the language of struggle in describing their experiences as ways of reclaiming their masculinity. They also pioneered direct, nonviolent action as a strategy against the injustices that they faced in prison and elsewhere. Stewart-Winter points out that World War II resisters like Bayard Rustin and Dave Dellinger, who later became leaders of the civil rights and antiwar movements of the 1950s and 1960s, learned "non-violent belligerence" as "an effort to invent forms of peace activism suited to an age in which soldiering was the normative task of men."[43] Through its actions with groups like the Catholic Worker Movement, the Council for Non-Violent Action (CNVA), and the Congress of Racial Equality, this cohort became a major influence on the postwar civil rights and antinuclear movements.[44]

The 1950s was, therefore, a period of ferment in the pacifist movement. Organizations like the CNVA, the National Committee for a SANE Nuclear Policy, the Catholic Worker Movement, and Women Strike for Peace directly challenged the federal government's nuclear and civil defense policies. Members organized public protests, testified before Congress, and staged acts of civil disobedience to publicize their cause. At the same time, the CCCO, the National Interreligious Service Board for Conscientious Objectors (NISBCO), and the Metropolitan Board for Conscientious Objectors (MBCO), all of which were formed during or immediately after World War II, worked to ensure the rights of COs. They counseled individual men seeking CO status, helped men appeal unfavorable decisions, and petitioned presidents Truman, Eisenhower, and Kennedy to grant blanket amnesty to all violators of what they saw as unfair Selective Service laws.[45]

Activists particularly objected to the strict religious guidelines laid down by the Selective Service laws. They believed that such a narrow interpretation of belief denied men their constitutional right to freedom of religion. Many men with sincere religious or philosophical objections to war were hurt by the "supreme being" clause. One young man told an MBCO attorney that he was withdrawing his application for CO status because "I had based my desire to become a conscientious objector on a philosophical rather than a religious basis. I have come to feel that for me to be a conscientious objector in any sort of effective way would involve too great a compromise of my views on the situation."[46] Such dilemmas prompted MBCO officials to initiate a legal strategy to overturn the "supreme being" clause of the Selective Service Act of 1948 and its successor, the Universal Military Training and Service Act of 1951.[47] According to MBCO executive secretary Frieda Langer Lazarus, "The whole question as to what constitutes 'religion' must be clarified in a test case, as the present wording in the S.S. Act of 1948 would appear to be definitely unconstitutional."[48] Over time, test cases did wend their way through the court system. In 1965, the Supreme Court nullified the sections of the draft law outlining qualifications for conscientious objector status, finding in *United States* v. *Seeger* that a CO applicant did not have to show belief in a god or supreme being in order to qualify, as long as he could demonstrate a "sincere and meaningful belief" that occupied a place "parallel to that filled by the God of those admittedly qualified for the exemption."[49] Further, in *Welsh* v. *United States* (1970), the Court found that even an atheist could qualify as a conscientious objector, provided he could pass a test of moral and ethical beliefs.

Though the Supreme Court sent down the *Seeger* decision in the same month that President Johnson ordered ground troops to Vietnam, the case was not a direct outgrowth of the war in Southeast Asia. Rather, it culminated almost twenty years of campaigning against the Selective Service on the part of pacifists, and its effects were far-reaching. It forced the Selective Service to shift to a secular understanding of conscientious objection, making it easier for prospective COs to obtain positive rulings just as the Vietnam War intensified and draft calls skyrocketed. Applications for CO status jumped from approximately 18,000 in 1964 to more than 40,000 in 1970.[50] Between 1965 and 1970, more than 170,000 registrants qualified for CO status, exceeding the World War II total. In 1972, more men were classified as COs than were inducted into the military.[51] Many men genuinely objected to all wars on moral grounds, but the Supreme Court's rulings allowed some the latitude to qualify as COs even if their objections were less principled.

In the late 1950s and early 1960s, a new cohort of college students and young activists began to protest war and militarism. These activists objected to war as an immoral phenomenon and criticized the social and physical coercion inherent in the draft. In 1960, for example, a member of the Oberlin College chapter of the Student Peace Union penned a leaflet entitled "An Alternative to the Draft—A Statement to Young Men" which stated, "If conscience and a sense of reality . . . have become lost . . . we must stand alone in resisting the coercion, physical and moral, of the draft . . . for wars will cease only when men refuse to fight."[52] Using such tenets as a base, these men constructed their ideal of masculinity around the notion that strength of character was measured by an individual's desire and ability to stand up for his beliefs and principles, regardless of opposition or consequences. Though a small group initially, these men defined masculine citizenship as the responsibility to challenge the nation to live up to its ideals internally instead of physically combating outside foes.

As draft resistance became a core tenet of more activist organizations, including those of the New Left such as SDS, civil rights activists also transformed their stance on military service for African Americans. From the Revolutionary War onward, black Americans had commonly viewed equal service in the armed forces as a path toward full and equal citizenship in the civilian world. Accordingly, generations of civil rights leaders, from Frederick Douglass to W. E. B. DuBois to A. Philip Randolph, advocated military service for African Americans during times of national crisis, even as they fought against segregation and discrimination. During World War II, they drew attention to their two-track agenda through the "Double-V" campaign, and black veterans become prominent activists in the postwar struggle for racial justice.[53] But the hope of the early civil rights movement faded as it became clear that President Johnson's Great Society programs would have to take a back seat to funding the Vietnam War. Activists began to turn their anger on the system that was perpetrating military action in Southeast Asia.

One by one, civil rights organizations publicized their support for young black men who chose to avoid military service. In July 1965, after John D. Shaw from McComb, Mississippi, was killed in combat in Vietnam, activists

Joe Martin and Clint Hopson printed a leaflet encouraging black male citizens of Shaw's native town to reject the hypocrisy of a government that called for democracy in Vietnam but denied civil rights to its own citizens. "No Mississippi Negroes should be fighting in Vietnam for the White Man's freedom, until all the Negro People are free in Mississippi," they wrote. "Negro boys should not honor the draft here in Mississippi."[54] Martin and Hopson's leaflet was disseminated widely through movement publications. Similarly, after decorated Navy veteran Samuel Young was murdered in Tuskegee, Alabama, in January 1966 for using a whites-only restroom, members of the Student Nonviolent Coordinating Committee issued a position paper asking, "Where is the draft for the freedom fight in the United States?" It reiterated the organization's sympathy with and support for "the men in this country who are unwilling to respond to a military draft which would compel them to contribute their lives to United States aggression in Vietnam in the name of the 'freedom' we find so false in this country."[55] On April 4, 1967, Martin Luther King Jr. vocalized his disappointment with the continuing war in Vietnam at a Clergy and Laity Concerned meeting at Riverside Church in New York City. Although he did not advocate draft resistance, he challenged young men "with the alternative of conscientious objection" and encouraged all clergy members to relinquish their ministerial exemptions and seek CO status instead.[56] By the end of the decade, every major civil rights organization from the National Association for the Advancement of Colored People to the Black Panthers had come out against the war and military service for African Americans.

During the first half of the war, the press roundly condemned protesters' activities and values. In October 1965, for example, the newsmagazine *Time* referred to antiwar protestors as "Vietniks" and ridiculed them as misguided, "burning-eyed" zealots who offered "deep comfort" to Chinese communists.[57] Nevertheless, draft avoidance behavior continued to gain acceptance. More and more men looked for ways to avoid military service, either by applying for CO status or deferments or through outright draft evasion. John Whiteclay Chambers II estimates that between 1964 and 1973, 27 million young men reached draft age, of whom 16 million, or 60 percent, of those eligible did not serve. Of these, 15 million received legal exemptions or deferments and approximately 570,000 evaded the draft illegally, most frequently by failing to report for induction calls.[58] Though 209,517 were accused of violating the draft law, only 8,750 were found guilty and only 3,250 of the convicted went to prison, as juries became increasingly unwilling to convict young men for draft law violations, and judges appeared ready to reduce the sentences of those who were convicted.[59]

To avoid induction, men emphasized their physical, mental, and moral weaknesses. CO appeals discussed applicants' claims of homosexuality, drug use, and physical ailments with remarkable candor.[60] Draft counselors, like Manhattan's Irving Sadoff, taught young men how to highlight existing conditions in a believable manner so that their local draft boards would grant them deferments.[61] Appeals rates skyrocketed. While the Justice Department received 47 appeals per 1,000 men in 1953, it saw 102 per 1,000 in 1969.[62] The Selective Service rejection rate for physical ailments jumped from 24.2 percent in 1966 to 39.9 percent in 1971, indicating a sharp rise in the number of men asking for this type of exemption, learning how to work the system in order to obtain one, or both.[63] Student Homophile Leagues like Columbia University's were formed to help "students who consider themselves basically heterosexual but . . . [who were] interested in taking advantage of the 'homosexual exemption.'" This response prompted one writer for the *New York Times* to speculate in 1970 that "just as homosexuality is less scorned and feared by this generation of young men than it was by their elders, so is a category that might be summed up as 'weakness.' The stigma that once commonly attached to a 4-F military classification, and comparable attitudes toward the conscientious objector, have virtually disappeared."[64] These activists were clearly defining manhood separately from military service.

Conclusion

The decline of military masculinity in popular culture, combined with two decades of manpower policies that deemphasized the need for universal service, unbroken pacifist opposition to the draft, and the spread of the idealistic, individualistic values of the New Left, created a situation in which young men, regardless of their commitment to the peace movement, could openly reject the claim that military service was necessary to their masculine identity. As they actively sought ways to turn draft resistance from a liability into an asset, protest and draft avoidance ceased being seen as fringe activities. By 1968, *Time* had dropped its derisive use of the term "Vietnik" to describe antiwar protestors. In 1970, a young man named Neil A. Oxman testified before a congressional hearing on student views toward US policy in Southeast Asia that he would flee to Canada rather than serve in the US Army. "I am a man and my honor as a human being would be compromised should I support the present actions of my President," he stated.[65] As Oxman was the popularly elected student-body president of Villanova University, a Catholic institution not generally associated with radical causes, his testimony suggested that the idea that there was more personal honor in flight than in military service had now entered the mainstream.

By the early 1970s, many young men had ceased to accept unquestioningly the masculine ideal of the World War II generation that demanded defending nation and family from outside threats through military service. Instead, they constructed their masculinity on the belief that dying in an immoral war was futile, contending that they could better serve their country by challenging it to live up to its democratic ideals, or at least surviving in order to contribute meaningfully later. Men who rejected the possibility of enlistment found that they could still enjoy the privileges of masculine prerogative.[66] Unlike lovelorn "4-F Charlie," the draft resisters of the 1960s and 1970s discovered that "Girls say 'yes' to boys who say 'no.'"

Notes

1. Quoted in Bernard Rostker, *I Want You! The Evolution of the All-Volunteer Force* (Arlington, VA: Rand Corporation, 2006), 15.

2. See, for example, Rostker, *I Want You!*; David Cortright, *Soldiers in Revolt: GI Resistance During the Vietnam War* (New York: Anchor Books, 1975; rpt. 2005); Susan Jeffords, *The Remasculinization of America: Gender and the Vietnam War* (Bloomington: Indiana University Press, 1989); and Beth Bailey, *America's Army: Making the All-Volunteer Force* (Cambridge, MA: Belknap Press, 2009).

3. John Whiteclay Chambers II, "Conscientious Objectors and the American State from Colonial Times to the Present," in *The New Conscientious Objection: From Sacred to Secular Resistance,* ed. Charles Moskos and John Whiteclay Chambers II (New York: Oxford University Press, 1993), 40.

4. This essay assumes the existence of multiple masculinities, a theory that rejects binary notions of gender (i.e., masculinity vs. femininity). Instead, it argues that different groups of men and women define their masculinity and femininity in relation to one another. This allows, for instance, pacifist men to define their own masculinity differently from the ways that soldiers might. See Joan Scott, "Gender: A Useful Category of Historical Analysis," *American Historical Review* 91 (1986): 1053–75; Margaret R. Higonnet and Patrice L.-R. Higonnet, "The Double Helix," in *Behind the Lines: Gender and the Two World Wars,* ed. Margaret R. Higonnet et al. (New Haven, CT: Yale University Press, 1987); George Chauncey, *Gay New York: Gender, Urban Culture, and the Making of the Gay Male World, 1890–1940* (New York: Basic Books, 1994); and Paul Higate, ed., *Military Masculinities: Identity and the State* (Westport, CT: Praeger Press, 2003).

5. Christian G. Appy, "'We'll Follow the Old Man': The Strains of Sentimental Militarism in Popular Films of the Fifties," in *Rethinking Cold War Culture*, ed. Peter J. Kuznick and James Gilbert (Washington, DC: Smithsonian Institution Press, 2001), 74–105.

6. Walter Graebner, "How to Tell If a Jap Is Really Dead," *New York Times*, September 12, 1943, BR7.

7. Christina S. Jarvis, *The Male Body at War* (Dekalb: Northern Illinois University Press, 2004), 60.

8. David O. Selznick, *Since You Went Away*, Vanguard Films, 1944 (MGM Home Entertainment: 2004).

9. Appy, "'We'll Follow the Old Man,'" 76.

10. See Andrew J. Huebner, *The Warrior Image: Soldiers in American Culture from the Second World War to the Vietnam Era* (Chapel Hill: University of North Carolina Press, 2007), 130.

11. See Lizabeth Cohen, *A Consumer's Republic: The Politics of Mass Consumption in Postwar America* (New York: Vintage Books, 2003), esp. 144–50.

12. See Elaine Tyler May, *Homeward Bound: American Families in the Cold War Era* (New York: Basic Books, 1988); Jessica Weiss, *To Have and To Hold: Marriage, the Baby Boom, and Social Change* (Chicago: University of Chicago Press, 2000); and James Gilbert, *Men in the Middle: Searching for Manhood in the 1950s* (Chicago: University of Chicago Press, 2005).

13. See Gilbert, *Men in the Middle*, esp. chap. 7; Sloan Wilson, *The Man in the Gray Flannel Suit* (New York: Simon and Schuster, 1955).

14. George Q. Flynn, *The Draft, 1940–1973* (Lawrence: University Press of Kansas, 1993), 85.

15. Mulford Sibley and Philip E. Jacob, *Conscription of Conscience: The American State and the Conscientious Objector, 1940–1947* (Ithaca, NY: Cornell University Press, 1952), 498, 84.

16. Flynn, *The Draft*, 29.

17. This number is notoriously difficult to verify. Local Selective Service boards did not keep careful records, and different studies classify conscientious objection differently. In 1950, the Selective Service estimated the number to be approximately 72,000 (Selective Service System, *Conscientious Objection*, Special Monograph No. 11, 2 vols. [Washington, DC: US Government Printing Office, 1950], 315); however, other sources have questioned the Selective Service's estimates. The figure 138,000 comes from Carl L. Peterson Jr., *Avoidance and Evasion of Military Service: An American History, 1626–1973* (Bethesda, MD: International Scholars Publications, 1998), 101–2. Timothy Stewart-Winter, in "Not a Soldier, Not a Slacker: Conscientious Objectors and Male Citizenship during the Second World War," *Gender and History* 19 (2007): 519–51, here 542, places the number at 100,000, as do Sibley and Jacob in *Conscription of Conscience*, 84.

18. US House Committee on Armed Services, *Full Committee Hearings on Universal Military Training*, 80th Cong., 1st sess., 1947; US House Committee on Armed Services, *Subcommittee Hearings on Universal Military Training: Hearings on H.R. 4121*, 80th Cong., 1st sess., 1947; US House Committee on Armed Services, *Universal Military Training*, H. Rpt. 1107, Report to Accompany H.R. 4278, 80th Cong., 1st sess., 1947; US House Committee on Armed Services, *Universal Military Training: Hearings Before the Committee on Armed Services*, 82nd Cong., 1st sess., 1951; US Senate Committee on Armed Services,

Universal Military Training: Hearings before the Committee on Armed Services, 80th Cong., 2nd sess., 1948; US Senate Committee on Armed Services, *Universal Military Training and Service Act of 1951: Hearings Before the Preparedness Subcommittee of the Committee on Armed Services*, 82nd Cong., 1st sess., 1951; and US Senate Committee on Armed Services, *Universal Military Training and Service Act of 1951: Report of the Committee on Armed Services to Accompany S. 1*, Report No. 117, 82nd Cong., 1st sess., 1951.

19. See Michael S. Sherry, *Preparing for the Next War: American Plans for Postwar Defense, 1941–45* (New Haven, CT: Yale University Press, 1977), 88–9.

20. Samuel P. Huntington, *The Common Defense: Strategic Programs in National Defense* (New York: Columbia University Press, 1961), 240; "Poll of Women Favors Military Duty for Boys," *New York Herald Tribune*, December 4, 1944; "Opinion Survey: Universal Military Training, Weekly Surveys of Newspaper Opinion Concerning Universal Military Training and the Postwar Military Establishment, 1944–1945," entry 52, volumes 1 and 2 (390/10/13/1), Records of the Office of the Secretary of War (RG 107), National Archives and Records Administration, College Park, MD (hereafter NARA); and "Now or Never!," *Woman's Home Companion*, August 1945, 17.

21. Sherry, *Preparing for the Next War*, 75.

22. Informal Remarks of the President to his Advisory Commission on Universal Training, December 20, 1946, President's Advisory Commission on Universal Training, box 3, Commission Kit—2nd Meeting, 12-28-46, Harry S Truman Library, Independence, MO (hereafter Truman Library).

23. "Universal Military Training," n.d., Assistant Chief of Staff (G-2), Intelligence, Administrative Div., Document Library Branch, Publications "P" Files, 1946–51, Universal Military Training, box 3672, Records of the Army Staff (RG 319), NARA.

24. Even at the height of the Korean War in 1952, 48 percent of the American population rejected the principle of drafting men with children. See Flynn, *The Draft*, 127.

25. Laura McEnaney, *Civil Defense Begins at Home: Militarization Meets Everyday Life in the Fifties* (Princeton, NJ: Princeton University Press, 2000), 76–7.

26. "Reports of the Scientific Advisory Committees," in M. H. Trytten, *Student Deferment in Selective Service: A Vital Factor in National Security* (Minneapolis: University of Minnesota Press, 1952), 92.

27. Flynn, *The Draft*, 106.

28. Edward A. Suchman, Robin M. Williams, and Rose K. Goldsen, "Student Reaction to Impending Military Service," *American Sociological Review* 18, no. 3 (June 1953): 293–304.

29. Flynn, *The Draft*, 143.

30. Ibid., 125–26.

31. Ibid., 128.

32. "Induction Statistics," US Selective Service, http://www.selectiveservice.us/military-draft/8-induction.shtml.

33. "Estimated Number of Males Reaching Age 18, 1948–65," May 2, 1947, President's Advisory Commission on Universal Training, box 4, First Princeton Meeting, May 7–9, 1947, Truman Library.

34. Flynn, *The Draft*, 147, 153.

35. Michael S. Foley, *Confronting the War Machine: Draft Resistance During the Vietnam War* (Chapel Hill: University of North Carolina Press, 2005), 38.

36. A total of 15,586 men received II-A deferments in fiscal 1955 and 112,000 received II-A deferments in fiscal 1962 (see United States Selective Service System, *Annual Report of the Director of Selective Service* [Washington, DC: US Government Printing Office, 1955], 22; and ibid., 1963, 11); Dee Ingold to the Director and attachments, February 13, 1958, 105 Advisory Committee (Ala-Wyoming), 1963-48, box 34 and Memo, re: Amendments to Selective Service Regulations, November 16, 1962, 110 General, 1963-1955, box 35, both in Central Files, Records of the Selective Service System (RG 147), NARA.

37. "Channeling," Orientation Kit, Selective Service System, July 1, 1965, 6.

38. Flynn, *The Draft*, 127.

39. Article 6(j) of Title I of the Selective Service Act of 1948 and its successor, the Universal Military Training and Service Act of 1951, laid out the criteria for certification as a conscientious objector, exempting men who objected to all wars based on "religious training and belief," but defining this as "an individual's belief in a relation to a Supreme Being involving duties superior to those arising from any human relation, but . . . not includ[ing] essentially political, sociological, or philosophical views or a merely personal moral code" (Universal Military Training and Service Act of June 19, 1951, 65 Stat. 75, 86).

40. Chambers, "Conscientious Objectors and the American State," 37; Stewart-Winter, "Not a Soldier, Not a Slacker," 521.

41. Because neither the military nor the Selective Service kept exact records on the types of men who served as noncombatants, it is impossible to know exactly how many pacifists served in this capacity, although they made up the largest number of conscientious objectors during World War II (see note 17 above).

42. Stewart-Winter, "Not a Soldier, Not a Slacker," 521.

43. Ibid., 532.

44. Radical pacifists, as historian James Tracy calls these men, introduced nonviolent direct action, "an experimental protest style that emphasized media savvy, symbolic confrontation with institutions deemed oppressive," and a decentralized, nonhierarchical organizational structure to the New Left. It was Bayard Rustin, for example, who introduced the idea of nonviolent action to Martin Luther King, Jr. during the 1955 Montgomery, Alabama bus boycott. See Tracy, *Direct Action: Radical Pacifism from the Union Eight to the Chicago Seven* (Chicago: University of Chicago Press, 1996), quote on xiii.

45. The literature on American pacifism between World War II and the Vietnam War is relatively thin, but see Tracy, *Direct Action*; Peterson, *Avoidance and Evasion of Military Service*; Lawrence S. Wittner, *Rebels Against War: The American Peace Movement, 1941–1960* (New York: Columbia University Press, 1969); Charles DeBenedetti, *The Peace Reform in American History* (Bloomington: Indiana University Press, 1980); and Mel Piehl, *Breaking Bread: The Catholic Worker and the Origin of Catholic Radicalism in America* (Philadelphia: Temple University Press, 1982). Gender historians have looked at the role of women in the movement; see Amy Swerdlow, *Women Strike for Peace: Traditional Motherhood and Radical Politics in the 1960s* (Chicago: University of Chicago Press, 1993); and Dee Garrison, "'Our Skirts Gave Them Courage': The Civil Defense Protest Movement in New York City, 1955–1961," in *Not June Cleaver: Women and Gender in Postwar America, 1945–1960*, ed. Joanne Meyerowitz (Philadelphia: Temple University Press, 1994), 201–28.

46. Conrad Brandfonhiner [?] to Mr. Siteman, Sept. 26, 1950, Metropolitan Board for Conscientious Objectors, Series B, General Records, 1946–ca.1980, Box 14, Siteman,

Stephen: General and Case Correspondence, 1950, Swarthmore Peace Collection, Swarthmore, Pennsylvania (hereafter SPC).

47. The Selective Service Act of 1948 required all men between the ages of eighteen and twenty-six to register with the Selective Service and set out the terms of their subsequent draft classifications. Men were classified based on their availability for service. Men classified as I-A were available, and if drafted, were liable for twenty-one months of service. Men who were classified as II-A and II-C had occupational deferments; those classified as III-A had deferments for dependents; and those classified as IV-F were deemed physically, mentally, or morally unfit. COs fell into two categories: I-A-O encompassed those who would serve in the military as noncombatants, usually as medics, and IV-E included those who would not serve in any capacity. The act also outlined the appeal process. The Universal Military Training and Service Act of 1951 amended the 1948 law to include a student deferment and extend the term of service to twenty-four months. It also included a provision for UMT if Congress passed a separate law to fund it and provided criteria for CO certification (see note 39, above).

48. Frieda Langer Lazarus to Chester Bruvold, September 20, 1948, Metropolitan Board for Conscientious Objectors, Series C: Files of Frieda Langer Lazarus, box 15, General Correspondence, 1948–49, SPC.

49. *United States v. Seeger,* 380 U.S. 163 (1965).

50. Michael Useem, *Conscription, Protest, and Social Conflict: The Life and Death of a Draft Resistance Movement* (New York: Wiley Press, 1973), 131.

51. According to Lawrence M. Baskir and William A. Strauss, members of President Gerald Ford's Clemency Board, close to 27 million men reached draft age during the Vietnam War. Of these, approximately 171,000 (0.63 percent) were certified as COs (Baskir and Strauss, *Chance and Circumstance: The Draft, the War and the Vietnam Generation* [New York: Vintage Books, 1978], 5, 30). Although this percentage is low, it is almost one-and-a-half times the comparable proportion (0.45 percent) from World War II, assuming that 100,000 men were certified as COs out of a draftable pool of 22 million men between the ages of eighteen and thirty-seven (Flynn, *The Draft*, 63). The 1972 statistic reflects a number of factors, including the decreased draft calls that came with President Nixon's policy of "Vietnamization" and the winding-down of the Vietnam War. It is telling, however, because it indicates that large numbers of men sought to avoid military service even as their likelihood of being conscripted diminished. Chambers, "Conscientious Objectors and the American State," 42.

52. Quoted in Michael Ferber and Staughton Lynd, *The Resistance* (Boston: Beacon Press, 1971), 14.

53. See, for example, Charles M. Payne, *I've Got the Light of Freedom: The Organizing Tradition and the Mississippi Freedom Struggle* (Berkeley: University of California Press, 1995); Lance Hill, *The Deacons of Defense: Armed Resistance and the Civil Rights Movement* (Chapel Hill: University of North Carolina Press, 2004); Steve Estes, *I Am a Man: Race, Manhood, and the Civil Rights Movement* (Chapel Hill: University of North Carolina Press, 2005); and Estes' chapter in this volume.

54. "McComb Antiwar Petition," reprinted in *Students for a Democratic Society Bulletin* 4, no. 1 (1965), 2.

55. "Student Nonviolent Coordinating Committee Position Paper: On Vietnam," reprinted through The Sixties Project, Institute for Advanced Technology in the

Humanities (IATH), University of Virginia, Charlottesville, VA, http://www2.iath
.virginia.edu/sixties/HTML_docs/Resources/Primary/Manifestos/SNCC_VN.html.

56. Martin Luther King Jr., "Beyond Vietnam—A Time to Break Silence," April 4,
1967, Riverside Church, New York City, reprinted at http://www.americanrhetoric.com
/speeches/mlkatimetobreaksilence.htm.

57. "The Vietniks: Self-Defeating Dissent," *Time*, October 29, 1965, 54.

58. Chambers, "Conscientious Objectors and the American State," 41.

59. Baskir and Strauss, *Chance and Circumstance*, 5.

60. See Correspondence on CO Appeals, Records Relating to Conscientious Objection,
box 2, RG 147, NARA.

61. Saul Braun, "From 1-A to 4-F and All Points in Between," *New York Times Magazine*,
November 29, 1970, 124.

62. Flynn, *The Draft*, 240.

63. Bernard D. Karpinos, "Draftees: Disqualifications for Military Service for Medical
Reasons—An Analysis of Trends over Time," Manpower Research Report No. MA
72-1, Office of the Secretary of Defense (Alexandria, VA: Human Resources Research
Organization, 1972), viii.

64. Braun, "From 1-A to 4-F," 125.

65. Ad Hoc Committee of Members of the House of Representatives, *Student Views
Toward United States Policy in Southeast Asia*, Hearings, 91st Congress, 2nd sess., May
21-22, 1970, 113.

66. This interpretation challenges the argument advanced by some scholars that
America's loss in Vietnam, coupled with other negative events of the 1970s, precipitated
a national "crisis of masculinity" during that decade. Although the United States certainly
faced shifting political, diplomatic, and economic conditions in the 1970s, not all
Americans viewed their nation's loss in Vietnam as a crisis. Yet the argument that masculine
citizenship became decoupled from military service in the decades leading up to the 1970s
reinforces the argument that the American military suffered a crisis of confidence during
the 1970s and needed to "remasculinize" its image during the 1980s. See Jeffords, *The
Remasculinization of America*; Susan Faludi, *Stiffed: The Betrayal of the American Man* (New
York: Harper Collins, 1999), esp. part III; and Natasha Zaretsky, *No Direction Home: The
American Family and the Fear of National Decline, 1968–1980* (Chapel Hill.: University of
North Carolina Press, 2007).

Chapter 8
Man the Guns: Race, Masculinity, and Citizenship from World War II to the Civil Rights Movement

Steve Estes

Stanley Dunham was a typical American GI. Hailing from Kansas and newly married, he enlisted shortly after the attack on Pearl Harbor. His wife worked on a Boeing assembly line, cranking out bombers for the war effort. Their only daughter was born in 1942, not long before Dunham was shipped overseas. He served in France with Patton's army, but saw little combat. After the war, Dunham sold furniture and insurance. "His was an American character," Dunham's grandson later wrote, "one typical of men of his generation, men who embraced the notion of freedom and individualism and the open road without always knowing its price, and whose enthusiasms could as easily lead to the cowardice of McCarthyism as to the heroics of World War II." Dunham was no red-baiting follower of Joseph McCarthy, but neither was he a war hero. He was the kind of ordinary GI that Tom Brokaw lionized in *The Greatest Generation*. Dunham did his duty, served overseas, and came back to lead an unremarkable life—except for one thing. His daughter married an African man, and their son would go on to become the first African American president of the United States.[1]

In his ordinary story with an extraordinary twist, Stanley Dunham is a symbol of the "Good War" and the good warriors who fought it. Nothing about Dunham's upbringing as a working-class white man from Kansas suggested that he would support the interracial marriage of his only daughter and then take pride in helping to raise his mixed-race grandson. Perhaps his wartime experiences explain this racial tolerance. In the hopeful narrative of the Good War, the victorious fight against Nazi bigotry and oppression made American men like Stanley Dunham more critical of injustices at home, gradually shifting their views in favor of expanded rights for ethnic minorities and women. Historians who view World War II as a watershed moment for civil rights and women's rights point to the executive order against racial discrimination in war industries, the heroism of African American military units, and the liberating symbolism of Rosie the Riveter. The racial integration of the US armed forces in the late 1940s and a string of civil rights victories for African Americans in the 1950s and 1960s also support a progressive analysis of the war.[2]

But what are we to make of Robert "Tut" Patterson, the former paratrooper who founded the white supremacist Citizens' Councils to battle school integration, or Byron De La Beckwith, the former Marine who returned home to Mississippi and assassinated civil rights organizer Medgar Evers? What about Strom Thurmond, the decorated D-Day veteran from South Carolina who filibustered a civil rights bill for more than 24 hours, or George Wallace, the Army Air Corps veteran who stood in the schoolhouse door to stop integration in Alabama? Are these men part of the "Greatest Generation," or part of a conveniently forgotten one? What are we to make of the war's legacy for them and for the story of the "Good War" in the American South and the rest of the nation?

This chapter explores the evolution of black and white soldiers' conceptions of race and manhood in World War II, laying a foundation for the African American civil rights movement, but it also looks at some of the soldiers who resisted the changes set in motion by World War II. Black veterans returned from fighting with a new sense of themselves as American men and citizens, an understanding that fueled their participation in the civil rights movement of the 1950s and 1960s. Some white American veterans, like Barack Obama's grandfather, may not have joined the movement, but the war did affect them in more subtle ways, broadening their horizons and changing their views of black men in particular and race relations in general. Yet many white southern veterans returned home little changed and continued to defend the South's segregated way of life. A strong regional tradition of military service all but demanded that southern men with political ambitions serve in the armed forces, so it is not surprising that many of the men who led the campaign against integration in the South were veterans.

World War II inspired a more progressive vision of race and gender relations for some Americans, but it did not have this effect on southern soldiers-turned-statesmen. These men returned from serving overseas to fight not for equality but for white supremacy.

The contested nature of World War II's legacy can only be understood by looking beyond the 1940s to the long postwar period. Other scholars have looked at how World War II affected the home front and how veterans influenced political struggles in certain states and locales in the years immediately after the war.[3] Scholars argue that these changes in domestic race and gender relations were "central to the whole campaign for civil rights" in the 1950s and 1960s, yet few have examined the connection between race and manhood and how these conceptions changed.[4] World War II shaped both black and white veterans' ideas about race and manhood in ways that influenced the struggle over civil rights long after the war. Historical connections among manhood, citizenship, and military service inspired black veterans and many white allies to support civil rights after the war as a natural extension of rights won by black soldiers who had survived the military's rite of passage and done their duty as American men. Yet some southern white veterans took a different lesson from the war that was no less steeped in tradition. They had survived the rite of passage into manhood through their service and returned home to take on traditional roles as protectors of their families and leaders of their communities—families and communities that were based on white male supremacy. These competing views of manhood and citizenship that emerged from World War II became a subtext for the racial conflicts of the civil rights movement.

This chapter begins with a brief analysis of the wartime experiences of US troops, both black and white, focusing on how the war shaped their conceptions of race and manhood. It then investigates how wartime experiences and racial/gendered rhetoric affected the politics of the early postwar period, particularly the evolution of an increasingly divided Democratic Party, and how veterans deployed new conceptions of race and gender in the civil rights movement of the 1950s and 60s. Finally, it looks at how memories of both the war and the movement became incorporated into the myth of American exceptionalism at the end of the twentieth century. This chapter is intended to complicate our understandings of the ways that World War II affected America's "Greatest Generation" and the ways that this generation shaped the postwar period.

"Man the Guns"

"I spent four years in the Army to free a bunch of Dutchmen and Frenchmen," one black US Army corporal said in 1945, "and I'll be hanged if I'm going to let the Alabama version of the Germans kick me around when I get home. No sirreee bob! I went into the Army a Nigger; I'm coming out a man!" Though he fought in the Pacific theater thousands of miles away, Michigan native Raymond Carter could not have agreed more. For Carter, the most memorable moment in the war was the day his ship, the *U.S.S. Gregory*, took fire in the South Pacific. The *Gregory* was supporting the American invasion of Guadalcanal in the midst of a bloody island-hopping campaign to retake the Pacific from the Japanese. Carter was part of the crew, manning a four-inch deck gun. When a Japanese cruiser landed a devastating hit on the *Gregory*, crippling the vessel, all hands had to abandon ship. Like his fellow sailors, Carter scrambled onto one of the life rafts. Feeling lucky to be alive, he later described the bond that formed between the men. "Talk about togetherness; we were straight out of *The Three Musketeers*, all for one and one for all." Such combat-forged camaraderie is a common theme in stories from the Good War. Yet it does not tell the whole story of Carter's wartime experiences or the experiences of other black men and women who served during World War II.[5]

Ray Carter enlisted in the Navy early in the 1940s as a fresh-faced nineteen-year-old. Perhaps he had seen a poster urging young recruits to "Man the Guns." More likely, posters and newspaper stories featuring the black World War II hero Dorie Miller inspired Carter to sign up. Miller was a messman on the *U.S.S. West Virginia* stationed in Pearl Harbor on December 7, 1941. During the Japanese surprise attack that morning, Miller risked his own life to drag his dying captain out of harm's way, before manning a deck-mounted machine gun. Perhaps hoping to follow Miller's example and to man the guns himself, Carter joined the Navy.[6]

Because of his tan complexion, the Navy recruiter asked Carter about his nationality and was clearly surprised when Carter responded that he was "colored." The white officer quickly crossed out Carter's original duty assignment and wrote "steward" on the recruiting forms. It was official policy of the Navy in the early 1940s that "colored men are enlisted only in the messman branch" as cooks and personal attendants for white officers. It was a "waste of time and effort," the Navy reasoned, to recruit and train black sailors for other positions that were assumed to be beyond their capacity. "Oh man, was I a real dum-dum!" Carter later recalled. "I had enlisted to fight for my country and my great contribution to the war effort was to wait on whites."[7]

More than one million African Americans served in the US Armed Forces during World War II, and hundreds of thousands more contributed to the war effort by working in defense industries. Though many black soldiers were relegated to labor battalions in the early years of the war, manpower needs and political pressure eventually brought thousands of them into combat. Similarly, many war industries had initially hired white men only, but when white American men went off to war, positions opened up for white women and African Americans.

Although it is certainly not the only defining experience for boys becoming men, military service—especially during a time of war—has traditionally been viewed as a rite of passage into manhood. In the context of wartime service, "man" becomes not just a noun, but a verb; not just an identity, but an action as soldiers and sailors are ordered to "man the guns." Military action, then, shapes a masculine identity. The tests of physical prowess, courage, and mettle in the military are supposed to harden young boys into men and prove that they can fulfill their traditional roles as husbands and fathers, protecting their families and communities from harm. On a political level, wartime military service has also been seen as an obligation of citizenship in modern republics and democracies. Citizen-soldiers must protect and defend the state in return for the right to have a say in how the state is run. Well into the twentieth century, the segregation of the armed forces and the relegation of women and minority men to noncombat roles denied them the rights of citizenship by excluding them from this "band of brothers." Still, there was a sense among African American men that participation and valorous service in war could uplift their race and gain them respect and recognition as men.[8]

When they returned from fighting overseas, these men brought back a revolutionary new sense of themselves and their comrades. One black chaplain stationed in the Pacific gave a final sermon to his men at the conclusion of hostilities that urged a new militancy among black troops. "We have won the military battle for democracy," he said, "but the fight is not over. Don't be satisfied with the way things were . . . . Don't let anyone ever again tell you, you are inferior because you are black . . . . Be a man! We owe it to ourselves." Black troops were not the only ones who saw racial injustice in a new light after the war. The scales had fallen from the eyes of a few white veterans as well. Captain Hyman Samuelson, a white officer from Louisiana who served with black troops, resolved to fight racism when he returned home. "Before

I die," he wrote in his diary in 1943, "I must help stamp out this crazy idea that the white man has about his superiority over the colored man . . . . It's wrong—damn wrong!"[9]

Samuelson's racial epiphany does support the idea of the Good War's beneficial effect on white soldiers, even southern ones. However, the political career of fellow southern veteran Strom Thurmond calls into question the whole notion of the Good War's influence on race, manhood, and civil rights. "One cannot always be a hero, but one can always be a man," read the caption under Strom Thurmond's Clemson University yearbook picture in 1923. During Thurmond's later service in World War II, his heroism and manhood became synonymous. The scion of a powerful and wealthy South Carolina family, he would go on to have one of the longest and most storied careers in American politics. Thurmond volunteered for active duty the day America declared war on Germany in 1941. He was already thirty-nine years old, yet World War II would become a defining moment in his path to manhood and not coincidentally, to political power.[10] During the D-Day invasion, Thurmond was part of a glider assault team that took fire over Utah Beach before crashing in France behind German lines. We "had so many narrow escapes," he wrote in a letter home to a South Carolina newspaper, "that it is a miracle to me that any of us who landed by glider are still alive." Thurmond traveled with the Allied forces across France and into Germany, enduring the Battle of the Bulge. For his service, Lieutenant Colonel Thurmond was awarded the Bronze Star, Purple Heart, and Croix de Guerre. Favorable coverage of his exploits in the South Carolina press laid the foundation for a successful postwar political career.[11]

Southern veterans like Strom Thurmond returned to a dramatically different South than the one they had left. During the war, more than three million people migrated from the rural South to southern cities or to other parts of the country. A third of the more than a million and a half southerners who left the region altogether were African Americans, pulled north and westward by the promise of jobs and relative freedom. Yet the war had also brought new industries to the South and revived local economies, some of which had been languishing since the Civil War. Echoing the Good War thesis, historian Morton Sosna argues that the war ultimately transformed the South from "a provincial backwater characterized by ruralism, agrarianism, poverty, and racial apartheid to a more recognizable modern society with patterns of urbanization, industrialization, and race relations similar to other parts of the United States."[12]

Southern veterans of both races facilitated these changes. While many black veterans sought to escape the South, others stayed and struggled to remake the region. In Mississippi, for instance, World War II veterans Amzie Moore, Aaron Henry, and Medgar Evers led grassroots voting drives in the 1950s and 1960s. As historian Jennifer Brooks argued in her excellent case study of Georgia politics after the war, black veterans "found their sense of manhood and citizenship magnified by meeting the challenges of military service and war." Brooks also recognized that African Americans were not the only southern veterans changed by their service. Some white veterans also displayed a new sense of themselves and their region. White newspapermen like Hodding Carter of Mississippi and Harry Ashmore of Arkansas, for example, returned from service overseas to lead moderate challenges to the racial and economic status quo. As one white Mississippi veteran put it in 1945, "I found out after I did some fighting in this war that the colored boys fight just as good as the white boys . . . . I've changed my ideas a lot about colored people since I got into this war, and so have a lot of boys from the South." Weighing such sentiment in support of the Good War thesis, historian Jim Cobb argues that despite some variations in veterans' views, "it was nonetheless possible to discern among them a widespread inclination toward a more 'modern' or 'progressive' approach to government and politics, one that stressed economic development and favored moderation over demagoguery on the racial issue."[13]

"To Secure These Rights"

As one of ten candidates in the sprawling South Carolina gubernatorial race of 1946, Strom Thurmond seemed to embody this new spirit in his first campaign after the war. If elected, Thurmond wanted to encourage business development, eliminate the poll tax, and provide more funding for education, but he also campaigned on his wartime heroism. Using his war record to beat up his opponents and buttress his claim as a good government reformer, Thurmond argued that the incumbent political machine was reminiscent of the "scheming, conniving, selfish men" whose lust for power had led to World War II. "I was willing to risk my life to stamp out such gangs in Europe," he said, and "I intend to devote my future to wiping out the stench and stain" of such corruption and greed in South Carolina. Voters believed the war hero. He was sworn into office with the Bible that he had carried to Europe.[14]

For Governor Thurmond, an early litmus test on race came just a few months into his term. Racial violence had been on the upswing across the South since the end of the war, as black veterans chafed at Jim Crow social strictures and white southerners sought to remind these black men of their "place" in the racial and gender hierarchy of southern society. Returning to his South Carolina home in 1946, black veteran Isaac Woodard asked the white bus driver if it would be possible to stop so that he could use the bathroom. "Hell, no!" the driver said. Still wearing the uniform that symbolized his service to his country, Woodard seethed: "Dammit, you've got to talk to me like a man." The driver then radioed ahead to the police, who pulled Woodard off the bus at the next stop and beat him until he was blind. The incident became a cause célèbre for the newly emboldened National Association for the Advancement of Colored People (NAACP), which had seen national membership grow nearly tenfold during the war. Thurmond remained studiously silent about Woodard during his gubernatorial campaign, but when a mob took another black man from a Greenville jail and lynched him in February 1947, the newly elected governor intervened. "Mob rule is against every principle for which we have so recently sacrificed so very much," Thurmond said, "and we expect to combat it with the same determination." The young governor used the ideals of the war to justify progressive intervention. He demanded the arrest and prosecution of two dozen white men for the lynching, but the men were later acquitted by an all-white jury.[15]

Such incidents of racial violence inspired President Harry Truman to take action on civil rights. In a letter to a friend, Truman explained that when white authorities "can take a Negro Sergeant off a bus in South Carolina, beat him up, put out one of his eyes, and nothing is done about it, . . . something is radically wrong with the system." Of course, there were political concerns as well. Truman knew that he would have to deal with such situations if he would have any hope of winning the support of the African American migrants who now voted in urban centers outside the South. The president created a commission to study race relations in 1946, and he received its report, "To Secure These Rights," the following year.[16]

"To Secure These Rights" mixed self-congratulation for the American advances made in race relations during World War II with a surprisingly frank indictment of the racial problems that still plagued the country. As part of its praise for American progress on the race issue, the report even singled out the South Carolina prosecution of the 1947 lynch mob as a positive step. Its main goal, however, was to show how the experiences and ideals of World War II mandated an end to segregation and prejudice. In making this case, the report laid the foundations for future civil rights rhetoric and the Good War thesis.[17]

World War II showed that "the majority and minorities of our population can train and work and fight side by side in cooperation and harmony," according to the president's committee. During the war, black platoons had fought in regiments in eleven white combat divisions, two of which comprised mostly white southerners. The report cited postwar surveys with these men indicating that two-thirds of the white veterans had experienced a change of heart about black soldiers. "When I heard about it, I said I'd be damned if I'd wear the same shoulder patch they did," said a white South Carolinian. "After that first day when we saw how they fought, I changed my mind. They're just like any of the other boys to us." A white veteran from Alabama first thought black soldiers would be "yellow," but he came to admire their courage and work ethic by the end of the war. Most of the veterans who remained prejudiced, according to the report, were more segregated from black troops or only saw them doing menial tasks that reinforced prewar stereotypes. The report portrayed segregation as a self-perpetuating social problem, easily broken down during the war by fair and equitable integration that was a military necessity. After the war, American foreign policy dictated the need for equal treatment. "The existence of discrimination against minority groups in this country," Secretary of State Dean Acheson explained, "has an adverse effect upon our relations with other countries." In this way, the report also previewed an argument that civil rights advocates would use during the Cold War.[18]

Truman's support for the proposals in "To Secure These Rights" set him on a collision course with southerners like Strom Thurmond in a battle over the legacies of World War II. Thurmond felt that it was his duty as a southern white man and a veteran to defend his vision of America and the South. But Thurmond struggled to use World War II to justify segregation. Whereas the authors of "To Secure These Rights" had returned again and again to the experiences and rhetoric of the war to push for civil rights, Thurmond had difficulty responding in kind. As he became the regional standard bearer for a dissident wing of southern Democrats, he honed his message into a stump speech that carried him to the 1948 presidential nomination of the States' Rights Democratic Party (more commonly known as the Dixiecrats). In Alabama, he warned that the federal government would use "Gestapo-like" tactics to force integration. "We have only recently seen in Europe how quickly liberty perishes under such a government." After President Truman issued an executive order integrating the armed forces in the summer of 1948, Thurmond complained that "the policy of having separate white and negro units which helped the United States win two world wars has been sacrificed on the altar of politics." Accepting the Dixiecrat presidential nomination in Mississippi, Thurmond underscored his fighting credentials: "I did not risk my life on the beaches of Normandy to come back to this country and sit supinely by and permit a bunch of hack politicians to whittle away your heritage and mine."[19]

These brief references to the war reveal how unfriendly this field of battle was for the segregationists. Since the ideology and rhetoric of World War II offered relatively little ammunition for Thurmond's crusade, he relied more on his military exploits and a gendered message to rally support and gain sympathy for the southern cause. The leading historian of the Dixiecrat campaign, Kari Frederickson, first noted the gendered component of this political conflict. After Dixiecrats depicted the liberal turn of the national Democratic Party as an act of personal betrayal, Frederickson argued, "resistance to civil rights and encroachments of the federal government became nothing less than a test of their manhood." Thurmond became central to this fight, in part, because he "personified the gendered components of the region's reactionary states' rights political culture." Little wonder then that one constituent echoed Thurmond's masculinist rhetoric in a 1948 letter, confiding, "As a South Carolinian, I am deeply interested in everything in South Carolina. As a man, I am deeply interested in States' Rights." Thurmond won the votes of men like the author of this letter, but he did not win many more in his 1948 campaign for the presidency. Though Thurmond's Dixiecrat campaign proved quixotic, his use of white manhood as a rallying point for defending segregation became a model for future massive resistance to integration in the South.[20]

"Be a Man—Fight for Civil Rights!"

When Harry Briggs came back to South Carolina after serving in the Navy, he did not set out to become a civil rights activist. He just did not want any of his five children to have to walk several miles every day to attend underfunded, segregated schools. "We ain't got no money to buy a bus for your nigger children," replied Roderick W. Elliot, the white chairman of the district's board of trustees. With support from Thurgood Marshall of the NAACP Legal Defense Fund, Briggs sued Elliot in 1949. *Briggs v. Elliot* was the first of five cases the NAACP filed to challenge school segregation. One of the lawyers for the state was a young white attorney and fellow World War II veteran named Fritz

Hollings. Years later, after he had served for three decades as a liberal senator, Hollings recalled an exchange with one of the NAACP lawyers about Briggs. "How in the world can you ask them to serve in the front lines in Europe and when they come home, ask them to sit in the back of the bus," the attorney asked. "As a veteran," Hollings said, "that struck me. I realized that just ain't right." Though Harry Briggs and his wife Eliza lost their jobs for challenging segregation, they ultimately won their case as part of the Supreme Court's landmark 1954 *Brown v. Board of Education* decision.[21]

In calling for massive resistance to the *Brown* decision, southern whites used both racial and gendered rhetoric. The Citizens' Councils, a grassroots, white supremacist organization just to the left of the Ku Klux Klan, led the way. Founded in Mississippi by a World War II paratrooper named Robert Patterson, the Councils were more than willing to use scare tactics that demonized black men as rapists and warned of the impending threat to white women from integration. This struggle was not just about black manhood, but white masculinity as well. Patterson spoke of the organization he founded in gendered terms, later recalling that he had no idea that the Citizens' Councils "would, in a few months time, expand miraculously into a virile and potent organization." As segregation battles heated up, personal attacks on southern leaders' racial loyalty and manhood eclipsed debates about the constitutionality of court decisions or the legacies of the Good War.[22]

Perhaps the most famous veteran of World War II, President Dwight Eisenhower, finally weighed in on the segregation debate in Little Rock, Arkansas, in 1957. Eisenhower was no racial liberal. In the mid-1940s, he had opposed integration of the armed forces, arguing that the military was unprepared "spiritually, philosophically, or mentally to absorb blacks and whites together." In the midst of the crisis over racial integration at Little Rock Central High School, the Citizens' Councils tried to appeal to Eisenhower as a veteran and a father by publishing an open letter to the president in their newspaper. In the letter, a former Air Force officer explained why he, as a father, had to fight against integration: "Do you think any American father with any red blood in his veins is going to allow his dear, little girl to be insulted, possibly sexually molested and exposed to disease" through integration? Publicly, Eisenhower supported integration, but privately, he sympathized with conservative, white southerners' feelings on the issue. "These [segregationists] are not bad people," Eisenhower once confided to Supreme Court Chief Justice Earl Warren. "All they are concerned about is to see that their sweet little girls are not required to sit in school alongside some big overgrown Negroes." Despite his private sympathies, however, the president felt an obligation to enforce the Supreme Court's *Brown* decision.[23]

Losses at the Supreme Court and confrontations like Little Rock forced segregationist veterans to reassess their strategies in the late 1950s and early 1960s. On the local level, segregationists in the Citizens' Councils turned to violence to thwart civil rights activities. A closer look at Mississippi reveals that the movement really could boil down to a fight between veterans over the legacies of the war and postwar definitions of American citizenship.

Born in Mississippi in 1925, Medgar Evers served in France with an all-black unit during World War II. When the state of Mississippi waived the poll tax for veterans in 1946, Evers tried unsuccessfully to register to vote. But Evers was able to attend college on the GI Bill, and after graduation he redoubled his efforts toward civil rights, becoming a field secretary for the NAACP. Many of Evers' NAACP recruits were other black veterans. Evers often began speeches and interviews by saying that he was a proud Mississippi veteran, simply demanding his rights. "I speak as a Native Mississippian," he said in a 1963 televised address. "I was educated in Mississippi schools and served overseas in our nation's armed forces in the war against Hitlerism and fascism." Less than one month after delivering this speech, Evers was dead, the victim of an assassin's bullet.[24]

Opponents of civil rights had been gunning for Evers—both figuratively and literally—for a long time. They found their trigger man in Byron De La Beckwith, a former Marine who had been wounded in the Pacific theater during World War II. After the war, Beckwith became a salesman in Greenwood, Mississippi. The Supreme Court's *Brown* decision inspired him to fight for white supremacy. By the early 1960s, Beckwith had joined the Citizens' Councils, Ku Klux Klan, and similar rightwing groups. "I believe in segregation like I believe in God," Beckwith had once written to the local paper. "I shall . . . bend every effort to rid the U.S.A. of integrationists." Though his gun was found at the scene, an all-white jury acquitted Beckwith in 1964.

The trial was over, but the contested nature of race, patriotism, and the war's legacy remained. Evers was buried at Arlington National Cemetery with full military honors. At the funeral, one speaker eulogized, "No soldier in this field has fought more courageously, more heroically than Medgar Evers." For this speaker, Evers' status as a veteran underscored the tragedy of his death and the justice of his cause. Nearly two decades after the end of the Second World War, two Mississippi veterans—one white and one black—fought over the meaning of the war for race and manhood in America.[25]

On the national level, segregationists officially eschewed the type of violence seen in Mississippi and they began shifting the debate about rights from the context of World War II to the Cold War. National debates concerning America's response to communism echoed the masculinist strategies that the Citizens' Councils brought to bear on the civil rights movement. As historian K. A. Cuordileone has argued, politicians of this era attempted to position themselves as "hard," manly Cold Warriors. Southern veterans like Senator Strom Thurmond brooked no quarter for communist "subversives" or for liberals who appeared "soft" on communism and African American demands. Leander H. Perez, a powerful Louisiana politician and Citizens' Council leader, made this point explicitly in 1960. "How can we preserve *our* constitutional rights, *our* liberty and freedom under law, *our* status as first class citizens, *our* self-respect and manhood," Perez demanded, "if we continue to run from the negroes" and bow to "the worldwide Communist conspiracy."[26]

Anticommunist rhetoric was certainly not new in the 1960s. Southern politicians had been attacking organized labor and racial liberals as communists or "fellow travelers" since the 1930s. In confronting integration campaigns in the postwar era, anticommunism proved more palatable for a national audience than overt racism or states' rights rhetoric. As historian George Lewis points out, unlike states' rights rhetoric, which had difficulty dealing with southern dissenters, anticommunism both forged alliances with a national conservative movement and marginalized southern civil rights protesters as "un-American." Mary Dudziak, Thomas Borstelmann, and others have argued that the Cold War mandated liberal (albeit gradual) progress on civil rights primarily because regressive policies like segregation hobbled American foreign policy in the contest with the Soviets. Yet the rhetorical terrain of the Cold War provided much better defensive positions for white supremacy than World War II ever had. Although segregationist veterans used their war records to fuel their campaigns and compared an interventionist government bent on forcing integration to European fascists, civil rights activists found much more support for their cause in Good War rhetoric than segregationists did.[27]

Perhaps more than any other single veteran of World War II, it was a southern president who really marshaled the rhetoric of the Good War to advance civil rights in American law. A Congressional representative from Texas in 1941, Lyndon Baines Johnson volunteered for active duty in the Navy shortly after the attack on Pearl Harbor. Johnson served less than a year before President Franklin Roosevelt recalled him from active duty to help govern in Washington. Johnson did not come back from the war a civil rights advocate, but neither was he a diehard segregationist. By the late 1950s he had become one of the region's more moderate voices on civil rights. When he assumed the presidency in 1963, it was an opportune time to lead the nation forward on civil rights as protests in the South were touching the conscience of the nation. In his public addresses, Johnson often referred to black military service and American experiences in World War II as further evidence that all Americans deserved equality. Perhaps Johnson—a staunch Cold Warrior himself—realized that anticommunist rhetoric muddied the waters of civil rights debates, while the fight against the Nazis clarified the moral mandate for racial equality. "Americans of every race and color have died in battle to protect our freedom," Johnson said when signing the Civil Rights Act of 1964. "Now our generation of Americans has been called on to continue the unending search for justice within our own borders." In advocating passage of a voting rights bill the following year, Johnson went further. He again commended American citizens of every color for serving their country as "guardians of our liberty," and then spelled out the American promise of equality. This was a "promise to every citizen that he shall share in the dignity of man. This dignity cannot be found in a man's possessions; it cannot be found in his power, or in his position. It really rests on his right to be treated as a man equal in opportunity to all others." Johnson called on fellow veterans, "men from the South, some of whom were at Iwo Jima, men from the North who have carried Old Glory to far corners of the world and brought it back without a stain on it, . . . men from every region who fought for us across the globe twenty years ago" to support voting rights for all Americans.

Though many southern veterans in Congress continued to oppose Johnson, the majority of the veterans present that night answered the president's call. How could they not? Johnson had wisely played to their vanity and their identity as men, an identity that had been forged during the war. The president used the "band of brothers" rhetoric to enshrine the ideals of the "Good War" into civil rights law just as Truman had tried to do with "To Secure These Rights." In short, manly courage and camaraderie during the war mandated racial equality afterward.[28]

By the time veterans of World War II had become elder statesmen, the Good War stood beside the "good" civil rights movement as unquestioned pillars of American politics. Many of the veterans who came to power from the late 1960s to the early 1990s harnessed these narratives for conservative political purposes. Presidents Richard Nixon, Ronald Reagan, and George H. W. Bush were World War II veterans in the Republican Party who pursued southern strategies and projected images as "hard" Cold Warriors to win national elections. These conservative political leaders rarely railed explicitly against the civil rights movement. In fact, they crafted a story of the movement as a moral triumph of Americanism not all that dissimilar to the trope of the Good War. In this story, the movement eliminated racial discrimination at home just as the Good War had defeated the odious bigotry of Nazism in Europe. By the time George H. W. Bush left office in 1993, both the Second World War and the African American civil rights movement had become the subjects of nostalgic narratives that spoke more to the myths of American progress and exceptionalism than to the continuing demands for reform and change. At this juncture of myth and memory, World War II and the African American civil rights movement ushered black men into the pantheon of American heroes, guaranteeing them equal rights as men and as citizens. The promotion of Colin Powell to chairman of the joint chiefs of staff under George H. W. Bush and Bill Clinton (and later to secretary of state under George W. Bush) and the election of President Barack Obama a little over a decade later suggested that there was more than a little truth in this myth. Yet the two public institutions where black men were overrepresented at the end of the twentieth century—American military units and prison cell blocks—suggested that connections between race and manhood remained as complicated at the end of the long postwar period as they were in 1945.[29]

Conclusion

The dissonance between the idealistic rhetoric of World War II and the reality of racism in postwar America created a new militancy among black veterans that spurred the early civil rights movement. While calls to arms reinvigorated traditional notions of manhood during the war, they further illuminated the gulf between what was expected of black men as soldiers and as civilians. Black men had fought to protect democracy in Europe even though they could not vote in Alabama or Mississippi. They were citizen-soldiers who did not enjoy the basic rights of citizenship. They joined up to "man the guns" in a segregated military that rarely treated them as men. Despite these paradoxes, World War II military service gave many black soldiers the opportunity to prove themselves as men in a very traditional sense. Having survived the rite of passage into manhood in military service, black veterans felt differently about themselves, even if many white Americans still did not. The discrimination against black veterans and massive resistance to early civil rights victories like the *Brown* decision revealed the limits of the positive legacies of black military service. The confidence and strength that black veterans gained as soldiers were simply a foundation for future struggle. Whites might reluctantly recognize black sacrifice, service, and even manhood during a time of military crisis, but when the crisis passed, they remained unwilling to fully recognize African Americans' civil rights. That fight would define the long postwar era in America.

On the other side of this struggle were conservative veterans, many of them southerners. World War II had shaped their identities as southern, white, American men, but it did not make them lifelong champions of freedom, equality, and justice for all. As pressure for civil rights grew, southern veterans struggled mightily to use "their" war to justify massive resistance to integration, but the Cold War contest against the left-wing philosophy of communism provided much better cover for an inherently conservative campaign to defend white male supremacy. For these veterans, the short postwar period gave way to a long Cold War that enabled them to find national allies in the fight against racial radicals and big government. By demanding that red-blooded American men join ranks to defeat communism (including the communist philosophy of racial equality), southern leaders tried to harness the "hard" masculinity of the Cold Warrior to defend segregation. Conversely, for several decades after the wars in Europe and the Pacific, black veterans and other civil rights activists were better served by looking back to the Second World War for ideological support and sustenance. In this vision of the long postwar era, civil rights supporters (including many historians) ignored the reality of segregationist veterans, hoping to emphasize what was good in the Good War and great in the "Greatest Generation." But this is not history; it is nationalistic nostalgia. A more critical historical analysis of race and masculinity in the long postwar era must reckon with the ways in which this period saw both a redefinition of black manhood and citizenship and a resurgence of traditional notions of white male supremacy.

Notes

1. Barack Obama, *Dreams from My Father: A Story of Race and Inheritance* (New York: Random House, 2005), 16; Tom Brokaw, *The Greatest Generation* (New York: Random House, 2001).

2. Neil A. Winn, "'The Good War': The Second World War and Postwar American Society" *Journal of Contemporary History* 31, no. 3 (1996): 463–82, and *The Afro-American and the Second World War* (New York: Holmes & Meier, 1993); Mary Pinick Motley, ed., *The Invisible Soldier: The Experience of the Black Soldier in World War II* (Detroit, MI: Wayne State University Press, 1975); Sherna Berger Gluck, *Rosie the Riveter Revisited: Women, the War, and Social Change* (Boston: Plume, 1987); Emily Yellin, *Our Mothers' War: American Women at Home and at the Front During World War II* (New York: Free Press, 2004); Studs Terkel, *The "Good War": An Oral History of World War II* (New York: New Press, 1984).

3. Pete Daniel, "Going Among Strangers: Southern Reactions to World War II," *Journal of American History* 77, no. 3 (December 1990): 886–911; Neil R. McMillen, ed., *Remaking Dixie: The Impact of World War II on the American South* (Jackson: University Press of Mississippi, 1997); John Dittmer, *Local People: The Struggle for Civil Rights in Mississippi* (Urbana-Champaign: University of Illinois Press, 1995); and Jennifer E. Brooks, *Defining the Peace: World War II Veterans, Race, and the Remaking of Southern Political Tradition* (Chapel Hill: University of North Carolina Press, 2004).

4. Quote from Wynn, *The Afro-American and the Second World War*, 21. See also Richard M. Dalfiume, *Desegregation of the US Armed Forces: Fighting on Two Fronts, 1939–1953* (Columbia: University of Missouri Press, 1969); and Daniel Kryder, *Divided Arsenal: Race and the American State During World War II* (Cambridge: Cambridge University Press, 2000).

5. Black corporal quoted in Robert Patterson, *Brown v. Board of Education: A Civil Rights Milestone and Its Troubled Legacy* (New York: Oxford University Press, 2002); Ray Carter interview from Motley, *Invisible Solder*, 106–8.

6. Miller's story was first mentioned in "Torpedo Hit the Arizona First," *New York Times*, December 22, 1941. See also "Navy Cross for Dorrie Miller," *Pittsburgh Courier*, May 16, 1942.

7. Navy Department Memorandum (September 1940) included in Bernard Nalty and Morris J. MacGregor, *Blacks in the Military: Essential Documents* (Wilmington, DE: Scholarly Resources, 1981), 135. Carter interview in Motley, *Invisible Soldier*, 106–8.

8. R. Claire Snyder, *Citizen-Soldiers and Manly Warriors: Military Service and Gender in the Civic Republic Tradition* (Lanham, MD: Rowan & Littlefield, 1999): 6–9. On the legacies of black service in the Civil War, see Eric Foner, *A Short History of Reconstruction, 1863–1877* (New York: Harper & Rowe, 1990), 4, 12. Carter quote from Motley, *Invisible Soldier*, 108.

9. Nelson Peery, *Black Fire: The Making of an American Revolutionary* (New York: The New Press, 1995), 271; Gwendolyn Midlo Hall, *Love, War and the 96th Engineers (Colored)* (Urbana: University of Illinois Press, 1995), 233. Diary entry from Christopher Moore, *Fighting for America: Black Soldiers, The Unsung Heroes of World War II* (New York: Presidio Press, 2005), 144–145. For similar epiphanies by white soldiers, see letter to the Chicago *Defender* reprinted in Phillip McGuire, *Taps for a Jim Crow Army* (Lexington: University of Kentucky Press, 1993), 175; and letter to the NAACP from a white North Carolinian in Walter White, *A Rising Wind* (New York: Doubleday, Doran, and Company, 1945), 126.

10. Nadine Cohodas, *Strom Thurmond and the Politics of Southern Change* (New York: Simon & Schuster, 1993), 33; See also "Biography of Strom Thurmond" (1948) in the J. Strom Thurmond Papers (Mss 100 11A.00175 #01171), Special Collections, Robert Muldrow Cooper Library, Clemson University.

11. For more on Thurmond's military record, see Cohodas, *Strom Thurmond*, 82–3; Jack Bass and Marilyn W. Thompson, *Ol' Strom: An Unauthorized Biography of Strom Thurmond* (Marietta, GA: Longstreet Press, 1998), 73–77; and "Biography of Strom Thurmond" (1948) in the Thurmond Papers (Mss 100 11A.00175 #01171).

12. Daniel, "Going Among Strangers," 886; Morton Sosna, "Introduction," in *Remaking Dixie*, xiv–xv.

13. Brooks, *Defining the Peace*, 4; and Jim Cobb, "World War II and the Mind of the South," in McMillen, ed., *Remaking Dixie*, 6–8. See also Harry S. Ashmore, *Civil Rights and Wrongs: A Memoir of Race and Politics, 1944–1996* (Columbia: University of South Carolina Press, 1997), 48–9.

14. Bass and Thompson, *Ol' Strom*, 80–2; and Cohodas, *Strom Thurmond*, 89.

15. Quotes from Woodard incident reported in George McMillan, "Race Justice in Aiken," *The Nation*, November 23, 1946, in Clayborne Carson, David Garrow, et al., eds. *Reporting Civil Rights: American Journalism 1941–1963* (New York: Library of America, 2003): 82–4; Kari Frederickson, *The Dixiecrat Revolt and the End of the Solid South, 1932–1968* (Chapel Hill: University of North Carolina Press, 2001), 54–5, 58–9; and Bass and Thompson, *Ol' Strom*, 84–85. See also "Willie Earle Lynching Case" (1947), Thurmond Papers (MSS 100 11A.00038 #00306).

16. David McCullough, *Truman* (New York: Simon & Schuster, 1993): 722; Frederickson, *Dixiecrat Revolt*, 54–5.

17. "To Secure These Rights: The Report of the President's Committee on Civil Rights," (December 1947), x, 23, 30–1; http://www.trumanlibrary.org/civilrights/srights1.htm.

18. Ibid., 83–4, 140, 146.

19. "Statement of J. Strom Thurmond: 'Segregation in the Armed Forces'"; McCormick, South Carolina (1950), Thurmond Papers (MSS 100 11A.00493 #01051); and "Address Before the States Rights Democratic Conference or Democratic Party Rally States Rights," Jackson, Mississippi (1948), Thurmond Papers (MSS 100 11A.00128 #00635).

20. Frederickson, *Dixiecrat Revolt*, 101–102; and Frederickson, "'As a Man, I am Interested in States' Rights': Gender, Race, and the Family in the Dixiecrat Party, 1948–50," in *Jumpin' Jim Crow: Southern Politics from Civil War to Civil Rights*, ed. Jane Dailey, Glenda Elizabeth Gilmore, and Bryant Simon (Princeton, NJ: Princeton University Press, 2000), 260–74, 270.

21. Darlene Clark Hine, "The *Briggs v. Elliot* Legacy: Black Culture, Consciousness, and Community before Brown, 1930–1954," *University of Illinois Law Review* 5 (2004): 1062–63; and Jack Bass and W. Scott Poole, *The Palmetto State: The Making of Modern South Carolina* (Columbia: University of South Carolina Press, 2009), 156–57.

22. Robert Patterson, *Second Annual Report, August 1956* (Winona: Association of the Citizens' Councils of Mississippi, 1956); Southern Pamphlet Folio 6860, Rare Book Collection, Wilson Library, University of North Carolina; and Steve Estes, *I Am a Man!: Race, Manhood, and the Civil Rights Movement* (Chapel Hill: University of North Carolina Press, 2005), 48–9.

23. Ashmore, *Civil Rights and Wrongs*, 86; *The Citizens' Councils*, 1956; Earl Warren, *The Memoirs of Earl Warren* (New York: Madison Books, 1977), 291–92.

24. Myrlie Evers-Williams and Manning Marable, eds., *The Autobiography of Medgar Evers: A Hero's Life and Legacy, Revealed through His Writings, Letters, and Speeches* (New York: Basic Civitas Books, 2005), 6–7, 12, 136, 280.

25. Harold H. Martin., "The Trial of 'Delay' Beckwith," *Saturday Evening Post*, March 14, 1964; David Stout, "Byron De La Beckwith Dies; Killer of Medgar Evers Was 80," *New York Times*, January 23, 2001; "Medgar Evers," www.naacp.org.

26. Kyle A. Cuordileone, "'Politics in an Age of Anxiety': Cold War Political Culture and the Crisis in American Masculinity, 1949–1960," *Journal of American History* 87, no. 2 (2000): 515–45. Emphasis in original of Perez quote in "The Challenge to the South and How It Must Be Met," a speech to the Louisiana Citizens' Councils, July 21, 1960, Citizens' Council Collection Box 3 (Folder 12), McCain Library, University of Southern Mississippi.

27. George Lewis, *The White South and the Red Menace: Segregation, Anticommunism, and Massive Resistance, 1945–1965* (Gainesville: University of Florida Press, 2004), 168–69; Mary Dudziak, *Cold War Civil Rights: Race and the Image of American Democracy* (Princeton, NJ: Princeton University Press, 2002); Thomas Borstelmann, *The Cold War and the Color Line: American Race Relations in a Global Context* (Cambridge, MA: Harvard University Press, 2003).

28. Monroe Billington, "Lyndon B. Johnson and Blacks: The Early Years," *Journal of Negro History* 62, no. 1 (1977): 26–42; Lyndon B. Johnson, "Radio and Television Remarks on Signing the Civil Rights Bill" (July 2, 1964), *Public Papers of the Presidents of the United States: Lyndon B. Johnson, 1963–64* (Washington, DC: Government Printing Office, 1965), 2:842–44. Lyndon B. Johnson, "Special Message to Congress: The American Promise" (March 15, 1965), *Public Papers of the Presidents of the United States: Lyndon B. Johnson, 1965* (Washington, DC: Government Printing Office, 1966), 1:281–87.

29. For more on the conservative uses of the civil rights narrative, see Jacquelyn Dowd Hall, "The Long Civil Rights Movement and the Political Uses of the Past," *Journal of American History* 91, no. 4 (March 2005): 1233–63. For more on race (and class) in the American criminal justice system and the all-volunteer military, see Michelle Alexander, *The New Jim Crow: Mass Incarcerations in the Age of Colorblindness* (New York: The New Press, 2012); and Amy Lutz, "Who Joins the Military? A Look at Race, Class, and Immigration Status," *Journal of Political and Military Sociology* 36, no. 2 (Winter 2008): 167–88.

Part III

Restoring Families and Recasting Welfare States

Chapter 9

White on Departure? Race and War Bride Immigration to the United States after World War II

Angela Tudico

Following World War II, thousands of war brides immigrated to the United States from around the world. Some 45,853 Japanese war brides arrived between 1947 and 1964. Along with 14,435 Filipinas, 6,000 Chinese, and 6,432 Koreans, these women composed the largest-ever wave of female immigration from Asia and caused a marked demographic shift in the United States—a 20 percent increase in the Asian-American population in less than fifteen years.[1] European war brides immigrated in even larger numbers. In just the first year following the Allied victory in Europe, for example, at least 35,000 British women came to the United States as new spouses.[2] Throughout the 1940s and 1950s women represented more than half of all immigration to the United States, in part due to the arrival of war brides and fiancées.[3] Though it is difficult to calculate the total number of war brides who arrived on American shores following World War II, the large demographic shift reflects the fact that the postwar era offered unprecedented possibility for migration, especially among women.[4] But not all spouses and fiancées of servicemen had the same opportunity to come to the United States. A series of laws called the War Brides and Fiancée Acts, first passed in 1945 and 1946 respectively, contained racially specific caveats. That is, only those persons who were racially eligible for citizenship were allowed to immigrate. Because of the way these laws were written, they initially excluded many

Japanese war brides. Even after the laws were reformed to be racially and ethnically neutral, however, implementation by Immigration and Naturalization Service (INS) officials violated the spirit of their terms. For European war brides and fiancées in particular, INS officials regulated the immigration process so as to preserve prewar racial and ethnic categories—that is, distinctions that favored northern over southern Europeans. Through an analysis of INS case files, this chapter examines the postwar immigration of European and Japanese war brides to the United States and the extent to which it was possible for women to use these laws as a way to gain entry to the United States and commence new lives with their American husbands.[5] These files suggest that prewar ideas about race and ethnicity, especially dramatic distinctions between northern and southern Europeans, remained powerful after the war.

This chapter first presents historians' views of the racial and ethnic context for immigration that was in place before the war, examining in particular arguments about how members of specific groups became "whitened." It then discusses prewar American immigration policy, with particular emphasis on the quota system established in the 1920s, as well as changes to that policy that began to emerge during the war years. The laws passed on behalf of war brides and fiancées in the immediate postwar era served to further erode the rigidity of American immigration law. It finally assesses how INS officials processed war bride and fiancée immigration from Europe and Japan to the United States, paying particular attention to the agency's treatment of British, German, Greek, Italian, and Japanese women. A comparison of these groups reveals immigration officials' insistence on maintaining ethnic specificity among European war brides and undermines the current understanding of World War II as a turning point in the whitening of second-wave immigrants (from southern and eastern Europe) in the United States.[6]

How Immigrants Become White

Historians have argued that World War II was a turning point in the "whitening" of second-wave immigrants in the United States. In *American Crucible: Race and Nation in the Twentieth Century*, for example, Gary Gerstle contends that the experience of military service rendered racial and ethnic differences less important than the bonds forged by men fighting together in the same unit. According to Gerstle, "The military became, in effect, an enormously important site for melting the many streams of Euro-Americans into one white race."[7] World War I, he argues, did not have the same impact on the whitening of southern and eastern European immigrants, because "the American soldiers were together for too short a time and involved in too little combat for the army-as-melting-pot to erase ethnic and regional differences."[8] Not until World War II were second-wave immigrants fully embraced by the racialized American nation that Gerstle describes in his work—a nation that still excluded African Americans, as was apparent by the segregation of the US armed forces that lasted until 1948.[9]

Although the military certainly offered one site in which second-wave immigrants were able to become white, the transition to whiteness, as historians such as James R. Barrett and David Roediger contend, was an uneven process for those who occupied an "in-between" status in the American racial hierarchy. In their article, "Inbetween Peoples: Race, Nationality and the 'New Immigrant' Working Class," Barrett and Roediger argue that during the early part of the twentieth century, second-wave southern and eastern European immigrants occupied a status between white and nonwhite. More important, this in-between status was not consistent. They explain, "The courts consistently allowed 'new [European] immigrants,' whose racial status was ambiguous in the larger culture, to be naturalized as 'white' citizens and almost as consistently turned down non-European applicants as 'nonwhite.'"[10] It is precisely the status of southern and eastern Europeans in the national state, specifically in terms of immigration policy, that this chapter seeks to address. Although all European war bride immigrants were nominally white, and Congress made no racial or ethnic distinctions in the war brides or fiancée acts when it came to Europeans, in practice the INS maintained racial and ethnic differences. This arm of the US state retained, then, the "in-between" status of southern and eastern Europeans.

Loosening Immigration Restrictions

The context for war bride legislation was the racially structured immigration system set in place by Congress in the 1920s, which itself built upon earlier immigration restrictions, most notably the Chinese Exclusion Act of 1882. Starting in 1924, US law completely excluded immigration from Japan and placed quotas on immigrants from other nations.[11] The number of immigrants annually admitted from any national group depended on that group's percentage of the US population in the nineteenth century.[12] Because of the composition of the population at that time, this system favored countries from northern and western Europe, such as Great Britain, and curtailed immigration from southern and eastern European countries like Italy and Greece. Meanwhile, immigration from Asia was virtually halted.

When the INS evaluated the quota system near the end of World War II, the agency explained how effective the 1924 law had been in changing the composition of immigrants coming to the United States. It acknowledged that with the quotas introduced in 1924, the goal of Congress was to "shift the trend in European immigration from a predominance of southern and eastern European immigration back to a predominance of northern and western European immigration, so as to admit immigrants who were considered more easily assimilable."[13] Nations in northern and western Europe constituted 81.9 percent of the total annual quota allotment, while southern and eastern European countries were granted only 16 percent.[14] This meant that a country such as Great Britain had an annual quota of 65,721 immigrants, while Italy received only 5,802. Other southern and eastern European nations had even lower quotas; for example, Greece had only 307.[15] Because northern and western countries enjoyed such a large proportion of the slots, they never exhausted their availability. Indeed, in regard to Great Britain, the INS reported, "with the exception of the fiscal years 1930 and 1931, at no time did the number admitted exceed 7 percent of the total number admissible."[16] As a whole, northern and western European countries never used more than 32 percent of their quotas between 1931 and 1944. The INS somewhat clinically noted that this level of fulfillment was relatively low, especially compared to southern and eastern European nations, whose quota fulfillments "rose sharply" and were "practically exhausted" each year.[17]

During the war years, even before it moved to change immigration law to accommodate war bride and fiancée immigration, Congress began to revise restrictive immigration policy. In 1943, Congress reversed its policy on excluding all Chinese immigrants, which had been in place since 1882, and set a tiny quota (105 people per year) for that nation. Immediately following the war, two separate but similar acts allowed for the immigration and naturalization of immigrants from India and the Philippines. These changes can be attributed to what historians have termed "a good behavior prize," as well as activism by Asian Americans in the United States.[18]

These laws began to break down long-established barriers to immigration from East and South Asia, but Congress did not move to accommodate the new wave of migrants produced by international marriages until GIs and their new wives and fiancées began to exert pressure. They quickly found that the American immigration system was ill equipped to handle a large influx of women from countries around the globe. Even before the war ended, the foreign wives of US citizens applied for nonquota visas to immigrate to the United States in such numbers that the INS reported the strain being placed on their office. The agency noted,

> . . . visa petitions filed by the servicemen to enable their wives to obtain non-quota visas are an indication of the numerical importance of that group. In the early part of the fiscal year 1944, seven-eighths of all visa petitions received at the Central Office were of this type.[19]

In 1944, most of these petitions being filed were on behalf of women in Great Britain, Australia, and New Zealand, where many GIs had been stationed. The INS indicated a simultaneous rise in petitions on behalf of Italian nationals, however, and correctly predicted a further increase from other southern and eastern European nations as the US armed forces moved across Europe as military action and postwar duty dictated. The INS also recognized the tenuous status of fiancées compared with wives of servicemen, who themselves were accorded nonquota status under immigration law.[20] Fiancées, they warned, had "no special rights or privileges under the immigration law."[21] With this in mind, the INS began to discuss the need for new legislation to facilitate the immigration of war brides and later fiancées. Administration officials consulted the INS as they worked to craft the legislation, various versions of which they would take to Congress throughout 1945.

An early version of the bill that would evolve into the War Brides Act of 1945 proposed making war brides citizens immediately upon their marriage to GIs. The proposed legislation would have applied only to those racially eligible for citizenship, thereby excluding Japanese war brides entirely. Nevertheless, the debate within the government surrounding this proposal revealed a range of attitudes toward these potential immigrants.[22] The debate took place among various government officials, including the secretary of war, attorney general, and INS officials who worked particularly hard to draft the legislation.

Surprisingly, most of the government officials favored automatic citizenship for these women. One INS official who largely favored immediate citizenship for war brides explained his support in pragmatic terms: "In declining to grant citizenship we merely put these wives to a great deal of trouble in accomplishing what can be accomplished under existing law in approximately two years."[23] In addition to explaining how this bill would amend the law to expedite the immigration and naturalization process for spouses of citizens, this official believed such revisions to existing laws were sound, because they benefited men and women serving their country during war. As he put it succinctly, "We would be justified in going the whole distance as a war measure and in behalf of our citizen service people."[24] Both of the justifications would be employed later that year to defend the legislation on behalf of citizen soldiers and war brides. It passed in December 1945 as Public Law (P.L.) 271, or the War Brides Act. Variations on the argument about citizens' service to the nation would reappear in the following years to justify passage of the Fiancée Act (June 1946), suggesting a connection between this idea and the passage of legislation on behalf of both war brides and fiancées.

The War Department did not make the same connection, however, and objected strongly to the first war bride legislation proposed. Secretary of War Henry Stimson issued the War Department's official position on the legislation to Richard B. Russell, chairman of the US Senate Committee on Immigration. Stimson's position reflected themes such as waging war efficiently and the moral character of these immigrant women. Stimson's first objection was to the purported immorality of potential immigrants; he questioned the "good moral character" of these women, whom he suspected of prostituting themselves to gain entry to the United States. Stimson lacked confidence even in the military's own screening process. GIs had to obtain permission from their commanding officers to marry, but Stimson did not believe this process was sufficient to weed out unworthy immigrants.[25] Stimson also relayed his fear that the war brides bill would serve as a distraction and undermine the effectiveness of military personnel overseas, thereby obstructing the chief objective of the military: winning the war.

T. B. Shoemaker, acting commissioner for the INS, discounted most of the concerns presented by Stimson and offered an argument in favor of automatic citizenship for war brides that again invoked the idea that the citizen soldier merited such treatment for services rendered to his (or her) country. "The bill," he noted, "by reason of the service rendered by the citizen, in his interests and not primarily that of the one he marries, would extend automatic citizenship to the one he marries."[26] Shoemaker thus attempted to refocus attention on the bill away from the unknown (and possibly dangerous or unwanted) war bride population to the citizen GI who had served his or her country honorably and deserved to be compensated by the government—in this case, by eliminating red tape from the long and involved naturalization process for his bride (or her bridegroom).[27] In effect, the INS shifted the focus to the GI and made him or her the prime beneficiary of the legislation, rather than the war bride or groom. This rhetorical re-visioning of the bill, along with support from other government officials, including Attorney General Francis Biddle,[28] would not be enough to convince the War Department to support this first version of war brides legislation or for Congress to pass it in this form, but it proved useful in debates on later legislation.[29]

In December 1945, Congress passed P.L. 271, the first of a series of war brides acts entitled, "A bill to expedite the admission to the United States of alien spouses and alien minor children of citizen members of the United States armed forces," commonly referred to as the War Brides Act (WBA). Notably, the House Report on the WBA reiterated the arguments previously used by the attorney general and some INS officials in support of these bills: "One of the reasons for the introduction of this measure is . . . that it is believed such strong equities run in favor of these service men and women in the right of having their families with them."[30] The new legislation allowed war brides and grooms to enter the United States as nonquota immigrants and offered them a moderately expedited immigration and naturalization process by eliminating the requirement for medical exams in their country of origin (preexaminations) and permitting them to begin paperwork overseas rather than in the United States. One of the most significant and radical aspects of this law was that it explicitly circumvented the quota system, which had been in place since the 1920s. Section 2 of the bill read, "Regardless of section 9 of the Immigration Act of 1924, any alien admitted under section 1 of this Act shall be deemed to be a nonquota immigrant as defined in section 4(a) of the Immigration Act of 1924."[31] Further, the ensuing renewals of the bill allowed the liberalized provisions to be in place for the next twenty years. With the passage of the WBA, a new window of opportunity opened for immigration from countries whose quotas had long been overburdened.

However, although the WBA represented a significant shift in immigration law, it stopped short of circumventing all of the restrictions of the 1920s—particularly the complete exclusion of specific racial groups, including the Japanese. The bills drafted in 1945 stipulated that entry would be granted only to "any alien racially eligible to naturalization."[32] Since the then-current law (a holdover from earlier restrictive laws) excluded the Japanese, this meant that Japanese war brides would be automatically barred. By 1947, however, under pressure from thousands of international couples, Congress approved the first in a series of laws providing loopholes for Japanese war brides. P.L. 213, the Japanese War Brides Act, passed on July 22, 1947, as an amendment to the original WBA.[33] The act stated, "The alien spouse of an American citizen by a marriage occurring before thirty days after the enactment of this Act, shall not be considered as inadmissible because of race, if otherwise admissible under this Act."[34]

The law was only a partial victory for Japanese war bride couples, however, because it was mainly a temporary measure: the couple had to have married prior to July 22, 1947, or within one month of the passage of the bill. Nonetheless, it represented an important shift in US immigration policy: for the first time in more than twenty years, US immigration law admitted at least some Japanese to the United States. Moreover, Japanese spouses of American soldiers would have the same access to the WBA as spouses from Europe, allowing for a period (albeit brief) of equal treatment under American law.[35] Japanese war brides had another chance to come to the United States when Congress passed a second Japanese War Brides Act (P.L. 717) on August 19, 1950. This version was similar to the first, but it did not expire until February 1951, this time allowing couples a six-month window to marry and so making the wives eligible to immigrate. When this law expired, Congress extended it again, to March 1952.[36] Timetables became a hallmark of war bride legislation, and they were particularly crucial for Japanese war bride couples faced with a limited window to take advantage of changes in US immigration law.

The series of war brides acts did not allow for the immigration of servicemen's fiancées, only spouses. Fiancées were subject to quotas like any other immigrant. But in 1946, as the quotas for certain countries from which servicemen's fiancées originated became oversubscribed, Congress saw fit to pass a new set of laws: the fiancée acts. Congress and INS officials first focused on Australia and New Zealand, because those nations had extremely small quotas, about 100 people per year. Later they perceived a special need for a fiancée provision for women from countries such as Greece, a nation with a much larger quota than Australia or New Zealand but one that was still heavily oversubscribed. On June 29, 1946, six months after the passage of the initial War Brides Act, P.L. 471, "Admission of the Alien Fiancées or Fiancés of Members of the Armed Forces of the United States," became law.[37] P.L. 471, commonly known as the Fiancée Act, granted fiancées nonquota status, but like the WBA it restricted immigration to those who came from nations racially eligible for citizenship. Other strict provisions accompanied this nonquota status for fiancées. The couple had three months to marry once the fiancée arrived in the United States, or the potential spouse would face deportation. Additionally, the soldier had to post a $500 bond to cover the cost of potential deportation. Strict provisions aside, this law sidestepped the restrictive immigration policies of the prewar era and opened another avenue for postwar migration for the women and men romantically linked with American soldiers.

Ethnic Differences in the Implementation of Immigration Policies

By circumventing the existing tight quotas on migration from southern and eastern Europe, these laws provided an additional means by which people from those regions could immigrate to the United States, yet their very existence shows that the United States continued to make a distinction between southern and eastern Europe on the one hand and northern and western Europe on the other. Even though Italian war brides legally benefited from the new law the same way other European war brides did, they experienced heightened scrutiny from INS officials during the implementation of the WBA.

One basic difference concerned preexaminations before embarkation for the United States. On March 4, 1946, E. E. Salisbury, an INS official stationed in Tidworth, England, wrote a series of letters to the INS officials stationed in Europe—specifically Italy, France, and Ireland—on how to process war brides. The letter to Eugene Cole, the INS official primarily responsible for processing Italian war brides and stationed in Naples, differed from the other two letters: preexamination would stop in Tidworth, England; Le Havre, France; and Belfast, Ireland, but would continue in Naples.[38] Salisbury did not explain the need to continue preexaminations in Italy, but he did enclose copies of the revised procedures to be carried out in England and France for Cole's edification. The special directive issued by Salisbury had an impact on war brides from other nations as well. According to a report written by Cole in April, war brides from Italy and other places in the Mediterranean theater—specifically Greece, Egypt, Algiers, and Tunis—would ship through Naples.[39] War brides from western European nations such as Belgium, Germany, and the Netherlands would ship through Le Havre. In other words, Italian and Greek women were grouped with and treated the same as women from northern Africa rather than grouped with women from northern and western Europe, again suggesting that in practice they were deemed nonwhite.

In addition to creating differences in how southern and eastern European war brides were to be processed, the INS, and specifically Eugene Cole, questioned the very legitimacy of some of the marriages involving Italian women.

Cultural differences in acceptable marriage practices between the United States and southern European countries caused a problem for war bride couples trying to take advantage of the special legislation passed on their behalf. Proxy marriages, in which a man could marry via letter or messenger, were regarded as legitimate civil marriages under Italian law and were not unusual during wartime.[40] In several reports to his superiors, however, Cole cited proxy marriages as a problem. In the case of a marriage between an Italian woman and a GI from Ohio, Cole stated that he found it particularly troublesome because it involved a child, and he requested instructions from Salisbury. This case occurred in April 1946, before the fiancée act had been passed or any special dispensation had been created for fiancées, something that Cole stated he believed would have solved the problem.[41]

In another instance, Cole stated that he "refused to consider the case until an 'in person' marriage was performed."[42] War bride couples sometimes attempted to marry via proxy if the soldier's military unit had been reassigned to a different location before the couple had the chance to wed. Cole, however, did not recognize this practice because the 1924 immigration laws did not recognize proxy marriages as legitimate for the purposes of granting spousal privilege (and nonquota status) to potential immigrants. He did not think that the special circumstances of the postwar military justified a change of policy on such marriages. The continuing hold of the 1924 law in this way was exacerbated by the Italian legal system. According to Cole, "The Italian authorities hesitated to allow the second marriage because they recognized the proxy marriage and had regularly recorded it in the records of the commune."[43] These cultural differences in acceptable marriage practices caused a problem for war bride couples trying to take advantage of the special legislation passed on their behalf. Japanese war bride couples would experience similar problems with the WBA, but unlike the Europeans they would never be able to make use of the fiancée acts, since they were excluded from those entirely.

Cases involving Greek fiancées also demonstrate that women from southern and eastern Europe received closer scrutiny from INS officials than women from northern and western Europe. Although one would expect no differentiation among various groups of Europeans based on the war bride and fiancée laws as written, the implementation of the new legislation tells a different story. In the summer of 1947, some INS officials expressed concern that Greek nationals were taking unfair advantage of the Fiancée Act. The Chicago office initially raised the issue in June, about one year after the fiancée law passed. F. M. Symmes, chief in the Adjudications Division in

Chicago, called his superiors' attention to the large number of the cases he had handled for Greek American soldiers hoping to bring Greek fiancées to the United States. He described the pattern of these potential unions to the district director as follows:

> In practically all of the cases the soldier has never seen, nor talked with the girl . . . . Some relative of the girl in this country shows her picture to a discharged soldier and he is asked to bring that girl over and marry her. They correspond some but that is the extent of the acquaintanceship. In a number of the cases the relative puts up the bond for the soldier.[44]

The protocol these Greek American GIs and Greek women followed fell perfectly in line with the rules specifically outlined by the Fiancée Act; for the most part, Symmes conceded, the required $500 bonds were posted and the GIs went through with the marriage. In one case, however, a GI was promised a house and property by a Greek woman's American uncle if the two would marry. When he did not receive the house and property after the woman arrived, the GI refused to marry her, and the woman was deported when three months had elapsed and no wedding had taken place.

The "safeguards" put in place by the House of Representatives for the Fiancée Act ensured that such problems would not burden the United States but only the war bride couple, or in this case, one half of the couple. What Symmes most likely did not care for was the style of courtship and engagement among this group of American GIs and foreign women who were making use of the Fiancée Act; he felt it violated the spirit of the act. Although the Greek and Greek American couples followed the rules of the Fiancée Act to the letter, Symmes questioned whether these unions conformed to what he believed the intent of the law to be. "I am certain that the law was not intended to cover the cases mentioned above," he explained. "I have read it over carefully, but am at a loss as to how to stop such a clear misuse of the law. The American Consuls are the only ones who can stop it."[45] Symmes could not find a way to bar such unions, however, because they were perfectly legal under the Fiancée Act. The law itself did not specify the types of engagements.

Nevertheless, immigration officials construed these marriage customs as "abuses" of the US law. Symmes' fears that Greek Americans were trying to circumvent the Fiancée Act seemed (to him) to be confirmed by the actions of one Mrs. Askounes of the Immigrants' Protective League. This woman, he reported, "gave a radio speech in Greek and told her listeners that a G.I.

could bring over any Greek girl and marry her, even though he had never seen her before. This may account for the number of bonds being made for Greek girls lately."[46] Askounes' radio address may have indeed accounted for an increase of petitions among Greek fiancées, since she was informing the community about laws of which they may not have been aware. But in reality neither her actions nor those of the Greek community constituted a technical misuse of the Fiancée Act. What seems most evident is that the Greek American community was eager to bring in more immigrants from Greece than existing quotas allowed.

Various INS officials responded to the alarm that Symmes raised as his report worked its way through the agency until it finally reached headquarters. Not all INS officials reacted with the same level of anxiety as Symmes did, but they agreed that the situation required attention and possible action. The latter came from G. J. Haering, INS visa division chief, in the form of heightened scrutiny: "The Department is cautioning consular offices to be especially careful in reaching decisions in the cases of applicants for visas under Public Law 471," Haering wrote, "and it is hoped that the abuses, such as those reported by your Chicago office, may be obviated so far as it may be possible."[47] While more restrained than Symmes, Haering's response did produce the heightened scrutiny that Symmes had hoped for from consular offices. This greater scrutiny demonstrates that distinctions between southern and northern Europeans remained very much alive and meaningful among INS officials after the war. Prewar racial and ethnic categories were not dead or even blurred in this particular area of policy and experience: Greeks had not become fully white.

As a result, the immigration process for Greek American GIs with Greek fiancées became more rigorous. Furthermore, it seemed that all consular offices would be practicing heightened scrutiny, not just in Greece but in other southern and eastern European nations with oversubscribed quotas, such as Italy and Poland. Thus all couples hoping to benefit from the Fiancée Act would feel the repercussions of the alarm that Symmes had raised about Greeks. Yet Haering's response conceded that even this action would be inadequate to deal with the alleged problem—eliminating it as much as possible but not entirely. The records do not reveal whether the problem escalated further or whether the increased scrutiny from the consular offices solved it to the satisfaction of the visa division and central office.

The fact that war brides from northern and western Europe, specifically England and Germany, never experienced problems with the INS like those faced by war brides and fiancées from Italy and Greece indicates their status as preferred immigrants, just as in the prewar era. In fact, the INS worked to clarify the status of German immigrant women and ease their immigration process. German war brides in particular experienced few problems, even though they hailed from a former enemy nation. The INS clearly stated that this status would have no impact on the German war bride immigration experience. This throws into question the heightened scrutiny from INS officials faced by the women from Italy, North Africa, and Japan. In November 1948, a woman from Long Island, New York, requested information about the regulations regarding "enemy aliens entering this country" on behalf of a GI stationed in Germany (apparently her son) who hoped to bring his German fiancée to the United States.[48] The INS responded by saying, "The fact that she is German does not in itself affect her admissibility to the United States under immigration laws."[49]

Since Germans enjoyed a privileged place on the continuum of acceptable immigrants for the United States and thus garnered a large quota, German women did not even need the special provisions set up by the fiancée acts. The immigration quota for Germany was not oversubscribed, and in fact it was much easier for Germans to immigrate under the 1924 law because of the strict regulations set up under the Fiancée Act and the $500 bond required—a hefty sum in the immediate postwar era. INS officials specifically clarified this issue when some German fiancée couples posted bonds and attempted to immigrate under the Fiancée Act, even though it was unnecessary. Ironically, commercial airlines transporting German fiancées periodically misunderstood the regulations and would not allow the women to travel without evidence of the bond required by fiancées. When one INS official became aware of the problem, he wrote to various airline officials to explain the regulations.[50] Airline employees were not the only ones confused by the ins and outs of US immigration policy, however, and the INS routinely attempted to clarify these same rules to various parties, even within the agency.[51] In their explanations, INS officials frequently—and openly—made a distinction between women from nations such as Great Britain and Germany, who did not need the Fiancée Act, and women from Italy and Greece, who still did. The persistence of this distinction shows that while the war had created a new opportunity for migration for all European women (as well as men to a much lesser extent), those opportunities continued to be limited by prewar American ideas about race and ethnicity.

Further evidence of the privileged racial status of northern and western Europeans may be seen in the INS's treatment of desertion cases—instances in which war brides had been abandoned by American husbands who refused to accept the legitimacy of their marriages abroad and had possibly married someone else once back stateside. The most obvious example of contrasting treatment can be seen in the way that the agency handled cases of desertion for British and Italian war brides; the British women in such instances received greater assistance from INS officials, while the Italians were subjected to scrutiny. Desertion by GI husbands was a risk that all war brides faced, as Eugene Cole mentioned in one of his reports from Naples, noting cases in which "the serviceman refuses to request the wife's transportation or threatens divorce."[52]

Although women from many different countries suffered desertion, the INS investigated only the cases of British women, depriving the others of needed help. Assistance consisted mainly of interviewing husbands who had abandoned their British wives. In most of the cases, the husbands flatly refused to accept their British spouses, often because they had found new wives once back in the United States. Cases could become quite complicated. One former GI, for example, told an INS official that he wished to divorce his British war bride in order to marry the American woman he was then living with in Indiana. Asked if he wished his wife and son to come to the United States, the former soldier declared,

> No, I absolutely do not. . . . I don't think the child is mine and she forced me into marriage and she also failed to tell me of her mental condition before I married her. Therefore, I don't want them here and I am not able to support them if they do come. I further do not believe that she is a fit subject to come to the US and become a citizen.[53]

The outcome of these cases remains unknown. The significance lies, however, in the INS's pursuit of such cases—British war bride cases only. Rather than trying to prevent excess immigration from Great Britain, INS officials actually encouraged this immigration by attempting to resolve desertion cases for British women.[54] In these cases, it was the American husbands, not the immigrant war brides, who received heightened scrutiny from the INS.

Compared with their European counterparts, Japanese war brides encountered much greater difficulties. Japanese women were never able to take advantage of the fiancée acts because, unlike the WBA, they applied only to women and men "racially eligible for citizenship." Like Italian war brides, the legitimacy of their marriages was also routinely called into question. In the case of Japanese marriages, however, the Japanese government was the first to challenge their legitimacy. Many GIs and Japanese women participated in ceremonies that INS officials came to call "saki [*sic*] marriages," which were not recognized as legal until they were registered with the Japanese government.[55] Unlike the situation in Italy with wartime proxy marriages, both the husband and wife were present at the Japanese ceremonies, but since the Japanese government withheld legalization until the marriages were registered, the United States followed suit and also refused to recognize them for the purposes of the WBA.[56] The United States could claim that it was simply following the rule of law in the war bride's country, although this did not hold true for Italy, in which proxy marriages were perfectly legal. Yet the INS challenged the legitimacy of both types of marriages. For women from both countries, the results were similar: limiting their right to use the war brides acts and, as a result, curbing immigration from Italy and Japan.

Conclusion

Against the ravaged postwar landscape of death, devastation, and occupation that was reality for many Japanese and European women following World War II, the complex permutations of American immigration laws and the ways in which the INS chose to apply those laws may seem trivial. Yet for the thousands of women who found a unique opportunity for international courtship amid this setting and whose futures included marriages or engagements to American servicemen, the implementation of these laws determined whether their new lives would be possible, difficult to secure, or completely unfeasible. INS officials' stringent adherence to the prewar racial and ethnic order undergirded by earlier iterations of American immigration law—even in the face of explicit legal reforms—preserved the United States' preference for immigrants from northern and western Europe. Perhaps not surprisingly, Japanese war brides faced the greatest problems with immigrating to the United States, but the experiences of German women casts doubt on the assumption that it was merely Japan's enmity with the United States that lay at the root of their difficulties. Moreover, women from the countries of southern and eastern Europe—those that fought with as well as against the United States—encountered difficulties as well. Just as the war brides and fiancée acts opened new doors for immigration, they simultaneously exposed these women to a more stringent immigration process than that experienced by their Anglo-Saxon counterparts. These prejudicial holdovers from earlier immigration restrictions curtailed the potentially seismic transnational demographic shift that war bride and fiancée immigration might have produced and imposed a limit on the change that World War II brought about.

In many ways, the findings of this chapter are quite prosaic. It is not so surprising that World War II, though having wrought dramatic changes in gender and racial norms on the US home front, did not in and of itself completely upend the racial order. Just as Jim Crow and disenfranchisement survived the war intact, so did most of the racial imperatives that guided American immigration policy. It would take nearly twenty years following the end of World War II for a century-long civil rights movement to accomplish the major legislative victories of the Civil Rights Act and Voting Rights Act of the mid-1960s. In 1965, the same year that the Voting Rights Act passed, the new Immigration Act abolished the use of nation-of-origin quotas that had limited and racialized immigration since the 1920s.[57] American immigration laws and their application followed a similar trajectory as other postwar racial battles, and it may not be unexpected that the INS processed southern and eastern European immigrants differently than northern and western European ones. War brides and fiancées experienced a provisional and exceptional legislative status compared to other immigrants, but legislative victories do not always produce immediate egalitarian treatment. That some INS officials refused to grant special status to southern and eastern European war brides and fiancées, but instead treated them like other immigrants from those countries, reveals the lag between law and practice and the recalcitrance of prewar ideas about race, ethnicity, and immigration. It also suggests that the legislation passed to reward American soldiers who fought the good fight abroad was able to go only so far. Rhetoric surrounding the war brides acts and GI Bill was certainly persuasive (the laws passed, after all), but the application of such postwar benefits was uneven.[58] Not all American soldiers returning home benefited equally from such laws—and neither did their war brides and fiancées.

Notes

1. Caroline Chung Simpson, "'Out of an obscure place': Japanese War Brides and Cultural Pluralism in the 1950s," *Differences: A Journal of Feminist Cultural Studies* 10 (1998): 47–81, 51.

2. Jenel Virden, *Good-bye, Piccadilly: British War Brides in America* (Urbana-Champaign: University of Illinois Press, 1996), 3.

3. Martha Gardner, *The Qualities of a Citizen: Women, Immigration, and Citizenship, 1870–1965* (Princeton, NJ: Princeton University Press, 2005), 225.

4. It is difficult to calculate exact numbers for war bride and fiancée immigration to the United States, as these women did not always immigrate under these classifications. See, for example, the discussion of German fiancées later in this chapter, and also Susan Zeiger, *Entangling Alliances: Foreign War Brides and American Soldiers in the Twentieth Century* (New York: New York University Press, 2010), chaps. 3–5.

5. In 2003 the Immigration and Naturalization Service (INS) ceased to exist and was replaced by the US Citizenship and Immigration Services (USCIS). The USCIS History Office and Library continues to house INS records, as well as guides to INS records housed at the National Archives and Records Administration (NARA). Because the agency name was changed long after the time period covered in this project, I will refer to INS archival collections and case files, even though they are housed in the USCIS History Office and Library.

6. The title of this chapter specifically refers to *White on Arrival: Italians, Race, Color, and Power in Chicago, 1890–1945* (New York: Oxford University Press, 2003), in which Thomas Guglielmo argues that Italian immigrants were "largely accepted as white by the widest variety of people and institutions" (6).

7. Gary Gerstle, *American Crucible: Race and Nation in the Twentieth Century* (Princeton, NJ: Princeton University Press, 2001), 188. See also chapter 5, "Good War, Race War, 1941–1945."

8. Ibid, 88.

9. Similarly, Ira Katznelson argues that military service and particularly the GI Bill following the war favored white men more than African American men. Local implementation of benefits, for example, allowed white veterans greater access to home loans than African American veterans. See Katznelson, *When Affirmative Action Was White: An Untold History of Racial Inequality in Twentieth-Century America* (New York: Norton, 2005).

10. James R. Barrett and David Roediger, "Inbetween Peoples: Race, Nationality and the 'New Immigrant' Working Class," *Journal of American Ethnic History* 16 (1997): 3–44, 5.

11. The Immigration Act of 1924 was not the first time that the United States restricted immigration from Japan. The Gentleman's Agreement between the United States and Japan in 1907 halted the immigration of additional laborers from Japan, though it did permit wives of Japanese men already in the United States to immigrate. See Gardner, *Qualities of a Citizen*, 17.

12. For an excellent in-depth discussion of this quota system and how it came to be, see Mae M. Ngai, "The Architecture of Race in American Immigration Law: A Reexamination of the Immigration Act of 1924," *Journal of American History* 86, no. 1 (June 1999): 67–92. See also Ngai, *Impossible Subjects: Illegal Aliens and the Making of Modern America* (Princeton, NJ: Princeton University Press, 2004). Notably, Ngai argues that although all European immigrants were categorized as white by this system, there was a hierarchy of preferences within the categorization based on nationality, with northern and western Europeans given preference over southern and eastern Europeans.

13. Gertrude Krichefsky, "Quota Immigration, 1925–1944," *INS Monthly Review*, June 1945: 156–59, 156. *INS Monthly Review* was an in-house INS publication.

14. Ibid. The outstanding 2.1 percent of quota space was dispersed among Africa and Asia.

15. Ibid. 158.

16. Ibid., 159. Germany used as little as 5.1 percent of its annual allotment of quota immigration in 1933, for example.

17. Ibid.

18. Roger Daniels, *Coming to America: A History of Immigration and Ethnicity in American Life* (New York: Harper Collins, 1990), 328.

19. "Wives and Fiancées of Members of Our Overseas Forces," *INS Monthly Review*, December 1944: 78–79, 78.

20. Ibid. Wives of American citizens were granted nonquota status under immigration law.

21. Ibid.

22. This debate constituted an INS file that contained correspondence between various government officials. The file, number 56215/261, was titled, "Making citizens of US citizen spouses of US citizens serving honorably in armed forces during WWII." See Entry 9, RG 85, File 56215/261, NARA.

23. Shaughnessy to Carusi, March 19, 1945, Entry 9, RG 85, File 56215/261, NARA. Jenel Virden also discussed the fact that INS officials supported war bride immigration. See Virden, *Good-bye, Piccadilly*, 53–5.

24. Shaughnessy to Carusi, March 19, 1945, NARA.

25. Ibid.

26. Ibid.

27. Shoemaker had addressed the gendered implications of the proposed war brides bill in his first discussion of the legislation in March 1945. He explained that the bill would be applied equally to male and female citizens who had served honorably in the armed forces. He noted that this bill represented no groundbreaking legislation as far as foreign women were concerned, because "prior to September 22, 1922, alien women acquired citizenship immediately upon their marriage to male United States citizens." Shoemaker was right, as only in 1922 had the Cable Act revised immigration law in such a way that a wife's citizenship remained independent of her husband's. If war brides were granted automatic citizenship, it would simply restore earlier treatment of women's citizenship. Where foreign husbands were concerned, however, this legislation offered the possibility for something entirely new in US immigration law. As Shoemaker explained, "This is the first time that alien men will have acquired citizenship by virtue of marriage to female citizens (provided the bill is enacted into law). However, it is not seen where there would be any justification in drawing any distinction between the sexes." Even though this version of the war brides bill did not pass, the proposal remains significant for several reasons: the bill treated men and women in the armed forces equally, and the fact that the bill would have made foreign husbands automatic citizens upon marriage was never used publicly as an argument against the bill. The eventual war brides and fiancée acts followed this early bill, granting equal benefits to male and female citizen soldiers and their foreign spouses and fiancées. See T. B. Shoemaker to Hugh B. Cox, March 6, 1945, Entry 9, RG 85, File 56215/261, NARA.

28. Attorney General Francis Biddle to Secretary of War, March 1945, Entry 9, RG 85, File 56215/261, NARA. INS officials assisted Attorney General Biddle with the drafting of his letter in favor of the bill. See L. Paul Winings to Edward Shaughnessy, memorandum, March 30, 1945, Entry 9, RG 85, File 56215/261, NARA. Additionally, the INS and Biddle had been in contact with each other about war bride legislation prior to the drafting

of the letter. See, for example, Edward Shaughnessy to L. Paul Winings, March 6, 1945, Entry 9, RG 85 File 56215/261, NARA.

29. Gardner also notes that the war brides and fiancée acts "rewarded the sacrifices of soldiers by reuniting them with their foreign-born wives." See *Qualities of a Citizen*, 225.

30. House Report No. 1320, 79th Congress, 1st Session, *Congressional Record,* December 10, 1945, from Entry 9, RG 85, File 56226/527, NARA. In tandem with the idea of the honorable service provided by soldiers, the House report indicated that the idea of the family and reunion was a powerful concept in terms of supporting this bill. For a more detailed discussion of this idea see Gardner, *Qualities of a Citizen*, 223–25.

31. Act of December 28, 1945, Admission of Alien Spouses and Alien Minor Children of Citizen Members of the United States Armed Forces, United States Congress, USCIS History Office and Library.

32. See proposed H.R. 2650, for example, and the enacted H.R. 4857.

33. The Japanese War Brides Act passed the House and Senate without objection, just as the War Brides Act had. "Admission to the United States of Alien Spouses," 80th Congress, 1st Session, Congressional Record—House, June 16, 1947, and "Admission to the United States of Alien Spouses," 80th Congress, 1st Session, Congressional Record—Senate, July 16, 1947.

34. Act of July 22, 1947, *Admissibility of Alien Spouses of Citizen Members of the United States Armed Forces*, United States Congress, USCIS History Office and Library.

35. Gardner completely ignores this aspect of the war bride/fiancée acts in her work. She claims that Japanese women were never allowed under either set of laws, which is inaccurate. See *Qualities of a Citizen*, 224–231. Her narrative focuses on the fiancée acts and admission of only racially eligible immigrant women, but does not discuss laws like P.L. 213, which allowed for the admission of Japanese war brides. For other discussions of P.L. 213 and P.L. 717, see, for example, Regina Lark, "They Challenged Two Nations: Marriages between Japanese Women and American GIs, 1945–Present" (Ph.D. diss., University of Southern California, 1999); and Simpson, "'Out of an obscure place'."

36. Elfrieda Berthiaume Shukert and Barbara Smith Scibetta, *War Brides of World War II* (New York: Penguin Books, 1988).

37. Act of June 29, 1946, *Admission of Alien Fiancées or Fiancés of Members Armed Forces of the United States*, United States Congress, USCIS History Office and Library.

38. E. E. Salisbury to Eugene Cole, March 4, 1946, Entry 9, RG 85, File 56226/527, NARA.

39. Eugene Cole to E. E. Salisbury, report April 4, 1946, Entry 9, RG 85, File 56226/527, NARA.

40. For an in-depth discussion of the history of proxy marriages, see Ernest G. Lorenzen, "Marriage by Proxy and the Conflict of Laws," *Harvard Law Review* 32 (1919): 473–88. Lorenzen traces proxy marriage as a legal form of marriage back to the Roman Empire. Though not legal in modern Italy, several nations (including Italy, Belgium, and France) legalized proxy marriages during World War I, again for members of the military.

41. Eugene Cole to E. E. Salisbury, report, April 4, 1946, Entry 9, RG 85, File 56226/527, NARA.

42. Eugene Cole to E. E. Salisbury, report, May 9, 1946, Entry 9, RG 85, File 56226/527, NARA.

43. Ibid.

44. F. M. Symmes to Acting District Director, June 5, 1947, Entry 9, RG 85, File 56230/853a, NARA.

45. Ibid.

46. Ibid. It is noteworthy that Askounes addressed her audience in Greek rather than English, evidence that the Greek American community retained their Greek (rather than simply white American) culture, even in the public sphere. This reveals that the Greek American community was not completely assimilated by the immediate postwar era but rather maintained at least strong linguistic ties to their country of origin.

47. G. J. Haering to Joseph Savoretti, August 12, 1947, Entry 9, RG 85, File 56230/853a, NARA.

48. Mrs. Margaret Cook to United States Public Health Department, November 17, 1948, Entry 9, RG 85, File 56230/853a, NARA.

49. INS to Mrs. Margaret Cook, November 24, 1948, Entry 9, RG 85, File 56230/853a, NARA.

50. Ibid.

51. For example, see Chief, District Adjudications Division, Atlanta, Georgia, to Joseph Savoretti, July 16, 1947, Entry 9, RG 85, File 56230/853a, NARA.

52. Eugene Cole to E. E. Salisbury, report, May 9, 1946, NARA. For an in-depth discussion of desertion among British war brides, see Virden, *Good-bye, Piccadilly*, 89–94.

53. Sworn statement with Herbert Bowling, August 22, 1946, Entry 9, RG 85, File 56226/527, NARA.

54. Most likely, the husband divorced the war bride and the war bride never immigrated to the United States. As Jenel Virden explains, British women had little legal recourse in desertion cases under US law, especially once the husbands were back in the United States. Virden argued that the United States did little to help these women. Based on the evidence above, however, it appears that the INS followed up with British war bride desertion cases more than with those for war brides from any other country.

55. "Saki" (or sake) marriages were purely ceremonial, and thus a marriage had to be registered with the Japanese government to be legal. They usually occurred in private within the home of the bride's family. The bride and groom drank sake together as part of the ceremony, leading US officials to commonly use the term.

56. Operations Instructions, "Validity of marriages between United States servicemen and Japanese nationals," May 26, 1952, Entry 9, RG 85, File 56323/921, NARA.

57. Ronald Takaki, *Strangers from a Different Shore: A History of Asian Americans* (Boston: Little, Brown and Company, 1989), 419. A decade earlier, in 1952, the passage of the McCarran-Walter Act amended the 1924 Immigration Act that excluded Japanese immigration in favor of a quota system that allowed limited Japanese immigration and "placed Japan on the same quota system as European countries." See Izumi Hirobe, *Japanese Pride, American Prejudice: Modifying the Exclusion Clause of the 1924 Immigration Act* (Stanford, CA: Stanford University Press, 2001), 241. But the 1924 law was not completely reversed until 1965.

58. For an example of how a similar pattern held true for the GI Bill, see note 9 above.

Chapter 10
Hot Lunches in the Cold War: The Politics of School Lunches in Postwar Divided Germany

Alice Weinreb

World War II left in its wake a world in the grip of a global food shortage. The war's devastating impact on both the lands and the peoples of Europe ensured that agricultural production was in a state of crisis; compounding this dire state of shortage were the literally millions of people who had been displaced, imprisoned, and simply starved during the war. Indeed, for the men and women charged with rebuilding a devastated world after the war's end in 1945, nothing seemed more urgent, or harder to get, than food. It was out of this chaos, suffering, and desperate need that the 1948 Universal Declaration of Human Rights explicitly promised everyone in the world the right to "health and well-being, including food." In this moment of general emergency, particular attention was dedicated to restoring the physical and mental health of Europe's children.[1] International concerns with feeding the hungry children of postwar Europe—UNICEF was created in 1946 specifically for this purpose—came to focus special attention on the children of the former enemy nations, in particular Germany. Pity for the plight of German children, who were singled out by the Western Allies as in a particular state of need—"there are probably no children in Europe today more distressed than numbers of those in certain German towns"[2]—mingled with fear over the potential threat embodied in a generation of angry and malnourished German youngsters. As the British Jewish philanthropist Victor Gollancz ominously argued in his plea for increased food aid to Germany's children, "Hunger does terrible things to a man: it warps him, turns him into something very like a beast, and fills him with hatred for anyone who, rightly or wrongly, he thinks has inflicted it. And it does terrible things, particularly, to children who one day will be men."[3]

This unique combination of fear and empathy meant that restoring the health of Germany's children rapidly became one of the primary goals of the occupation authorities. Among the various strategies proposed to revive and restore German youth, school lunches were one of the earliest and most popular policies enacted by the governments in all four zones of occupation. Despite a general consensus on the poor dietary status of German school-children, however, the Allies as well as the German people lacked a clear consensus on the specific role that school lunches should play in repairing damaged health. Embedded within a nexus of concerns over the shape of the modern German family and the definition of the postwar welfare state, school meals (*Schulspeisung*) were an early issue of contention between the German peoples and their two governments. Indeed, the radically different trajectories of postwar German school lunch policy both reflected and reified gendered understandings of labor, production, and consumption that became defining distinctions between East and West Germany during the Cold War.

The "rubble years" that followed the capitulation of Germany in May 1945 were framed by a sense of chaos and "upside-down-ness." Known as the "Hour of the Woman," this was a time when women did men's work while men were injured, weak, or absent; children ran wild; and homes were reduced to piles of bricks and dust.[4] Nothing signaled the preeminence of traditionally female concerns as much as the fact that everyday life seemed to be reduced entirely to the *Magen-Frage*, or "stomach question."[5] Historians have long noted the significance of the food crisis for postwar Germans.[6] However, the bulk of this scholarship, usually focusing on the western zones, prioritizes private food consumption—the mythic struggles of individual women and children to gather and prepare food items for family consumption. Such scholarship has left underexplored collective feeding programs, a major source of food for the populations of all four zones during the occupation years. The catastrophic food and housing situation ensured that the majority of the population was at least partially dependent on some sort of mass feeding program, including the literally millions of "dependents" created by the war—the homeless, unem-ployed, ill, and elderly—as well as the largest category of collective eaters: school-age children. Despite their relative lack of historical attention, school meals are one of the best-remembered and most frequently mentioned aspects of education and childhood experience during the postwar years, being, in the words of historian Benita Blessing, "one of the dominant leitmotivs of the postwar school throughout all of Germany."[7]

This chapter argues that although school lunches did not have a strong prewar tradition in Germany, they acquired particular importance during the immediate postwar moment. As a result of this explosion in significance, the German school lunch was the object of especially fraught social policy in both the German Democratic Republic (GDR) and the Federal Republic of Germany (FRG) throughout the Cold War decades. In no other European country were school meals as closely linked with the devastating consequences of postwar hunger and related societal collapse as they were in occupied Germany. School meals represented both the promises and the potential threats of reconstruction and foreign aid, and in both the FRG and GDR they were linked with a remaking of labor systems and gendered familial structures. The particular power that school lunches acquired in postwar Germany is largely because school lunch programs had remained relatively underdeveloped in prewar and wartime Germany. While France and Great Britain had established large, centralized meal programs for impoverished children in many large cities by the turn of the century, in Germany early public feeding programs had remained decentralized, highly localized, and privately funded, usually organized by churches or individual philanthropists.[8] Late nineteenth and early twentieth century economists and social commentators opposed collective meals for children on economic, medical, moral, and social grounds, believing that they weakened the family and encouraged welfare dependency.[9] Early in the century, Hans Luther, later to become minister of nutrition during the Weimar Republic, warned of the "dangers of the dissolution of family life . . . that are automatically bound with every thought of mass feeding programs."[10] Indeed, Germany's first large-scale experiment with school lunches came only in the wake of World War I, when Great Britain's Hunger Blockade and the global Depression drew international attention to Germany's malnourished and psychologically vulnerable children.

Quakerspeisung, or the Quaker Feeding Program, was the system of hot lunch distribution for schoolchildren set up in Austria and Germany in 1919. Established under the personal supervision of United States Food Administrator and future US President Herbert Hoover, and carried out primarily by Quaker volunteers organized by the American Friends Service Committee, the program was intended to be both humanitarian and propagandistic, ensuring that "every day of every week and every week of every month until the next harvest this helpless mass of humanity must physically sit at a table spread with American food under the American flag."[11] Despite the program's tremendous success, distributing 687 million hot meals over the five years of its existence, the Weimar government refused to take on permanent responsibility for feeding Germany's children upon the program's closure. When the Quakers ceased providing supplies for these lunches in April 1925, mass feeding for German children ended as well. Although worsening economic conditions toward the end of the decade meant the constant threat of malnutrition, the German state steadily reduced or eliminated collective feeding programs. State officials perceived children's nutritional health as the responsibility of individual parents, above all the mother. Feeding children was seen as the core activity of the healthy family; replacing private home-cooked meals with collective ones threatened to create unhealthy children and also seemed to be encouraging women to abandon their families and join the workforce. Working women themselves, regardless of their level of poverty, consistently opposed mass feeding programs for their own meals and especially for those of their children, seeing them as a mark of poverty and an admission of their own inadequacy as wives and mothers. A contemporary social worker observed in frustration that, despite widespread hunger during the First World War, German women "would rather starve inside their own four walls than be seen going to a communal kitchen."[12]

While the rise of Nazism and the onset of war did result in a dramatic increase in participation in collective meals, school meals had no place within the conservative ideology of the National Socialist German Workers' Party (Nationalsozialistische Deutsche Arbeiterpartei, or NSDAP), which continued to promote the ideal of home-cooked and home-eaten meals for children. Despite the fact that increases in female employment and the near-universal participation of children in various Hitler Youth programs meant that many children were, in fact, being fed by the state or other collective organizations rather than by their mothers, the Nazi Party never officially promoted school lunches as an acceptable alternative to home cooking. Between 1933 and 1939, the NSDAP busily dismantled the scant remnants of Weimar mass feeding programs, closing the few remaining communal kitchens and distributing groceries for private consumption as a substitute.[13] A 1943 article in the *Zeitschrift für Volksernährung* titled "How can I manage my family's nutrition if I am employed?" acknowledged that "some women are tempted to get lunch [for their children] from a communal kitchen." However, "we have learned from the [First] World War that this is not an ideal solution, even if such kitchens cook better today than they did back then. Mass feeding has specific nutrition-physiological disadvantages."[14] The article concluded firmly that "whoever is able should continue to prepare daily meals for the family by applying the lessons of nutritional science."[15] Even during the last months of the war, when both food scarcity and collective meals were widespread, Third Reich nutritionists and social scientists continued the German tradition of associating a healthy family life with home-cooked and home-consumed meals.

The end of the Second World War was in many ways eerily evocative of the end of the First. If the sheer quantity of rubble and scale of physical devastation of the German landscape, in particular its cities, distinguished 1945 from 1918, in one important regard these moments of defeat were identical for German women and children: they ushered in times of widespread food shortages and collective meals. During World War I, German civilians had suffered from severe food shortages since the early months of the war. Indeed, many had blamed the collapse of the home front on the domestic food crisis. In contrast, during the Second World War the Nazi state managed to maintain adequate civilian nutrition until the final year of the war. In contrast to the famines spreading through much of the world in 1945, at the moment of its unconditional surrender, Germany's food economy was the strongest in continental Europe.[16] Nonetheless, just as in 1918, the end of the war for Germany meant the onset of a multiyear nutritional crisis. And, just as in 1918, German children became the objects of massive international feeding programs in the form of hot school lunches. While German children in the late 1940s, as in the early 1920s, would have experienced school meals as part of military defeat, foreign aid, and societal collapse, school meals in post–World War II Germany were profoundly different from the Quaker charity programs of the early Weimar years. After 1945, the legacy of the Third Reich, and the realities of division and occupation shaped school lunches in distinct ways, making them a revealing window into the gendered labor systems that developed in the two German states.

The rapid development of school lunch programs in the different zones of Germany between the years 1945 and 1949 was a defining aspect of the so-called "Hunger Years." Out of this shared experience, both postwar German states came to cast the presence or absence of a hot school meal as a key marker of a specifically German style of communism (in the east) or capitalism (in the west). Debates over the purpose and viability of the hot school lunch spoke to differing definitions of three key concerns: (1) the role of the state in domestic affairs, (2) the relationship between individual health and the national economy, and (3) the shape of the postwar German family. At stake were concerns over childhood nutritional health, maternal employment, familial stability, and German cultural identity. The school lunch was so important in these discussions precisely because it was explicitly connected to the postwar moment and the chaos and drama of defeat and occupation—a moment of both looking backward and looking forward.

School lunches went on to become a significant example of Cold War difference in divided Germany: they were canceled permanently in 1950 in the FRG and continually expanded in the GDR through 1990. By exploring both state policy and public discourse over school lunches during occupation and division, this chapter reconstructs the reasons and ramifications for this dramatic split in policy. Hot school meals are neither socially nor economically insignificant. They demand the physical remaking of school buildings, which must be renovated to include cooking and dining facilities; they need a system of funding and state regulation; and they accompany a redefinition of the purpose of education to include the consumption of a hot meal as part of the daily "school experience." Equally important, they require crucial shifts in the rhythm and time structure of German parents' and children's daily lives. Hot school meals meant that students would not return home for their midday meal; on the other hand, a lack of school lunches meant that children must be fed privately. Indeed, the absence of hot school meals was central to the structure of the West German school day, which ended in the early afternoon to allow children to return home to eat their hot lunch—requiring mothers to be at home and cooking. In East Germany, by contrast, school meals were deliberately expanded to allow children to stay away from the home for the entire day, thus enabling female participation in the workforce as well as increased productivity on the part of schoolchildren themselves.[17] In both East and West Germany, female employment was an issue that was inseparable from the presence or absence of school meals. As a result, hot school meals shaped women's employment patterns and daily lives in divided Germany. Unfortunately, historians have often overlooked school meals, seeing them at best as illustrative rather than causal factors in economic and social history.[18] This essay argues that school meals are especially important for understanding negotiations of the relationship between gender, family structure, and the state in postwar Germany. Mothers, children, nutritionists, and teachers argued first with Soviet and American officials and then with their own respective governments about the liberating and terrifying consequences of a hot school lunch.

232

Feeding German Children during the Occupation

A long tradition of mass feeding programs in Soviet Russia, along with an ideological commitment to collective meals, provided the context for the remarkable speed with which the Soviet Military Administration established large-scale feeding programs for the German population in its zone. The Soviets, working in tandem with local communists, began distributing food to schoolchildren in most of the major cities of the eastern zone within months of the defeat of the Nazi state. By October 1945, 60,000 schoolchildren in Leipzig were receiving hot meals five days a week; a year later, in September 1946, the Soviet administration passed a ruling requiring that all schoolchildren in the Soviet zone receive a daily snack of a hot rye roll and mug of coffee.[19] By the end of the year, about 50,000 children in the Soviet zone of Berlin were receiving a school meal, a number that almost doubled by the following March to include approximately half of the zone's schoolchildren.

These meals were aggressively promoted by the zonal government. As early as November 1945, the main East German newspaper, the *Berliner Zeitung*, placed school meals at the heart of the construction of a "new" Germany, one that was emerging, phoenix-like, out of the ashes of its fascist past: in the midst of ruined Berlin, a landscape of "absolutely hopeless destruction," stood "an oasis, for here behind these walls begins a new Reich . . . as every day that school meets, the boys and girls receive from Father Magistrate a warm and tasty meal."[20] In this socialist German state, it was not a mother's unpaid domestic labor but the "father" state's collective food system that best nourished Berlin's children. Such meals were distinct from earlier models of school lunches as charitable donations for a weakened population; instead, these lunches were the foundation of a new and antifascist Germany. In deliberately degendered language, not just mothers but all "clever parents" were encouraged to display their "prudence and practical good sense" by registering their children for the soups and simple casseroles that were increasingly (though still not universally) available in often rubble-filled classrooms and temporary schooling facilities.[21]

Indeed, early socialist rhetoric argued that school meals were a reward for both children and parents. Touting the fact that "school meals offer advantages and essential relief to parents and their children,"[22] both German communists and Soviet officials saw school meals as an expression of

the humanistic character of the socialist social structure, in which children are cared for and treated as a precious resource. Concern and care for the young generation is an essential part of the socialist state, and another site that reveals its superiority over capitalist society.[23]

The German communists who worked with the Soviets and went on to become leaders of the GDR were personally committed to school meals as a pedagogical tool, a way to monitor health and nutrition, and a means for restructuring the local and national economy. Far from the aggressive humanitarianism of Hoover's Quaker lunches, a model of collective feeding that explicitly encouraged feelings of impoverishment and dependence, East German school meals were recast as a necessary prerequisite for independence, productivity, and prosperity. School lunches represented a careful renegotiation of the relationship between citizens and the state; the (paternal) state promised to provide children with midday meals, something previously the provenance of mothers. In exchange, mothers were freed to focus on productive labor outside of the home rather than child-centered labor within it. Because food production and consumption were traditionally central to the creation and maintenance of gender difference, school meals seemed an especially effective way of overturning these patterns. Indeed, school meals were an evocative symbol of a specifically East German democratic ideal; they erased traditional differences between men, women, and children, wherein women cooked, men worked, and children ate. School meals meant that men, women, and children could all engage in parallel rather than divergent behavior. All would be productive outside of the home, and all would eat their state-provided lunches at their respective "workplace."

The symbolic valence of the school lunch was quite different in the western zones. The British, building upon their own long domestic tradition of school meals, were only weeks behind the Soviets in establishing school lunch programs.[24] In contrast, the American zone did not begin offering widespread school meals in Bavaria until the fall of 1946, where they were unpopular and poorly developed, reaching on average only 14 percent of the school-age population. The Americans' initial lack of success with feeding schoolchildren ended with the consolidation of the western zones into the "Bizone" in 1947 and the subsequent initiation of the *Hoover-Speisung* (Hoover Meals). Herbert Hoover had advocated for an American-led feeding program for German children since before the war had ended, citing military, economic, and humanitarian advantages. After touring postwar Germany in 1947 at the behest of President Truman, Hoover developed a massive school meal program which, in the words of his chief advisor, "helped save a whole generation of German youngsters."[25]

In actuality, more stringent qualification requirements and higher cost excluded tens of thousands of children from enjoying these higher quality meals. Hoover's lunches increased the calories and flavors of school meals but decreased the actual number of children receiving hot lunches.[26]

The June 6, 1948, currency reform dealt the final blow to school lunches in the western zone. The introduction of the deutsche mark was intended to stabilize the economy, limit inflation, and encourage industrial and economic development. The reform was instantly memorialized as the moment when empty window displays transformed overnight into overflowing cornucopias of consumer goods. Indeed, the currency reform was perceived as marking the end of the postwar crisis years and ushering in the beginning of a prosperous postwar society. However, the immediate impact of the reform on the average German civilian was far from positive. Skyrocketing prices, decreases in the value of wages, and the loss of savings held in the now defunct Reichsmark meant huge increases in unemployment and poverty for hundreds of thousands of West Germans. One of the most dramatic effects of the currency reform was the rapid reduction in school meal program participation. School lunches became too expensive for parents scrambling to feed themselves, their children, and unemployed, elderly, or ill relatives.[27] By the time the FRG was founded in 1949, the school meal program was in a state of near collapse.

In Bad Taste: School Lunches during the West German *Wirtschaftswunder*

The American food donations that had provided supplies for West German school lunches had long been scheduled to end in June 1950, which meant that the costs for these meals would be transferred entirely to the new FRG government. As the deadline for cancellation approached, passionate debates broke out in the West German cabinet over the meal program's future. Health and education experts cited grim medical statistics warning of the devastating long-term impacts of hunger on growing children, quoting already high rates of malnourishment and underweight throughout the country.[28] The ministries of finance and agriculture argued against school lunches, refusing to fund "wasteful" and "unnecessary" school meals that contradicted assertions of a prosperous and healthy West German society. The Dairy Board, hoping to find an outlet for a massive milk surplus, attacked the very principle of canteen food, asserting that:

it has been proven that providing children with school meals from a canteen is not healthy, as both the cooking of the food and its transport in thermal cans spoil the food. On the contrary, milk is natural and pure, and that is much more important than the current meal based on reconstituted powdery substances.[29]

Many cited the horrors of Nazism as a central reason to reject school meals; collective eating, they claimed, was only one step away from fascism as well as from communism. Even those who were in favor of maintaining school lunches continued to conceptualize them as a form of charity or emergency relief. No one suggested that they be freed from their association with poverty and ill health to become a normal part of the West German school day. With conservative governing officials who were openly hostile toward collective eating of all kinds, and under pressure from a booming dairy industry, the federal government voted to end hot school meals and replace them with subsidized milk or cocoa.[30] Horrified by what was seen as "the deliberate sabotage of the school children's meal program,"[31] West German doctors and educators saw the decision to end the national school meal program as catastrophic, a decision motivated solely by the desire "to dispose of the excess production of milk" and to create a new generation of heavy milk drinkers.[32]

Despite assertions from dissident cabinet members and charity workers that "in the wealthiest countries in the world school meals have become self-evident,"[33] the federal government and much of the population remained convinced that school meals were a sign of poverty, a policy that, by providing inferior foodstuffs and encouraging poor parenting, created rather than alleviated childhood hunger. In this context, the decision to end the school lunch program was not based simply on economic expediency, nor was it only the result of a powerful dairy lobby. Although both of these aspects were significant factors in the cancellation of the school lunch program in 1950, just as important was the development of a West German national narrative within which the school lunch was made a symbol of postwar crisis and occupation.[34] The FRG's transformation into a free-market economy was officially elided with a permanent end of German hunger—and without hunger, there was no place for school lunches. Thus the FRG came to understand itself as a country that by definition could not have a national school lunch program. Although West German nutritionists explicitly modeled their nutritional education programs on the United States, they made school lunches a dramatic exception, due to, they claimed, low levels of female employment, short distances between homes and schools, and the fact that "German parents want to have their children at home for their meals for educational reasons and to strengthen family life, a psychological aspect that is far less significant to American families." For these reasons, they claimed that school meals could never be part of the country's nutritional policy.[35] Even those few progressive West German nutritionists who advocated state-sponsored meals regretfully acknowledged that "an ideal model like that of Sweden, where children receive complete meals [at school], will never be realized here, although such a program would provide an optimal linkage of nutritional theory and praxis."[36]

One of the foundations of West German national identity was that of a shared origin in mass, even universal, poverty—something crystallized in the Hunger Years that were defined by school lunches. This collective poverty and hunger acquired its constructive power through contrast to current and future well-being, the *Wohlstandsgesellschaft* (society of prosperity). As Minister of Economics Ludwig Erhard announced in 1956, during the founding years of the FRG, "the people were led from poverty to a new well-being."[37] Almost immediately upon its formation, the Adenauer cabinet had declared its aim to "shift emphasis from the control and rationing of food to that of increasing food production."[38] School meals were one of this policy's first victims. [39] The fate of school meals was quickly mythologized, smoothly incorporated into a narrative of West German modernization and economic development. In his propaganda booklet *Sechs Jahre Danach* (*Six Years Later*), published in the same year that the school meal program came to end, Chancellor Adenauer was already reminiscing about a program that sounded as if it belonged years, rather than months, earlier in German history:

> If one wants to describe the overcoming of the nutritional difficulties of the past years, one cannot avoid the school feeding program, a program that will go down in history as the greatest aid ever provided to West Germany.[40]

By relegating school lunches to the German past, the absence of school meals became an important part of the West German state's attempt to create a national sense of prosperity, while locating childhood nutrition in the private, familial sphere. West German thoughts of school meals rapidly dwindled to fond and fading memories of the beloved *Hoover-Speisung*. Here the state protected the family rather than the (potentially hungry) child, and school meals remained associated both with material poverty and with a disrupted or perverted family life. Throughout the 1950s and 1960s, medical studies claimed that school lunches actually worsened children's health and weakened the stability of the family.[41]

The West German schoolchild's diet became highly standardized: a light breakfast, a mid-morning sandwich eaten at school (*Schulbrot*), a complete hot meal in the early afternoon, a late-afternoon sandwich (*Vesperbrot*), and the final early evening supper. Needless to say, all of these meals were prepared by the mother. Indeed the very structure of the school day was premised on a mother's ability and desire to feed her child. The half-day school, releasing children in the early afternoon (usually between 1:00 and 2:00 p.m.), required not only that mothers be at home to care for their children during the afternoon, but that these hungry schoolchildren be greeted with a fresh warm meal.[42]

This normalization of home cooking in postwar West Germany, however, did not automatically result in satisfactory childhood health. Despite continued insistence that their children did not "need" school meals, concerns over the health of German children grew steadily over the postwar years. A 1953 housewife's consumer guide reported that "the health of our children is a subject that causes us grave concerns." Without making any explicit reference to the federal elimination of school meals, the authors noted that "since 1950 we have been unable to document any real improvements [since] the poor economic conditions of many parents render them unable to provide their children with the essential high-quality, protein-rich foods."[43] The paper concluded, however, not with a call for school food distribution, but with a request for private and corporate donations to support milk distribution, as even the subsidized price remained too high for many parents. A year later, the nationally renowned pediatrician Dr. Hans Hoske, in an essay titled "Healthy Nutrition as a Social Responsibility," sounded a dramatic warning over the state of Germany's children:

> the health of our youth is in a precarious situation. After the war, we assumed that the youth would recover after a few years of improved living standards. Observation at first seemed to confirm this belief. Only experienced scientists realized that this was an illusion that we were only too willing to believe in order to escape the worries of the war and postwar years.[44]

His solution to this vague but dire situation was an extensive cookery program for mothers: home-cooked meals needed to be improved rather than replaced with alternate nutritional models. School meals went entirely unmentioned in the study.

In the mid-1960s, nationwide debates over schoolchildren's nutrition in the FRG broke out again in the wake of the "Düsseldorf Sandwich Test." The test, sponsored by the Market Research Group for Grain and Cereal Products, was intended to determine children's bread preferences by providing free breakfasts to schoolchildren in Mainz and Düsseldorf. Although the original goal of the test was to establish guidelines for mothers to prepare healthy breakfasts for their children before school began, the test produced unexpected results: 25 percent of the surveyed children arrived at school without having eaten any breakfast at all. The results unleashed a sense of real crisis across the country. A few months after these results were published, West German president Heinrich Lübke gave a speech on the National Day of Bread inspired by the "horrifying results" of the survey. Rather than endangering the physical health of children, Lübke claimed that inadequate maternal feeding

> represents the degeneration of the family [which] no longer consumes meals together. . . . Next to love, it is after all the fact that members of a family share bread with one another that provides one of the strongest bonds [*Kräfte des Zusammenhaltes*].[45]

Although a national survey of housewives done in connection with the original *Schulbrot*-test unexpectedly revealed that, "regardless of income and regional traditions," 77 percent of participants favored a state-sponsored school breakfast, the mainstream medical establishment remained firmly convinced of an inherent tension between childhood health and school meals.[46]

Dr. Werner Droese, director of the Institute for Child Nutrition in Dortmund, wrote in 1970 of the feeding dilemmas faced by the small number of West German full-day schools that provided midday meals to their pupils. Warning that "it is almost impossible for a school's collective feeding program to appropriately acknowledge the different appetites and individual tastes of the schoolchild," Droese feared the negative impact of such meals on the fragile body and more fragile ego of the growing child.[47] His solution was predictable: children "as much as possible must be sent home for lunch. The belief that the majority of children cannot receive a warm lunch at home is . . . not accurate."[48] Indeed, a parallel study done in Nordrhein-Westphalen found that 92.5 percent of West German mothers could and did prepare a warm midday meal for their children.[49] Interviews and surveys repeatedly confirmed that parents, especially mothers, accepted responsibility for their children's diet; most West German adults asserted that good mothering was equated with good home cooking.[50] The FRG's "society of prosperity" had no room for mothers who either could not afford to provide a healthy lunch for their child or were incapable of doing so because of work or other obligations.

The few West Germans who spoke out for school lunches during the 1970s and 1980s were not nutritionists but feminists, who argued that providing children with hot lunches *at school* was central to struggles for female emancipation. Only if school meals were provided by the state could the West German school day be expanded beyond its postwar schedule. Feminist sociologist Helga Pross pointed out in the mid-seventies that

> regardless of whether the mother prepares a modest snack or a full warm meal, in any case she is forced into the kitchen because of the half-day school system. Because Germany has no full-day schools, mothers must spend the afternoon cooking; that is how the country can afford to remain with half-day schools.[51]

Such criticisms, however, remained on the fringes of the West German establishment. Throughout the duration of the Cold War, West German mothers were cast as both the cause of and the solution to poor childhood nutritional health. Traveling home to eat lunch seemed both nutritionally and socially advantageous for children, and the consumption of a mother's home-cooked meal remained a central and irreplaceable part of West German childhood. The FRG's early cancellation of school lunches supposedly confirmed the linkage of state-provisioned meals for children with poverty and maladjustment. Just as the FRG had moved out of the occupation period and into the economic miracle (*Wirtschaftswunder*), so too had Germany's children "outgrown" school lunches. Indeed, throughout the duration of German division, school meals were stigmatized not only by nutritional and educational experts but also by the West German population at large. Even when there was limited popular mobilization for school lunches during the social and economic unrest of the 1970s, these meals were explicitly reserved for "children of working parents, half-orphans, and children from divorce with working mothers."[52] Mothers did not demand lunches for their own liberation, nor for the health of their children, but rather for the good of particular populations of disadvantaged children.

Thus, the 1950 decision to cancel the school lunch program was not only a definitional act in the formation of a West German state; it was also destined to become one of the longest-lived and most significant social policies for everyday life in West Germany. It reflected the ideal separation of the home sphere—which revolved around the interdependence of mother and child—and the workplace, which was ultimately intended for men. When, in 1975, the German Society for Nutrition (Deutsche Gesellschaft für Ernährung e.V.) sponsored an international symposium on school feeding programs, the West German speakers were the only participants to consistently assert the incompatibility of widespread school lunches with their national character. After having interviewed many parents about their attitudes toward their own children's potential participation in a school meal program, a Dr. R. Gutezeit asserted that, for West Germans,

> eating, above all at the midday meal, seems to us [West Germans] to have the character of a very intimate, private atmosphere that one does not want regulated. Perhaps here is a last piece of autonomy that must be defended, something that above all mothers feel in regard to their children and state institutions.[53]

Rejecting school meals was a crucial part of defending the healthy, intact, middle-class family—and the class and gender structures that framed it. As in the GDR, a healthy national economy required a healthy domestic economy; in the FRG, however, these two systems were held separate along both gendered and generational lines.

Lunches for All: School Meals and the Making of a New Germany

The story was dramatically different in the eastern half of the divided country. Here the end of occupation and the official founding of the GDR did not lead to the end of school meals but to their increased political, economic, and cultural value, as they were actively integrated into the new socialist state. While the East German government and its medical and education authorities assumed that this new prioritization of school lunches would be embraced by the population, in fact it took over a decade for the general public, especially mothers, to accept school meals as part of their children's daily diet. Indeed, the social and economic goals of school meals as well as their cultural meaning changed over the early postwar years due to pressures from mothers and children as well as changing economic realities.

Immediately after the war, high rates of female employment in all four zones were driven by necessity. The absence of men, most of whom had been recruited into the war effort and were not located on German territory at the end of the war, meant that women were responsible for the initial, exhausting work of reconstruction. In the western zones, these numbers dropped dramatically as soon as husbands and sons returned from the front, as the FRG adopted a conservative Christian societal model based on the integrity of the single-income nuclear family. The Socialist Unity Party of Germany (Sozialistische Einheitspartei Deutschlands, or SED), by contrast, claimed that the new ubiquity of female labor was the beginning of a positive and permanent shift in labor patterns—and the hot school lunch was understood as pivotal to this development. For East German leaders, school lunches were integral to the construction of a modern socialist state, because they transformed both mother and child into productive members of society. The children who consumed these meals gained physical vitality and a sense of collective productivity, while their mothers were able to cease cooking midday meals for their children and reorient their time and energy toward working in the public sphere; as a 1968 article in the women's magazine *Für Dich* pointed out: "It is, after all, the school meal program that first made it possible for many mothers to pursue their careers in peace."[54]

On March 30, 1950, the SED passed the Decree for the Execution of School Lunches (Anordnung zur Durchführung der Schulspeisung).[55] The 1950 law formally announced the integration of a state-regulated lunch into the standard school day, and explicitly linked the end of the occupation and the founding of a "new" Germany with an existential change in the form and purpose of school lunches. By mandating hot cooked meals as a replacement for the previously widespread cold meals of bread with jam or cold cuts, the bill unapologetically aimed at making school meals the schoolchild's primary meal of the day. It was expected that mothers would celebrate the reduction in time and money spent on feeding their children, children themselves would enjoy tasty, nutritionally standardized meals consumed with their peers, and the national economy as well as educational quality would show immediate improvements.

To the consternation of both nutritionists and economists, however, the mandated hot school meals were condemned by parents and rejected by their children as both unnecessary and unwanted. It was not self-evident to the populace that remaking the national economy required remaking the domestic, familial economy. East German women did accept, albeit begrudgingly, the necessity of working outside the home, but they challenged the equation between female employment and a universal school lunch. Even if they accepted the older, bread-based cold lunch model, many mothers opposed hot school meals composed of a grain, vegetable, and occasional meat. These meals seemed an encroachment on their rights as parents and a threat to the well-being of their children. Women often voiced their fear that hot school meals would render mothers' cooking unwanted or redundant, something that was the explicit goal of the state but not necessarily East German parents:

> Experience has shown that children were either so full from this [hot school] meal that, when they arrived home in the afternoon, they did not want the hot meal their mothers had provided for them, or that there were mothers who from laziness did not prepare a warm meal for their children because they believed that they had received enough to eat in school.[56]

Parents and community leaders wrote numerous letters requesting exemptions for their children, claiming both the desire and the ability to feed their children better than "Father Magistrate."[57] Despite official rejection of all appeals for exemption—"the cold school meal does not satisfactorily fulfill the political content of the demands of the law"[58]—the East German state struggled for years to convince its youthful citizens to consume these hot collective meals and their working mothers to allow them to do so.

Over the subsequent decade, the state's appropriation of school meals as a central symbol of the successes of a socialist economy drew attention to their persistent limitations. The end of rationing in 1958, intended to mark the economic recovery of the GDR and improvements in the quality of life, only highlighted

> the discrepancy between the good nutritional situation of the population and the inadequate feeding of children by means of the school meals. We want to guarantee our children a good education, a high level of cultural development. As a result, children rightfully expect us to ensure them a good diet.[59]

Struggling to catch up with continually rising expectations, the SED passed a series of bills that resulted in gradual but decisive improvements in East German school canteens. Constant complaints over the quality of school meals along with parents' refusal to allow their children to partake of these meals forced regular funding increases, which improved meals' quality and reach.

Rather than disputing East German mothers' ability to control and regulate their children's diets, school lunch policy in the GDR gradually cast these meals as a necessary complement to the traditional family repast. A healthy family life required that all members of the family (parents and children) eat in workplace canteens and school cafeterias as well as at home. East German scientists and policymakers, the vast majority of them men, did not question traditional gender dichotomies within the home, where women were the producers of food and men and children were the consumers. Advisors made sure to point out that the development of mass feeding programs, particularly school meals, was intended "to reduce individual food production in the household,"[60] but not to eliminate it. Home-cooked meals, especially those prepared by a loving and nutritionally well-informed mother, continued to be a crucial part of a child's diet. However, their importance was not due to their central role in maintaining children's health, but in their symbolic ability to strengthen the connections between the domestic and the national economies. Sundays and holidays were set aside for crucial family meals, which were "not an individual but a familial issue. All who eat the meal must also play a role in creating it," an obligation that demanded from women the new task of delegating the labor of cooking.[61] Such ostensible egalitarianism, however, was qualified with reminders that "of course the housewife has the last word—and ultimately primary responsibility—in tasting and flavoring the dishes."[62] What was conceptualized as the real cooking, the creative and productive aspects of preparing meals, remained in the hands of women, while the busywork and supplemental labor (salads, desserts, and vegetable cleaning), and especially the cleanup, could be left to husbands and children.

At the same time, East German nutritionists denied any tension between school meals and maternal love, contending that a woman's ability to properly mother her children actually depended upon her child's consumption of a school lunch. School lunches promised to increase mothers' abilities to control and "optimize" children's diets. The East German discourse on school lunches thus maintained a traditional bourgeois emphasis on the mothers' preeminence over the nutrition of her child, positing the state as a necessary intermediary but not a replacement for mothers' authority. Nutritionists advised

any mother who is worried about the school lunches of her children not to accept poor conditions and, resigned, resume her own cooking;

244

instead she should make use of her democratic rights and obligations, and help to create an atmosphere of impatience toward the non-fulfillment of state-regulations [for school meals].[63]

This argument remade the traditional German model of mothering. A good mother did not need to actually cook for her child. She did, however, remain the ultimate guardian of her child's diet, expressing a specifically socialist maternity not by feeding her own children but by ensuring that the state feed all children better. The continued series of bills to improve school lunch quality was as much an attempt to address the concerns of mothers as the needs of children.

These changes in both real meal quality and in the East German state's maternalist rhetoric were ultimately successful.[64] Between 1960 and 1970, participation in school lunches increased by 160 percent.[65] East German school meals were heavily regulated and controlled, largely through the work of the Central Institute of Nutritional Sciences, which designed menus, trained school chefs, and monitored health and nutrition among children and adults. Despite the greater social prestige and financial support allotted workers' canteens, nutritionists acknowledged that "in no other category of collective feeding are there comparably high rates of development" as in school meals.[66] Consistent funding gradually overcame many major obstacles to school lunches, particularly inadequate technological and sanitary facilities.[67] By the 1980s, more than 85 percent of East German schoolchildren were eating at least one hot meal a day at their schools, and mothers who cooked midday meals for their children had become a dramatic anomaly.

As was the case in the FRG, the fate of school meals in the GDR was quickly mythologized, cast as a turning point in the development of a modern postwar state. Here, however, it was not the elimination of school lunches that symbolized entrance into a prosperous, Christian, and capitalist world. Instead, a radical expansion and redefinition of school lunches defined the GDR as a progressive and modern socialist state: in the proud words of a 1958 nutritional report, "In the years following 1945, the school lunch program in the GDR acquired a scope never before experienced in Germany."[68] School meals were ultimately accepted by the population as a positive and definitionally socialist attribute of East German society. School meals incorporated children into a work-centered and productivity-oriented social economy and allowed their mothers to work outside the home, while at the same time confirming a traditional bourgeois emphasis on food and maternal care as central for the health of the German family. Despite initial resistance on the part of children and especially mothers, women in the GDR came to accept and ultimately support school lunches as a part of daily life and a key responsibility of the state.

One can perhaps best see the popularity of East Germany's school lunches in the tremendous reaction to the program's reduction and ultimate cancellation after reunification. Newspapers from the former GDR were rife with anger and fear over the negative impacts on both childhood health and maternal economic independence that the end of school lunches seemed to portend.[69] So constant and passionate were the concerns over the fate of East German children's hot school lunches that they inspired a lengthy article in the conservative West German newspaper *Frankfurter Allgemeine Zeitung* titled "As if School Meals Were the Most Important Thing," published in March 1990.[70] The West German author, Kurt Reumann, complained that in the wake of reunification, East Germans, and especially East German women, seemed only to care about afterschool care (*Hort*) and, especially, school meal programs.[71] Ultimately, few aspects of daily life in the GDR had become as popular as the once-controversial hot school lunch.

Conclusion

In 1945, in the face of a global food crisis, millions of undernourished children, and fragmented families, postwar reconstruction required a school meal program. This was true throughout Europe and indeed throughout much of the world. In occupied Germany, however, the specific political realities of defeat and division ensured that school lunches were especially politicized and contested. School lunches were a matter of state policy, but they were also at the heart of private family life; indeed, these collectively consumed soups, casseroles, and stews represented more than any other product of the postwar moment the intersection of national and familial economies. School meals helped delineate the parameters of appropriate parenting, and especially good mothering. In addition, by determining the daily work rhythms of both schoolchildren and mothers, the presence or absence of school lunches could either mandate or render impossible full-time female employment.

The impressive scope of East German school lunches only highlights the ways in which the meaning of these meals changed over time. In the immediate postwar years, communists argued that feeding children at schools linked the reconstruction of bodies and minds, repairing the damages of National Socialism through a collective diet. By the mid-1950s, when the basic nutritional needs of the population had been met, school lunches became a site of contact and conflict between the East German state and mothers. While the state tried to claim responsibility for children's nutrition, it was ultimately forced to recognize mothers' higher authority in that realm. Official discourse claimed that children's consumption of school lunches would preserve a strong familial economy while enabling women to work outside of the home. Women accepted this new labor model upon the condition that it did not eliminate mothers' productive power within the home—a power dependent on her control over her children's diets.

In the western zones, the relationship between feeding and schools was quite different. Here, the idea of German children receiving foreign aid in the form of school-distributed meals was a marker of crisis, but also a sign of paternalistic healing and a marker of innocence. As such, it was initially enthusiastically embraced, one of the few aspects of occupation policy that met with near-universal support. After the formation of the FRG in 1949, however, attitudes began to change. Precisely because school meals were associated with emergency relief, their presence, regardless of their objective value for German youth, signified the condition of the country as one of crisis and dependency. By insisting upon German mothers' ability to provide meals for their children, the West German government, supported by nutritional experts, standardized a specific model of familial and social relations. The decision to end school meals was more than simply a conservative insistence on the primacy of a mother's position at the kitchen stove; it was also an important element in the West German project of "overcoming the past" and its larger ambition to distinguish itself from the socialist GDR. It was also one of the earliest, most contested, and longest-lasting attempts on the part of the West German state to formalize the separation between the home and the workplace. Women, and especially mothers, were the central targets of this project—and mandating daily cooking seemed the most effective method of regulating their labor.

Thus, when it came to school lunches, the Cold War shaped divided Germany in complex ways. In the wake of the war and during the misery of the Hunger Years, German men, women, and children demanded hot school meals from the Allies and their respective zonal governments. Cautiously and with varying degrees of success, the Soviets and then German communists negotiated with the population of the GDR to develop what became a massive school meal program. Simultaneously, however, they accepted popular insistence on traditional gender roles in terms of maternal responsibility for childhood health. In contrast, in the FRG, school lunches retained associations with poverty, maternal inadequacy, and childhood ill health. School meals were seen as incompatible with healthy children and nurturing families. As a result, unusually in the postwar landscape, in West Germany moving into the Cold War meant moving away from hot school lunches.[72]

Notes

1. Tara Zahra, *The Lost Children: Reconstructing Europe's Families after World War II* (Cambridge, MA: Harvard University Press, 2011).

2. Dorothy Macardle, *Children of Europe; a Study of the Children of Liberated Countries: Their War-Time Experiences, their Reactions, and their Needs, with a Note on Germany* (Boston: Beacon Press, 1951), 13.

3. Victor Gollancz, *Leaving Them to Their Fate: The Ethics of Starvation* (London: V. Gollancz Ltd, 1946), 43.

4. Elizabeth Heinemann, "The Hour of the Woman: Memories of Germany's 'Crisis Years' and West German National Identity," in *The Miracle Years: A Cultural History of West Germany, 1949–1968*, ed. Hanna Schissler (Princeton, NJ: Princeton University Press, 2001).

5. For more on the politically fraught nature of food concerns during the Allied occupation, see Alice Weinreb, "For the Hungry have no Past, nor do they belong to a Political Party: Debates over German Hunger after World War II," *Central European History* 45 (2012): 1–29.

6. One of the best of these studies is Rainer Gries, *Die Rationen-Gesellschaft: Versorgungskampf und Vergleichsmentalität: Leipzig, München und Köln nach dem Kriege* (Münster: Westfälisches Dampfboot, 1991).

7. Benita Blessing, *An Antifascist Classroom: Denazification in Soviet-Occupied Germany, 1945–1949* (New York: Palgrave Macmillan, 2006), 54. See also, for example, Klaus-Dieter Kraus, *Vom Kaugummi und der Schulspeisung bis hin zum Brausepulver* (Bochum, MA: Paragon, 2001).

8. See Keith Allen, "Schul- und Armenspeisung in Berlin 1880–1914: Der Menschenfreund Hermann Abraham und seine Kritiker," in Hans-Jürgen Teuteberg, ed., *Die Revolution am Esstisch: Neue Studien zur Nahrungskultur im 19.–20. Jahrhundert* (Munich: Franz Steiner Verlag, 2004).

9. For a discussion of particularly female resistance to collective meal programs even during the extreme food shortages of World War I, see Belinda Davis, *Home Fires Burning: Food, Politics, and Everyday Life in World War I Berlin* (Chapel Hill: University of North Carolina Press, 2000), 141.

10. Cited in Keith Allen, *Hungrige Metropole: Essen, Wohlfahrt und Kommerz in Berlin* (Hamburg: Ergebnisse, 2002), 70.

11. Herbert Hoover, *Central European Relief* (New York: American Association for International Conciliation, 1921), 110.

12. Cited in Davis, *Home Fires Burning,* 141.

13. Peter Zolling, *Zwischen Integration und Segregation: Sozialpolitik im "Dritten Reich" am Beispiel der "Nationalsozialistischen Volkswohlfahrt" (NSV) in Hamburg* (Frankfurt/M.: P. Lang, 1986), 176.

14. "Wie meistere ich die Familiennahrung trotz Berufsarbeit?" *Zeitschrift für Volksernährung* 6 (March 1943), 73.

15. Ibid., 73

16. Gustavo Corni, *Brot, Butter, Kanonen: die Ernährungswirtschaft in Deutschland unter der Diktatur Hitlers* (Berlin: Akademie Verlag, 1997).

17. For a comparative discussion of the political importance of the time structure of child care and national educational structures in postwar East and West Europe, see Karen Hagemann, Konrad Jarausch, and Cristina Allemann-Ghionda, eds., *Children, Families, and States: Time Policies of Childcare, Preschool, and Primary Education in Europe* (New York: Berghahn Books, 2011).

18. There are some important recent exceptions, especially in Anglo-American history. See James Vernon, "The Ethics of Hunger and the Assembly of Society: The Techno-politics of the School Meal in Modern Britain," *The American Historical Review* 110 (2005): 693–725; and Susan Levine, *School Lunch Politics: The Surprising History of America's Favorite Welfare Program* (Princeton, NJ: Princeton University Press, 2008).

19. Gries, *Die Rationen-Gesellschaften,* 113.

20. "Mutter hat eine Sorge weniger. Die Schulspeisung ist im Gange," *Berliner Zeitung,* November 24, 1945, 4.

21. "Kluge Eltern sind für die Schulspeisung," *Berliner Zeitung,* March 12, 1946, 2.

22. "Warum Nicht Alle? Schulspeisung, ein Vorteil für Kinder und Eltern," *Berliner Zeitung,* March 19, 1946, 4.

23. Cited in *Die Rationen-Gesellschaften,* 113.

24. By the end of 1946, about 12 percent of the area's children were receiving the 300-calorie portion of soup, and by 1948 up to 80 percent of the children in the British Zone were receiving a hot meal at least three days a week; see Michael Wildt, *Der Traum vom Sattwerden: Hunger und Protest, Schwarzmarkt und Selbsthilfe* (Hamburg: VSA Verlag, 1986), 80–99.

25. Under these new, more restrictive policies, approximately 1.7 million children out of a total of 2.15 million British-zone and 1.4 million American-zone schoolchildren qualified to participate in the Hoover Meals program.

26. Louis Paul Lochner, *Herbert Hoover and Germany* (New York: Macmillan, 1960), 181.

27. Hilde Thurnwald, *Gegenwartsprobleme Berliner Familien: Eine soziologische Untersuchung an 498 Familien* (Berlin: Weidmann, 1948), 48.

28. A Bavarian study found that 712,000 of an examined 962,000 schoolchildren were underweight and called the current 350-calorie school lunch "a welcome enrichment of the diet"; "Die Schulspeisung muss fortgesetzt werden: 35 percent aller Schulkinder speisungsbedürftig – das Hilfswerk für die Jugend darf nicht aufhören," BArch B 142 / 447.

29. "Betr. Auszug aus dem Protokoll der Dienstbesprechung vom 18.2.1950," BArch B 142 / 447. The Ministry of Agriculture, supporting the Dairy Board, recommended

an exclusively milk-based school breakfast due to the "substantial savings in preparation." The associated Administration of Nutrition, Agriculture and Forestry strongly lobbied for the transition to an exclusively milk-based school meal program in order to promote childhood health and to guarantee a market for steadily increasing milk production ("Betreff: Dienstbesprechung am 18 Febr. 1950 in Frankfurt," BArch B 142 / 447).

30. 80. Kabinettssitzung am 4. Juli 1950, 6. Kinderspeisung, BMI (Kabinettsprotokolle der Bundesregierung online), http://www.bundesarchiv.de/cocoon/barch/0000/k/k1950k/kap 1_2/kap2_48/para3_12.html.

31. "Gesundheitsbehörde der Hansestadt Hamburg," BArch B 142 / 447.

32. "Die Schulspeisung muss fortgesetzt werden," BArch B 142 / 447.

33. "Betrifft: Schulkinderspeisung [Standtpunkt der Gesundheitsverwaltung]," BArch B 142 / 447.

34. For example, out of the tens of thousands of schoolchildren in Frankfurt, only 3,100 children were receiving school lunches within months of the passing of the resolution. Jutta Heibel, *Vom Hungertuch zum Wohlstandsspeck* (Frankfurt/M.: Verlag Waldemar Kramer, 2002), 231. In Bavaria, out of the 320,000 participants at the beginning of 1950, only 112,000 continued to receive a free lunch after the bill, and this number dropped steadily over the following months. Winfried Müller, *Schulpolitik in Bayern im Spannungsfeld von Kultusbürokratie und Besatzungsmacht 1945–1949* (Munich: Oldenbourg, 1995), 95.

35. Heinrich Kraut and Willy Wirths, *Mehr Wissen um Ernährung. Berichte über Studienreisen im Rahmen der Auslandshilfe der USA* (Frankfurt/M.: Verlag Kommentator, 1955), 104.

36. Hans-Dietrich Cremer and E. Peppler, "Fragen der modernen Gemeinschaftsverpflegung," *Deutsches Medizinisches Journal* 15 (1964): 319.

37. Cited in Stephan Leibfried and Lutz Leisering, *Time and Poverty in Western Welfare States* (New York and Cambridge: Cambridge University Press, 1999), 176.

38. Hubert G. Schmidt, "Postwar Developments in West German Agriculture, 1945–1953," *Agricultural History* 29, no. 4 (1955): 153.

39. The idea that the existence of school meals was a sign of collective poverty and Communism was specific to the FRG. In the United States, for example, school lunches were promoted as a way of both eliminating poverty and fighting Communism. Virginia representative John Flannagan Jr., one of the most passionate advocates of the original 1945 School Lunch Act, claimed in defense of school meals that "the dictator nations exist upon hungry bodies and befuddled minds. If you want to dispel the gloom of Nazism and Communism from the face of the earth, the thing to do is to feed and educate the people of these nations. A full stomach and a trained mind will never embrace either Nazism or Communism." Cited in Levine, *School Lunch Politics*, 82.

40. Presse- und Informationsamt, Germany (West), *Sechs Jahre Danach: Vom Chaos zum Staat* (Wiesbaden: Limes Verlag, 1951), 40–1.

41. Hans Breuer, "Das Schulfrühstück und seine Bedeutung im Rahmen der Ernährung des Kindes" (Phil. Diss., Georg-August Universität Göttingen, 1968).

42. Karen Hagemann, "Between Ideology and Economy: The 'Time Politics' of Child Care and Public Education in the Two Germanys," *Social Politics* 13 (2006): 217–60, 247.

43. Liane Haskarl and Wolfgang Clauss, *Die Macht der Hausfrau: Eine ernährungswirtschaftliche Fibel für d. Verbraucher* (Kiel: Verlag der Kieler Druckerei, 1952), 21.

44. Hans Hoske, "Befund: Jugendernährung Unzureichend!," *Ernährungs-Umschau* 4 (1954): 93.

45. Werner Steller, *Der Düsseldorfer Schulbrot-Test* (Bonn: Mühlenstelle, 1965) 3.

46. "Die Ergebnisse der Schulbrotteste in der Bundesrepublik Deutschland," BArch B 116 / 30525.

47. Werner Droese and Helga Stolley, "Die Ernährung des Schulkindes," *Ernährungs-Umschau* (1970): 519.

48. Werner Droese, "Erste Erfahrungen über das Mittagessen in Ganztagsschulen: Zugleich ein Beitrag zur Gemeinschaftsverpflegung von Kindern," *Deutsche Medizinische Wochenschrift* 98, no. 35 (1973): 1567.

49. Ibid.

50. Ruth Werner, *Schulverpflegung aus der Sicht von Schülern und Eltern: Einstellung von Schülern und Eltern zur Mittagsmahlzeit in der Ganztagsschule und der Beurteilung des Speisenangebotes durch den Schüler* (Bonn: Bundesministerium für Ernährung, Landwirtschaft und Forsten, 1977), 117.

51. Cited in Alois Wierlacher, *Vom Essen in der deutschen Literatur: Mahlzeiten in Erzähltexten von Goethe bis Grass* (Stuttgart: W. Kohlhammer, 1987), 23.

52. "Schöneberg will Schulspeisung in neuer Form beleben," *Der Tagesspiegel*, November 24, 1966.

53. R. Gutezeit, "Rückwirkungen der Schulverpflegung auf das Elternhaus," *Internationale Arbeitstagung Schulverpflegung*, ed. Deutsche Gesellschaft für Ernährung e.V. (DGE) (Frankfurt/M.: DGE , 1976), 192.

54. Rolf Henschel, ". . . Nun Lasst es euch Schmecken," *Für Dich* 6 (1968): 11.

55. Cited in Karin Opelt, *Volkshochschule in der SBZ* (Opladen: Leske + Budrich, 2004), 66.

56. "Schulspeisung—warm oder kalt?," BArch DR 2 / 2422.

57. For many examples, see BArch DR 2 / 2422.

58. "Protokoll über die Sitzung am 15.3.1951," Barch DR 2 / 725.

59. M. Boenheimm and I. Leetzi, "Wird die Schulspeisung ihrer Aufgabe gerecht? Teil I," *Das Deutsche Gesundheitswesen* 13, no. 45 (1958): 1463.

60. Arthur Scheunert, *Ernährungsprobleme der Gegenwart* (Leipzig: Hirzel, 1952), 19.

61. Anonymous, *Gesunde Küche leicht gemacht: ein Taschenbuch für die werktätige Hausfrau* (Berlin: Zentralstelle f. Werbung d. Lebensmittelindustrie, 1963), 32.

62. Ibid.

63. Henschel, "Nun Lasst es euch Schmecken," 10.

64. For a discussion of "socialist maternalism," see Donna Harsch's chapter in this volume.

65. Herbert Grossmann, Manfred Möhr, and H. Hölzer, "Die Schul- und Kinderspeisung in der Deutschen Demokratischen Republik: inhaltliche und organisatorische Aspekte," *Die Nahrung* 15, no. 2 (1971): 133–40.

66. Manfred Möhr, "Entwicklung der Schülerspeisung in der DDR seit 1945," *Ernährungsforschung* 30, no. 4 (1985): 105.

67. See "Berliner städtische Großküchen VEB," BArch DR2 / 4449.

68. "Der derzeitige Stand der Schulkinderspeisung in der DDR und Vorschläge zu ihrer weiteren Verbesserung" BArch DR2 / 1967.

69. East German newspapers ran countless articles bemoaning reductions in scope and increases in prices of school lunches in the regions of the former GDR throughout 1990

and 1991. See for example Gabriele Oertel, "Geschmacklose Kost aus den Rathäusern," *Neues Deutschland*, December 14, 1990; Gabriele Oertel, "Na dann, Mahlzeit!" *Neues Deutschland*, January 31, 1991; Heide Schlebeck, "Doch nur ein Windei zum Frühstück," *Berliner Zeitung*, September 21, 1990.

70. Kurt Reumann, "Als sei Schulspeisung das Wichtigste: Was Schüler und Eltern in der DDR gegenwärtig am meisten bewegt," *Frankfurter Allgemeine Zeitung*, March 13, 1990.

71. Faced with working mothers' concerns over their children's diets, Reumann condemned what he considered East German parents' inappropriate "hysteria," and suggested that worried mothers "stay at home so that they themselves could be responsible for their own children's upbringing." Reumann, "Als sei Schulspeisung das Wichtigste."

72. A 1951 UNESCO study of childhood health in most of eastern and western Europe, North America, and much of Asia found that school meal programs were being expanded in every country studied with the exception of the FRG. International Bureau of Education, *School Meals and Clothing* (Paris: UNESCO, 1951), 57–8. Even today, Germany is one of the few industrialized countries with half-day schools and no school lunch program.

Chapter 11
Women, Family, and "Postwar": The Gendering of the GDR's Welfare Dictatorship

Donna Harsch

Between 1949 and 1989, the arc of communist rhetoric about socialism in the German Democratic Republic (GDR) followed a gradual but striking trajectory. At the beginning, the Socialist Unity Party of Germany (Sozialistische Einheitspartei Deutschlands, or SED) trumpeted a loud promise of a glorious future built on socialist production; toward the end, it made a relatively muted claim to provide East Germans with "social safety and security" in the here and now. The arc was also real: over time, state monies shifted from disproportionate investment in heavy industry to expensive outlays for consumer goods, apartments, maternal leave, and universal child care. The first signs of these revisions appeared in the mid-1950s under First Secretary of the Politburo Walter Ulbricht, but changes remained fitful and fragmentary through the 1960s. The shift became substantial and lasting after the ascension to power of Erich Honecker in 1971. In typically hyperbolic language, Honecker dubbed his program the "unity of economic and social policy," pairing social policy equally with economic.[1] This trajectory was not part of the original plan. What explains the GDR's transition to a "welfare dictatorship"?[2]

Among interpretations, two predominate. One emphasizes the external situation of East German competition with West Germany, while the other focuses on the internal relationship between restless workers and an SED anxious about their discontent.[3] This chapter accepts the scholarly consensus that the transition was a response to the GDR's external context and domestic constraints, but argues for a partial redefinition of both interpretations. The external condition emphasized here is the Cold War confrontation (i.e., German-German rivalry writ large). I address the Cold War competition from the vantage point of political economy, rather than the more common political/national perspective on the antagonistic relationship between the GDR and the Federal Republic of Germany (FRG). The internal constraint highlighted here is Stalinist gender relations, a variation on the social-class viewpoint that typically characterizes studies of relations between state and society under Stalinism. The chapter explores interaction between these domestic and external conditions in order to illuminate their mutually reinforcing influence on the transition to a welfare dictatorship in the postwar GDR.

The first section addresses the Cold War context. Following Tony Judt's argument in *Postwar: A History of Europe Since 1945*, it assumes that after the mid-1950s East European communists revised their economic policies in a consumerist direction in reaction to the unexpected economic success of the "European model" of capitalism.[4] *Postwar* evocatively portrays the characteristics and economic context of the semi-consumerist path taken in Eastern Europe but does not elucidate it. The new path cannot be explained, this chapter argues, within *Postwar*'s theoretical understanding of the Cold War. The capitalist West and socialist East, Judt posits, told "separate and non-communicative stories" about themselves. Attention to gender relations suggests that, in fact, the systems were not separate; that is, they were not completely distinct and different. Their gendered similarities facilitated effective and, indeed, powerful communications about consumption from the West to the East.

The second section considers the internal workings of the Stalinist system and, in particular, the triangular relationship between the Stalinist state/economy, the family, and women. It makes several points. The family constituted a primary and unreconstructed social structure which Stalinism simultaneously ignored, needed, and exploited. State neglect magnified the importance of the family for ordinary people, amplified women's role in the family, and enhanced the appeal of Western-style consumption. Over time the SED-state became increasingly interested in women as reproducers, producers, and consumers and attuned to the unforeseen consequences of women's family-based decisions.[5]

The third section details some of the daily negotiations and tensions between unorganized women, with their domestic concerns, and the dictatorial party/state, with its productivist agenda. It reflects on how the Cold War confrontation, Stalinist structures, and SED demands on women combined to influence women's behavior, which, in turn, forced the SED-state to revise its productivist policies. The chapter concludes that this process was both particular to Stalinism and comparable to developments elsewhere, for significant parallels can be found in the relationship among women, the family, economics, and state policy in capitalist democracies.

East Germany and the Cold War Confrontation

Tony Judt frames his outstanding historical survey of Europe after 1945 within "[t]he Cold War confrontation; the schism separating East from West; the contest between 'Communism' and 'capitalism'; the separate and non-communicating stories of prosperous Western Europe and the Soviet bloc satellites to the East."[6] Many scholars consider the Cold War to be central to postwar European history. Judt goes further. He sees "postwar" and "Cold War" as mutually constitutive. The Cold War defined postwar Europe, but the Cold War came out of the Second World War—and was a *postwar* phenomenon. From our post–Cold War perspective, we realize, he argues, that what seemed permanent was an "interim age: a postwar parenthesis, the unfinished business of a conflict that ended in 1945 but whose epilogue had lasted for another half century."[7]

This interpretation fits the GDR well. As did the FRG and West Germans, the GDR and East Germans experienced the Cold War confrontation directly and intensely. Political leaders in each state saw their "Germany" as the national incarnation of the East/West schism. The central political legitimization of SED rule was, moreover, antifascism—the unchanging bedrock around which social-economic discourse evolved.[8] In staking both the GDR's legitimacy and its own claim to power on antifascism, the SED insisted on an intrinsic (counter) association between "Hitler fascism" and the war, on one side, and the "New Germany," on the other. Ironically, this binary relationship turned out to be real, if not in the way the SED meant. The New Germany was *the* postwar state that lived and died with the Cold War. The GDR was the interim state of an interim age.

Judt frames the Cold War within the politics of the Second World War but attributes Cold War rivalries as much to economic competition as to ideological antagonism. This perspective too throws light on the evolution of state socialism. Victors and vanquished, whether of the Right or Left, emerged from the war conscious of the dismal failures of Depression-era capitalist economies, Judt reminds us. Postwar scarcity seemed to foreshadow the return of economic malaise after the horrible hiatus of the war. Many Europeans, and certainly communists, were aware of the rapid development of Soviet socialized industries in the interwar years. The dual consciousness of capitalist failure and socialist success motivated the Marshall Plan and, in occupied West Germany, the currency reform of 1948. As communists maneuvered to gain power in Eastern Europe, they were the confident actors, convinced that the future was on the side of socialized production. Communists, including members of the SED, witnessed with genuine surprise (if also denial) the rising prosperity and the new features of postwar capitalist Europe: increasing cooperation among West European economies, especially France and West Germany; high employment levels; increasingly efficient mass production; mass consumerism and commercial services; Keynesian fiscal mechanisms; and social democratic redistributive policies.[9]

These features developed incrementally, Judt argues, creating a "European model" that combined elements of American-style market capitalism with the higher levels of state intervention associated historically with continental capitalism. The gradual (and never complete) Americanization of private consumption was a striking feature of postwar Europe in the popular imagination.[10] Among the many inefficiencies and scarcities that came to plague state-socialist economies, a major difficulty, as everyone knows, was their consumption shortages. As prosperity spread in Western Europe, private consumption came to define the economic differences between the systems. After Vice President Richard Nixon presented the marvels of American consumerism to Nikita Khrushchev, First Secretary of the Soviet Communist Party and Chairman of the Soviet Council of Ministers, at the "kitchen debate" in 1959, touting them as proof of capitalism's superiority, the Soviet leader countered with the promise that the USSR would soon offer more and better private consumption to Soviet citizens. Interestingly, Walter Ulbricht, first secretary of the SED and later also chairman of the GDR Council of Ministers, had made a comparable competitive claim a full year *before* the kitchen debate. The GDR, he announced only three months after the state finally ended rationing in 1958, would soon surpass levels of consumption in the FRG. Ulbricht's prediction was preposterous but not just phrase-mongering. In the 1960s, production of consumer durables such as washing machines jumped upward.[11] By the late 1960s, Judt points out, communist rulers all over Eastern Europe "opted . . . to treat their subjects

256

as consumers and replace the socialist utopia of tomorrow with material abundance today."[12]

Why, though, did powerful communist dictatorships opt to do this? To analyze, rather than just describe, the relationship between neo-Stalinist consumerism and the Cold War confrontation, we have to assume that capitalism communicated with Stalinism. Everyone recognizes, of course, that each side spun stories about itself that aimed to transmit something appealing to ordinary people in the other system. Such communications included blatant propaganda from on high, as disseminated by Nixon on the one side and Khrushchev on the other. In addition, there occurred popular communication about consumption (and other issues) between Westerners and Easterners, and between Easterners and Easterners. All of these types of communication, but especially the latter two, were particularly frequent, not surprisingly, between Germans in East and West. Not only did they share the same language but, before August 1961, a permeable border and, after that, airwaves that the SED found hard to block. Travel across the border was not just by East Germans escaping, never to return (although three million of them did just that). There were thousands of two-way crossings as Easterners crossed to West Berlin and back, Westerners to the East and back, to visit, shop, work, or conduct business.

Tens of thousands of East Germans also received big doses of Western propaganda of exactly the kind Khrushchev got in the kitchen debate—and ordinary East Germans received them much earlier than did the Soviet leader. This explains why the German communist leader Ulbricht took up the consumption gauntlet before Khrushchev. In 1952, for example, the United States organized a West Berlin exhibition of American consumer goods whose aim was to confront East Germans with capitalist plenty. Around 200,000 East Germans (and 300,000 West Germans) visited this exhibition. Its crowning glory was a roofless, scale-model two-bedroom home peopled by a "family" of four who acted out the daily routine of the happy American household. The jewel in the crown was an all-electric kitchen outfitted with every modern appliance and gadget; the model mother/housewife demonstrated its wonders to visiting masses who circled the outer house walls on a raised platform.[13]

The display broadcast powerful messages about private consumption and the ideal family, and about gender and the rationalized household. These communications tell us much about what American zone administrators wanted Easterners to believe and desire.[14] They do not tell us why East Berliners were so eager to hear these messages. Certainly, all Germans (and other Europeans) yearned for nice and useful things for the home after the war. Unless we assume, however, an innate human desire for the all-electric kitchen, the extraordinary popularity of the exhibition requires further explanation. East Germans were receptive because, generally speaking, postwar Europeans lived in systems that were related in important ways, including many gender norms, gender roles, gendered structures, and gendered policies. Gendered norms and institutions were not the only common features between the systems, nor were all aspects of gender relations in the two systems similar. Still, the gendered overlap was particularly significant. Early in the postwar / Cold War era, the intersection was largest in the realm of domestic relations, the organization of the family, and the natalist policies of European states. Cultural bonds were obviously tightest between the two Germanys. The general point about gender relations is meant to apply, however, to Stalinism and capitalism as European systems, not only to the German-German case.[15] The nuclear family provided a medium through which flowed American communications about consumption, housework, and the good life. Women were particularly receptive to messages about labor-saving devices, due to their role in the family, on the one hand, and their increasing participation in wage labor, on the other. In the Stalinist East, women responded on similar, though modified, grounds: they felt more deprived as household consumers; under state socialism, mothers entered the workforce, as a rule, earlier than in the West.

Stalinism and the Family

The "classical socialist system" had, according to the economist János Kornai, an "ambivalent" relationship to the family.[16] This ambivalence arose from Stalinist ideology's indifference to domestic needs and desires combined with the Stalinist economy's unacknowledged dependence on the material and emotional labors performed by the nuclear family.[17] Orthodox Stalinists, including leaders of the SED, drastically squeezed consumption and exploited unpaid domestic labor to accumulate capital for investment in production, especially basic and heavy-industrial production. The SED aimed also to mobilize the wage labor of mothers of young children, while promoting high fertility and, for two decades, restricting women's access to birth control. Institutional child care was provided, although its quantity and quality were extremely insufficient through the 1960s.

The domestic structure that the communist state exploited was, basically, the family it inherited in 1945, a family forged by cultural traditions, capitalism, the Third Reich, and war.[18] The SED did not attempt to transform domestic arrangements, whether understood as family labor (the totality of work/care performed in the family) or gender relations (the division of domestic labors).[19] The neglect of the domestic was not just pragmatic but also philosophical, resting on the assumption that the family was of secondary social significance. Communists recognized, certainly, that women's oppression was grounded in the patriarchal family. They supported civic and social equality for women and, once in power, eliminated the legal privileges of husbands/fathers. They believed, however, that female emancipation and familial change depended fundamentally on woman's participation in wage labor. As wage workers, women would gain autonomy, cast off their parochial concerns, and become class conscious.[20]

Early Marxists, of course, recognized that woman could not realize her productive potential unless she was freed from domestic drudgery. A socialized economy, argued Marxist theorists like Friedrich Engels, August Bebel, and V. I. Lenin, would transfer most consumption, child care, and housework out into the socialized sector and, thus, free women.[21] Three points require emphasis here. First, communists denied social meaning to domestic work. Housework was not potentially emancipatory, because it was unwaged, private, individualized, unproductive, and (according to the Marxist definition) unskilled. It did not function as real *labor*. Nor did the great Marxist theorists attribute much significance to the emotional work of the family as a communal exercise in the development of human character. They assigned that role to the production collective.[22] Second, they premised the socialization of housework and consumption on the prior transformation of the relations of production. Socialized wage labor, production, and workers would over time automatically transcend private unwaged labor, consumption, and housewives. Third, they did not envision a redistribution of labor within the family as a provisional, much less long-term, solution to women's domestic burdens. Reapportionment would not reduce the total demands of the household on its members' time, effort, and attention.[23] Redistribution would constitute, in fact, a step backward, for it would saddle men with the repetitive daily routines of the home and the vital but tedious concerns of consumption.

Instead, the early Bolsheviks envisioned communalization of the household and socialization of the family, not just displacement of its work to socialized services. Taken aback by the unwanted results of radical social reforms, on the one hand, and increasingly interested in the family as an anchor of stability and source of unpaid labor, on the other, the Stalinized Soviet Communist Party retreated from social experimentation.[24] After 1945, leading German communists, like their East European comrades, reflexively adopted the staid, even conservative, Stalinist understanding of the family.[25] The SED did not officially question the nuclear family as the form of domestic life under socialism.

Stalinism's ambivalent relationship to the family was related to its inconsistent relationship to consumption, especially private consumption. The SED elite, like other communist elites, wanted to satisfy the people's legitimate needs and raise workers' standard of living. The Stalinist labor regime, in fact, stoked workers' interest in consumption by tying super-high production quotas (Stakhanovism) to the quantity and quality of food and clothing available to high-performing workers at shops inside producer-goods factories and in state stores.[26] Consumers' desires were piqued, meanwhile, by advertisements in dailies and illustrated weeklies, articles in women's weeklies and, somewhat later, advice books on domestic living.[27] Simultaneously, though, communist leaders delivered stern lectures about the dangers of "bourgeois" consumerism, frivolity, spending, and personal indulgence, and the benefits of "proletarian" production, asceticism, saving, and collective investment. German communists were part of a European intellectual tradition on both the Left and Right that disdained the vulgarity, extravagance, and emptiness of American consumerism. Antipathy to consumerism was grounded in the supply-side bias of classical economics. Unlike ever more Western economists and politicians after 1945, communists still did not recognize the growth-generating potential of individual demand and consumer industries.[28] The Stalinist relationship to *social* consumption was contradictory in a different way. In theory, communists wanted to increase it immeasurably. In practice, services were expensive; investment in them subtracted from basic industry, the foundation of prosperity and socialism.

Stalinists, in sum, operated according to a production-based understanding of political economy and social transformation and downplayed or even disdained domesticity and consumption. This ranking of priorities led the SED to socialize production and upend class relations but leave the organization of individual consumption and private gender relations basically as it was.[29] The contradiction between dynamic production and stagnant consumption had the ironic effect of enhancing the material and affective importance of the family for its members. East Germans depended on a family unit that worked hard to compensate for scarce provisions, cheap clothing, crumbling housing, poor services, and, at least initially, skimpy public welfare.[30]

The state's reliance on family labor and private networks of support affected women in direct and diverse ways: women organized most elements of family consumption; women carried out the great bulk of household labor; women bore and nurtured children; women performed much of the care for infirm and aged relatives. The gendered distribution of labor in the family, combined with state neglect of domestic needs, led to a second set of ironic consequences. Women's domestic role was continually reproduced, which, in turn, strengthened their orientation toward consumption, the home, children, and marriage, while also reinforcing men's assumption that such an orientation was natural. Certainly, men and women were both immersed in the family and dedicated to its survival. Not just mothers but also fathers contested state policies that restricted consumption and their ability to raise their children. Male workers saw themselves as the breadwinner whose "family wage" should support the family. This belief fueled their opposition to low wages and their antagonism to the integration of women workers into better-paid occupations. Many husbands told wives how to run the household and rear the children. Men had much invested in the family. Still, both women *and* the SED assumed that consumption, reproduction, and the home were women's affairs.[31]

The interaction between private domesticity and socialized production caused a third unexpected effect: the small family generated needs and desires that the socialist economy could not satisfy.[32] East Germans and, more generally, Eastern Europeans increasingly contrasted this failure with the rising success of the West German and West European "democratic market" model. In sum, the intermeshing of public upheaval and private continuity paradoxically strengthened popular interest in the nuclear family, individual consumption, conventional gendered personas, and things "over there."

The Stalinist economy did, of course, modify private lives. The family and public gender norms changed as married mothers began to enter and to stay in the GDR's labor force in large numbers in the later 1950s. Joining the single mothers who had preceded them into waged work, these women became less willing to perform hard labor at home. The structures of wage labor altered the family but, mediated through women's decisions, mainly in ways the SED did not like, such as a rising rate of divorce, a declining rate of fertility, growing demands for time-saving household technologies, and pressure to create part-time positions. Party and state officials began to fret about such unplanned trends in the late 1950s, when a vexing scarcity of labor increasingly plagued the GDR. The labor shortage was caused, on the one hand, by the inefficiencies of all command economies and, on the other, by the hemorrhaging of East German workers to the West. Like every Stalinist economy, the GDR depended on the mobilization of new sources of labor to maintain rapid growth.[33] The SED became eager to improve the productivity of *current* workers by raising skill levels. The party leadership also recognized the need for more and better-educated children who would become the *next generation* of workers. The insatiable appetite of state-socialist structures for more and higher-quality labor concentrated attention on women. By the late 1950s, housewives constituted the only remaining pool of non-employed labor; women workers comprised by far the larger pool of unskilled labor; women bore all the babies and did most of the childrearing; wives performed most housework. The party became attuned to the importance of domestic affairs as the weight they loaded onto women began to impinge on its production and reproduction goals.[34]

Women and the State

Like other social histories of Stalinism, this chapter rejects the classic version of the totalitarian thesis and assumes that society under (neo-)Stalinism was differentiated, active, and even effective, despite being atomized, repressed, and oppressed.[35] Ordinary East Germans struggled to find levers of influence within the dictatorial system and contested state policy in numerous ways: passive resistance, letters of complaint, flight to the FRG, individual sabotage, work stoppages, small protests, and a massive strike wave. These resistances, social historians argue, made a difference, causing the state to modify its policies at the point of production, attend to consumption, and revise the Plan. They point, above all, to the workers' rebellion of June 1953, which forced policy changes at the time and haunted the SED ever after.[36]

Like male workers, female workers opposed production and wage policies, although they did so less effectively on average, for women workers had less experience on the shop floor, exercised little power within shop-floor organizations, and were therefore more vulnerable to pressure from above.[37] When it came to everyday life and the family, in contrast, women had lots of experience and could mobilize support from private networks. They knew what had to be done and did not shy from acting on that belief. Without the right to challenge the SED in public, much less to organize, East German women thwarted its plans through daily evasions and resistances, including decisions about consumption, marriage, reproduction, the care of children, job training, and hours of work.[38]

The Cold War context and, in particular, proximity to the FRG influenced popular opinion and complaints about the quality and quantity of private, especially household, consumption in East Germany. Evidence for this association and for its gendered expression is plentiful from the immediate postwar years through to 1989.[39] During the High Stalinist period between 1948 and 1953, women's complaints about acute shortages and unfair distribution of basic foods and clothing were an important feature of popular discontent. Because the gendered division of labor of the early postwar years was "conventional" both at home and in production, women tended to articulate their anger in and around stores, while men expressed their fury in and around the workshop. Unrest of both types reached a peak during the multisided crisis of 1952–53, brought on by the SED's drive to build socialism rapidly by accelerating collectivization, ratcheting up production quotas, and repressing even basic consumption. At factory meetings, women were publicly shamed for shopping in the West but defended their actions as practical. As they often pointed out, butter was cheaper in West Berlin. Standing in line and on the streets, female shoppers contrasted (if cautiously) shortages in the GDR with better conditions in the "West."[40]

In response to unrest and rebellion in 1953, the state worked to improve the food situation. As they and their families ate better, consumers directed their antennae toward new "needs." In the case of clothing, women lamented, above all, the poor quality and lack of style. Because shoppers disdained its goods, the textile and garment industry had to deal, ironically, with surplus: huge piles of fabric and clothing moldered in warehouses because women refused to buy them and instead made their own knockoffs of Western styles.[41] Young textile workers were especially astute connoisseurs of Western fashion. In 1960, they flounced through mill gates in "stiletto heels and petticoats," much to the consternation of SED women sent in to interview them about their production ethic. Textile workers presumably learned what to wear from photographs of "so-called romantic heroes, movie stars, singers, and other painted apes of the Western world" tacked up around their workstations.[42] To tempt women with socialist couture, the GDR's Institute for Clothing Culture staged remarkable numbers of extremely well-attended fashion shows in factories and at outdoor fairs. Women picked up fashion tips at these shows but, if they could, bought fabric and ready-made clothes in West Berlin.[43]

The family shopper crossed into the western zone to purchase much else as well: shoes, spare parts for bikes, kitchen knives, light bulbs, razor blades, zippers, and toilet paper.[44] They also bought bananas, oranges, chocolate, coffee, toys, and, of course, fashion magazines. In 1954, East Germans made *monthly* purchases worth 200 million marks in West Berlin.[45] Such amounts awoke state planners to what one historian has termed the "stimulating power of people's consumer needs."[46] In the 1960s, the state decided finally to update the GDR's shockingly old textile and garment mills, importing expensive technologies and high-quality materials from the West in order to produce modern synthetics and Western styles.[47]

East German women's interest in the mechanized household, as we have seen, long predated Khrushchev's encounter with Nixon. At meetings of the GDR Women's League in the mid-1950s, women talked about their desire for vacuum cleaners, ovens, washing machines, floor waxers, mixers, blenders, toasters, and bread slicers. Women's League officials did not discourage these wishes. Instead, they relayed upward women's discontent with the scarcity, expense, and awkward design of GDR appliances. Indeed, they expanded on the complaints of ordinary women, contrasting, for example, the display of classy appliances at Cologne's trade show in 1956 to the sad assortment on view at Leipzig's exhibition.[48] Activity and opinions from below were, again, stirred up by things "over there." Consumer complaints only effectively got the ear of state officials and planners, however, when they intersected with an economic concern from above. As in the case of lost textile sales, planners realized that sales of nonperishable consumer goods could generate impressive revenues for the state.[49]

In addition, the shortage of labor, especially skilled labor, led East German economists and planners to revise their negative attitude toward the rationalized private household. The state was increasingly determined to mobilize married women with young children for wage labor and also eager to convince women workers, the vast majority of whom were unskilled or semiskilled, to train for skilled labor. Women's constant talk about appliances led officials to conclude that consumer durables were attractive (and expensive) enough to entice nonemployed wives into paid labor. They also hoped that the all-electric kitchen would increase the efficiency of the employed woman at home, so that she could manage to train for a skilled position.[50] In 1962–63, production of household durables jumped and, after 1965, leaped upward.[51]

Neo-Stalinist consumerism was, we see, not a straightforward or automatic response from on high to Cold War competition or to the successes of the European model. It emerged out of a complex process in which economic considerations and "communications" from below each played a role. Attitudes from below were, meanwhile, shaped by communication between the West and ordinary Easterners.

Women also actively pressed for the expansion of socialized services. In this area of interaction with the party-state, they acted, almost always, as workers, not as consumers, and, in most cases, as working mothers. There is little evidence that women's demands for better services were motivated by the Western model. Instead, they insisted that the communist state fulfill its unmet promises. The most frequent focus of irritation, indeed, anger, was the inadequacies of institutionalized child care. Women workers, supported enthusiastically by SED women but often snubbed by factory managers, complained bitterly throughout the 1950s and 1960s about inadequate facilities for children, especially infants and toddlers, whose mothers either had to work or wanted to. Less constantly but also frequently, mothers expressed worries about the quality of child care, again, especially for very young children. Any number of women did not work for wages because they did not want to put their children in the weekly homes—institutions where children lived from Monday morning through Saturday afternoon (during their mother's work week) and on which the state relied heavily, especially in the 1950s. Women's agitation around child care was a significant factor in the expansion and improvement of crèche care. Their concerns about their children's development also sparked state attention, including psychological studies of children in various kinds of child care and a gradual decline in weekly and, above all, long-term institutional care.[52]

Women, then, intentionally challenged particular state policies toward consumption, both private and social. More typically, though, women acted in their personal or family interest without intending to contest state policies but with the effect of prompting officials to investigate and address the causes of the unwanted behavior. The rise in the divorce rate in the 1960s, almost completely propelled by employed wives, is one example. Even more upsetting to the state was the leveling off and then decline of the fertility rate in the 1960s. A third trend that troubled the state was the substantial retreat by full-time employed wives into part-time work in the 1960s. In the late 1950s, after much debate inside the Ministry of Labor and the SED, part-time work was expanded to attract housewives into wage labor. In response, however, already employed wives barraged factory managers with demands that they, too, be allowed to work short hours since, as they pointed out ad infinitum, they had the same burden of housework as nonemployed housewives. Given the acute shortage of labor, managers acceded to these requests because they preferred to retain at least part of a worker's time, rather than lose her to another factory.

Pressure from the SED to stop the trend had no effect. Investigations by party and trade union women into the reasons women retreated to part-time work all came up with the same explanations: women did it for their children (sometimes due to a teacher's "suggestion"); they did it under pressure from their husbands to maintain an orderly and comfortable home; they did it to relieve themselves and their families from some of the stress of two-spouse, full-time employment. They did it, in other words, because of the labors they had to perform at home. The reports make clear that SED and trade union women were stunned by the amount of time these women spent working for the family and by the highly unequal domestic relationships of these mainly unskilled women workers (many of whom were married to skilled workers and, indeed, party and union functionaries).[53]

Conclusion

These social and economic trends were critical to the emergence of state maternalism—policies that massively expanded the number of day nurseries, after-school care, and the duration of paid maternity leaves—that became the core of the SED's welfare dictatorship as it emerged in the 1960s and 1970s.[54] Unlike neo-Stalinist consumerism, the revisions to social policy cannot be directly traced to the Cold War confrontation. Yet many of the social trends that provoked state intervention in state-socialist economies ran parallel to trends in the West, including the postwar rise, then fall, in the birthrate; climbing rates of divorce; the ascent of single motherhood; and the increase in women's employment. In *Postwar*, Judt notes the continual if gradual increase in Western women's workforce participation. It is striking that many Western states developed comparable solutions to the GDR's: natalist and maternalist policies and child care institutions, although some Western states relied more on commercialized than on state services.[55]

The parallels are much more noticeable if the GDR is compared to a range of Western European states rather than only to the FRG. Ironically, the FRG, not the GDR, was the anomalous German state within the realm of West European family policy. For reasons that lie outside the scope of this essay, West German social policies were much less oriented toward employed mothers and young families than were the welfare policies of France, Sweden, Finland, and some other Western states.[56] Feminist scholars have argued that the family "warrants consideration as an independent variable" in the origin and evolution of the Western welfare state. Changes inside the family, including divorce rates, number of children, and wives' labor force participation, influenced state policy, not only vice versa. Since the wife/mother typically initiated familial change, feminists reason, women's private decisions (not to mention public demands by women's organizations for gender-balanced policies) produced political consequences, if often indirectly.[57]

The two sides in the Cold War were, then, not completely distinct, even though they were intensely antagonistic. For most of the major European countries on both sides, an intense wave of industrialization characterized the early postwar era. Industrialization was fostered both by wartime destruction and by pressure from the Cold War superpowers, each of which encouraged its European "satellites" to follow a hyper-industrialist plan of development. This wave brought comparable and massive social changes in its wake: urbanization, expanded access to and levels of education, and women's entry into paid labor and, if much more gradually, into skilled and professional employment. Not only the rising standard of living but these social trends, in turn, stimulated higher levels of consumption and, eventually, (the desire for) mass consumerism. These economic and social trends interacted with the natalist policies implemented by virtually every European state on both sides of the so-called Iron Curtain.

Last but far from least, the shared institution of the small family and its gendered division of labor significantly structured the dynamic communications between gender norms and roles, economic exigencies, and state policies within both socialist and capitalist economies as well as between them. It is hard to disentangle the relative significance of competitive Cold War (systematic-political) forces versus convergent postwar (social-economic) factors in this process. Not only did both matter, but they also influenced each other. Whatever the precise combination of causes, the resulting constellation of women's demands and state responses built a solid, if underappreciated, connection between the (Western) "European model" and (East European) neo-Stalinism.

Notes

1. On the GDR's evolution, see André Steiner, "Zwischen Frustration und Verschwendung," in *Wunderwirtschaft: DDR-Konsumkultur in den 60er Jahren*, ed. Neue Gesellschaft für Bildende Kunst (Cologne, Weimar and Vienna: Böhlau, 1996), 25; André Steiner, "Zwischen. Konsumversprechen und Innovationszwang: Zum wirtschaftlichen Niedergang der DDR," in *Weg in den Untergang: Der innere Zerfall der DDR, ed.* Konrad Jarausch and Martin Sabrow, (Göttingen: Vandenhoeck & Ruprecht, 1999), 163; Beatrix Bouvier, *Die DDR: Sozialstaat? Sozialpolitik in der Ära Honecker* (Bonn: JHW Dietz Nachfolge, 2002), 68, 70–71; Judd Stitziel, "Fashioning Socialism: Clothing, Politics and Consumer Culture in East Germany, 1945–1971" (PhD diss., Johns Hopkins University, 2001), 509; Winfried Thaa et al., *Gesellschaftliche Differenzierung und Legitimitätsverfall des DDR-Sozialismus: Das Ende des anderen Wegs in der Moderne* (Tübingen: Franke Verlag, 1992), 53–55; Manfred G. Schmidt, "Grundzüge der Sozialpolitik in der DDR," in *Am Ende des realen Sozialismus*, ed. Eberhard Kuhrt, vol. 4: *Die Endzeit der DDR-Wirtschaft: Analysen zur Wirtschafts-, Sozial- und Umweltpolitik* (Opladen: Westdeutscher Verlag, 1999), 274–80, 284–87.

2. Konrad Jarausch coined this term; see Jarausch, "Care and Coercion: The GDR as Welfare Dictatorship," in *Dictatorship as Experience: Towards a Socio-cultural History of the GDR*, ed. Jarausch (New York and Oxford: Berghahn Books, 1999).

3. Scholars often combine the two explanations but weight one more heavily than the other. Work that emphasizes rivalry with the FRG includes: Schmidt, "Grundzüge," 286; Bouvier, *Die DDR*, 202, 221; Gerhard Wettig, "Niedergang, Krise und Zusammenbruch der DDR: Ursachen und Vorgänge," in Kuhrt, ed., *Die Endzeit*, 383–384. Work that emphasizes state/society relations includes: Steiner, "Konsumversprechen," 165; André Steiner, *Von Plan zu Plan: Eine Wirtschaftsgeschichte der DDR* (Munich: Deutsche Verlagsanstalt, 2004); Stephan Merl, "Sowjetisierung in der Welt des Konsums," in *Amerikanisierung und Sowjetisierung in Deutschland 1945–1970*, ed. Konrad Jarausch and Hannes Siegrist (Frankfurt/M.: Campus Verlag, 1997); Peter Hübner, "Balance des Ungleichgewichtes: Zum Verhältnis von Arbeiterinteressen und SED-Herrschaft," *Geschichte und Gesellschaft* 19 (1993): 25–8; Peter Hübner, *Konsenz, Konflikt und Kompromiß: Soziale Arbeiterinteressen und Sozialpolitik in der SBZ/DDR 1945–1970* (Berlin: Akademie Verlag, 1995); Jeffrey Kopstein, *The Politics of Economic Decline in East Germany, 1945–1989* (Chapel Hill: University of North Carolina Press, 1997).

4. Tony Judt, *Postwar: A History of Europe Since 1945* (London: Penguin, 2005).

5. To focus the argument on gender relations per se, here I treat "women in the family" as if they were an undifferentiated group. They were not. Distinctions in family income and women's level of education influenced decisions about employment and childbearing. Also significant were real and perceived distinctions based on marital status and the presence of children. For discussion of these distinctions, see for example Gunilla-Friederike Budde, *Frauen der Intelligenz: Akademikerinnen in der DDR 1945 bis 1975* (Göttingen: Vandenhoeck & Ruprecht, 2003); Donna Harsch, *Revenge of the Domestic: Women, the Family, and Communism in the German Democratic Republic* (Princeton, NJ: Princeton University Press, 2007); Elizabeth D. Heineman, *What Difference Does a Husband Make? Women and Marital*

Status in Nazi and Postwar Germany (Berkeley: University of California Press, 1999); Carola Sachse, *Der Hausarbeitstag: Gerechtigkeit und Gleichberechtigung in Ost und West 1939–1994* (Göttingen: Wallstein Verlag, 2002). Despite these distinctions, the vast majority of women in the GDR lived in a version of the nuclear family in which the kinds of housework and care for children and the elderly that adult women performed were basically the same, whether they were working class or professional; single mothers, married mothers, or childless wives.

6. Judt, *Postwar*, 1–2.

7. Ibid.

8. On antifascism, see Jeffrey Herf, *Divided Memory: The Nazi Past in the Two Germanys* (Cambridge, MA: Harvard University Press, 2000); and Sigrid Meuschel, *Legitimation und Parteiherrschaft in der DDR* (Frankfurt/M.: Suhrkamp, 1992). See also Catherine Epstein, *The Last Revolutionaries: German Communists and their Century* (Cambridge, MA: Harvard University Press, 2003), 131–33; Corey Ross, *Constructing Socialism at the Grass-Roots: The Transformation of East Germany, 1945–1965* (London: St. Martin's Press, 2000); 178–81; and Jonathan R. Zatlin, *The Currency of Socialism: Money and Political Culture in East Germany* (Cambridge, UK: Cambridge University Press, 2007), 7–8.

9. Mark Landsman, *Dictatorship and Demand: The Politics of Consumerism in East Germany* (Cambridge, MA: Harvard University Press, 2005), 4–5, 38–9.

10. See, for example, Mary Nolan, "Varieties of Capitalism und Versionen der Amerikanisierung," in *Gibt es einen deutschen Kapitalismus? Tradition und globale Perspektiven der sozialen Marktwirtschaft*, ed. Volker R. Berghahn and Sigurt Vitols (Frankfurt/M.: Campus, 2006); Konrad Jarausch and Hannes Siegrist, eds. *Amerikanisierung und Sowjetisierung in Deutschland 1945–1970* (Frankfurt/M.: Campus, 1997); Victoria de Grazia, *Irresistible Empire: America's Advance through Twentieth-Century Europe* (Cambridge, MA: Harvard University Press, 2006).

11. Harsch, *Revenge of the Domestic*, 183–88.

12. Judt, *Postwar*, 580–581. Also see Katherine Verdery, *What Was Socialism, and What Comes Next?* (Princeton, NJ: Princeton University Press, 1996).

13. Greg Castillo, "Domesticating the Cold War: Household Consumption as Propaganda in Marshall Plan Germany," *Journal of Contemporary History* 40 (2005): 267–70. Also see Castillo, *Cold War on the Home Front: The Soft Power of Mid-Century Design* (Minneapolis: University of Minnesota Press, 2010); Karin Zachmann, "Küchendebatten in Berlin? Die Küche als Kampfplatz im Kalten Krieg," in *Konfrontation und Wettbewerb: Wissenschaft, Technik und Kultur im geteilten Berliner Alltag (1948–1968)*, ed. Michael Lemke (Berlin: Metropol Verlag, 2008), 181–205. On the Soviet case through the internal lens, see Susan E. Reid, "Cold War in the Kitchen: Gender and the De-Stalinization of Consumer Taste in the Soviet Union under Khrushchev," *Slavic Review* 61 (2002): 211–52.

14. In his astute analysis, Greg Castillo shows that such propaganda from the United States was not new to the postwar era but seems to have hit its mark only after 1945 (Castillo, "Domesticating the Cold War"). On Weimar Germany and Americanization, see Mary Nolan, *Visions of Modernity: American Business and the Modernization of Germany* (Oxford: Oxford University Press, 1994); Nancy R. Reagin, *Sweeping the German Nation: Domesticity and National Identity in Germany, 1870–1945* (Cambridge, UK: Cambridge University Press, 2007). Also see Erica Carter, *How German Is She? Postwar German Reconstruction and the Consuming Woman* (Ann Arbor: University of Michigan Press,

1997); Jennifer A. Loehlin, *From Rugs to Riches: Housework, Consumption, and Modernity in Germany* (Oxford and New York: Berghahn Books, 1999); Christine von Oertzen, *Teilzeitarbeit und die Lust am Zuverdienen: Geschlechterpolitik und gesellschaftlicher Wandel in Westdeutschland 1948–1969* (Göttingen: Vandenhoeck & Ruprecht, 1999).

15. Books that have studied German-German relations from a gendered perspective include Heineman, *What Difference Does a Husband Make?*, and Sachse, *Hausarbeitstag*. Also see Uta G. Poiger, *Jazz, Rock and Rebels: Cold War Politics and American Culture in a Divided Germany* (Berkeley: University of California Press, 2000).

16. János Kornai, *The Socialist System: The Political Economy of Communism* (Princeton, NJ: Princeton University Press, 1992), 106–7. Also see Thaa et al., *Gesellschaftliche Differenzierung und Legitimitätsverfall*, 25–7, 49.

17. Kornai, *Socialist System*; see also Alena Heitlinger, *Women and State Socialism: Sex Inequality in the Soviet Union and Czechoslovakia* (London and Basingstoke: MacMillan, 1979), 194.

18. On the German family in the interwar era, see, for example, Karen Hagemann, *Frauenalltag und Männerpolitik: Alltagsleben und gesellschaftliches Handeln von Arbeiterfrauen in der Weimarer Republik* (Bonn: JHW. Dietz Nachfolge, 1990); Heineman, *What Difference*; Reagin, *Sweeping the German Nation*.

19. This point is made in the feminist scholarship on the GDR, including Christine Külke, "Die Berufstätigkeit der Frauen in der industriellen Produktion der DDR: Zur Theorie und Praxis der Frauenarbeitspolitik der SED" (Phil. diss., Freie University Berlin, 1967); Gabriele Gast, *Die politische Rolle der Frau in der DDR* (Düsseldorf: Bertelsmann Universitätsverlag, 1973); Gisela Helwig and Hildegard Maria Nickel, eds., *Frauen in Deutschland 1945–1992* (Berlin: Akademie Verlag, 1993); Gisela Helwig, "Frauen im SED-Staat," *Materialien der Enquete-Kommission 'Aufarbeitung von Geschichte und Folgen der SED-Diktatur in Deutschland,'* vol. 3.2: *Rolle und Bedeutung der Ideologie, integrativer Faktoren und disziplinierender Praktiken in Staat und Gesellschaft der DDR*, ed. Deutscher Bundestag (Frankfurt/M.: Campus, 1995); Gisela Helwig, *Zwischen Familie und Beruf: Die Stellung der Frau in beiden deutschen Staaten* (Cologne: Verlag Wissenschaft und Politik, 1974); Gesine Obertreis, *Familienpolitik in der DDR 1945–1980* (Opladen: Westdeutscher Verlag, 1986); Birgit Bütow and Heidi Stecker, eds. *EigenArtige Ostfrauen: Frauenemanzipation in der DDR und den neuen Bundesländern* (Bielefeld: Kleine Verlag, 1994); Heike Trappe, *Emanzipation oder Zwang? Frauen in der DDR zwischen Beruf, Familie and Sozialpolitik* (Berlin: Akademie Verlag, 1995); Ute Gerhard, "Die staatlich institutionalisierte 'Lösung' der Frauenfrage: Zur Geschichte der Geschlechterverhältnisse in der DDR," in *Sozialgeschichte der DDR*, eds. Hartmut Kaelble, Jürgen Kocka and Hartmut Zwahr (Stuttgart: Klett-Cotta, 1994).

20. See Grit Buehler, *Mythos Gleichberechtigung in der DDR: Politische Partizipation von Frauen am Beispiel des Demokratischen Frauenbunds Deutschlands* (Frankfurt/M.: Campus Verlag, 1997), 14–16, 30; Susanne Diemer, "Die 'neue Frau', aber der 'alte Mann'? Frauenförderung und Geschlechterverhältnisse in der DDR," in *Politische Kultur in der DDR*, ed. Hans-Georg Wehling (Stuttgart: Verlag W. Kohlhammer, 1989).

21. Alena Heitlinger, "Marxism, Feminism, and Sex Equality," in *Women in Eastern Europe and the Soviet Union,* ed. Tova Yedlin (New York: Greenwood Publishing Group, 1980), 10–11.

22. Irene Dölling, "Gespaltenes Bewusstsein—Frauen- und Männerbilder in der DDR," in Helwig and Nickel, *Frauen in Deutschland,* 26; Heitlinger, "Marxism," 11–15.

23. Helga Ulbricht et al., *Probleme der Frauenarbeit* (Berlin: Verlag Neues Leben, 1963), 28. Early on, leading communist men, most prominently Walter Ulbricht, explicitly endorsed the conventional division of domestic labor and, especially, the kitchen as a woman's room, in response to Communist women who suggested methods for reforming the division of labor in the home and, especially, the kitchen. See Zachmann, "Küchendebatten in Berlin?"

24. See Wendy Z. Goldman, *Women, the State and Revolution: Soviet Family Policy and Social Life, 1917–1936* (Cambridge, UK: Cambridge University Press, 1993); Lisa Kirschenbaum, *Small Comrades: Revolutionizing Childhood in Soviet Russia, 1917–1932* (New York: Routledge, 2000); and Heitlinger, *Sex Inequality.*

25. Heitlinger, *Sex Inequality,* 136; Lynn Haney, *Inventing the Needy: Gender and the Politics of Welfare in Hungary* (Berkeley: University of California Press, 2002), 62.

26. Harsch, *Revenge of the Domestic,* 178–82.

27. See Ina Merkel, *Utopie und Bedürfnis: Die Geschichte der Konsumkultur in der DDR* (Cologne: Böhlau, 1999); Ina Merkel, . . . *und Du, Frau an der Werkbank: Die DDR in den 50er Jahren* (Berlin: Elefanten Press, 1990); Annette Kaminsky, *Kaufrausch: Die Geschichte der Konsumkultur in der DDR* (Cologne: Christian Links Verlag, 1999); Heineman, *What Difference*; Harsch, *Revenge of the Domestic*; Stitziel, *Fashioning Socialism.*

28. Landsman, *Dictatorship and Demand,* 4–9; Dietrich Mühlberg, "Von der Arbeitsgesellschaft in die Konsum-, Freizeit- und Erlebnisgesellschaft. Kulturgeschichtliche Überlegungen zum Bedürfniswandel in beiden deutschen Gesellschaften," in Christoph Klessmann, Hans Misselwitz, and Günter Wichert, eds., *Deutsche Vergangenheiten—eine gemeinsame Herausforderung: Der schwierige Umgang mit der doppelten Nachkriegsgeschichte* (Berlin: Ch. Links Verlag, 1999), 191–92; Rita Felski, *The Gender of Modernity* (Cambridge, MA: Harvard University Press, 1995); Poiger, *Jazz,* Chapter 1.

29. On the "ideological neglect" of consumption, see Landsman, *Dictatorship and Demand,* esp. 86.

30. Kornai, *Socialist System,* 106–8; Thaa et al., *Differenzierung,* 97–8.

31. Nancy Reagin's fascinating study of the German culture of housework and its relationship to national identity describes a highly gendered and labor-intensive housework regime that presumably shaped domestic norms and roles in West and East Germany (Reagin, *Sweeping the German Nation*). Historians of the GDR who emphasize women's role in consumption and the gendered rhetoric of official discourse about consumption include Kaminsky, *Kaufrausch*; Merkel, *Utopie*; Katherine Pence, "'You as a Woman Will Understand': Consumption, Gender and the Relationship between State and Citizenry in the GDR's Crisis of 17 June 1953," *German History* 19 (2001): 218–52; Stitziel, *Fashioning Socialism*; and David Crew, ed., *Consuming Germany in the Cold War* (Oxford and New York: Berg Publishers, 2003).

32. Sachse makes a comparable point about the connections between consumption, housework, and household; see Sachse, *Hausarbeitstag,* esp. 33–4, 273–91, 303. Scholars of consumption also draw the connection. Typically, however, historians have ignored the family/household as a "source of influence" on "ways of life" in the GDR; quotes from Mühlberg, "Arbeitsgesellschaft," 186–89.

33. Kornai, *Socialist System*, 204, 211, 214–15.

34. For a similar point, see Hans Günter Hockerts, "Grundlinien und soziale Folgen der Sozialpolitik in der DDR," in Kaelble, Kocka and Zwahr, *Sozialgeschichte der DDR*, 519; Gisela Helwig, "Einleitung," in Helwig and Nickel, *Frauen in Deutschland*, 15; Horst Laatz, "Vom Klassenkampf zur individuellen Wertorientierung: Zur Entwicklung der soziologischen Frauenforschung in der DDR von 1960 bis 1980," in Dieter Voigt, ed., *Qualifikationsprozesse und Arbeitssituation von Frauen in der Bundesrepublik Deutschland und in der DDR* (Berlin: Duncker und Humbolt, 1989), 182.

35. For an overview of debates about totalitarianism and *Alltagsgeschichte* (everyday history) in the GDR, see Bernd Faulenbach, "Acht Jahre deutsch-deutsche Vergangenheitsdebatte," in *Deutsche Vergangenheiten—Eine gemeinsame Herausforderung: Der schwierige Umgang mit der doppelten Nachkriegsgeschichte*, ed. Christoph Klessmann, Hans Misselwitz, and Günter Wichert (Berlin: Christian Links Verlag, 1999), esp. 19, 21–3. For works on the GDR that incorporate social history, see Richard Bessel and Ralph Jessen, eds. *Die Grenzen der Diktatur: Staat und Gesellschaft in der DDR* (Göttingen: Vandenhoeck & Ruprecht, 1996); Mary Fulbrook, *Anatomy of a Dictatorship: Inside the GDR, 1949–1989* (Oxford: Oxford University Press, 1995); Hübner, *Konsens*; Jarausch, *Dictatorship as Experience*; Patrick Major and Jonathan Osmond, *The Workers' and Peasants' State: Communism and Society in East Germany under Ulbricht 1945–1971* (Manchester and New York: Manchester University Press, 2002); Thomas Lindenberger, ed., *Herrschaft und Eigensinn in der Diktatur: Studien zur Gesellschaftsgeschichte der DDR* (Cologne: Böhlau, 1999); Lutz Niethammer, Alexander von Plato, and Dorothee Wierling, *Die volkseigene Erfahrung: Eine Archäologie des Lebens in der Industrieprovinz der DDR* (Berlin: Rowohlt, 1991); and Kaelble, Kocka, and Zwahr, *Sozialgeschichte der DDR*.

36. Kopstein, *Economic Decline*, 11; Ross, *Constructing Socialism*, 57–9; Hübner, *Konsens*; Merl, "Sowjetisiereung," 182; and Schmidt, "Grundzüge der Sozialpolitik in der DDR," 284.

37. Harsch, *Revenge of the Domestic*, chaps. 5 and 7.

38. For a similar perspective, see Budde, *Frauen der Intelligenz*, 15.

39. On the immediate postwar era, see Harsch, *Revenge of the Domestic*, chap. 1; and Paul Steege, *Black Market, Cold War: Everyday Life in Berlin, 1946–1949* (New York: Cambridge University Press, 2007).

40. Harsch, *Revenge of the Domestic*, 63–69; Pence, "'You as a Woman'," 227, 230, 218–22, 249. Also see Landsman, *Dictatorship and Demand*, 115, 118, 120.

41. Stitziel, 62–64, 81, 86, 151, 156, 226, 230.

42. SAPMO-BArch, DY30/IV/2/17/37, Bl. 104-111, 5.5.61, Einschätzung . . . der Lage der jungen Arbeiterinnen in der Textilindustrie; DY30/IV2/17/70, Bl. 99, Bericht . . . Leipziger Baumwollespinnerei vom 28.11- 2.12.61.

43. Landsman, *Dictatorship and Demand*, 143. For evidence of the popularity of fashion shows among women workers, see SAPMO-BArch, DY30/IV2/17/65, Bl. 199-200, 25.2.59, Die Arbeit des FA in Leuna; DY30/IV2/17/69, Bl. 116–17 Bericht . . . VEB Kunstseidenwerk "Siegfried Rädel" im Kreis Pirna, 17.6.59.

44. See, e.g., SAPMO-BArch, DY30/IV2/5/968, Bl. 55, SED Plauen, an ZK u. Bezirksleitung der SED, 24.4.56; DY30/IV2\17\35, Bl.1, Bericht . . . IG Metall am 7.12.56; DY30/IV2/17/72, 6.10.62, I. Einige Fragen zum Nationalen Dokument, Bl. 42.

45. Landsman, *Dictatorship and Demand*, 201; Annette Kaminsky, *Wohlstand, Schönheit, Glück: Kleine Konsumgeschichte der DDR* (Munich: C. H. Beck Verlag, 2001), 62.

46. Mühlberg, "Arbeitsgesellschaft," 195.

47. On the old mills, see Harsch, *Revenge of the Domestic*, 103–4. On modernization, see Stitziel, *Fashioning Socialism*, 127, 335–39, 341–42.

48. SAPMO-BArch, DY30/IV2/17/33, Bl. 22, Info. der Arbeitsgruppe Frau über die Probleme der allseitigen Erleichterung der Hausarbeit; DY30/IV2/17/33, Protokoll . . . 5.10.56; 39/120/5865. [1957]. Also see SAPMO-BArch, DY30/IV2/17/41, Frauenkonferenz . . . "Schwarze Pumpe" am 28/29.6.58, 4; DY34/A2080. Bericht . . . Senftenberg und Finsterwalde [1958], S.8; DY30/IV2/17/37, Bl.135, Information . . . Haushaltsgeräte [1957]; Bl.139–141, Anlage: Auswertung des Besuches der Kölner Haushaltsmesse, September 1956; DY31/338, Einschätzung . . . Handelskonferenz . . . ., 5–6; *Frau von heute*, 21.5.54, Was unsere Männer für den Haushalt konstruierten; 3.9.54, Praktische Neuheiten für die Frau; 21.9.56, Noch einmal Leipziger Allerlei für die Hausfrau; Katherine Pence, "Schaufenster des sozialistischen Konsums: Texte der ostdeutschen 'consumer culture'?" in Alf Lüdtke und Peter Becker, eds., *Akten. Eingaben. Schaufenster. Die DDR und ihre Texte* (Berlin: Akademie Verlag, 1997), 114.

49. Hübner, *Konsens*, 169; Steiner, "Frustration," 26, 35.

50. Külke, "Berufstätigkeit der Frauen," 46–47; Obertreis, *Familienpolitik*, 185; Helga Ulbricht et al., *Probleme der Frauenarbeit*, 28.

51. Harsch, *Revenge of the Domestic*, 183.

52. Ibid., 168–73; Helwig, "Frauen im SED-Staat," 1233.

53. Harsch, *Revenge of the Domestic*, 250–54, 299–300.

54. See the feminist scholarship cited in note 19 above.

55. For a comparative survey, see Sonya Michel, *Children's Interests/Mothers' Rights: The Shaping of America's Child Care Policy* (New Haven: Yale University Press, 1999), 282–96.

56. Karen Hagemann, Konrad H. Jarausch, and Cristina Allemann-Ghionda, eds., *Children, Families, and States: Time Policies of Childcare, Preschool, and Education in Europe* (New York and Oxford: Berghahn, 2011).

57. Quote is from Jane Lewis, "Gender and Welfare Regimes: Further Thoughts," *Social Politics* 4, no. 2 (Summer 1997): 161–62. Also see Susan Pedersen, *Family, Dependence, and the Origins of the Welfare State: Britain and France, 1914–1945* (Cambridge: Cambridge University Press, 1993); Seth Koven and Sonya Michel, eds., *Mothers of a New World: Maternalist Politics and the Origins of Welfare States* (New York: Routledge, 1993); Diane Sainsbury, ed., *Gender and Welfare State Regimes* (Oxford: Oxford University Press, 1999); and Haney, *Welfare in Hungary*.

Chapter 12

The Soldier-Breadwinner and the Army Family: Gender and Social Welfare in the Post-1945 US Military and Society

Jennifer Mittelstadt

World War II and its aftermath disrupted gender roles across a wide range of American institutions—the labor market, politics, and the home. One of the unrecognized arenas in which this contest played out was the military, particularly the US Army—and its growing role in providing social welfare. Of course, the army had always functioned as a social welfare institution since its origins in the Revolutionary War, especially for veterans and survivors of fallen soldiers.[1] But in the late twentieth century, with the switch to the All-Volunteer Force (AVF), the army transformed into a much larger and more intensive social welfare institution than ever before. Starting in the early 1970s, the United States military began building a robust social welfare system for active-duty military personnel and their families. For the nearly ten million Americans who volunteered for active duty after 1973—and their tens of millions of family members—the volunteer force provided a wide array of unprecedented programs: medical and dental insurance and service; housing assistance; subsistence payments; commissary and post exchange privileges; tax advantages; education and training; dozens of family welfare programs; child care; and social services ranging from financial counseling to legal aid.[2]

These programs were not considered rewards for citizens for the sacrifice of military service. They constituted primary lures for individuals to join the military and, even more important, once in, to remain. Spending on these programs grew to constitute the largest or often the second largest portion of the Defense Department budget.[3] The social welfare programs within the military both reflected and reinforced the gendered politics of civilian social welfare. Because the military occupied a central role in American life in the last half of the twentieth century, understanding these internal dynamics sheds light on the broader politics of gender and social welfare in the long postwar period.

Two military decisions in the postwar era accounted for the growth of military welfare. First, the advent of the Cold War prompted American policymakers to maintain a large standing army and a draft after World War II. This decision brought growing numbers of married men, many with children, into the military, whereas before World War II the ranks had consisted overwhelmingly of single young men. The presence of these families changed the military profoundly, although they were generally ignored by official military leadership. That is, until a second shift in military policy: the turn to the AVF in 1973. At that point, forced to recruit and retain personnel rather than conscript them, the military altered its approach toward families. The military increasingly developed and promoted itself as a significant source of social security for soldiers and their families. It expanded its social welfare apparatus through all ranks, to all military families, and into many new areas of social support. Though this occurred in all branches of the service, the army changed most; the largest of the services, it was the destination for most military families.

Married young heads of households stood at the core of this new apparatus. Army policy explicitly aimed at helping male heads of households—referred to in this chapter as soldier-breadwinners—support their families through a widening range of benefits and supports.[4] The army pleaded the case of the soldier-breadwinner before Congress to fund new programs, and it advertised the prospect of stable male-headed families to potential enlistees and soldiers it wished to retain. The connection of army benefits and social services to a male-breadwinner ideology served not merely to solve manpower problems by appealing to recruits, but also to restore the tarnished image of the army in the wake of the highly unpopular Vietnam War. The army touted its function as an imagined family and its adherence to familial hierarchies and "family values" associated with male-headed households in hopes of bringing a sense of order, loyalty, and cohesion to the institution itself.

That male-breadwinning ideology powerfully shaped the growth of social welfare functions in the military is, perhaps, not surprising. As the military transitioned to the volunteer era, it continued to be an overwhelmingly male-dominated institution, and it invested more deeply in masculinity and monitored threats to it.[5] At the same time, the United States experienced a resurgence in male-breadwinner ideology in the 1970s and 1980s. Just as the country shifted to the volunteer force, the press and many politicians identified a "crisis" of male breadwinners and proposed a raft of programs to aid them.[6] Then in the 1980s, under President Ronald Reagan, male-breadwinning ideology folded into a new Christian Right agenda favoring so-called traditional families: two-parent, mother-at-home families hewing to what the Christian Right called "family values." The military's embrace of a male soldier-breadwinner ideology followed these trends, both shoring up the ideology and at the same time strengthening the social, cultural, and political position of the military. The particular ways in which male-breadwinning ideology played out in the policies, practices, and politics of the military in the late twentieth century thus merit close attention.

This chapter describes the construction of a military social welfare apparatus as an important phenomenon shaping constructions of gender and the function of both the military and social welfare in American postwar society. It identifies the military decisions that led to this development and describes in detail the expansive, gendered social welfare apparatus that emerged. It analyzes the male soldier-breadwinner identity essential to this apparatus, concluding with a discussion of the repercussions of this distinctive gendered notion of family and social welfare for both the military and broader American politics and society.

Families and Social Welfare Needs in the Postwar Army

For centuries, the US Army had met its manpower goals by either accepting only single soldiers or ignoring the families of soldiers. In the period from the American Revolution through the antebellum period, single men filled the army's ranks.[7] It lured soldiers with monetary rewards and promises of land, which they might use as the basis for supporting a family, but army regulations did not mention family members and did not officially provide anything for them. Then in 1847, Congress prohibited married men from enlisting in the army, and policies discouraged marriage for nearly a century after that.[8] It was only the massive manpower demands of World War II that changed this tradition. Military leaders determined that an unprecedented 16 million service personnel would be needed to avoid risking defeat. To meet this demand for manpower, they had to allow husbands and fathers into their ranks. Beginning in 1942, married men and men with children entered the military.

This trend might have ended as quickly as it began had it not been for the beginning of the Cold War and the decision of American policymakers to retain a large peacetime military and a draft. This 1948 manpower decision forced the army to continue to draft men with wives and children. By 1960, this policy had produced a revolution in military life. The bastion of single males was so transformed that military "dependents"—spouses and children—outnumbered military personnel.[9]

Even though the postwar army had so many family members in its midst, it nevertheless seldom assisted them. A 1955 study of the armed forces explained that while the military was "prepared in terms of tradition and organization to care for its own personnel," to some degree, it had "only recently become—on any large scale—a family affair," and had not yet developed the will or capability to care for families.[10] The army performed minimally for most families and not at all for those of many junior enlisted soldiers—nearly half its force. The branch's routine disregard reflected the classic soldiers' joke: "If the army had wanted you to have a family, it would have issued you one."

Decades of neglect ended in 1973 when President Richard Nixon abandoned the draft and switched to the AVF. The change pushed the number of families higher than ever before. Unlike the draft-era force, which had relied on a small cadre of career soldiers augmented by large numbers of one-term draftees, the volunteer force hinged on a much larger cohort of career personnel. Moreover, because the army was simultaneously entering a more technologically advanced era, the cost to train soldiers rose, and thus the need to retain them became more acute.[11] The resulting emphasis on career personnel reinforced the demographic trend toward soldiers with families. First-termers in the draft army had been unlikely to be married or have children, but first-termers in the volunteer army were far more likely to be married.[12] Moreover, career soldiers who were not married at the time of enlistment were more likely to marry over time. By 1983, there were one and a half times as many family members as actual military personnel.[13]

Record numbers of families in the army did not alone compel its leaders to expand social welfare. It was the need to recruit and retain soldiers in the volunteer era that finally forced the army to embrace programs to assist soldiers and their families. No longer able to compel men to join, the army had to *convince* them. All of this meant that the army would have to fight to recruit and retain career personnel—with families. This required finally doing more to meet their needs.

The Soldier-Breadwinner and Social Welfare in the Volunteer Army

Gender conventions within the armed forces and in American society at large shaped the army's effort to meet the needs of soldiers and families. Explicitly and implicitly, symbolically and in practical terms, a kind of new social compact emerged in the volunteer era between the army and soldiers. It consisted of a promise to allow young men who volunteered for service both to be soldiers and to have and support families at a decent standard of living—to be soldier-breadwinners.

The focus on male soldier-breadwinners clearly derived from the overwhelmingly male character of the armed forces. On the eve of the volunteer force, women constituted less than 2 percent of army personnel. Yet that figure changed drastically over the next several years as the army realized the necessity of bringing women into the volunteer force; there was literally no way to recruit the numbers of men necessary to sustain the force. The volunteer army thus recruited women heavily, and by 1978 the proportion of female soldiers had risen to 6.6 percent of enlistees.[14] Still, no matter the increase in women's numbers, they remained overwhelmed by the ocean of men around them. Women were symbolically overwhelmed, too, by the thoroughgoing male culture of the military, which resisted incorporating women into the ranks. Indeed, it may have been in part because of the growing numbers of female enlistees that men, not women, remained the focus of army leaders' plans for a more robust support system as the army made the switch into the volunteer era. The army did not emphasize its increasing feminization.[15]

The focus on male soldier-breadwinners was due not only to the sex of most soldiers but also to the perceived threat to their breadwinning status. The need to preserve the status of the male soldier-breadwinner emerged from the debates over compensation and benefits that accompanied the switch to the volunteer force. Advocates for the volunteer force argued that low pay and insufficient benefits and services stood as the primary obstacles to the success of a volunteer force. To make this point, members of Congress took to the floors of their chambers and the editorial pages of newspapers to expose the difficulties facing married male soldiers and their families. They told a story of male soldier-breadwinners in crisis.

Poverty and lack of services imperiled the families of the new recruits. Republican Congressman William Steiger of Wisconsin insisted, "For today's young soldier . . . his wife and children are dependent for survival upon a military compensation system that is a national disgrace."[16] Pennsylvania Republican Senator Richard Schweiker decried the hardships of the typical junior enlisted soldier posted to Germany. Lacking a military allowance to pay for his wife and children to join him, he would "float a loan" and bring them on his own dime. "This economic burden of indebtedness," Schweiker explained, "immediately puts him behind the eight ball not only economically but mentally . . . . [W]e see a lot of mental breakdowns that are directly attributable to the fact that the GI is here without his family or if he is here [with family] the marriage is in serious trouble because a soldier has to live in a constant state of poverty and indebtedness."[17]

Poverty forced some married soldiers to turn to government welfare programs like Aid to Families with Dependent Children (AFDC), food stamps, and general assistance to make ends meet. This phenomenon became a central motif of the struggling soldier-breadwinner narrative.[18] It accentuated the gendered and racialized assumptions about both welfare and the military in play at the time. Welfare—the term a stand-in for public assistance programs—had long been stigmatized for indiscriminately helping the supposedly undeserving poor.[19] Congressional and media observers painted welfare receipt as an especially ignominious status for a soldier, whose worthiness ought to be unquestioned. This degradation was compounded by the fact that in the public imagination, welfare was not only stigmatized but also feminized and racialized. It was symbolized by the stereotype of the African American "matriarch" popularized in Daniel Patrick Moynihan's controversial and widely disseminated 1965 memo for the Department of Labor, *The Negro Family: The Case for National Action*. Joining the matriarch image was the new rhetoric of the late 1960s antiwelfare backlash: the "breeder," a promiscuous woman who had children just to garner a larger welfare check.[20] The soldier, with his masculinized imagery of bravery, independence, strength, and sacrifice, fit nowhere in such a demeaned, feminized landscape.

The image of soldiers dragging wives and children to welfare lines captured media attention. The Associated Press reported, "From New Jersey to California . . . public welfare agencies are supplementing allotment checks from Vietnam, paying the rent of married draftees or buying groceries for families whose breadwinners are overseas."[21] A *New York Times* headline decried "Poverty in Uniform"—the "married recruit" with wife and children receiving public assistance. "These families—now numbering in the tens of thousands—who must depend on food stamps and other forms of welfare to make ends meet" needed far more support.[22] Overall, the image of soldiers on welfare generated shock and disgust. "That a man with or without a child has to be on welfare while serving his country," Republican Senator Mark Hatfield of Oregon exclaimed, "should put the Senate to shame."[23]

Soldiers themselves made it clear that they felt the pinch of supporting families in a difficult economy. In 1975, Staff Sergeant D. L. Manley wrote a letter to the *Army Times*, complaining that the army "turn[ed] its back on the service members' needs. If a sergeant cannot afford the basic needs of his family now," he asked, "what is to be expected in the future?"[24] Army studies of the 1970s reported soldiers' complaints that "frequent moves, family separation, and lack of housing" made their lives difficult.[25] They indicated that that this general "dissatisfaction over living conditions was one of the main objections to Army life."[26] Army investigators asked what the branch might do to remedy matters, and soldiers answered with demands for a decent standard of living for their wives and children: they wanted economic security, protection against unforeseen events, health care, more support for their families, and job training for the future.[27]

Studies conducted at several posts around the country echoed the importance of broader quality-of-life issues not only to soldiers, but also to their wives. A survey at Fort Benning, Georgia, revealed army wives' interest in programs that improved overall family security and standard of living. Between 69 and 77 percent of wives of enlisted personnel reported that the army's educational programs, which allowed soldiers to increase their earning potential, exerted "some or strong influence" on them to recommend that their husbands stay in the army.[28] In addition, 55 to 65 percent of these women said they believed that the army would be "much or a little better" with programs like family housing, better medical benefits, and better educational benefits.[29] If these benefits were improved, wives said, they would be more inclined to have their husbands reenlist.

The Crisis of the Male-Breadwinner Family

The challenges facing male soldiers and their families assumed urgency in part because they echoed society-wide fears of the erosion of male breadwinning and the difficulty facing working-class families—the group from which most soldiers originated. In the 1970s, the lives of the working classes were widely perceived as having descended into, as the title of Lillian Rubin's 1976 classic analysis of working-class families put it, "worlds of pain."[30] Declining economic fortunes in the industrial sector of the economy hit working-class men hard, with unemployment rates as high as 10 percent in industrial states like Massachusetts and New Jersey.[31] A spate of scholarly and journalistic investigations of the "forgotten man"—the white, blue-collar, male bread-winner—described his seeming downward trajectory, his inability to support his wife and children, and his accompanying loss of self-respect and dignity. As historian Marisa Chappell points out, opinion makers believed that these "'stable breadwinners, churchgoers, voters, [and] family men' had a tremendous investment in their role as provider."[32] Her research shows that a broad coalition of policymakers, scholars, journalists, and members of civil rights organizations wanted much more public attention paid to "the hard-working, father-dominated families" that "constitute the great majority."[33]

The perceived crisis generated a host of national policy proposals to shore up a male-breadwinning ideal for members of the working class.[34] One of the top priorities of the War on Poverty, for example, was creating jobs for men through programs like the Job Corps. Nixon's Family Assistance Plan would have provided an income floor to supplement the wages of low-income working families, particularly those with male breadwinners who had previously been slighted by the nation's emphasis on welfare for nonworking mothers and children. African American civil rights leaders like Dorothy Height, Vernon Jordan, Coretta Scott King, and Roy Wilkins changed tack from fighting for poor African Americans to supporting seemingly "majoritarian issues" like progressive tax reform and full employment—policies aimed at working male heads of households.[35] Perhaps the most important example of this was the failed Full Employment and Balanced Growth Act (the Humphrey-Hawkins Bill), which emphasized jobs for male breadwinners.[36] Together these proposals constituted a broad agenda to shore up the male breadwinner in a time of crisis.

If the problems facing working-class men were urgent in the civilian world, they were perceived as dire in the context of the military. In a volunteer era, images of soldiers and their families standing in welfare lines could doom the military. As Secretary of Defense Melvin Laird told Congress, "From the standpoint of morale, the standpoint of equity, and from the standpoint of attracting and keeping men and women in our military services that are necessary to meet our national security needs," something had to be done.[37]

Social Welfare for Soldier-Breadwinners and Traditional Families

By the mid-1970s the army finally had begun to weave what would become an extensive social safety net for the soldier-breadwinner and his family. Army policymakers emphasized those issues and areas that enhanced soldiers' abilities to have their families with them and to support them at a better standard of living. The initial expansion bestowed upon junior enlisted soldiers' families—the bulk of the volunteer force—the same benefits already provided to the families of career personnel and officers. Over time, the army went beyond expanding existing coverage and created wholly new family-centered offices, programs, and services.

The most important early expansion of soldier benefits was related to Junior Enlisted Travel: the army term for travel provisions for junior enlisted soldiers. The term "travel," with its possible connotations of vacations or airline tickets, was misleading. In fact, "travel" denoted a host of payments and entitlements related to the relocation of soldiers and their families to new posts—and support of families once there. The most important of these concerned command-sponsored, accompanied overseas tours, foreign billets in which a soldier brought his wife and children at the army's expense. Prior to the onset of the volunteer force, "accompanied" tours were viewed as the perquisites of long-term career service, necessary only for higher-ranking soldiers who both had families and had earned the privilege of the army's sponsorship. Only soldiers above the rank of corporal qualified, which left more than 40 percent of the army in the cold.

Though command-sponsored, accompanied tours might have been historically a privilege of rank, leaders of the modern volunteer army of the 1970s redefined them as necessary to maintain soldiers' satisfaction. "This type of situation," a member of the House Armed Services Committee pointed out, "is hardly conducive to force morale and retention and we are losing some very good people as a result."[38] The new entitlements provided dependent travel, storage of household goods, shipment of privately owned vehicles and up to 1,500 pounds of household goods, and movement of a house trailer for service members in the ranks of corporal (with less than two years' service) and below.[39] "The long-range benefits of this action," argued Rep. Bill Nichols, the Republican from Alabama who chaired the Armed Services Compensation Subcommittee, "include potential better reenlistment rates, less attrition before completion of enlistment and longer overseas tours."[40]

The army's new programs for solider breadwinners also included family housing. Historically, the army had provided no family housing except to senior noncommissioned and commissioned officers. In the 1950s it began providing limited family housing to additional officers and some senior enlisted personnel. But this was woefully inadequate, and, for the enlisted personnel, often dilapidated. With the switch to the volunteer force in the early 1970s, the lack of family housing and its poor quality became a serious problem. As Congress reported, "Adequate family housing . . . was one of the primary factors influencing the retention of qualified married military personnel in the services."[41] If the army was to keep its married soldiers it needed more family housing. In 1973, housing improvements for soldiers and families became the "largest single program authorization for the military."[42]

While the army extended its privileges to junior enlisted soldiers and families, it also began to build a social service apparatus for them. This initiative expanded the limited programs offered by the service's official social service institution, Army Community Service (ACS), which since 1966 had offered fairly minimal, volunteer-staffed services. The new programs included orientation, family counseling and support, child and youth education and recreation, financial counseling, legal services, and more.[43] These "model programs" were "developed and tested for adaptation" at specific posts and then expanded across army installations in the next few years.[44]

The early expansion of existing programs to young enlisted soldiers and families presaged a massive expansion of new family-focused programs for the whole army in the early and mid-1980s. In 1984, the army issued the first "Army Family Action Plan" (AFAP), a set of policy prescriptions for improving the lives of the families of soldiers.[45] Remarkably, soldiers and families themselves wrote these prescriptions. AFAP developed as an annual army-wide review process at each post in which all families and soldiers could participate. By 1987, 270,000 family members were attending them.[46] These symposia sent up recommendations for review first to the post commander and then, when broader policy solutions were required, to the Department of the Army. By the mid-1980s, the army had changed into a large and diversified provider of social welfare. Its new programs and services allowed soldiers with families to enjoy a decent standard of living, with an economic and social security previously unknown, particularly for junior enlisted soldiers.

As army family programs multiplied in the 1980s, they became more closely entangled with a new version of male-breadwinning politics: Christian Right "family values" during the Reagan administration. Reagan created closer ties with the increasingly politicized religious right than any president before him.[47] With the help of the Christian Right, Reagan emphasized the legitimacy of traditional, two-parent, mother-at-home families in policies, speeches, and law.[48] At the same time, Reagan opposed policies and laws benefiting nontraditional families such as AFDC and federal child care programs. Supporting "traditional" families and opposing those not exhibiting "family values" animated Reagan's politics across a range of social institutions.

The army's programs reflected this social engineering. The chief architect of its family programs in the 1980s, Chief of Staff General John Wickham, was a committed "born again" Christian.[49] He and other army commanders drew directly on evangelical Christian leaders and their doctrines to shape the army's growing array of family services. In 1983, Wickham turned to friends in the evangelical religious right community to help shape army family programs, notably James Dobson, head of Focus on Family, a well-known religious organization dedicated to the "preservation of the family and the propagation of traditional, pro-family views." Wickham and religious conservatives steered army services toward Christian Right notions of family.[50] This ideology trickled throughout military family programs, in videos purchased to help families with deployments, in family counseling, and in the promotion of chaplaincy as a major component of family support.[51] It reinforced not only the gender divisions in economic roles typical of male-breadwinning families, but also social and cultural norms of male "leadership" and female "submission" to husbands' authority typical of Christian Right "family values." Army programs of the 1980s shaded toward and benefited from a conservative evangelical Christian political agenda.

The Army Family and the Relegitimization of the Army

As the Army embarked upon its expansion of social welfare, it simultaneously worked to publicize these new benefits. Its multimillion-dollar advertising budget devoted funds not merely toward recruiting new soldiers but also to retaining those it already had. For those already in the ranks, the army drew attention to the soldier-breadwinner model and its support programs. In 1975, it placed full-page advertisements in the *Army Times* directed specifically at officers. In bold letters, it told them to "ASK YOUR MEN TO ASK THEIR WIVES ABOUT RE-ENLISTING." In smaller print, it suggested: "Remind [your man] to ask his wife if she likes the housing, the day care centers, the medical care, and all the other things" the army had done for her family.[52] By the early 1980s, these ads had become commonplace, shrewdly directed at the various demographics of army families. Each ad pictured a husband in uniform with a wife and child. One typical ad featured a white soldier with wife Connie and son Ronnie Lee standing proudly in front of a new brick single-family housing unit intended for an army family. "Because we're in the Army," the soldier explained, "people may not expect us to live this well. But . . . Connie and I feel that the Army's really come a long way . . . in taking care of its people."[53] The army hoped other soldiers would agree.

A raft of glossy new brochures sent to posts across the world complemented the advertisements and touted the benefits now being provided. "The Army Family—A Partnership" described in four languages—English, German, Korean, and Spanish—the "services for your family" on most installations throughout the world. Photos of happy army wives of Asian, Latina, and European descent accented each page.[54] To be sure, the advertisements and the outreach materials had practical connections to manpower goals: to "make all benefits more visible so service members and their families are aware and understand what they have and what it's worth," as the deputy chief of staff for personnel put it.[55] After all, the soldier had to be reminded that he was receiving this support from the army for the medical care, housing, and social services to have their intended effect. But the advertisements signaled far more. As the army reached out to recruit and retain soldier-breadwinners, it simultaneously drew on the rhetoric associated with the soldier-breadwinner to redefine itself as an institution.

And in the 1970s, the army was in dire need of redefinition. At the height of the Vietnam War, before the transition to the volunteer force, the army had reached an institutional nadir. Well-publicized incidences of crime, alcohol and drug abuse, overt racism, and resistance to authority plagued the army of the late 1960s and early 1970s. Events as dire as the My Lai massacre—and its cover-up—and the killing of superior officers by their own soldiers (known as "fragging"), as well as commonplace practices such as binge drinking and smoking marijuana, undermined the army's professionalism and effectiveness. Its leaders "became increasingly convinced that the professional fabric of the institution was unraveling."[56]

As the army abandoned the draft and entered the volunteer era, a spate of books reported on the "anguish" of the Army with its "tarnished shield" and even forecast its death as a viable institution. Alongside the many public reports of shocking and unseemly army actions, these books reduced the army's legitimacy.[57] Its leaders were acutely aware of "the extent to which the Army's public image had declined." Its surveys revealed that even among its own soldiers, the army had a bad reputation: "70 percent of Army veterans advised prospective volunteers to join services other than the Army."[58]

The army's embrace of male-headed families helped it restore its image over the course of the 1970s and 1980s. It coincided with an effort to portray itself as an institutional family. In the early 1970s, the army revived one of its traditional maxims and adapted it to the emerging soldier-breadwinner framework. Secretary of the Army Martin Hoffman testified to Congress, "The old Army leadership adage 'Take care of your people and they will take care of you' was never more true." The army now provided "the assurance that when . . . in a combat environment or separated from family that the army will provide for medical care, commissary and exchange privileges, assistance with personal problem and survivors benefits," a raft of supports to "take care" of the soldier's family.[59]

To breathe life into the promise to take care of its own, the army resurrected another traditional phrase—the "Army family." The "Army took care of its own" because of an "Army family" ethos. Deputy Chief of Staff Harold Moore used his annual status reports in the 1970s to revive the phrase. "As we moved through the second year of the volunteer force we . . . took a hard look at where we need to go to improve personnel management for members of the Army family."[60] Moore spelled out the army family's broad constituency, making the case for "*all* elements of the military 'family,'" including wives and children.[61] In Moore's terms—terms that became commonplace—soldiers joined the volunteer army, and because the army was a "family," it, in turn, took care of the soldier's family.

In the 1970s, the army utilized the respectable image of an "army family" taking care of its members to contrast with the perceived chaos of the Vietnam-era force. This framing was evident in the late 1970s, when a few budget-cutting members of Congress fruitlessly opposed the extension of travel benefits to junior enlisted personnel. Army commanders revolted, fearing that leaving families behind in the United States would inflame personnel problems from the Vietnam era. They argued that the increasing family-friendliness of the army quelled all manner of bad soldier behavior. "At three dozen major U.S. military bases in West Germany," *Time* magazine reported, the presence of "dependent families" served as "a moderating influence" on soldiers. "Married men," General John W. Pauley explained, "tend to be more stable and much less subject to the dangers of alcohol, drug abuse and sexual adventures with the locals, provided family are with them at these overseas posts." An army of families, in which one overarching US Army family took care of them all, produced a more professional, obedient, responsible and honorable army. These were characteristics that were found lacking in the army during the Vietnam draft era and that the army was at pains to promote in the new era of the volunteer force.

Family rhetoric complemented increased emphasis on discipline and order, too. The "army family" that "took care of its own" reinforced the hierarchy of army life by modeling the gendered relations of the traditional male-breadwinner family. In the "army family," the army assumed the highest place at the top of the ladder—the symbolic head of household. The army took care of its "dependents" below, providing authority but also sustenance. The soldier stood one rung below the army, serving and obeying, but also caring for his own family. His care for them—as breadwinner—was supplemented, but not supplanted, by the army's supports for the family. And below the soldier stood the family—wives, essentially—dependent on both soldiers and the army for their care, yet serving both husband/soldiers and the army through their loyalty and care work. The army family model exemplified military discipline and hierarchy, but set it in a human, understandable context.

The army family model also provided precisely the symbolism and metaphor for the kind of institutional goals the army was at pains to promote in the new era of the volunteer force: unity, cohesion, commitment, and loyalty. These goals worked internally to increase soldiers' sense of connection to the military, a connection that army leaders hoped would translate into the decision to make a career of military service. But they also worked externally to represent the military as an institution epitomized by these virtues—virtues in large part associated with traditional male-headed households.

This was especially true in the 1980s, with the Christian conservative turn within army family programs. Conservatives in the civilian world laid claim to the army. As they told the story, in a society that some viewed as drifting from the values of the traditional family, the army's choice to emphasize the male-breadwinner family made it "an enclave of virtue," setting it apart from—and above—other American institutions.[62] As General Wickham put it, "ideas of family cohesion and family values within our military community" offered a model to which the rest of the nation could aspire: "There is a dimension of the American dream, the notion of strength," he explained, "that is tied to the military family . . . and we have a great opportunity to influence and perpetuate that dream."[63] By the end of the 1980s some army officers trumpeted their "family values" as exceptional as compared to civilians', and proclaimed their moral superiority.[64] The army's evolving family model helped lift the army's reputation and revive its social and political standing.

Conclusion

The army's new social welfare apparatus shows how changing gender roles in postwar American life played out in a military context in the United States. Imperatives of the military and those of American politics and society fused male breadwinning to the fate of the volunteer force. Their linkage magnified the impact of male-breadwinner ideology inside and outside of the military, while simultaneously helping the military regain legitimacy and achieve even greater influence in American life. The results, for both soldiers and their families and for American politics and society, have been profound.

Within the military, the male soldier-breadwinner model served many people poorly, particularly women. It eclipsed the realities they faced as both soldiers and spouses. Female soldiers and their male spouses fit uneasily, if at all, into the male soldier-breadwinner model. Indeed, Air Force Lieutenant Sharron Frontiero would have to sue the Defense Department in a case that rose all the way to the Supreme Court to force the military to provide benefits to her male spouse.[65] Nor did the soldier-breadwinner model necessarily benefit army wives, whose economic dependence on their spouses and the army paid fewer dividends than they hoped. The model continued to impose economic difficulties on soldiers' wives and their families. As much as many male soldiers—and their wives—did identify with male-breadwinning and traditionally gendered family roles, many enlisted families could not afford to keep wives out of the labor market. Not only did these women often need to work to make ends meet, many of them wanted to work in any case. But finding work was difficult. In 1972, only 27 percent of military wives were in the labor force, far fewer than the number of married civilian women.[66] Soldiers' wives had (and still have) special challenges finding and keeping jobs: long hours worked by soldier husbands, deployments, and frequent moves. These women asked the army for assistance in dealing with these challenges beginning in 1980, but got little response.[67] In keeping with the soldier-breadwinner imagery, and because of the benefits already being provided to families, army leaders persisted in imagining most soldiers' wives as stay-at-home caregivers who did not need or want work.

As the army's investment in the social politics of restoring and protecting traditional and conservative models of male breadwinning grew during the 1980s, it affected more than just those in uniform. It also became entangled with the emerging conservative politics of "family values" in the United States. Amid the nation's changing political climate, the army's effort to support male breadwinning and create an "Army family" model of social welfare fostered the army's growing association with political conservatism, an association that secured the military's position on the conservative agenda. Social conservatives who lauded the symbolism and substance of the army's family programs helped assure increased budgetary support in the Reagan years and beyond, as well as political legitimacy that has remained largely unchallenged—and perhaps even grown—since then.

Notes

1. Sondra Albano, "Military Recognition of Family Concerns: Revolutionary War to 1993," *Armed Forces and Society* 20 (1994): 283–302, 284, 286, 287. Benefits for veterans—those who are not part of the active duty army (or military)—are provided by the Veterans Administration after separation from service. They constitute a separate but important form of social welfare not considered here.

2. Department of Defense, Office of the Under Secretary of Defense for Personnel and Readiness, "Population Representation in the Military Services," FY 2006, http://www.defenselink.mil/prhome/PopRep_FY06/.

3. In the 1970s, the manpower budget exceeded 50 percent of the defense budget; Sar Levitan and Karen Cleary Aldeman, *Warriors at Work: The Volunteer Armed Force* (Beverly Hills, CA: Sage Publications, 1977), 95. Moreover, this figure underestimates total manpower costs. It is drawn from the Department of Defense personnel budget, but many costs of benefits and social services are in other parts of the defense budget, including operations and maintenance, military family housing, and general construction.

4. I use the term "soldier-breadwinner" to capture the connection of this debate to the long history of male-breadwinner politics and ideology in the United States. See Alice Kessler-Harris, *In Pursuit of Equity: Women, Men and the Quest for Economic Citizenship in Twentieth-Century America* (New York: Oxford University Press, 2001).

5. For a recent analysis of this institutional culture, see Carol Burke, *Camp All-American, Hanoi Jane, and the High-and-Tight: Gender, Folklore, and Changing Military Culture* (Boston: Beacon Press, 2004).

6. Marisa Chappell, *The War on Welfare: Gender, Family, and the Politics of AFDC in Modern America* (Philadelphia: University of Pennsylvania Press, 2009); Natasha Zaretsky, *No Direction Home: The American Family and the Fear of National Decline, 1968–1980* (Chapel Hill: University of North Carolina Press, 2007).

7. Albano, "Military Recognition," 284.

8. Ibid., 284–85, 286.

9. Ibid., 289.

10. National Committee on Social Work in Defense Mobilization, *The Military Program and Social Welfare* (New York: National Committee on Social Work in Defense Mobilization, 1955), 23, 23–5.

11. David R. Segal, *Recruiting for Uncle Sam* (Lawrence: University Press of Kansas, 1989); and Charles Moskos, John Allen Williams, and David R. Segal, *The Postmodern Military: Armed Forces after the Cold War* (New York: Oxford University Press, 2000).

12. Levitan and Aldeman, *Warriors at Work*, 56.

13. General John Wickham, "The Army Family" (Washington, DC: US Army, Chief of Staff, Department of the Army, 1983), 5.

14. Office of the Assistant Secretary of Defense, Manpower, Reserve Affairs, and Logistics, "America's Volunteers: A Report on the All-Volunteer Armed Forces," (Washington, DC: US Defense Department, December 31, 1978), 70.

15. Beth Bailey, *America's Army: Making the All-Volunteer Force* (Cambridge, MA: Harvard University Press, 2009), 130–71.

16. William Steiger, "America's Poverty-Level Fighting Men," *Los Angeles Times*, May 16, 1971, F2.

17. U.S. Congress, Senate, Committee on Armed Services, "Hearings on Selective Service and Military Compensation," 92nd Congress, first session, February 2, 4, 8, 9, 10, 19, and 22, 1971, 46.

18. A common figure cited was 20,000. David Rosenbaum, "Senate Bars Plan Designed to Bring Volunteer Army," *New York Times*, August 26, 1970, 16.

19. There is a voluminous literature on the stigmatization of welfare provision, beginning even before the founding of the Republic. See, for example, Ruth Herndon, *Unwelcome Americans: Living on the Margin in Early New England* (Philadelphia: University of Pennsylvania Press, 2001); Seth Rockman, *Welfare Reform in the Early Republic: A Brief History with Documents* (Boston: Bedford/St. Martin's, 2002); Gwendolyn Mink, *The Wages of Motherhood: Inequality and the Welfare State* (Ithaca, NY: Cornell University Press 1995); and Joanne Goodwin, *Gender and the Politics of Welfare Reform: Mothers' Pensions in Chicago, 1911–1929* (Chicago: University of Chicago Press, 1997).

20. US Department of Labor, Office of Policy Planning and Research, *The Negro Family: The Case for National Action* (Washington, DC: US Government Printing Office, 1965); Ange-Marie Hancock, *The Politics of Disgust: The Public Identity of the Welfare Queen* (New York: New York University Press, 2004), 57–63; Lisa Levenstein, "From Innocent Child to Unwanted Migrants and Unwed Mothers: Two Chapters in the Public Discourse on Welfare in the United States, 1960–1961," *Journal of Women's History* 11 (2000): 10–33.

21. "Low Pay, High Costs Put Soldiers on Welfare," *Los Angeles Times*, November 13, 1969, A9.

22. "Poverty in Uniform," *New York Times*, June 1, 1971, 38.

23. Rosenbaum, "Senate Bars Plan," 1.

24. S.Sgt. D.L. Manley, letter to the editor, *Army Times*, August 13, 1975, 13.

25. Robert Griffith, *The U.S. Army's Transition to the All-Volunteer Force, 1968–1974* (Washington, DC: US Army Center of Military History, 1997), 30–3.

26. Department of the Army, *Historical Summary: Fiscal Year 1972* (Washington, DC: US Government Printing Office, 1972), 93.

27. Griffith, *U.S. Army's Transition*, 39.

28. Ibid., 18.

29. Ibid., 26.

30. Lillian Rubin, *Worlds of Pain: Life in the Working-Class Family* (New York: Basic Books, 1976).

31. Unemployment rates are from 1976; Department of Labor, Bureau of Labor Statistics, "Local Area Unemployment Statistics: Current Unemployment Rates for States and Historical Highs/Lows," last modified December 18, 2008, http://www.bls.gov/web /lauhsthl.htm.

32. Chappell, *War on Welfare*, 210–11.

33. Hamill and Robert Hill of the National Urban League, quoted in Chappell, *War on Welfare*, 211–12.

34. Chappell, *War on Welfare*, 196–98.

35. Ibid., 208.

36. Ibid., 231, 222.

37. US Congress, Senate, Committee on Armed Services, "Hearings on Selective Service," 92nd Congress, first session, February 2, 4, 8, 9, 10, 19, and 22, 1971, 46.

38. Rep. Bob Wilson (R-CA), quoted in "Jr. EM Travel Pay Pushed," *Army Times*, May 29, 1978, 22.

39. Department of the Army, *Historical Summary: Fiscal Year 1979*, 93–94.

40. "Jr. EM Travel Pay Pushed," 22.

41. *Congressional Quarterly Almanac*, 1973 (Washington, DC: Congressional Quarterly, Inc., 1973), 149.

42. Ibid., 919.

43. Department of the Army, *Historical Summary: Fiscal Year 1971*, 49; William B. Fulton, Director of the Army Staff, to Assistant Secretary of the Army for Manpower and Reserve Affairs, memorandum, January 23, 1976, folder 11, box 13, series II, All-Volunteer Army collection, Military History Institute, Carlisle Barracks, PA (hereafter referred to as MHI), 5.

44. Department of the Army, *Historical Summary: Fiscal Year 1971*, 49. By 1975, the deputy chief of staff for personnel reported that many of these programs had been adopted across the army by the chief of staff. Harold G. Moore, "A Busy Year of the 'Hard Look' at People Policies," *Army Magazine* 10, (October 25, 1975), 45.

45. US Army, Office of the Deputy Chief of Staff for Personnel, "Army Family Action Plan," (Washington, DC: US Army Chief of Staff, 1984).

46. Albano, "Military Recognition of Family Concerns," 292.

47. Gary Scott Smith, *Faith and the Presidency: From George Washington to George W. Bush* (New York: Oxford University Press, 2006), 318; D. Michael Lindsay, *Faith and the Halls of Power: How Evangelicals Joined the American Elite* (New York: Oxford University Press, 2007),18.

48. An antipornography effort, opposition to federal day care programs, and antiabortion stands, among other initiatives, indicated the power of the Christian Right in Reagan's administration. This work culminated in 1987 in "The Family," Reagan's executive order pledging to strengthen traditional family values across all his cabinet departments.

On Bauer and the White House Working Group on the Family that drafted the order, see Glen H. Utter and John Woodrow Storey, *The Religious Right: A Reference Handbook*, 2nd edition (Santa Barbara, CA: ABC-Clio, 200), 73l; Susan Faludi, *Backlash: The Undeclared War Against American Women* (New York: Random House, 1991), 275; White House Working Group on the Family, "The Family: Preserving America's Future" (Washington, DC: US Government Printing Office, 1986).

49. Anne Loveland, *American Evangelicals and the U.S. Military, 1942–1993* (Baton Rouge: Louisiana State University Press, 1996), 275. "Interview with *Soldiers* magazine," September 1983, in John A. Wickham Jr., *Collected Works of the Thirtieth Chief of Staff, United States Army* (Washington, DC: US Army Center of Military History, 1987), 338. For references to God, see Wickham, *Collected Works*.

50. James Dobson to Ronald A. Mlinarchik, February 19, 1986, folder "Task Force on Soldiers and Families," box 51, Papers of John Wickham, MHI; Loveland, *American Evangelicals*, 274–286.

51. For the video, see James Dobson to Ronald A. Mlinarchik, February 19, 1986, MHI. This video was in wide use even before Wickham became army chief of staff. See reference in "Interview with *Soldiers* magazine," in Wickham, *Collected Works*, 341. On counseling, see Comptroller of the Army, "The Army Budget: Fiscal Year 1985" (Washington, DC: US Department of the Army, 1984), 90. The overall chaplain's activities budget came to between $15 and $19 million in each of these years, with a small portion, $200,000, reserved specifically for coordinating the chaplaincy's growing family life centers. On the chaplaincy's increased role in family support, see "OC of CH Policy or Precedent: Subject: Family Life Ministry/Family Life Unit Ministry Team, November 9, 1990," Folder—MACOM Staff Chaplain, Family Life Ministry/Family Life Unit Ministry Team, Chief of Chaplains Policy, 9 Nov 90, Center of Military History Collection.

52. Advertisement in *Army Times*, September 24, 1975, 17.

53. Advertisement prepared by N. W. Ayer for *Army Times* distribution, 1985, US REE 609909; courtesy of Beth Bailey.

54. Headquarters of the Army, Department of the Army, "The Army Family—A Partnership/ Die Heeresfamilie—Eine Partnerschaft," (Washington, DC: US Department of the Army, 1985).

55. Fulton to Assistant Secretary of the Army, January 23, 1976, MHI, 3.

56. Griffith, *U.S. Army's Transition*, 25, 69.

57. Edward L. King, *The Death of the Army: A Pre-Mortem* (New York: Saturday Review Press, 1972); George Walton, *The Tarnished Shield: A Report on Today's Army* (New York: Dodd, Mead & Co., 1973); William L. Hauser, *America's Army in Crisis: A Study in Civil-Military Relations* (Baltimore: Johns Hopkins University Press, 1973); Haynes Johnson and George C. Wilson, *Army in Anguish* (New York: Pocket Books, 1972).

58. Griffith, *U.S. Army's Transition*, 37.

59. Cited in Fulton to Assistant Secretary of the Army, January 23, 1976, MHI, 2. The phrase "The Army Takes Care of Its Own" originated during World War II.

60. Moore, "A Busy Year," 38.

61. Harold Moore, "On Pay and Benefits: A 'Balanced Approach,'" *Army Magazine*, October 26, 1976: 10, 101(emphasis in original).

62. Andrew Bacevitch, *The New American Militarism: How Americans Are Seduced by War* (New York: Oxford University Press, 2005); Loveland, *American Evangelicals*, 298.

63. Chief of Staff of the Army General John Wickham, "Address at the Army Community Services Workshop," Arlington, Virginia (August 17, 1984), in Wickham, *Collected Works*, 64.

64. Bacevich, *New American Militarism*, 141. These notions took hold beyond General Wickham, in an increasingly conservative Christian officer corps in the 1980s. See also Thomas Ricks, *Making the Corps* (New York: Scribner, 1998); David King and Zachary Karabell, *The Generation of Trust: How the U.S. Military Has Regained the Public's Confidence since Vietnam* (Washington, DC: American Enterprise Institute Press, 2003), 61–9; Loveland, *American Evangelicals*; and Ole R. Holsti, "Of Chasms and Convergences: Attitudes and Beliefs of Civilians and Military Elites at the Start of a New Millennium" in *Soldiers and Civilians: The Civil-Military Gap and American National Security*, ed. Peter D. Feaver and Richard R. Kohn (Cambridge, MA: MIT Press, 2001), 27.

65. *Frontiero v. Richardson*, 411 U.S. 677 (1973).

66. Mady Wechsler Segal and Jesse J. Harris, "What We Know about Army Families," (Alexandria, VA: US Army Research Institute for the Behavioral and Social Sciences, 1993), 36.

67. "The Army Family: Analysis and Appraisal" (proceedings of a symposium sponsored by the Association of the US Army and the Army Officers' Wives' Club of the Greater Washington Area, October 11–12, 1980), iii.

Part IV

Forging New Sexualities and Creating New Gender Identities

Chapter 13

The Liberal 1950s? Reinterpreting Postwar American Sexual Culture

Joanne Meyerowitz

For more than twenty years now, historians have written about the sexual conservatism of the postwar United States. In her 1988 book *Homeward Bound*, Elaine Tyler May drafted the outline of this now-common interpretation. May borrowed the word "containment" from the foreign policy of the Cold War and repositioned it as a broader postwar cultural ethos that applied as well to gender and sexuality. In May's influential rendition, middle-class Americans saw uncontrolled sexual behavior as a dangerous source of moral decline that would sap the nation's strength. In postwar America, she wrote, "fears of sexual chaos" made "non-marital sexual behavior in all its forms . . . a national obsession." Various officials, experts, and commentators "believed wholeheartedly," she claimed, in "a direct connection between communism and sexual depravity." Accordingly, they attempted to police sexual expression and "contain" it within marriage.[1] Over the past two decades, other historians have followed May's lead, elaborating on the Cold War "containment" of sexuality and suggesting its impact on policy, politics, citizenship, masculinity, femininity, and sexual behavior. And yet they have simultaneously undermined the "containment" thesis. As they expanded their base of evidence, they stretched the dominant interpretation and poked a passel of holes—sometimes inadvertently—in the story it tells.

Mounting historical evidence now suggests that the postwar years were not as conservative as sometimes stated. In 1988, the same year that May published *Homeward Bound*, for example, John D'Emilio and Estelle Freedman first presented a somewhat different argument. In *Intimate Matters*, they accepted the sexual conservatism of postwar American culture but also posed the postwar years as a time of "sexual liberalism." For D'Emilio and Freedman, sexual liberalism involved "contradictory patterns of expression and constraints." It "celebrated the erotic, but tried to keep it within a heterosexual framework of long-term monogamous relationships." With this formulation of moderate liberalism, they pointed to limited change during a conservative era. Since the publication of May's and D'Emilio and Freedman's books, other historians have made more direct assaults on the notion of postwar sexual "containment." In her 1999 book, *Sex in the Heartland*, Beth Bailey wrote of an increasingly "sexualized national culture" in the postwar years, with a rumbling "dissonance" between "public norms and . . . private acts." In colleges, she found, young adults engaged in "widespread covert violation" of conservative sexual norms, and college officials retreated from earlier policies that aimed to enforce sexual abstinence. More recently, in *The Permissive Society*, Alan Petigny pushed the argument even further. From the rising rates of nonmarital pregnancy, he detected an "appreciable upswing in premarital sexual behavior" in the postwar years. For Petigny, World War II "helped usher in an era of increased sexual liberalism." In his view, the "permissive society" and the "sexual revolution" bubbled up conjointly in the 1940s, not the 1960s. Taken collectively, a number of recent works—on Germany, Britain, and other nations as well as the United States—suggest that, with regard to sexuality, the postwar era harbored surprisingly liberal leanings.[2]

What should we make of this? Were the postwar years an age of resurgent sexual conservatism, or were they forward strides in the long march of the sexual revolution? Although the debate is hardly over, the obvious answer, it seems, is "both." This chapter draws on the recent literature on the postwar era to present the evidence for both sexual conservatism and sexual liberalism, and argues that the postwar years in the United States were in fact more liberal than often conceded, not only with regard to premarital heterosexual intercourse but also in other areas, including published erotica and obscenity law, gay and lesbian life, and interracial sex and marriage. It was not just that pockets of liberalism flourished beneath a conservative surface or that erotic celebration worked to promote long-term monogamous heterosexuality. In the postwar era, I contend, sexual conservatives confronted powerful assertions and overt arguments in favor of various forms of nonnormative sexual expression. The ensuing debates sometimes erupted into open battles that took place mostly within the middle class. Conservatives did not always hold the upper hand in these battles, and their defensive maneuvers set the stage for the "culture wars" that still rage today.

Sexual Liberalism, Sexual Conservatism

"Sexual liberalism" and "sexual conservatism" have no inherent meaning, and so they require definition. In my usage, American postwar "sexual liberalism" endorsed sexual expression more than sexual restraint. It was not necessarily politically progressive or sexually liberating. It had many strands, ranging from the radically democratic, utopian, and ecstatic to the commercial, corporate, crass, elitist, misogynist, sexist, racist, orientalist, and exploitative. And, like sexual containment, it was also, at least in part, implicated in "biopolitics," that is, multifaceted attempts to manage and administer the life and health of populations at the level of daily life and intimate interaction.[3] Simply put, sexual liberalism involved various incitements to and endorsements of sexual expression and display, and these helped constitute a liberal reformist version of modern sexuality that aimed to create, channel, and sustain vital and healthy bodies and a vital and healthy nation.

In other words, it is not that "bad" conservatives tried to manage and suppress sexuality and "good" liberals tried to free it via frankness. Sexual liberals, too, engaged in the management of populations; they, too, had particular—if different—visions of how sexuality constituted healthy bodies and healthy nations. Rightly or wrongly, sexual liberals associated various forms of sexual expression and display with health, fun, nature, beauty, freedom, democracy, and individual rights, and conversely linked various forms of sexual "repression" to mental and physical illness, "prudish" moralism, and antidemocratic authoritarian politics. They endorsed greater sexual expression, especially for the educated middle class, and they generally supported reproductive restraint via birth control.

American postwar sexual conservatism also had multiple strands. Those who espoused it usually hoped to "contain" or eliminate what they saw as damaging forms of sexual behavior, but they did not necessarily agree on exactly what needed to be contained or why, nor did they share a common outlook on other political issues. Where they concurred was in their advocacy of sexual regulation and their distrust of modern sexual incitements. They worried that vernacular sexual cultures, mass-produced and commercialized sexual products and services, nonnormative and nonmarital sexual expression, and sexually liberal ideals undermined the moral, social, and reproductive order. As one woman put it in 1956, "We can commercialize [sex] and degrade it to the extent that we destroy our own happiness, our marriages, our homes and even our nation."[4] When sexual conservatives attempted to control and manage sex, they had little choice but to talk about it, and their repeated warnings of sexual danger threatened to subvert the very goal of containment. Investigations, exposés, and morality tales could easily serve as unintended or unconscious sexual incitements, and direct arguments against sexual liberalism could advertise the views of one's opponents. In any case, sexual conservatives often pushed for containment inconsistently. In theory and practice, a single person could be liberal on one sexual issue (say, legalizing erotica) and conservative, contradictory, ambivalent, or apathetic on another (say, interracial sex and marriage). But on a number of issues, various groups of sexual liberals and sexual conservatives lined up on opposing sides and made their competing cases for sexual expression and sexual restraint.[5]

Containment

It is easy enough to supply ample evidence that the postwar years were sexually conservative. As May and others have related it, the postwar discourse was rife with commentary that pathologized various forms of nonmarital sexual expression. Psychologists and psychiatrists, who won impressive cultural clout during and after the war, played a central role in drawing the lines between "normal" and "abnormal" sexual behavior. American postwar psychoanalysts, in particular, defined nonnormative sexuality and portrayed it as psychotic, neurotic, arrested, and immature. Various experts and their popularizers cast gay men, lesbians, unwed mothers, and other women who had sex outside of marriage as psychically damaged individuals who could, in turn, harm others.[6] Such formulations appeared not only in clinical case studies, but also in newspapers, magazines, fiction, and film. From the mass media crime reports to the novels of Mickey Spillane to the movies of Alfred Hitchcock, postwar popular culture served up a range of crude and subtle narratives that depicted a populace threatened and weakened by sexually dangerous women and men.[7]

At the same time, the top-down policing of sexualized behavior escalated. In the 1950s, the state especially clamped down on homosexuality. Throughout the postwar years, the federal government, recent histories attest, fired thousands of gay men and lesbians from their jobs, expelled them from the military, and denied them veterans' benefits, and after 1952, denied queer immigrants entry and naturalization. A number of politicians, including the Democratic presidential candidate Adlai Stevenson and the Republican senator Joseph McCarthy, found themselves tainted by rumors of homosexuality that wended their way through the postwar media. The "lavender scare" at the federal level had its counterpart locally in cities across the nation. Employers dismissed workers suspected of homosexuality, and police surveillance teams investigated gay life, raided parks and bars, and arrested scores of men and women under the guise of laws against vagrancy, lewdness, disorderly conduct, and obscenity. The police actions and the subsequent press reports were the most public part of the postwar "flood of suspicion" that stigmatized gay men and lesbians and pushed them into the social margins.[8]

The regulation of what was called "vice" expanded in other areas as well. Before the 1940s, the police rarely enforced the statutes that made abortion illegal, it seems, except when a woman had died, but in the 1940s and 1950s, they undertook new campaigns to target, investigate, and arrest abortionists, some of whom had practiced freely for decades without attracting the arm of the law. Newspapers reported on raids on "abortion rings" in a wide array of cities. As one arrested abortionist described it, the politicians and police hoped to win positive publicity—"a harvest of headlines"—from their campaigns against "vice."[9]

Local authorities also took a renewed interest in obscenity laws. The Catholic Church, middle-class clubwomen, and other concerned citizens organized local campaigns and joined nationwide organizations, such as Citizens for Decent Literature, that protested the sale of erotic books and magazines in drugstores and on newsstands. FBI director J. Edgar Hoover endorsed the local campaigns, which spoke to a broader fear that a sexualized mass culture was corrupting the nation's youth. In response to the outcry, state and municipal officials tightened and enforced the laws that restricted the sale of erotic literature. Several cities—New York, Houston, Minneapolis, Cincinnati, and others—conducted raids, seized books and magazines, and arrested the retailers who sold them. At the federal level, the Senate and House of Representatives conducted their own investigations of obscenity and its distribution.[10]

The heightened concern with "vice" shaped racial politics, too. The sexual behavior of African Americans, Puerto Ricans, Mexican Americans, and Asian Americans was often depicted as vice-ridden—"wild, unstable, and undomesticated"—and in need of constraint. While nonnormative sexual behavior could be cast as an individual psychological problem, it was simultaneously understood as group-wide cultural pathology. In the postwar era, as before, white segregationists, for example, routinely portrayed blacks as "immoral, criminal, and diseased," and attempted to cordon off the perceived threat to "white civility."[11] In the face of the rising civil rights movement, southern whites expressed horror at the prospect of interracial sexual relationships, and they policed them through laws, religion, censorship, intimidation, and violence. In a number of western states as well, laws against interracial marriage remained on the books and frequently barred marriages between whites and Asians and whites and Native Americans as well as between whites and blacks.

In the northeastern and midwestern states, regulation was often more subtle but still severe. Universities, for example, forbade interracial dating, and family and friends punished it through shame, stigma, and ostracism. In 1952, to give just one minor example, Earlham, a racially integrated Quaker liberal arts college in Indiana, made the national news when its president and board of trustees publicly opposed the engagement of two of its students, a black woman and a white man. The college asked the man to leave campus and complete his courses by mail.[12]

Interestingly enough, historians have no single explanation for all the containing, constraining, denouncing, and policing. Twenty years ago, when women's history stood on the cutting edge, historians focused on fears of changing gender roles for women as the critical source of sexual conservatism. More recent interpretations, in line with recent historiographic trends, point to the containment of men's sexuality as often as women's—to fears of sexualized men who seemed to threaten the nation, including overly masculine "sadists" and insufficiently masculine "sissies." Historians now also address changing race relations to help explain the postwar obsession with sex. In a provocative recent interpretation, scholars argue that sexuality, not race, became the explicit legal marker of the worthy citizen. As racial definitions of citizenship, which legalized second-class status for people of color, began to break down, the government gradually redrew the lines of citizenship with heteronormative sexual behavior as a critical sign that separated respectable, healthy citizens from the undeserving.[13] Despite the changes in emphasis, however, the new historical literature—with its current concern with masculinity, the state, race, and citizenship—bolsters the same overarching argument of conservative containment.

302

Historians, then, have provided enough accounts of containment in multiple domains and enough interpretive frameworks to overdetermine the conservative outcome. The history of postwar sexuality could—and often does—end there. But we might borrow instead from Helen Horowitz's book *Rereading Sex*, which reconstructs the American discourse on sexuality in the nineteenth century. Horowitz addresses sexual regulation, but she does not pose the evolving conservative position, seen especially in the Comstock Act of 1873, as monolithic or inevitably dominant. She sees it instead as part of a multivoiced conversation, in which sexual conservatives engaged in open debate and legal battles with sexual reformers and vernacular traditions.[14] Let me suggest that we imagine the postwar era similarly, not only as constraint and crackdown, but as an era of competing ideals, multiple voices, and vocal debate. In this view, the postwar sexual conservatives responded to, argued with, and denounced competing visions of sexuality, which they saw as threatening. They did not just argue with the past or an imagined present or future; they actively resisted other members of the postwar middle class and a commercial economy that stood to profit from sexual liberalism. In short, we cannot understand the conservatives unless we look at what and whom they opposed.

The Sexually Liberal Postwar Era

If we listen for "multiple voices," who else spoke in the postwar era? Whom did the conservatives oppose? What bothered them and provoked their outrage? Historians who write of sexual liberalism give pride of place to the Kinsey reports, the two massive volumes compiled by Alfred Kinsey and his colleagues, *Sexual Behavior in the Human Male*, published in 1948, and *Sexual Behavior in the Human Female*, published in 1953. These best-selling collections of statistics made it abundantly clear that Americans engaged in all sorts of nonmarital sexual behavior. Kinsey and his colleagues conducted thousands of interviews and reported that both men and women defied the normative expectations with striking regularity. The Kinsey reports brought startling publicity to everyday sexual practice. They attracted national (and international) attention and inspired vocal arguments among experts. As his critics knew and his biographers have shown, Kinsey and his colleagues were not dispassionate or impartial investigators; they actively advocated sex without guilt as a sign and source of freedom and health. As ardent sexual liberals, they attacked the moralism of sexual conservatives and the legal constraints on the sexual behavior of consenting adults. Not surprisingly, sexual conservatives found the reports appalling. One biographer writes, "Kinsey's most vociferous critics were deeply religious people who feared that this work would undermine traditional morality."[15]

The Kinsey reports have come to symbolize the sexualization of American culture, but they represent only one tiny piece of the postwar explosion of sexual literature. A vernacular sexual culture was also making its way into the mainstream publishing industry, as publishers discovered, once again, that sex sold. Sensational tabloid newspapers and trashy magazines showcased sexual scandal and exposé, and new pulp paperbacks narrated risqué stories of sex outside of marriage. As queer studies scholar Michael Bronski notes, postwar publishers produced "huge numbers of original novels focusing on illegal or taboo sex." In addition, "girlie" magazines, with photographs of nude women, built on the tradition of pin-ups popularized during World War II. Most famously, *Playboy* magazine directly attacked the sexual containment of middle-class white men as the prudish repression of male health, freedom, and vitality. The success of *Playboy*, which first appeared in 1953, spawned dozens of imitators, most of them short-lived, including *Cabaret, Jaguar, Jem*, and *U.S. Male*. The publishing industry also moved into other niche markets in the postwar years. *Duke* magazine, inspired by *Playboy*, attempted to court African American heterosexual male readers with photos of nude African American women, and body-building magazines, such as *Physique Pictorial* and *Vim*, featured beefcake photos of nearly nude men for a gay male readership. Sexual conservatives complained about the proliferation of sexual imagery, especially the "severely distorted sexuality . . . reflected in the cult of the female nude." But they had little success in containing it.[16]

At the highbrow end of the market, the writings of Norman Mailer, Vladimir Nabokov, Allen Ginsberg, and others also pushed the boundaries of erotic literature. Most of the sexualized literature was by men and for men. The sexual liberalism of the postwar years harbored an aggressive masculinism, seen among soldiers during World War II and in veterans afterwards; it often construed nonmarital sexual expression as an assertion of male autonomy, which could include hostility to or subordination of women. But women were represented as readers and authors as well. Two especially sexual women's novels—Kathleen Winsor's *Forever Amber* and Grace Metalious's *Peyton Place*—sold millions of copies with tales of nonmarital sex, and both reappeared in new form as popular Hollywood films. These works, too, provoked the ire of sexual conservatives, who continued to protest the growing market in erotica, but millions of other Americans read the books and watched the movies that the conservatives decried.[17]

The explosion of erotic publications included a brisk mass market in lesbian and gay pulp novels, which attracted queer readers as well as straight ones. Pulp fiction was one sign, among many, of the growing visibility of gay and lesbian subcultures in the postwar years. Through the 1950s, gay and lesbian bars and queer drag shows attracted customers in every major city. In New York City, gay bars and gay street culture flourished in multiple neighborhoods: African Americans in Harlem, Puerto Ricans on the Upper West Side, and upper-class whites on the Upper East Side created their own gay circles, while hustlers in Times Square and street queens in Greenwich Village sustained a vibrant commercial culture of male prostitution. Philadelphia, San Francisco, Los Angeles, New Orleans, and other major cities had parallel urban geographies, in which certain neighborhoods and outposts were centers of lesbian and gay life. The visibility of gay locales attracted the attention of municipal politicians who promised to clean up "vice," but despite the periodic sweeps, raids, and arrests, they could not eliminate the not-so-hidden sites of urban queer life.[18]

New York was also the center (but not the only locale) of a thriving gay arts scene. James Baldwin, Truman Capote, Carson McCullers, Gore Vidal, and Tennessee Williams, among others, brought gay sensibilities to American literature. Elsewhere in the arts, Leonard Bernstein, John Cage, Stephen Sondheim, Alvin Ailey, Merce Cunningham, Lincoln Kirstein, Jasper Johns, and Robert Rauschenberg—all gay—stood at the center of modern music, dance, and painting. Various commentators noticed the gay arts scene and found it disturbing. Postwar critics complained of the gay influence on trends and tastes in arts and letters—what one called "a gradual corruption of all aspects of American culture." But here, too, the protests scarcely made a dent. As Michael Sherry writes, "the success of gay figures was stunning. . . . [G]ay artists helped create the sights, sounds, and words of modern American culture."[19] Queers remained undeniably central to the postwar urban American modernist and avant-garde movements.

But neither queer life nor sexual liberalism was ever exclusively urban. Even in the most remote rural regions, flourishing mail-order markets brought liberal sexual science, gay literature, pulp novels, physique magazines, and pornography to isolated readers. *Sexology*, a magazine that popularized liberal sexual science, published letters to the editor (on every imaginable sexual topic) from all over the United States. And the Haldeman-Julius booklets, published not in New York but in Girard, Kansas, were well known in the mail-order market. Founded by "freethinking" socialists in the 1910s, the Haldeman-Julius firm had shifted the center of its operations from politics to sex education and popular sexology by the 1930s. In the postwar era, it produced hundreds of sexual pamphlets that sold by mail for 35 cents a copy. Typical titles included *Voyeurism: A Form of Sexual Behavior, Male Homosexuals Tell Their Stories, Questions and Answers on the Sex Life and Problems of Trans-Sexuals, Questions and Answers about Cunnilingus,* and *Unconventional Modes of Sexual Expression.*[20]

Mail-order materials traversed the nation, usually without legal threat when protected by the cover of science. And people, too, traveled in search of what was billed as sexual adventure. By the 1950s certain vacation destinations had established themselves as sites of sexual tourism. Within the United States, Las Vegas had a risqué allure, while outside the borders, Tijuana and Havana capitalized on a prevalent racialized sexual stereotype of hot-blooded Latins. For the gay niche market, there were other well-known vacation spots: outside New York and Boston, middle- and upper-class gays expanded their space for summer escapades to Fire Island and Provincetown, which became known as gay vacation enclaves.[21]

Within this context a few gay men and lesbians created the first American gay rights movement. Donald Webster Cory set the stage for the movement with his 1951 book, *The Homosexual in America,* in which he argued that homosexuals were an oppressed minority. He associated gay life with democracy, freedom, and healthy expression, and opposed it to totalitarianism. Homosexuals, he claimed, "are seeking to extend freedom of the individual, of speech, press, and thought to an entirely new realm." In California, activists created new gay rights organizations in direct response to the "lavender scare" and police harassment. The Mattachine Society, a gay male group founded in 1951, and the Daughters of Bilitis, founded in 1955 to advocate for lesbians, eventually had local chapters across the nation. Along with One, Inc., a splinter group established in 1952, these small organizations were known collectively in their day as the "homophile movement." They published magazines, called for civil rights, and attempted to educate the public.[22] The movement adopted the language of sexual liberalism, which presented sexual expression as an individual right and a sign of freedom. As one author stated directly in 1955, "We might consider ourselves as part of a liberal, modern movement towards greater personal freedom."[23]

At the same time, as Renee Romano and others have shown, the mass media was increasing its focus on—and its pronouncements defending—

heterosexual interracial romance, love, sex, and marriage. After World War II, racial liberalism won greater national attention, inspired in part by revulsion against the racist policies of the Nazis and even more by the civil rights movement within the United States. While many racial liberals consciously avoided the delicate topic of interracial sex, others used its illicit, and therefore titillating, status to attract attention to the evils of racial segregation. The 1944 best-selling novel *Strange Fruit*, the 1949 box-office hit movie *Pinky*, and the sensational 1949 Broadway musical *South Pacific* all protested racism with moving stories of thwarted interracial love. In *Strange Fruit*, a young southern white man rejects his pregnant black girlfriend, and the tragic affair ends in murder and lynching; in *Pinky*, an African American nurse who had passed as white refrains from marrying her white fiancé; and in *South Pacific*, a white Navy officer spurns his Polynesian lover but then regrets his racism before he dies in battle. Despite the ill-fated couplings, all three stories tugged on the heartstrings and invited readers and viewers to root for interracial love.

In 1956, Hollywood revised its production code to permit films that depicted abortion, prostitution, and interracial relationships, another sign of sexual liberalization. The following year, *Island in the Sun*, a film that featured an interracial couple whose love was not thwarted, was a major money-making success. Set on a Caribbean island, the film depicts two interracial romances, one of which ends happily as the couple leaves to marry in England. (Like *South Pacific*, *Island in the Sun* drew on the racialized association between tropical locales and freer sexual expression.)

As with other forms of tabooed love, the risqué topic of interracial romance came under attack. *Strange Fruit*, for example, was banned in Boston for its obscene language, and the board of censors in a town in Texas prohibited theater owners from showing the film *Pinky*. Despite the attacks (or maybe, in part, because of them) the book and film attracted readers and viewers. *Strange Fruit* sold three million copies in the 20 years after its publication, and *Pinky* brought in more than $4 million the year it debuted.[24]

Meanwhile, the new African American mass-circulation magazines *Ebony* and *Jet* repeatedly publicized and defended interracial relationships and attempted to bring black-white heterosexual love within the scope of the heteronormative, healthy, and acceptable. Like the homophile publications, these magazines promoted a version of sexual liberalism that cast love as a "private affair" or a "personal matter." Interracial love was "normal and natural," and racial difference was an artificial barrier or a superficial factor that should not abridge the "right of individuals." Marriage, one author wrote, was "an individual choice . . . in a nation that was founded on the principles of human dignity and freedom." The northern white press also paid some attention. In 1951, for example, both *Life* and *Harper's Magazine* carried sympathetic articles on interracial heterosexual couples. And in the Earlham College episode in which officials publicly opposed the engagement of two of its students, the mostly white student body protested and both black and white newspapers covered the story. With the headline "Love in a Democracy," the *Chicago Defender*, an African American newspaper, responded with the credo of sexual liberalism: "Love and marriage should be an individual matter in a democracy. . . .[I]ndividual liberty is the cornerstone of our democracy."[25]

The sexual liberals who defended various forms of sexual expression—from erotica to gay and lesbian rights to interracial heterosexual relationships—often adopted or fashioned an urbane outlook in which sexual expression and sexual variation were understood as the modern "spice of life" or the sophisticated rejection of bland conformity. Like Kinsey and his colleagues, they sometimes presented a pluralist view that expanded the boundaries of the acceptable and the normative. In 1954, the celebrity transsexual performer Christine Jorgensen took this stance publicly when she told an interviewer, "I think that much that has been classified as abnormal for many years is becoming accepted as normal." At least as often, sexual liberals also used the political language of democracy in defense of sexual "freedom" and "individual rights." As Hugh Hefner said in a 1955 interview, his magazine, *Playboy*, was "a kind of argument for a liberal democratic society with emphasis on the freedom of the individual." Increasingly, scholars, artists, lawyers, and others defended the right to erotic expression as a hallmark of a vital democracy and denounced sexual restriction as a sign of totalitarianism. In their 1959 book, *Pornography and the Law*, for example, the anticensorship advocates Eberhard and Phyllis Kronhausen used the language of the Cold War not to contain sexual expression but to defend it. "The more actual democracy a society allows," they wrote, "the more sexual freedom is granted to its members. The more authoritarian the political organization of a society. . . the less sexual freedom."[26]

But explicit demands for freedom and rights were only the tip of the iceberg. The outspoken advocates of sexual liberalism were bolstered all along by a burgeoning marketplace that profited from sexually liberal ideals. And here less politicized incitements to sexual expression were just about everywhere. They appeared widely in the growing youth subcultures of the postwar era, not just in the well-publicized unconventional circles of the Beat poets and authors in New York and San Francisco, but also more generally in the jazz, rhythm and blues, and rock 'n' roll that attracted youth throughout the United States (and else-where) with sexualized music, lyrics, and dancing. In the 1950s, the "racy" lan-guage of black working-class vernacular culture moved into mainstream white middle-class rock 'n' roll and, via the radio, into middle-class homes. To its opponents, the music symbolized vice, excess, and rebellion, but to its advocates it signified freedom and fun. In the late 1950s, to give just one among many examples, the rock 'n' roll pioneer Little Richard sang top-ten hits with openly heterosexual lyrics, such as the infamous (and still well-known) hit, "Good Golly, Miss Molly," which used the vulgar slang verb "ball" to celebrate sexual intercourse. Although Little Richard hid (and still hides) his homosexuality, he used and even flaunted sexual innuendo to enhance his popular appeal. Postwar critics decried the sexualization of middle-class youth culture, from the lyrics in songs to the pictures in comic books to the pelvic grinds of Elvis Presley, and expressed dismay at the all-too-eager responses of young women and men. Their pressure tactics led to self-regulation in radio broadcasts, comic books, and television, but they could not stop the heavy investment in sex in the growing youth consumer culture.[27]

The postwar sexual display and the postwar arguments in favor of it began to have impact in the legal profession and on the law. In 1948, the California Supreme Court overturned the state law forbidding interracial marriage and, as Peggy Pascoe writes, "jump-started the post-World War II campaign to eliminate the [miscegenation] laws once and for all." This landmark decision argued that the state law violated the rights of individuals and "arbitrarily and unreasonably" discriminated. In the wake of the California decision, seven other western states repealed their miscegenation laws in the 1950s. The liberal approach, which upheld sexual expression as an individual right, showed up elsewhere in the legal arena. In 1955, the American Law Institute published sections of its Model Penal Code that called for the decriminaliza-tion of sodomy between consenting adults, and two years later a municipal court in San Francisco won national publicity when it declared that Allen Ginsberg's poem *Howl*, which had graphic homosexual references, was not legally obscene. More important, the federal courts steadily chipped away at obscenity laws. The long list of notable cases involved, among others, the men's magazine *Esquire* (1946), the Hollywood film *Pinky* (1952), the Kinsey Institute's collection of erotica (1957), and the homophile publication *ONE* (1958). In those and other cases, federal courts, despite vocal conservative opposition, gradually defended and expanded the right to publish, exhibit, import, and mail various kinds of erotica.[28]

The Long Sexual Revolution

Historians' emphasis on the postwar "containment" of sexuality has underplayed the concomitant liberalization of sexual mores, and their accounts of "sexual liberalism" have only begun to touch on the extent of the postwar endorsement and incitement of various forms of sexual expression. Historians of the African American civil rights movement have extended the timeline of that movement and now write of a "long civil rights movement" that began earlier than we used to think. Perhaps, as some historians have suggested, we should talk about a "long sexual revolution" as well. It might begin in World War II, the 1920s, or even after the Civil War, and though it was by no means a linear progression (and the 1950s moment, of course, differed substantially from the 1960s one), historians could trace genealogies, with their multiple branches, over the course of decades and also track the opposition all along the way. In this view, postwar attempts to "contain" sexuality might appear less as signs of muscle-flexing by triumphant conservatives and more as an episodic panic—a desperate rally to the defense—by the losers in a long war over the meanings of modern sex and healthy populations. In the postwar era, various sexual conservatives tried to apply the brakes to the widely publicized sexual expression and display that had marked the war years; they may have slowed the momentum of sexual liberalism, but they could neither stop nor derail the train.[29]

However we define or date the sexual revolution, a genealogical view of postwar sexuality invites us to turn our attention to the long-term trends that linked the 1940s, 1950s, and 1960s. A number of critical trends encouraged sexual expression and display, and not sexual containment. First, by 1950, in the capitalist American economy, sex-for-sale had undergone its own industrialization. If we borrow a labor history model, we might say that the center of sex-for-sale had changed over the course of a century from the customized craftwork of prostitution to the commercial production of leg shows, burlesque shows, and strip tease to the industrialized mass production of pornography seen in postcards, books, magazines, and films. The shift seems to have entailed more impersonal relations of production and consumption, or to put it another way, an aggregate generational shift in sex-for-sale, in which men moved, partially and gradually, from sex with prostitutes to masturbation with pictures, that is, from touching others to touching themselves. And it evoked protests from those who feared that the free market and its masturbatory mass culture were infiltrating the nation's homes and corrupting the nation's youth. But like other forms of industrialization, it was not easy to reverse, curtail, or contain. From the early twentieth century on, then, the industrialization of sex-for-sale, especially the proliferation of mass-produced erotica, encouraged the display and celebration of nonmarital sexual expression. In this area as in others, the trajectory of modern capitalism encouraged desire and longing, created and expanded markets, and mass-produced standardized goods and services that were once handcrafted and custom made.[30]

Second, by the 1950s, various scholars had been protesting for decades against the harmful effects of "repression," and their arguments had made their way into the popular culture. By mid-century, "repression" was understood as psychologically damaging. To various authors, simply put, repression caused frustration, which in turn caused neurosis and aggression. Social scientists and their popularizers explained militarism, fascism, criminality, racism, mental illness, and a host of other social ills by pointing in part to repression, including sexual repression and its attendant frustrations. Freud had introduced the language of repression to American intellectuals decades before, but for Freud, sexual repression created not only neuroses but also civilization. Some of his followers were less optimistic. Austrian and German radical émigrés such as Wilhelm Reich and Herbert Marcuse were among the key thinkers who espoused the antirepression thesis in the United States. Reared in heavily patriarchal cultures and watching (with horror) the rise of fascist dictatorships, these and other European leftists tended to blame early childhood sexual repression on authoritarian fathers. From the 1920s on, American-born sexually liberal authors, including Margaret Mead and Alfred Kinsey, produced their own condemnations of a sexually repressive culture that damaged its own youth. Writing from a different social context, the Americans tended to blame repression on domineering or prudish mothers. In the pop psychology that followed, the antidotes to repression included more permissive child-rearing, liberal sex education, and a rejection of the alleged constraints of the "Puritan" and "Victorian" past. By the 1950s, it was routinely assumed that self-expression and "self-actualization" were good and healthy, and repression was bad and damaging. In 1954, one critic of this trend wrote: "Repression came to have a bad name, and everyone so disposed went in for nonrepression. It was good for the health . . . [and] it was in line with the general quest for self-expression and self-enhancement." In sum, a popularized version of Freud posited sexual repression as unhealthy and associated it with individual ill health, social malaise, and dangerous politics. It posed the "containment" of sex as bad and damaging to the individual and the nation.[31]

Third, in politics and the law, sex had become a critical test case for free speech in a democracy. From at least the 1920s on, a tiny transnational

European and American movement had called for "sexual freedom." This international network of sex advocates differed from the older "free love" movement of the nineteenth century. They did not call for freeing love from economics and marriage but insisted instead on freedom of sexual expression, with or without love. From the 1920s on, the American Civil Liberties Union began to back this position, recognizing sexual speech (though not yet sexual behavior) as part of its civil liberties domain.[32] Various commentators began to associate freedom itself with the lifting of conventional sexual restrictions. That is, by the postwar era, sexual speech and the individual rights of consenting adults had already become part of the political discourse. In the 1950s, the Cold War language of containment had its counterpart in a Cold War language of individual freedom in a "free society," and the advocates of sexual expression also borrowed successfully from racial liberalism and its language of individual rights. From the 1930s on, then, sexual expression and the right to engage in some nonmarital forms of it became a critical part of the liberal political discourse on freedom and rights in a democracy.

The long-term trends help explain the sexual liberalism of the postwar years. But the war, too, had its impact. As many historians have noted, World War II—with its disruptive mass migration, "live-for-the-moment" ethos, assertion of the virility of soldiers, escalation of prostitution, proliferation of sexual imagery, interracial sex in war zones, and same-sex intimacy in the sex-segregated military—challenged traditional sexual standards.[33] In the postwar years, the memories of wartime sexual expression did not inspire a cultural consensus; instead, they informed competing visions of sexual order. Some Americans attempted to "contain" the wartime challenge, but others expanded, celebrated, and defended it. In niche and mainstream markets, entrepreneurs continued to lure consumers with sexual services, products, and fantasies, and the sexual marketplace supported (and was supported by) evolving liberal conceptions of health, freedom, and individual rights.

Conclusion

Why do we need a new overarching interpretation of postwar U.S. sexuality? What do we gain if we move away from the insistence on "containment" and look instead for the debates that pitted sexual liberals against sexual conservatives? We are reminded, first, that the sexualization of wartime culture provided openings for change that were not closed off in the postwar era.

Wartime changes did not simply lead to a backlash that insisted on reasserting an imagined traditional order. Rather, the wartime challenge amplified a multifarious conversation about what constituted a healthy sexual regime for a modern nation. The debates show, second, that the stereotype of the conservative postwar era is a one-sided account that erases historical complexity. The story of the "bad old days" of the 1950s fits too neatly with an overly simple progressive generational model in which the young rebels of the 1960s allegedly liberated themselves from repression, conformity, and conservatism. Just as the bohemians of the 1920s conjured a myth of Victorian sexual repression, so the activists of the 1960s constructed their own myth of postwar sexual containment. The emphasis on postwar conservatism also works to support another simplistic model, one in which the nation swings between seemingly liberal eras, like the 1960s and 1970s, and seemingly conservative ones, like the 1950s and 1980s. This model, too, erases the buzz of political conflict that animated the sexual discourse of past decades—and continues to animate it today.

In recent years, the "sex wars" have reappeared in new form in the conflicts between the Christian Right and its opponents over pornography, abortion, feminism, gay rights, and same-sex marriage. In the 1950s, these battles did not align with a right-left split. Both sexual conservatives and sexual liberals used the language of the Cold War, arguing on one side about the sexual threat that weakened home and nation and on the other about individual rights in a free world. Those who advocated sexual "containment" were not necessarily Republicans, and those who advocated "sexual liberalism" were not necessarily left-of-center. Since the 1970s, the political valence of the sexual arguments seems to have shifted, but the battles continue, and so do the long-term economic, intellectual, and political trends toward public sexual expression and calls for sexual "freedom." As recent events have shown, the peculiar sexual liberalism that blossomed in the second half of the twentieth century is still a source of divisive debate—and not just in the United States. In various parts of the world today, the liberal sexualized society, found in various incarnations in the United States and Europe, has become a symbol of cultural imperialism, capitalist corruption, decadence, decline, secularism, and amorality. And in other parts of the world, it has come to stand for modernity, health, democracy, self-expression, freedom, and individual rights. Sex in the abstract has been detached from its mundane performance and elevated to bear heavy symbolic weight in defining the characters of peoples and nations and in constructing competing fantasies of good and bad societies.[34]

We need to attend to the debates of the 1940s and 1950s, then, because they capture the complexity of the long postwar era and reveal crucial historical roots and context for current rifts and conflicts within the United States and on the international stage. The postwar debates (and the current ones as well) tell us as much about the world we live in and our varied attempts to manage it as they tell us about our sexual practices and sexual ideals.

Notes

1. Elaine Tyler May, *Homeward Bound: American Families in the Cold War Era* (New York: Basic, 1988), 93–4.

2. John D'Emilio and Estelle B. Freedman, *Intimate Matters: A History of Sexuality in America*, 2nd ed. (Chicago: University of Chicago Press, 1997), 276, 300; Beth Bailey, *Sex in the Heartland* (Cambridge, MA: Harvard University Press, 1999), 40, 44, 49; Alan Petigny, *The Permissive Society: America, 1941–1965* (New York: Cambridge University Press, 2009), 103, 132. See also Susan K. Freeman, *Sex Goes to School: Girls and Sex Education before the 1960s* (Urbana-Champaign: University of Illinois Press, 2008); and R. Marie Griffith, "The Religious Encounters of Alfred C. Kinsey," *Journal of American History* 95 (2008): 349–377. On other nations, see, for example, Elizabeth Heineman, *Before Porn Was Legal: The Erotica Empire of Beate Uhse* (Chicago: University of Chicago Press, 2011); Frank Mort, *Capital Affairs: London and the Making of the Permissive Society* (New Haven: Yale University Press, 2010); and Heike Bauer and Matt Cook, eds., *Queer 1950s: Rethinking Sexuality in the Postwar Years* (New York: Palgrave Macmillan, 2012).

3. On biopolitics, see Michel Foucault, *The History of Sexuality*, vol. 1: *An Introduction* (New York: Random House, 1978), part 5. The term "liberal" here is not anachronistic: postwar "sexual liberals" often used the word "liberal," as later quotations in this essay attest, to describe their views on sexuality.

4. Quoted (from *Ladies' Home Journal*) in Joanne Meyerowitz, "Women, Cheesecake, and Borderline Material: Responses to Girlie Pictures in the Mid-Twentieth-Century U.S.," *Journal of Women's History* 8, no. 3 (1996): 9–35, 25.

5. For an overlapping definition of current "sexual liberals" and "sexual conservatives," see Kristin Luker, *When Sex Goes to School: Warring Views on Sex—and Sex Education—since the Sixties* (New York: Norton, 2006), chap. 4. For Luker, the dividing line between "sexual liberals" and "sexual conservatives" is "whether any kind of sex besides heterosexual married sex should be morally and socially acceptable. . . . [F]or conservatives, sex is *sacred*, while for liberals, it's *natural*"; Luker, *When Sex Goes to School*, 98–99. For the postwar era, Miriam Reumann draws a distinction between "sexual pessimists, who foresaw the decline and collapse of the nation in changes in the sexual status quo, and idealists, who envisioned a new sexual order as liberating and empowering"; Reumann, *American Sexual Character: Sex, Gender, and National Identity in the Kinsey Reports* (Berkeley: University of California Press, 2005), 9.

6. Estelle B. Freedman, "Uncontrolled Desires: The Response to the Sexual Psychopath, 1920–1960," *Journal of American History* 74 (1987): 83–106; Rickie Solinger, *Wake Up*

Little Susie: Single Pregnancy and Race before Roe v. Wade (New York: Routledge, 2000); Carolyn Herbst Lewis, "Waking Sleeping Beauty: The Premarital Pelvic Exam and Heterosexuality during the Cold War," *Journal of Women's History* 17, no. 4 (2005): 86–110; Kenneth Lewes, *Psychoanalysis and Male Homosexuality* (Northvale, NJ: Jason Aronson, 1988); Jennifer Terry, *An American Obsession: Science, Medicine, and Homosexuality in Modern Society* (Chicago: University of Chicago Press, 1999); and Kevin Allen Leonard, "Containing 'Perversion': African Americans and Same-Sex Desire in Cold War Los Angeles," *Journal of the History of Sexuality* 20, no. 3 (2011): 545–567. For a well-known primary source, see Ferdinand Lundberg and Marynia F. Farnham, *Modern Woman: The Lost Sex* (New York: Harper, 1947). For an intriguing account of psychoanalytic influence on postwar sexuality, see Rachel Devlin, *Relative Intimacy: Fathers, Adolescent Daughters, and Postwar American Culture* (Chapel Hill: University of North Carolina Press, 2005).

7. May, *Homeward Bound,* chap. 4; Robert J. Corber, *In the Name of National Security: Hitchcock, Homophobia, and the Political Construction of Gender in Postwar America* (Durham, NC: Duke University Press, 1993); Gabriele Dietze, "Gender Topography of the Fifties: Mickey Spillane and the Post-World-War-II Masculinity Crisis," *Amerikastudien* 43 (1998): 645–56; and Corber, *Cold War Femme: Lesbianism, National Identity, and the Hollywood Cinema* (Durham, NC: Duke University Press, 2011).

8. Michael S. Sherry, *Gay Artists in Modern American Culture: An Imagined Conspiracy* (Chapel Hill: University of North Carolina Press, 2007), 52. On the postwar regulation of homosexuality, see John D'Emilio, *Sexual Politics, Sexual Communities: The Making of a Homosexual Minority in the United States, 1940–1970* (Chicago: University of Chicago Press, 1983); Allan Bérubé, *Coming Out under Fire: The History of Gay Men and Women in World War Two* (New York: Free Press, 1990); Robert D. Dean, *Imperial Brotherhood: Gender and the Making of Cold War Foreign Policy* (Amherst: University of Massachusetts Press, 2001); David K. Johnson, *The Lavender Scare: The Cold War Persecution of Gays and Lesbians in the Federal Government* (Chicago: University of Chicago Press, 2004); K. A. Cuordileone, *Manhood and American Political Culture in the Cold War* (New York: Routledge, 2005); Andrea Friedman, "The Smearing of Joe McCarthy: The Lavender Scare, Gossip, and Cold War Politics," *American Quarterly* 57 (2005): 1105–29; Margot Canaday, *The Straight State: Sexuality and Citizenship in Twentieth-Century America* (Princeton, NJ: Princeton University Press, 2009); Fred Fejes, "Murder, Perversion, and Moral Panic: The 1954 Media Campaign against Miami's Homosexuals and the Discourse of Civic Betterment," *Journal of the History of Sexuality* 9 (2000): 305–47; Stacy Braukman, "'Nothing Else Matters but Sex': Cold War Narratives of Deviance and the Search for Lesbian Teachers in Florida, 1959-1963," *Feminist Studies* 27 (2001): 553–75; and Whitney Strub, "The Clearly Obscene and the Queerly Obscene: Heteronormativity and Obscenity in Cold War Los Angeles," *American Quarterly* 60 (2008): 373–98.

9. Rickie Solinger, "Extreme Danger: Women Abortionists and Their Clients before *Roe v. Wade,*" in *Not June Cleaver: Women and Gender in Postwar America, 1945–1960,* ed. Joanne Meyerowitz (Philadelphia: Temple University Press, 1994), 352. See also Leslie J. Reagan, *When Abortion Was a Crime: Women, Medicine, and the Law in the United States, 1867–1973* (Berkeley: University of California Press, 1997), chap. 6. On the postwar regulation of "vice," see also Amanda H. Littauer, "The B-Girl Evil: Bureaucracy, Sexuality, and the Menace of Barroom Vice in Postwar California," *Journal of the History of Sexuality*

12, no. 2 (2003): 171–204; and Josh Sides, *Erotic City: Sexual Revolutions and the Making of Modern San Francisco* (New York: Oxford University Press, 2009), chap. 1.

10. D'Emilio and Freedman, *Intimate Matters*, 279–285; Meyerowitz, "Women, Cheesecake, and Borderline Material"; and Andrea Friedman, "Sadists and Sissies: Antipornography Campaigns in Cold War America," *Gender & History* 15 (2003): 201–27.

11. Roderick A. Ferguson, *Aberrations in Black: Toward a Queer of Color Critique* (Minneapolis: University of Minnesota Press, 2004), 87; and Susan K. Cahn, *Sexual Reckonings: Southern Girls in a Troubling Age* (Cambridge, MA: Harvard University Press, 2007), 284–85.

12. See also Jane Dailey, "Sex, Segregation, and the Sacred after *Brown*," *Journal of American History* 91 (2004): 119–44; Whitney Strub, "Black and White and Banned All Over: Race, Censorship and Obscenity in Postwar Memphis," *Journal of Social History* 40 (2007): 685–715; Renee C. Romano, *Race Mixing: Black-White Marriage in Postwar America* (Cambridge, MA: Harvard University Press, 2003); and Peggy Pascoe, *What Comes Naturally: Miscegenation Law and the Making of Race in America* (New York: Oxford University Press, 2009).

13. See especially Siobhan Somerville, "Queer *Loving*," *GLQ: A Journal of Lesbian and Gay Studies* 11 (2005): 335–70.

14. Helen Horowitz, *Rereading Sex: Battles over Sexual Knowledge and Suppression in Nineteenth-Century America* (New York: Vintage, 2002).

15. James H. Jones, *Alfred C. Kinsey: A Public/Private Life* (New York: Norton, 1997), 576. On religious sexual liberals who supported Kinsey, see Griffith, "The Religious Encounters of Alfred C. Kinsey." See also Jonathan Gathorne-Hardy, *Sex the Measure of All Things: A Life of Alfred C. Kinsey* (Bloomington: Indiana University Press, 2000); Paul Robinson, *The Modernization of Sex: Havelock Ellis, Alfred Kinsey, William Masters and Virginia Johnson* (Ithaca, NY: Cornell University Press, 1989, originally 1976); Reumann, *American Sexual Character*; and James Gilbert, *Men in the Middle: Searching for Masculinity in the 1950s* (Chicago: University of Chicago Press, 2005), chap. 5.

16. Michael Bronski, *Pulp Friction* (New York: St. Martins, 2003), 2; Lundberg and Farnham, *Modern Woman: The Lost Sex*, 297. See also D'Emilio and Freedman, *Intimate Matters*, 279–85; Meyerowitz, "Women, Cheesecake, and Borderline Material"; and Maria Elena Buszek, *Pin-Up Grrrls: Feminism, Sexuality, Popular Culture* (Durham, NC: Duke University Press, 2006). On *Playboy*, see especially Barbara Ehrenreich, *The Hearts of Men: American Dreams and the Flight from Commitment* (New York: Doubleday, 1983), chap. 4; and Elizabeth Fraterrigo, *Playboy and the Making of the Good Life in Modern America* (New York: Oxford University Press, 2009).

17. Lynette Carpenter, "The Censorship of a Wartime Heroine, or Taking the 'Forever' out of *Forever Amber*," unpublished essay, c. 1988, in author's possession; Ardis Cameron, "Open Secrets: Rereading Peyton Place," introduction to Grace Metalious, *Peyton Place* (Boston: Northeastern University Press, 1999). On postwar popular sexualized fiction and women readers, see also Regina Kunzel, "Pulp Fictions and Problem Girls: Reading and Rewriting Single Pregnancy in the Postwar United States," *American Historical Review* 100 (1995): 1465–87.

18. On gay and lesbian pulp fiction, see, for example, Bronski, *Pulp Friction*; Yvonne Keller, "'Was It Right to Love Her Brother's Wife So Passionately?': Lesbian Pulp Novels

and U.S. Lesbian Identity, 1950–1965," *American Quarterly* 57 (2005): 385–410; Susan Stryker, *Queer Pulp: Perverted Passions from the Golden Age of the Paperback* (San Francisco: Chronicle Books, 2001); and Regina Kunzel, *Criminal Intimacy: Prison and the Uneven History of Modern Sexuality* (Chicago: University of Chicago Press, 2009), chap. 3. On postwar gay urban life, see George Chauncey, *The Strange Career of the Closet: Gay Culture, Consciousness, and Politics from the Second World War to the Gay Liberation Era* (book in progress); Elizabeth Lapovsky Kennedy and Madeline D. Davis, *Boots of Leather, Slippers of Gold: The History of a Lesbian Community* (New York: Routledge, 1993); Marc Stein, *City of Sisterly and Brotherly Loves: Lesbian and Gay Philadelphia, 1945–1972* (Chicago: University of Chicago Press, 2000); Nan Alamilla Boyd, *Wide Open Town: A History of Queer San Francisco to 1965* (Berkeley: University of California Press, 2003); and Lillian Faderman and Stuart Timmons, *Gay L.A.: A History of Sexual Outlaws, Power Politics, and Lipstick Lesbians* (New York: Basic Books, 2006).

19. Alfred Towne, "Homosexuality in American Culture: The New Taste in Literature," *American Mercury*, August 1951: 3–9, 9; Sherry, *Gay Artists*, 47. See also Robert J. Corber, *Homosexuality in Cold War America: Resistance and the Crisis of Masculinity* (Durham, NC: Duke University Press, 1997); Nadine Hubbs, *The Queer Composition of America's Sound: Gay Modernists, American Music, and National Identity* (Berkeley: University of California Press, 2004); and Martin Duberman, *The Worlds of Lincoln Kirstein* (New York: Knopf, 2007).

20. On gay life outside of big cities, see especially John Howard, *Men Like That: A Southern Queer History* (Chicago: University of Chicago Press, 1999). On Haldeman-Julius, see Joanne Meyerowitz, *How Sex Changed: A History of Transsexuality in the United States* (Cambridge, MA: Harvard University Press, 2002), 42. On mail-order erotica in postwar West Germany, see Heineman, *Before Porn Was Legal*, chap. 3.

21. Red Vaughan Tremmel, "Sin City on The Hill: Play, Urban Conflict, and the Rise of Commercial Liberality, 1900–1960" (Ph.D. diss., University of Chicago, 2008); Louis A. Pérez Jr., *On Becoming Cuban: Identity, Nationality, and Culture* (Chapel Hill: University of North Carolina Press, 2000); Esther Newton, *Cherry Grove, Fire Island: Sixty Years in America's First Gay and Lesbian Town* (Boston: Beacon, 1993); and Karen Christel Krahulik, *Provincetown: From Pilgrim Landing to Gay Resort* (New York: New York University Press, 2007).

22. Donald Webster Cory, *The Homosexual in America: A Subjective Approach* (New York: Greenberg, 1951), 229. See also John D'Emilio, *Sexual Politics, Sexual Communities*; Martin Meeker, *Contacts Desired: Gay and Lesbian Communications and Community, 1940s–1970s* (Chicago: University of Chicago Press, 2006); Marcia M. Gallo, *Different Daughters: A History of the Daughters of Bilitis and the Rise of the Lesbian Rights Movement* (Emeryville, CA: Seal Press, 2007); Daniel Hurewitz, *Bohemian Los Angeles and the Making of Modern Politics* (Berkeley: University of California Press, 2007); and Douglas M. Charles, "From Subversion to Obscenity: The FBI's Investigations of the Early Homophile Movement in the United States, 1953–1958," *Journal of the History of Sexuality* 19, 3 (2010): 262–87.

23. Carle, "The Fifth Freedom," *ONE*, October 1955, 25.

24. See Romano, *Race Mixing*, 33–8, 165.

25. Jack Johnson, "Does Interracial Marriage Succeed?" *Negro Digest*, June 1945, 3; "Do Negro Stars Prefer White Husbands?" *Ebony*, May 1954, 90; Thyra Edwards Gitlin

and Murray Gitlin, "Does Interracial Marriage Succeed?" *Negro Digest*, March 1945, 63; Roi Ottley, "No Color Line for Frauleins," *Negro Digest*, February 1947, 11; Ilka Chase, "The Hazards of Interracial Marriage," *Negro Digest*, September 1948, 13; Dr. Nathaniel O. Calloway, "Mixed Marriage Can Succeed," *Negro Digest*, March 1949, 27; and "Love in a Democracy," *Chicago Defender*, May 17, 1952, 10. See also Richard L. Williams, "He Wouldn't Cross the Color Line," *Life*, September 3, 1951, 94; and "My Daughter Married a Negro," *Harper's Magazine*, July 1951: 36–40.

26. Jorgensen quote (from *True Confessions* magazine) in Meyerowitz, *How Sex Changed*, 52; Hefner quote in Fraterrigo, *Playboy and the Making of the Good Life*, 13; and Eberhard and Phyllis Kronhausen, *Pornography and the Law: The Psychology of Erotic Realism and Pornography* (New York: Ballantine, 1959), 283–84. See also Joanne Meyerowitz, "Sex, Gender, and the Cold War Language of Reform," in *Rethinking Cold War Culture*, ed. Peter J. Kuznick and James Gilbert (Washington, DC: Smithsonian Institution Press, 2001), 106–23.

27. See, for example, Cahn, *Sexual Reckonings*, chap. 9. On somewhat similar battles over youth culture, sexuality, and jazz and rock music in postwar Germany, see Uta G. Poiger, *Jazz, Rock, and Rebels: Cold War Politics and American Culture in a Divided Germany* (Berkeley: University of California Press, 2000).

28. Pascoe, *What Comes Naturally*, 206; *Perez v. Sharp*, 32 Cal. 2d 732 (1948). On state miscegenation laws, see Pascoe, *What Comes Naturally*, 243. On the American Law Institute, see Stein, *City of Sisterly and Brotherly Loves*, 131–32. On *Howl*, see D'Emilio and Freedman, *Intimate Matters*, 275–76. For federal court cases, see *Hannegan v. Esquire, Inc.*, 327 U.S. 146 (1946); *Gelling v. Texas*, 343 U.S. 960 (1952); *United States v. 31 Photographs*, 156 F. Supp. 350 (S. D. N. Y. 1957); and *One, Incorporated, v. Oleson*, 355 U.S. 371 (1958).

29. On British history, see, for example, Hera Cook, *The Long Sexual Revolution: English Women, Sex, and Contraception, 1800–1975* (New York: Oxford University Press, 2004). See also Petigny, *The Permissive Society*, chap. 3. Some American postwar commentators themselves wrote, as did Wilhelm Reich, of a sexual revolution. See, for example, Pitirim F. Sorokin, *The American Sex Revolution* (Boston: Porter Sargent, 1956).

30. On this point, see Joanne Meyerowitz, "Transnational Sex and U.S. History," *American Historical Review* 114 (2009): 1273–86, 1284.

31. Abram Kardiner, *Sex and Morality* (Indianapolis: Bobbs-Merrill, 1954), 51. On American mother-blaming, see Rebecca Jo Plant, *Mom: The Transformation of Motherhood in Modern America* (Chicago: University of Chicago Press, 2010); on the different emphases on maternal responsibility in Europe and the United States, see esp. 14–15. On the myth of Victorian "repression," see Foucault, *History of Sexuality*, vol. 1; Christina Simmons, "Modern Sexuality and the Myth of Victorian Repression" in *Passion and Power: Sexuality in History*, ed. Kathy Peiss and Christina Simmons (Philadelphia: Temple University Press, 1989), 157–77.

32. On the ACLU, see Leigh Ann Wheeler, *How Sex Became a Civil Liberty* (New York: Oxford University Press, 2013).

33. See, for example, John Costello, *Virtue under Fire: How World War II Changed Our Social and Sexual Attitudes* (Boston, MA: Little Brown, 1985); Bérubé, *Coming Out under Fire*; Beth Bailey and David Farber, *The First Strange Place: The Alchemy of Race and Sex*

in World War II Hawaii (New York: Free Press, 1992); Leisa D. Meyer, *Creating GI Jane: Sexuality and Power in the Women's Army Corps during World War II* (New York: Columbia University Press, 1996); Marilyn E. Hegarty, *Victory Girls, Khaki-Wackies, and Patriotutes: The Regulation of Female Sexuality during World War II* (New York: New York University Press, 2008); and Mary Louise Roberts, *What Soldiers Do: Sex and the American GI in World War II France* (Chicago: University of Chicago Press, 2013).

34. See, for example, Jasbir K. Puar, *Terrorist Assemblages: Homonationalism in Queer Times* (Durham, NC: Duke University Press, 2007), introduction.

Chapter 14
Private Acts, Public Anxieties: The Fight to Decriminalize Male Homosexuality in Postwar West Germany[1]

Robert G. Moeller

On a spring afternoon in April 1958 in a room in Passau in southern West Germany, a group of twenty-six men and two women convened to discuss what happened when adult men got together for the purpose of mutual masturbation. Was it comparable to anal sex? Fellatio? Rubbing one's erect penis between the legs of another man until ejaculation was achieved? Was it as good as coitus in heterosexual sexual relations? The participants in this discussion were not the editorial staff of a magazine aimed at a male homosexual readership considering how best to boost circulation, nor were they representatives of the Volkswartbund, a rabidly homophobic organization connected to the Catholic Church, which since its origins in the Kaiserreich had battled "moral decline" and had labeled male homosexuals as Public Enemy Number One.[2] Rather, they were members of a commission appointed by the West German Ministry of Justice, joined by other legal experts, to offer advice on a proposed reform of the criminal code. On that day in April, their long march through the massive draft law had reached the provisions that applied to homosexuality.

In the reform proposal, the relevant statute bore the number 363, but most Germans would have known that this represented simply a renaming of Paragraph 175, the provision that had outlawed male homosexual sexual relations since it became part of the Penal Code (Reichsstrafgesetzbuch) of the unified German

Reich in 1871.[3] This chapter focuses on calls for reform of the law in the 1950s and 1960s in the Federal Republic of Germany (FRG) and offers an explanation of why the law was significantly revised in 1969. An analysis of debates over the reform reveals much about where West German politicians and policymakers set the limits between private acts and public behavior. It illuminates why they viewed the progression of adolescent males to normative heterosexuality to be a process fraught with risk and danger. It focuses our attention on the ways in which changing conceptions of male *heterosexuality* influenced discussions about adult male *homosexuality*, suggesting that we can understand and explain the reshaping of *hetero*sexual relations—the focus of most of the chapters in this volume—only if we also consider how conceptions of *homo*sexual relations changed during the "long postwar." When we separate gender from sexuality, and heterosexuality from homosexuality, we are also reminded that after 1945, change did not happen at the same pace for everyone. The chapter offers insights into how changing conceptions of paternal responsibility and normative heterosexual masculinity were parts of the redefinition of citizenship in the wake of the defeat of German fascism, and how these conceptions heightened anxieties about homosexual men. It describes how lawyers, doctors, and politicians understood and discussed homosexual men, not how homosexual men understood and discussed themselves or responded to proposals for legal reform. The continued criminal prosecution of male homosexuality set limits to how actively homosexual men could openly represent their own interests without fear of retribution, leaving them objects of a discussion of homosexuality in which they were not welcome as participants.

The chapter has four parts. First, it examines why in the 1950s in West Germany—a liberal democracy—the criminal penalties prohibiting male homosexual activity that had been significantly expanded by the Nazis remained in place. Second, it considers the draft law that the experts who gathered in Passau ultimately produced. Third, it looks at the reform initiatives of the 1960s that led to a rejection of their recommendation to maintain the status quo and the adoption of sweeping revisions of the law. Finally, it offers some reflections on why the outcome of this process would not seem like a triumphant sexual revolution to many homosexual men.

The Limits to Reform in the 1950s

At the end of the Second World War, the victorious Allies demanded the abolition of all laws with specifically National Socialist content, but they stopped short of suspending Paragraph 175, leaving it to the new West German state (and its East German counterpart) to sort out whether the Nazis' significant expansion of the laws regulating male homosexual relations should remain in place. Before 1935, the law had criminalized homosexual sexual relations between men, but by the 1920s the police had largely reduced their prosecution of male homosexuality to investigations of third-party complaints, while in the parliament momentum for reform of the law reached a crescendo, leading to a draft proposal that recommended suspension of restrictions on adult consensual sex.

When the Nazis came to power, they brought to an end any discussion of progressive reform, instead criminalizing a much wider range of physical male homosexual acts and dramatically intensifying arrests. Before 1935, prosecution had required evidence of penetration. As historian Geoffrey Giles puts it, until 1935, "mutual masturbation was, from a legal point of view, safe sex." After 1935, it was not.[4] The revised law also introduced specific provisions to allow prosecution of adult men charged with seducing Germany's male youth. "A male over twenty-one years of age who seduces a male person under twenty-one years of age to commit a sex offence with him" could be sentenced to up to a decade in jail.[5] Nazi medical authorities were not the first to emphasize that homosexual men "preferred boys and youths," but the specter of the older men—"beasts" who were "evil personified"—preying on and morally corrupting the young permeated the language of legal reform, court proceedings, and the press more than ever before. As historian Stefan Micheler concludes, "Nearly all Germans came into contact with Nazi homophobic propaganda."[6] The breadth of popular support for Nazi policy is suggested by the fact that as many as one-third of criminal prosecutions were initiated by third-party denunciations—Germans voluntarily turning in other Germans.[7] Although legal experts also debated whether to criminalize lesbianism, they concluded that women were less likely to seduce other women, and, as one expert explained, "if a woman is seduced she will not for that reason lastingly withdraw from normal sexual relations, but will be useful as before in terms of population policy."[8]

At the end of World War II, the Allies offered no opinion about whether the 1935 version of Paragraph 175 was a specifically Nazi law. Although the immediate postwar period witnessed a revival of a homosexual male subculture in many West German cities—a clear indication that many homosexual men were convinced that dramatic changes were at hand—the Nazi revision of Paragraph 175 remained the law of the land. Most courts upheld it, and well-publicized police round-ups of homosexual men in Frankfurt in 1951 made clear that for many West Germans, sexual activity between adult men was still a crime.[9]

To be sure, in the FRG men who violated Paragraph 175 were not sent to concentration camps, they did not wear the pink triangle that the Nazis used to identify homosexual offenders in the camps, and no one was "rehabilitated" with invasive medical procedures. Yet the 1935 version of the law remained on the books.[10] From 1951 until the end of the decade, the rate of convictions for violation of Paragraph 175 rose by 44 percent, and in the 1960s, the number remained as much as four times higher than it had been in the last years of Weimar.[11] Thus it was entirely possible that those who had made arrests and some of those arrested for violating Paragraph 175 under the Nazis would meet in court again in a democratic FRG.

A 1957 decision by the Federal Constitutional Court went even further. The Court reviewed a case in which two men appealed to overturn their conviction under Paragraph 175 on three separate grounds: in its Nazi version, it embodied principles of National Socialist racial teaching (*Rassenlehre*); it represented a "striking violation of democratic principles"; and by criminalizing male, but not female, sexual behavior, it was at odds with the constitutional guarantee of the equality of women and men. The court concluded that homosexuality was a phenomenon particularly characteristic of periods of social chaos and instability. All men were more aggressive and predatory than women, and, according to the court, the "homosexual man is a 'man.'" Lesbianism need not be criminalized precisely because the "homosexual woman is a 'woman,'" less likely to be predatory and aggressive, freed from the "excess of sexual drives" that characterized men; even for lesbians, "feminine, motherly feelings predominate." Lesbianism might violate nature, but it did not present the same threat to society as male homosexuality.[12]

Although the constitution guaranteed Germans an "inviolable arena of human freedom . . . exempt from being influenced by any form of public authority," that arena did not include the places in which men engaged in homosexual acts. In the court's judgment, the Nazi expansion of the law was completely consistent with a "democratic political order." Quite simply, "homosexual activity unequivocally violates the moral law"; moral law could establish a "*legal* boundary to the right to the free development of personality"; it legitimated "an intervention by the lawgiver into the individual's freedom"; and it left the plaintiffs with no grounds for appeal.[13]

Many lawyers, doctors, and some politicians continued to lobby for the revision of the law, calling in particular for the decriminalization of sex acts between mutually consenting adult men. However, even those who favored reform remained concerned that young men required particular protection from the dangers of homosexuality and worried that behavior decriminalized in private might pour out into the public sphere, offending some and dangerously tempting others to sample forbidden fruit. Thus the Hamburg jurist Heinrich Ackermann, who supported an end to the criminalization of sex between consenting adult males when he addressed the German national lawyers' meeting (Juristentag) in 1951, saw no inconsistency in adding that "homosexuality and its practice violated the sense of shame and morality of the overwhelming majority of those in the German community of law" and presented a particular threat to youth. Particularly in big cities, "the breeding ground of homosexual drives," police should remain vigilant, ensuring that young people in particular, their "psyches easily influenced, sexually volatile or not unequivocally heterosexual," were protected from the "early stages of sexual immorality" including "hugging, kissing, and other forms of affection among men, men dancing together, men publicly wearing women's clothing, the operation of public clubs for homosexuals, men serving guests in women's clothing, the shameless activities that take place in toilets, the disgusting graffiti on the walls of toilets, the distribution of homosexual publications and pictures, and singing homosexual songs or presenting poems in homo-clubs."[14] "If, on the one hand," Ackermann concluded, "the lawmaker should tolerate homosexual activity in private . . . , then, on the other hand, it is all the more essential that the majority of the people who are horrified by homosexuality, remain unmolested."[15] Thus even advocates of the reform of Paragraph 175 wanted to make certain that what might be permissible in private spaces not invade the public sphere.

The Criminal Code Commission and Paragraph 175

Against this background, the legal experts in the criminal code commission (Strafrechtskommission) continued to debate the future of Paragraph 175. First convened in 1954, the commission was charged with critically examining the very concepts of retributive justice, crime, and punishment. Despite the constitutional court's ruling that Paragraph 175 did not violate the new West German constitution, the Basic Law (Grundgesetz), from May 1949, it too was up for revision. The fact that the law was not unconstitutional did not mean that it should forever remain in force. It was the commission's job to advise the Ministry of Justice and Chancellor Konrad Adenauer about the form that new laws should take.[16]

All members of the commission agreed that in the form promulgated by the Nazis, the legal prosecution of male homosexuals had gone too far, but there was no consensus on how to right past wrongs.[17] They judged homosexual sexual activity to be "immoral," but commission members were almost equally divided between those who resisted reform and those who favored suspending the criminal penalties for such immorality when it was practiced in private between consenting adults. They debated at length what additional laws might be required to protect adolescents and young adult males. With near unanimity, commission members voted to maintain provisions that penalized the homosexual man who was eighteen or older who "pursued immorality" with a man younger than twenty-one. Members of the commission also expressed fears that additional measures were needed to mitigate against the "dangers of the creation of [homosexual] cliques" within the highest levels of the government and military, recalling the so-called Eulenburg Affair, the scandal that, particularly in the years 1907–09, had surrounded some of Wilhelm II's closest advisors, who were allegedly engaged in homosexual acts, and the Nazis' 1934 murder of Ernst Röhm, the leader of the Stormtroopers (*Sturmabteiling,* or SA), who made no secret of his homosexual activity, and hinting at Cold War fears that homosexuals might be easily blackmailed and thus become agents of the Soviet Union.[18] Commission members worried that decriminalizing consensual sex between men would open the floodgates to a burgeoning male homosexual subculture. Those who argued that revising Paragraph 175 represented the acknowledgment that a secular state should not mandate morality were reminded that it was precisely the process of secularization that made it more imperative than ever for the state to provide clear moral guidelines and specify a proper gender order.[19]

Once the commission's recommendations percolated up through the Ministry of Justice in 1960, emerging by 1962 as a full-blown draft law, homosexual men were given no hope that the law that criminalized their sexual relations would soon be reformed. The final version dismissed the arguments of commission members who favored permitting consensual sex between adult males, and maintained penalties for "coitus-like behavior," leaving it to the courts to determine which sex acts filled the bill.[20] It also left in place provisions that established a higher age of consent for men who engaged in homosexual sex acts—twenty-one for males, compared to sixteen for heterosexual females and males—and criminal penalties for men who used their superior position in the workplace to coerce another male employee to engage in homosexual activity.

Adenauer's Justice Ministry determined that moving beyond a rollback of the worst excesses of the 1935 legislation would create the impression that the state approved of behavior that "the vast majority of the German population viewed as a despicable aberration."[21] In eugenic categories that dated back to the late nineteenth century but that were particularly prominent under the Nazis, the draft law also maintained that lifting criminal penalties on consenting adult male homosexuals was a threat to the "purity and health of sexual life," which were the essential prerequisites for the "survival of the Volk,"[22] echoing language that could have been heard in the Third Reich.

Enlightenment Breezes

With new national parliamentary elections imminent—and an octogenarian Konrad Adenauer, the chancellor who had headed a conservative coalition government since 1949, on his way out—parliament postponed action in 1962, and the debate over the draft law continued for another seven years. By the end of the decade, the West German parliament (Bundestag) was ready to reject much of what Adenauer's Justice Ministry had proposed. What had changed? Scholars who have written about criminal law reform during this period have noted that the progressive movement, which triumphed by the end of the 1960s, was one of many forces pushing West Germany to modernize. Much had changed in the meanwhile, and calls for a complete overhaul of the criminal code were part of a much broader set of social and political processes.[23] Particularly important was that the Social Democratic Party (Sozialdemokratische Partei Deutschlands), long the loyal opposition to Adenauer's government, came to power, first in 1966 as part of a broad coalition that also included Adenauer's Christian Democratic Union (Christlich Demokratische Union), and by 1969 with a parliamentary majority that drew only on the support of the liberals of the Free Democratic Party (Freie Demokratische Partei). Since the late 1890s, the Social Democrats had supported reform of the criminal code and suspension of the criminal penalties that prohibited sex between adult men. Now they were in a position to make key appointments in the Ministry of Justice. The departure of the Christian Democrats from power also diminished the influence of organized Christianity on politics at the national level. In the 1950s, Adenauer had allowed Church spokesmen to influence debates over reform of those parts of the civil code that addressed the family and those parts of the criminal code that regulated sexuality.[24] By the second half of the 1960s, neither the Catholic nor the Protestant church had a direct line to the chancellor's office.

In ways that would be difficult to quantify, fifteen years of prosperity had also convinced many West Germans that Western civilization was on firm enough ground that it would not be undermined by what homosexual men did behind closed doors. The importance of population size as a marker of national strength had resounded throughout the discourse on the legal regulation of sexuality since the late nineteenth century and was central to Nazi policy. It was still present in the 1950s as West Germans continued to fear that a declining birthrate, combined with the civilian and military deaths of the Second World War, could mean that Germans would "die out." By the 1960s, these demographic anxieties had abated.[25] A rising gross domestic product was viewed as more important than a rising birthrate, and homosexual men were no longer charged with undermining the vitality of the nation if they did not reproduce at all.

How this altered context translated into the discourse of legal reform can be illustrated by looking at the September 1968 national meeting of German lawyers (Deutscher Juristentag), the functional equivalent of the American Bar Association meetings, held in Nuremberg, where the revision of the criminal law regulating male homosexuality was extensively discussed. This debate previewed everything that parliamentarians would say in 1969 when they finally agreed to decriminalize sexual activity between consenting adult males. With few exceptions the assembled denounced anyone who wanted to maintain Paragraph 175 in its entirety. What had prompted West German lawyers to become "almost rebels," as one headline called them?[26] What had caused the "fresh breeze of the Enlightenment," in one reporter's words, to blow away the cobwebs encumbering an outdated criminal code?[27]

When it came to sexuality, speakers in Nuremberg argued, an enlightened future should be one in which the state intervened only in cases that involved force or the abuse of minors. The state's job was to protect society from harm, but sexual practices between consenting adults harmed no one. The "mature citizen" (*mündiger Bürger*) did not need the state's instruction to formulate moral judgments. What the state needed to protect was not moral attitudes but rather the "sphere of intimacy," a "space that cannot be penetrated by the state,"[28] in which consenting adults could do whatever they pleased. The state that had attempted to equate morality with law and respected no one's privacy had been bombed into oblivion by the spring of 1945. Some twenty years later, West Germans had come of age and were ready to embrace a truly pluralistic democracy in which individual citizens, not the state, made moral judgments. Reform advocates rejected the regulation of morality by the Nazi "community of the people" (*Volksgemeinschaft*), but they found no more acceptable the patriarchal order of the Imperial Kaiserreich or the ideal of a "Christian West," based on a "theocratic understanding of the state,"[29] offered by some Christian Democrats in the 1950s. Those pushing for reform thus sought to distance themselves from National Socialism, but they also associated themselves with progressives who had railed against the forces of conservatism since the late nineteenth century.[30]

National comparisons were also relevant. Ernst-Walter Hanack, a lawyer who presented one of the most comprehensive position papers in Nuremberg, pointed out that earlier in the year East Germany had already managed to get rid of Paragraph 175.[31] Moreover, the willingness of other European nations to permit adult men to engage in consensual sex had not led to the decline of Western civilization. As the Social Democrat Gustav Heinemann, the minister of justice who would soon become the West German president, put it, twenty years after the passage of the United Nations Charter on Human Rights, it was high time for the FRG to get in step with the rest of the world.[32]

Those calling for reform invoked another hallmark of the modern by insisting that their views were founded on the basis of scientific research. Religious beliefs might shape moral values, but science, not scripture, should inform discussions of legal precepts. The medical doctors, psychiatrists, and psychologists to whom reform-minded jurists listened most carefully agreed that homosexuality was an unalterable condition, shaped by a combination of genes and milieu—nature and nurture—not a sign of excessive lust or desire that had simply run amok. Reformers cited scientific studies according to which no more than 3 to 5 percent of men engaged in "homosexual practices" and research concluding that there was no increase in male homosexual activity in countries where it had been decriminalized.[33]

A year later, the discussions in parliamentary subcommittees that anticipated the final vote on the reform sounded like variations on themes that had been rolled out in Nuremberg. On May 9, 1969, twenty-four years after the collapse of Third Reich, the spokesman for the conservative Christian Democratic Union / Christian Social Union expressed his pleasure that the "intellectual heritage" of nineteenth-century reformers was coming to fruition after the "ghostly" misadventure of National Socialism, and he joined Social

Democrats and Free Democrats in supporting the abolition of criminal penalties against consensual sex between adult men. An overwhelming parliamentary majority voted to abolish key provisions of Paragraph 175.[34]

The Limits of Reform

The 1969 reform marked a watershed in the history of sexuality in postwar West Germany. However, if Enlightenment winds blew in Nuremberg and Bonn, they did not exactly lift the sails of the gay liberation movement or propel most West Germans in the direction of accepting homosexual acts or homosexual identities. From a story of progressive political reform, let me turn to one about the homophobic undertones that could be heard throughout the debates over Paragraph 175 in the 1960s. I want to focus on what was *not* said, and how what *was* said carried no endorsement of homosexuality as a legitimate sexual identity.

Most reformers agreed that decriminalizing sexual relations between adult men was not the same as advocating an acceptance of homosexuality. Reform represented an insistence on the limits that should be set to the state's ability to shape its citizens' behavior, not an endorsement of sexual liberation for homosexual men. Reformers sought to protect the concept of a "private sphere of intimacy," essential to the creation of a liberal political system. Advocates of reform maintained that not all forms of immorality should be subject to criminal prosecution, and that it was up to a "mature citizenry" to judge homosexuality however they chose in their hearts and minds, just not in their courts.

Jürgen Baumann, a leading reform advocate, reassured those made anxious by the suspension of Paragraph 175 by emphasizing that West Germans would not respond like a pack of "dogs let off the leash," eager to engage in all "shameful acts" simply because those acts were no longer subject to criminal penalties.[35] Others who supported reform countered conservative visions of a homosexual tidal wave by emphasizing that precisely because homosexuality was so distasteful to the general public, there was little chance that decriminalizing it would present a "serious danger" or have a "seductive influence" on young men.[36] In fact, claimed Baumann, suspending Paragraph 175 would reduce the number of homosexuals, because the place where homosexuality was most widespread was in prisons that accommodated violators of Paragraph 175.

Advocates of change emphasized that legal reformers should take their cue from science—doctors, sociologists, psychologists—not religion. However, the science on which they relied also tended to present homosexuality as an unfortunate abnormality. Consider, for example, the case of Theodor Adorno. In a collection of essays, published in 1963 and widely circulated and cited, the distinguished philosopher and social theorist railed against the "repulsive homosexual paragraph" while also presenting homosexuals as "frequently neurotic," the product of an unresolved Oedipal complex and the result of an "extreme identification with the mother."[37] In a major study of homosexuality, Hans Giese, the sexologist most frequently cited by advocates of reform, spent most of his time discussing the disturbingly pathological types of behavior—promiscuity, desire for ever younger sexual partners, boundless pursuit of sexual pleasure—in which homosexual men often seemed to engage. "Homosexuality," he concluded, was not a crime but "a faulty attitude, sometimes also an illness." Suspending the law would improve the chances for therapeutic treatment.[38]

Other voices at the time might have offered an alternative view. The American sex researcher Alfred Kinsey's study of male sexuality appeared on the edges of reform discussions, but no one in the West German debate drew on his findings to argue that homosexuality existed on a spectrum of normal forms of sexual activity. And Kinsey's conclusion that of men "between the ages of 16 and 55," 10 percent were "more or less exclusively homosexual . . . for at least three years," another 8 percent were "exclusively homosexual . . . for at least three years," 4 percent of "white males" were "exclusively homosexual throughout their lives," and 37 percent of males had at least some same-sex experience was one West Germans seemed to avoid.[39] Abiding fears of homosexuality were also expressed in the support most reformers gave to maintaining laws that specified that young men needed at least two, if not five, years more to make decisions about their sexuality than young women and young men who were secure in their heterosexuality.[40] In short, even among advocates of the suspension of penalties for consensual sex between adult men, there was deep ambivalence about homosexuality. Why? The record of reform debates yields no explicit answers, but let me offer some thoughts about how we might read the silence.

Perhaps the tendency of supporters of reform to stigmatize homosexuality stemmed in part from the belief that the masculinity that was appropriate to a democratic political order should be grounded in families, and that being a proper man meant being a proper father. A growing historical literature describes how this new version of paternal responsibility was on display in the first two postwar decades. I have written about the return of the last German prisoners of war, veterans of the Second World War, from the Soviet

Union in the fall of 1955 and how the popular press presented them as men who wanted most to embrace wives and children, not guns, and who could shed tears to express their happiness at finally returning to the Vaterland.[41] Till van Rahden describes advice literature from the 1950s and 1960s which recommended that real men should push baby carriages and change dirty nappies, aspects of the "ideal families" that grew out of companionate marriages.[42] Heide Fehrenbach describes popular movies in which the "cultural rehabilitation of German fathers" was acted out in the form of melodramatic *Bildungsromane* in which the "German family is healed by the father's belated recognition of his paternal devotion and duties."[43] Father did not always know best, yet a man's role as father was central to his existence as a citizen of a liberal democracy.

Expanding on his research on homosexuality in West Germany in the two and a half decades after World War II, historian Clayton Whisnant describes how politicians, sociologists, medical experts, and the media also emphasized that heterosexual families were the foundation of a post-1945 democratic polity. The good German father was juxtaposed to the "corrupting homosexual,"[44] and corrupting homosexuals thwarted the progression of young men to democratic fatherhood, a goal that homosexual men could never reach. Sexual outsiders would remain political outsiders in a society where political rights, defined by the sexual contract that accompanied the liberal social contract, as well as men's claims to citizenship were grounded in their identities as husbands and fathers.[45]

This "family-centered masculinity" stood in sharp contrast to the alternative of a militarized masculinity that had been elevated by the Nazis. Cultural analyst Susan Jeffords, borrowing from film scholar Steven Cohan, compares West Germany with the United States, where post–World War II military expansion gave rise to conceptions of a "hard" masculinity, the prerequisite for an aggressive defense of American interests in the Cold War. Cohan contrasts this with the "soft" masculinity of the domestic sphere that defined an "orderly, responsible home life."[46] A "hard" militarized masculinity did not reappear in West Germany even when West Germans rearmed after 1955 as part of the National Atlantic Treaty Organization. The liberal weekly newsmagazine *Der Spiegel* reported that "the handsomest man in the nation is no longer—as a hit song at the start of the First World War declared—a soldier, but rather a civilian." The magazine reported results of a poll according to which few West Germans felt pride or pleasure when confronted with a "military habitus."[47] Military reformers emphasized that Germans would henceforth be "citizens in uniform," grounded first and foremost in their families, not in a "hard" Prussian military tradition. Perhaps West German anxieties that this "soft" masculinity might become too soft made it even more essential to police the border between heterosexual tenderness and a homosexual excess that expressed itself in women's clothing and red fingernail polish, between the caring male hands that cradled a child and the menacing grip of the homosexual seducer.[48]

Homosexuals did not benefit from the changing attitudes that accompanied the sexual revolution of the 1960s. By the end of that decade, many West Germans showed a growing acceptance for different forms of families, (unmarried couples, single-parent households headed by women), for changing *hetero*sexual roles (as well as premarital sex and even marital infidelity), and for popular culture that celebrated heterosexual pleasure and desire. The availability of the pill and information about birth control had profound consequences for sexual practice.

By the 1960s, the heterosexual household was the site not only of citizenship, but increasingly of steamy sex. "Enlightenment" films offered public displays of how to achieve private pleasures, and, as historian Elizabeth Heineman demonstrates, by the late 1950s, customers "hoped [that] mail-order erotica would enhance stability and pleasure within the family."[49] The moral landscape was shifting, but even as attitudes toward heterosexual sexual activity changed, popular assessments of homosexuality did not. A 1969 public opinion poll registered that nearly half of those asked believed that homosexuality should still be subject to criminal penalties, and far greater numbers—82 percent of men and 81 percent of women—said they considered homosexuals more despicable than prostitutes.[50] In short, the sexual revolution of the 1960s was a *hetero*sexual revolution. An antipathy toward male homosexuality, still viewed by many as at best an unfortunate pathological condition, continued to hold sway in the Federal Republic even as key parts of Paragraph 175 were suspended.

Those who sought to decriminalize sex between consenting adult males also refused to acknowledge that homosexual men were among the victims of the Third Reich. Some, like Hans Giese, a supporter of reform, had survived the early 1940s as Nazi party members and chose not to offer their perspectives on this part of the past.[51] Arguing from analogy, reform advocates maintained that discrimination against homosexuals in the FRG was like discrimination against Jews under the Nazis, but almost no one wanted to address the lines of continuity from Third Reich to Bonn Republic that defined the legal persecution of male homosexuals.[52] In public deliberations over the reform of the criminal code, there was no reflection on the fact that Nazi legal provisions had remained in force for over twenty years after the obliteration of the Third Reich. Some things that the Nazis had identified as criminal behavior should remain crimes. Only in the mid-1980s would homosexual men join the "mosaic of victims" of the Third Reich, and when they did, it would largely be thanks to the Green Party. Few homosexual victims of National Socialism would ever receive either monetary or moral recognition for what they had suffered.[53]

The silence in the 1950s and 1960s surrounding the Nazi persecution of homosexual men was not complete, but the exceptions remained at the margins of debate. Some homosexual men who had been persecuted by the Nazis called their treatment in the Third Reich a "shocking example of inhumanity and a source of shame that every self-respecting German should not forget."[54] But such voices resounded in magazines aimed primarily at a male homosexual readership, and laws that sought to prevent the endangerment of youth and to ensure that the public was not exposed to "filth" were invoked to put these publications out of business.[55] Ostensibly, the pictures of thinly clad young men and the personal ads the magazines carried caused offense, but by banning them, other truly offensive memories—of the Nazis' persecution of male homosexuals—were also pushed to the margins. Individual petitioners sought to convince the Justice Ministry that Paragraph 175 was a "crime against humanity."[56] Ironically, those expressing these opinions were sometimes writing from their prison cells where they were serving sentences imposed by Paragraph 175.

Limited in their ability to talk about their past experiences, homosexual men were also not invited to testify about their circumstances in the present. Those who sought to reform Paragraph 175 in the 1960s made no attempt to solicit testimony or opinion from those whom the reform of the law most directly affected. As one petitioner put it to Justice Minister Heinemann, no other legal question had been so exhaustively discussed as the reform of Paragraph 175, but the discussion was about "homosexuality," not "homosexual human beings."[57] The formation of any sort of public, political movement to advance the rights of homosexuals in the 1950s and 1960s was stymied by fears of criminal prosecution under the same laws that had driven homosexual men into hiding from 1933 to 1945.[58]

The significance of the absence of open advocacy of homosexual rights by homosexuals in the German public sphere from 1933, when Hitler came to power, until 1969, when Paragraph 175 was reformed, is suggested by a brief detour to the United States. The 1950s were certainly not free of homophobic prejudice in America, and scholars have illuminated the chilling effects of the "lavender scare" and the aggressive pursuit of "sexual perverts" thought to be threats to national security. But the two decades after the end of World War II also witnessed the emergence of the Mattachine Society and the Daughters of Bilitis, part of the "homophile movement" which argued that individual freedom of sexual expression was a fundamental civil right. Drawing on the research of social scientists like Kinsey, it also maintained that homosexuality was not abnormal. Openly homosexual citizens were openly demanding their rights.[59] At the same time in West Germany, no one was asking homosexual men to speak for themselves, attempts at organization among homosexual men were significantly hampered by the existence of Paragraph 175 and fears of surveillance and persecution, and nowhere could homosexuals effectively organize to influence the shape of a national discussion. It would not be until the 1970s that a homosexual rights movement would reemerge in West Germany, often with little historical sense of precedents that had flourished in the 1920s.

Seen as half full, the glass poured by the judges and lawyers in Nuremberg and a year later by parliamentarians in Bonn was a remarkable testimony to the liberal reform consensus that dominated West German politics by the late 1960s. But for homosexual men, the glass remained half empty. When the gay liberation movement appeared in the 1970s, enabled not least by the legal change of 1969, it spent little time expressing its gratitude to those who had brought about the reform.

Conclusion

By the late 1960s, many West Germans were ready to embrace a version of modernity that set clear limits to the state's right to regulate sexuality. The changes in Paragraph 175 championed by reformers are indications of what much recent literature on the sixties has shown—it did not take the student radicalism of 1968 to propel the Federal Republic forcefully out of the rubble of the Third Reich into structures of democratic political governance.[60] Modernity meant acknowledgment of a "private sphere of intimacy" where the state had no business. Reform advocates clearly rejected not only the legacy of the interventionist Nazi state but also a much longer tradition, according to which the state had the responsibility to dictate morality. Private life and public policy should be kept distinct, and the "mature citizen" should be free to make her or his own moral judgments. However, reform advocates also made clear that if homosexual men come out of the closet, they should not stray beyond the bedroom door.

The gay liberation movement would directly challenge this conception of the public/private divide, demanding that openly gay men be free to enter the streets, political parties, universities, public and privately owned work-places, legally sanctioned "marriage-like relationships," night clubs, and what-ever other spaces they chose to inhabit, donning high heels, leather, mascara, business suits, blue jeans and tank tops, military uniforms, dresses, or what-ever else they chose to wear, and claiming their constitutional right to the "free unfolding of [their] personalit[ies]," however they chose to interpret that right. The movement would insist, "it's not the homosexual who is perverse; rather, it's the situation in which he lives," as the title of a 1972 film by the gay activist Rosa von Praunheim put it.[61] The gay liberation movement also adopted the pink triangle as a political symbol, visibly associating continued oppression in the present with Nazi persecution in the past.[62]

This was not what the reformers in the late 1960s had in mind. The iden-tity politics of the seventies and eighties would clash head-on not only with Christian conservative views of sin and morality, but also with leftist con-victions that questions of sexual identity should be subordinated to the *real* political agenda of overthrowing capitalism, as well as liberal conceptions of homosexual rights that sanctioned only a "private sphere of intimacy" and lib-eral anxieties that any discussion of the complete abolition of Paragraph 175 raised the discomforting specter of pederasty and predatory older homosexual men. In the late 1960s, West German lawmakers agreed that consensual sex acts between adult men should not be criminalized. But they and many other West Germans continued to believe that male homosexuality was a patho-logical condition that could present a threat to Germany's male youth. The state's exit from the regulation of what happened behind closed doors between consenting adults also failed to bring widespread tolerance or acceptance of homosexuals. Indeed, most lawmakers agreed that Germans were able to find homosexuality morally distasteful without any instruction from the state. As West German society showed an ever-increasing tolerance for different forms of *hetero*sexual practice, it would continue to offer a far more restricted space for those who chose to march to the beat of a different drummer.

Notes

1. My thanks to Frank Biess, Jane Caplan, Jennifer Evans, Heide Fehrenbach, Elizabeth Heineman, Dagmar Herzog, Mia Lee, Lynn Mally, Rachel O'Toole, Uta Poiger, Todd Presner, Ulrike Strasser, Marilyn Young, and Jonathan Zatlin, who offered useful comments on earlier drafts of this article. The article appeared in a longer version in *Feminist Studies* 36 (2010): 528–52, and appears here with permission of the editors.

2. Joanna Gotzmann, "Der Volkswartbund: Die bischöfliche Arbeitsstelle für Fragen der Volkssittlichkeit im Kampf gegen Homosexuelle," *"Himmel und Hölle": Das Leben der Kölner Homosexuellen 1945–1969*, ed. Kristof Balser et al. (Cologne: Emons Verlag, 1994), 169–83.

3. "Grosse Strafrechtskommission, Niederschrift über die 82. Sitzung am 28. April 1958 in Passau," Bundesarchiv (hereafter BA), B 141/82159, Bl. 53–111. The proceedings of the commission were published as *Niederschriften über Sitzungen der Grossen Strafrechtskommission*, Vol. 8, Besonderer Teil, 76. bis 90. Sitzung (Bonn: Bundesdruckerei, 1959).

4. Geoffrey J. Giles, "The Institutionalization of Homosexual Panic in the Third Reich," in *Social Outsiders in Nazi Germany*, ed. Robert Gellately and Nathan Stoltzfus (Princeton, NJ: Princeton University Press, 2001), 240.

5. The translation of the law is in *Hidden Holocaust? Gay and Lesbian Persecution in Germany 1933–45*, ed. Günter Grau, trans. Patrick Camiller (London: Cassell, 1995), 66.

6. Stefan Micheler, "Homophobic Propaganda and the Denunciation of Same-Sex-Desiring Men under National Socialism," in *Sexuality and German Fascism*, ed. Dagmar Herzog (New York: Berghahn Books, 2005), 116, and in general, 95–130.

7. Micheler, "Homophobic Propaganda," 95–130.

8. See "Academy of German Law. Work preparation subcommittee of the Committee on Population Policy. Extracts from the minutes of discussions held on 2 March 1936," in Grau, *Hidden Holocaust?*, 72.

9. Dieter Schiefelbein, "Wiederbeginn der juristischen Verfolgung homosexueller Männer in der Bundesrepublik Deutschland: Die Homosexuellen-Prozesse in Frankfurt am Main 1950/51," *Zeitschrift für Sexualforschung* 5 (1992): 59–73; Clayton J. Whisnant, *Male Homosexuality in West Germany: Between Persecution and Freedom, 1945–1969* (New York: Palgrave Macmillan, 2012), 29–36; and Jennifer V. Evans, *"Bahnhof* Boys: Policing Male Prostitution in Post-Nazi Berlin," *Journal of the History of Sexuality* 12 (2003): 605–36.

10. Dagmar Herzog, *Sex after Fascism: Memory and Morality in Twentieth-Century Germany* (Princeton, NJ: Princeton University Press, 2005), 88–95; Christian Schulz, *Paragraph 175. (abgewickelt): Homosexualität und Strafrecht im Nachkriegsdeutschland. Rechtsprechung, juristische Diskussion und Reformen seit 1945* (Hamburg: MännerschwarmSkript, 1994); Andreas Pretzel, "Die gescheiterte Entnazifizierung des Rechts," in *NS-Opfer unter Vorbehalt: Homosexuelle Männer in Berlin nach 1945*, ed. Andreas Pretzel (Münster: Lit Verlag, 2002), 71–82; Robert G. Moeller, "'The Homosexual Man is a 'Man,' the Homosexual Woman is a 'Woman': Sex, Society, and the Law in Postwar West Germany," *Journal of the History of Sexuality* 4 (1994): 395–429; Whisnant, *Male Homosexuality in West Germany*; and Hans-Georg Stümke and Rudi Finkler, *Rosa Winkel, Rosa Listen: Homosexuelle und "Gesundes Volksempfinden" von Auschwitz bis heute* (Reinbek/Hamburg: Rowohlt, 1981).

11. Edward Ross Dickinson, "Policing Sex in Germany, 1882–1982: A Preliminary Statistical Analysis," *Journal of the History of Sexuality* 16 (2007): 204–50, 208, 236.

12. Moeller, "'The Homosexual Man is a 'Man,'" 419.

13. Ibid.

14. Whisnant, *Male Homosexuality in West Germany*, 57–61; and on perceptions of youth culture in the 1950s in general, see Uta G. Poiger, *Jazz, Rock, and Rebels: Cold War Politics and American Culture in a Divided Germany* (Berkeley: University of California Press, 2000).

15. Heinrich Ackermann, in comments to the 1951 national meeting of West German lawyers, copy sent to Ministry of Justice, October 5, 1951, BA, B141/4072; and Ackermann, "Welche Erweiterung des geltenden Strafrechts fordert die Aufhebung des §175?," reporting the meeting of the organization's subcommittee on criminal law on February 14, 1953, BA, B141/82157.

16. Petra Gödecke, "Die Strafrechtsreform zwischen Vergeltung und Resozialisierung, rigider 'Sittlichkeit' und vorsichtiger Toleranz," in *Recht und Justiz im gesellschaftlichen Aufbruch (1960–1975)*, ed. Jörg Requate (Baden-Baden: Nomos, 2003), 261–73.

17. See the memo from Rotberg (Justice Ministry), February 8, 1951, BA, B141/82156.

18. Clayton J. Whisnant, "Styles of Masculinity in the West German Gay Scene, 1950–1965," *Central European History*, 39 (2006), 372; and, in general, Richard Gatzweiler, *Das Dritte Geschlecht: Um die Strafbarkeit der Homosexualität* (Cologne: Klettenberg, 1951).

19. For quotations from the commission debates, see "82. Sitzung, 25. April 1958," in *Niederschriften über Siztungen der Grossen Strafrechtskommission*, Vol. 8, 226–42; and "142. Sitzung, 18. Juni 1959," ibid., vol. 13, 535–54.

20. See "CDU/CSU-Fraktion des Deutschen Bundestages, Arbeitskreis für Allgemeine Rechtsfragen, Niederschrift über die Eichholzer Tagung 'Strafrechtsreform' v. 24.9.– 26.9.62," BA, B141/82161.

21. See "Auszüge aus der Bundestagsdrucksache, IV/650 vom 4. Oktober 1962 (Regierungsentwurf eines Strafgesetzbuches—E 1962)," in *Sexualität und Verbrechen: Beiträge zur Strafrechtsreform*, ed. Fritz Bauer, Hans Bürger-Prinz, Hans Giese, and Herbert Jäger (Frankfurt/M.: Fischer Bücherei, 1963), 407; and the discussion of the reform in Whisnant, *Male Homosexuality in West Germany*, 166–203.

22. "Auszüge aus der Bundestagsdrucksache," 405–6, 409–10, 398–99; also Justice Ministry, "Entwurf eines Strafgesetzbuches (StGB) E 1960 mit Begründung (Kabinettsvorlage) (April 1960)," BA, B141/82160. See also the discussion in "Auszug aus der Niederschrift über die 253. Sitzung des Rechtsausschusses von Montag, den 18. Juni 1962 bis Mittwoch, den 20. Juni 1962, in Bonn, Bundeshaus," BA, B141/82161.

23. See, for example, Michael Kandora, "Homosexualität und Sittengesetz," in *Wandlungsprozesse in Westdeutschland: Belastung, Integration, Liberalisierung 1945–1980*, ed. Ulrich Herbert (Göttingen: Wallstein: 2002), 379–401.

24. Robert G. Moeller, *Protecting Motherhood: Women and the Politics of Postwar West Germany* (Berkeley: University of California Press, 1993).

25. Wolfgang Kretschmer, "Homosexualität und Gesellschaft," *Frankfurter Allgemeine Zeitung*, June 16–17, 1967; and Moeller, *Protecting Motherhood*, 109–41.

26. Claus Preller, "Beinahe Rebellen," *Hamburger Morgenpost*, September 21, 1968.

27. Rudolf Gerhard, "Der Richter ist kein Sittenwächter," *Frankfurter Allgemeine Zeitung*, October 3, 1968.

28. See, for example, comments of Adolf Arndt, *Verhandlungen des siebenundvierzigsten deutschen Juristentages, Nürnberg 1968*, vol. 2, *Sitzungsberichte*, ed. Ständige Deputation des deutschen Juristentages (Munich: C.H. Beck'sche Verlagsbuchhandlung, 1969), J35.

29. Adolf Müller-Emmert, "Verstaubte Moral oder rationales Recht? Zur Reform des Sexualstrafrechts," *Vorwärts*, October 17, 1968.

30. "Freiheit in der Intimsphäre: Auf dem Wege zur Reform des deutschen Sexualstrafrechts," *Pariser Kurier*, October 12, 1968.

31. Ernst-Walter Hanack, "Empfiehlt es sich, die Grenzen des Sexualstrafrechts neu zu bestimmen?" in *Verhandlungen des siebenundvierzigsten deutschen Juristentages, Nürnberg 1968*, ed. Ständige Deputation des deutschen Juristentages, vol. 1: *Gutachten* (Munich: C. H. Beck'sche Verlagsbuchhandlung, 1968), A1–8; also, Karl-Heinz Lehmann, in *Verhandlungen des . . . Juristentages*, 2: K 116–17.

32. For Gustav Heinemann's comments, *Verhandlungen des . . . Juristentages*, 2: H22.

33. Jürgen Baumann, *Verhandlungen des . . . Juristentages*, 2: K 107–8.

34. Quotation from Richard Sturm, Deutscher Bundestag, 5. Wahlperiode, Stenographischer Dienst, 130. Sitzung des Sonderausschusses für die Strafrechtsreform, Bonn, 16. January 1969, 2624; and from Max Güde, *Verhandlungen des Deutschen Bundestages*, 5. Wahlperiode, Stenographische Berichte, Vol. 79 (Bonn, 1969), 232. Sitzung, 12827, 12831–2.

35. Baumann, *Verhandlungen des . . . Jursitentages*, 2: K 109.

36. Fritz Pallin, *Verhandlungen des . . . Jursitentages*, 2: K 61.

37. Theodor W. Adorno, "Sexualtabus und Recht heute," in *Sexualität und Verbrechen*, 308–9.

38. Hans Giese, "Geschlechtsunterschiede im homosexuellen Verhalten," in *Mensch, Geschlecht, Gesellschaft: Das Geschlechtsleben unserer Zeit gemeinverständlich dargestellt*, ed. Hans Giese, 2nd ed. (Baden-Baden: Verlag für angewandte Wissenschaften, 1961), 876–77. See also Hans Giese, *Der homosexuelle Mann in der Welt*, 2nd revised ed. (Stuttgart: Ferdinand Enke, 1964).

39. Alfred C. Kinsey, Wardell B. Pomeroy, and Clyde E. Martin, *Sexual Behavior in the Human Male* (Philadelphia: W. B. Saunders, 1948), 650–1.

40. Manfred Bruns, "Das Sexualstrafrecht und der Jugendschutz," in *Die Geschichte des § 175: Strafrecht gegen Homosexuelle*, ed. Freunde eines Schwulen Museums in Berlin, e.V. in Zusammenarbeit mit Emanzipation e.V. Frankfurt am Main (Berlin: Verlag Rosa Winkel, 1990), 165–71.

41. Robert G. Moeller, *War Stories: The Search for a Usable Past in the Federal Republic of Germany* (Berkeley: University of California Press, 2001), 88–122.

42. Till van Rahden, "Demokratie und väterliche Autorität: Das Karlsruher 'Stichentscheid'-Urteil von 1959 in der politischen Kultur der frühen Bundesrepublik," *Zeithistorische Forschungen*, Online-Ausgabe, 2, 2 (2005), http://www.zeithistorische -forschungen.de/16126041-Rahden-2-2005.

43. Heide Fehrenbach, "Rehabilitating Fatherland: Race and German Remasculinization," *Signs* 24 (1998):107–27, quotations, 118.

44. Whisnant, "Styles of Masculinity," 359–93.

45. Carole Pateman, *The Sexual Contract* (Cambridge: Polity Press, 1988).

46. Susan Jeffords, "The 'Remasculinization' of Germany in the 1950s: Discussion," *Signs* 24 (1998): 163–169; and Steve Cohan, *Masked Men: Masculinity and the Movies in the Fifties* (Bloomington: Indiana University Press, 1997), xii. See also the chapter by Amy Rutenberg in this volume.

47. *Der Spiegel,* October 5, 1955, 22.

48. See also the chapter by Friederike Brühöfener in this volume.

49. Herzog, *Sex after Fascism,* 143–4; Elizabeth D. Heineman, "The Economic Miracle in the Bedroom: Big Business and Sexual Consumption in Reconstruction West Germany," *Journal of Modern History* 78 (2006): 874; and in general, Heineman, *Before Porn Was Legal: The Erotica Empire of Beate Uhse* (Chicago: University of Chicago Press, 2011); also Sibylle Buske, *Fräulein Mutter und ihr Bastard: Eine Geschichte der Unehelichkeit in Deutschland 1900–1970* (Göttingen: Wallstein Verlag, 2004), 231–364.

50. "Späte Milde," *Der Spiegel,* May 12, 1969.

51. Hans Giese entry in Bernd-Ulrich Hergemöller, *Mann für Mann: Biographisches Lexikon zur Geschichte von Freundesliebe und mannmännlicher Sexualität im deutschen Sprachraum* (Hamburg: MännerschwarmSkript, 1998), 277–78.

52. For an important exception, see Hans-Joachim Schoeps, "Überlegungen zum Problem der Homosexualität," in Hermanus Bianchi, et al., *Der homosexuelle Nächste: Ein Symposium* (Hamburg: Furche-Verlag, 1963), 74–114.

53. Claudia Schoppmann, *Nationalsozialistische Sexualpolitik und weibliche Homosexualität* (Pfaffenweiler: Centaurus, 1991), 257–58.

54. See, for example, Weltbund für Menschenrechte angeschlossen an die internationale Freundsloge Bremen, "Wir rufen Euch," published in *Die Insel: Monatsblätter für Freundschaft und Toleranz* 2, no. 2 (February 1952), 24–25.

55. See, for example, Justice Ministry to Ministry of the Interior, memorandum, June 2, 1953, BA, B141/4667, Bl. 64.

56. Quotations from W. A. Schmitt to Justice Ministry, petition, January 2, 1951; also Helmut Meier to Thomas Dehler, Justice Minister, petition, February 19, 1951, BA, B141/4072. There are many other individual petitions in this volume and in BA, B141/4071.

57. M. Mischnick-Tartara to Heinemann, June 12, 1968, BA, B141/90244.

58. Andreas Pretzel, "Aufbruch und Resignation: Zur Geschichte der Berliner 'Gesellschaft für Reform des Sexualrechts e.V.' 1948–1960," in Pretzel, *NS-Opfer unter Vorbehalt,* 287–338; Klaus Müller, "Totgeschlagen, totgeschwiegen? Das autobiographische Zeugnis homosexueller Überlebender," in *Nationalsozialistischer Terror gegen Homosexuelle: Verdrängt und ungesühnt,* ed. Burkhard Jellonek and Rüdiger Lautmann (Paderborn: Ferdinand Schöningh, 2002), 397–418; and the discussion of the West German homophile movement in Whisnant, *Male Homosexuality in West Germany,* 64–111.

59. David K. Johnson, *The Lavender Scare: The Cold War Persecution of Gays and Lesbians in the Federal Government* (Chicago: University of Chicago Press, 2004). See also the chapter by Joanne Meyerowitz in this volume; John D'Emilio, "The Homosexual Menace: The Politics of Sexuality in Cold War America," in D'Emilio, ed., *Making Trouble: Essays on Gay History, Politics, and the University* (New York: Routledge, 1992); and in general,

Margot Canaday, *The Straight State: Sexuality and Citizenship in Twentieth-Century America* (Princeton, NJ: Princeton University Press, 2009).

60. See, for example, Herbert, *Wandlungsprozesse in Westdeutschland*.

61. Rosa von Praunheim, *50 Jahre pervers: Die sentimentalen Memoiren des Rosa von Praunheim* (Cologne: Kiepenheuer & Witsch, 1993), 138.

62. Erik Jensen, "The Pink Triangle and Political Consciousness: Gays, Lesbians, and the Memory of Nazi Persecution," *Journal of the History of Sexuality* 11 (2002): 319–49.

Chapter 15

Homosexuality and the Politics of Masculinity in East Germany[1]

Jennifer V. Evans

On August 24, 1961, eleven days after temporary barbed wire fencing cordoned off the eastern portion of Berlin from its western half, Günter Litfin attempted in vain to swim across the River Spree. Noticed by transport police, he was shot several times and ultimately drowned. One of 70,000 workers with addresses in the east and jobs in the west, Litfin had been crisscrossing the internal boundary without incident until that fateful day.[2] To counter negative press reports in West Germany about the Wall's first victim, the eastern media painted Litfin in stark hues. He was an "indolent element known under the nickname 'dolly-boy' in homosexual circles in West Berlin."[3] The Wall had "separated him from his lovers" in the West, leaving him "unable to ply his trade."[4] Forgetting that the German Communist Party had supported the decriminalization of homosexuality in the 1920s, the leader of East Germany's Socialist Unity Party (Sozialistische Einheitspartei Deutschlands, or SED) and chairman of the German Democratic Republic (GDR) Council of Ministers, Walter Ulbricht, used Litfin's death to remind Germans that the building of the Berlin Wall was an absolute necessity to "close the holes through which the worst enemies of the German people could creep." The Wall would prevent "counter-revolutionary vermin, spies and saboteurs, profiteers and human traffickers, prostitutes, spoiled teenage hooligans and other enemies from sucking the life force from our people."[5] Twenty-eight years later, in June 1989, another young man found himself at the center of a smear campaign within the internal correspondence of the

343

SED's Central Committee. In a petition to the party, a junior officer of the East German People's Police (Volkspolizei) described his shock at being outed by colleagues for his "homosexual disposition." Labeled "a security risk out of fear of blackmail," he tried in vain to secure alternative employment, but word of his "disposition" followed him to every interview. Now, aware of radio reports trumpeting liberalization, he sought clarification.[6]

These two cases bound the short history of the Berlin Wall with tales of transgression. They underscore the fact that the decriminalization of homosexuality after 1957, which culminated in the abolition of the antisodomy paragraph of the East German Criminal Code in 1968, did not give rise to a sexual revolution in East German society.[7] Even as the East German police no longer enforced Paragraph 175 of the German Criminal Code (*Reichstrafgesetzbuch*) from 1871, which had made homosexual acts between males a crime, for adults after 1957, same-sex desire remained a hot-button issue throughout the history of the GDR. Indeed, the communist east played host to homophobic vitriol, relying on images of espionage, secret societies, effeminacy, and treason to link same-sex desire with stunted or degenerate political maturation.[8] Far from eradicating "the problem" of "unnatural desire" (*widernatürliche Unzucht*), decriminalization politicized the age of consent, drawing a line between consensual adult encounters and intergenerational sex. No longer was sexual deviance regulated via the judicial system. Instead, the state drew upon a raft of educators, psychologists, and therapists to promote responsible sexual practices, especially among the nation's youth.[9]

This chapter seeks to do three things. First, it will bring to light the uneasy relationship between prudishness and changing social mores that failed to dissipate after the decriminalization of homosexuality; second, it shows that explanatory devices involving biology were central instruments of state power in East Germany; and third, it suggests that efforts at controlling sexual desire backfired in significant ways, enabling subcultural self-determination and emboldening citizens after 1968 to take the regime to task for failing to live up to the spirit of the new law. Such an approach shows that while the postwar period may have ushered in new definitions of gender expression, challenging assumptions and the rigidity of social roles, men and youths perceived as effeminate or gay were not uniformly afforded the benefits of sexual enlightenment and social citizenship. In East Germany, homophobia continued to shape official and private life and the roles set out by the state for its citizens, who internalized, embraced, or rejected these norms and rules for their intimate realm.

Pre- and Postwar Discourses on Homosexuality

Fears concerning sexual deviance and seduction have a long history in Germany, as elsewhere, surfacing in sexual scandals, medical texts, psychiatrists' notations, the columns of newspapers and boulevard press, and debates about the criminalization of same-sex relations. By the end of the Weimar Republic, both opponents and supporters of decriminalization agreed that adolescents were particularly vulnerable to seduction by adult male homosexuals. The Nazis relied on this idea when they expanded Paragraph 175 in 1935 and substantially increased prosecutions. Just as Nazi Germany expanded the German criminal code from 1871 as part of its social revolution, Stalin's Soviet Union likewise treated homosexuality as suspicious activity linked to sabotage, espionage, and a lack of political reliability. The Soviet Union's most celebrated playwright, Maxim Gorky, was unequivocal in seeing homosexuality as antithetical to the tenets of communism: "exterminate homosexuals and fascism (itself) will disappear," he wrote in 1934.[10] Homophobia ran rampant across the political spectrum. Like the Nazis, Soviet People's Commissar of Justice Nikolai Krylenko thought homosexuals were sexual pariahs who, "in filthy little dens and hiding places," made elaborate plans to corrupt the innocence of youth through seduction.[11] In the volatile 1930s, both the fascist and Stalinist regimes relied on similar notions of youth endangerment, rendering the male homosexual a danger to the moral and material integrity of the state.

Following the collapse of the Third Reich, the Allied occupation, and the creation of the two Germanys in 1949, how did the GDR deal with this twofold inheritance: the Nazi past and the Soviet presence? Mass rape, prostitution, displaced populations, and the destruction of the family created what many observers felt was a significant moral vacuum in both Germanys. Children were forced to bear adult burdens at an early age, and conditions of scarcity and lawlessness renewed debates surrounding the dangers of sexual impropriety. Defeat and occupation, together with what some experts gauged might be between 10 and 20 percent of returning soldiers having experimented with homosexuality during the war, brought the very definition of normative masculinity back into focus.[12] In the midst of a deepening Cold War, fear over the moral condition of male youth was at the same time a concern with the roles young East or West German men would be required to play in state and society.[13]

Decriminalization, Discrimination, and Early Postwar Politics

As increasing numbers of refugees fled across the internal boundary from East to West Germany, the nation's youth as "the bearers of hope for the Party" (*die Hoffnungsträger der Partei*) held a particularly important place for the realization of new social and political norms in the GDR of the 1950s.[14] East German advice literature attempted to inculcate a socially responsible form of hetero-sexuality to help channel pleasure-seeking impulses for the collective strug-gle. While youth services hurried to discipline and reeducate deviations from prescribed norms, institutions like the state youth organization Free German Youth (Freie Deutsche Jugend, or FDJ) and, from the mid-1950s, the National People's Army steeped young men in traditions of duty and respect for author-ity.[15] Homosexuality, like delinquency and rowdiness (*Rowdytum*), called into question the smooth transition from fascism to "real existing socialism."

Alongside such fears, the postwar crisis gave rise to the voices of East Germans who regarded sexual expression as a fundamental freedom, one that was embedded in a broader vision of radical social and political change in the first postwar years. Dresden psychiatrist Rudolf Klimmer reignited the debate over decriminalization of homosexuality between men and began to seek sup-port for his view, based on the work of German sexologist Magnus Hirschfeld, that there existed a bias in nature for homosexual desire.[16] Although the occu-pying forces—Great Britain, the United States, and France in the western zones, the Soviet Union in the eastern—refused to revoke Paragraph 175, and although German courts in the western zones and after 1949 in the newly founded Federal Republic of Germany (FRG) continued to prosecute homo-sexuals according to the 1935 Nazi law, the GDR took a more lenient stance.[17] A reform commission set up at the behest of the Ministry of Justice went so far as to suggest that homosexuality should be decriminalized entirely, and after 1957 consensual acts among adults were no longer prosecuted, unless there was a perceived threat to public order or "the social good."[18] Legal wrangling and state pressure delayed criminal code reform until the late 1960s, but by reverting to the pre-1935 definition of homosexuality and then discontinuing the prosecution of most adult infractions, the GDR took a bold step away from West German jurisprudence.

Paragraph 175a governing male prostitution and intergenerational sex, however, was not considered tainted by the fascist stain. East German courts declared the legality of this facet of the Nazi legislation, because it was rooted in "progressive ideas in that it defended sexual integrity and thus the healthy

346

development of youth."[19] Spurred on by the evolving debate on both sides of the German-German boundary over the early onset of puberty and its implications for age-of-majority discussions, the East German regime and courts paid particular attention to masculine comportment.[20] Before a consensus could be reached, however, the events of 1953—both inside and outside East Germany—halted the project of legal reform.[21]

In the wake of Stalin's death, the introduction of intense economic restructuring in the spring of 1953 resulted in a wave of labor unrest all across the country. Legions of young workers, angered by increased production norms and what amounted to wage cuts, went on strike. Faced with revolt by the very emblems of the revolution, the regime changed its course almost overnight. Gone were the halcyon days of utopianism; as the Soviet Union had done in the mid-1920s when it backed away from sexually progressive policies as Stalin tightened his grasp on power, East German leaders set in motion a series of socially conservative policies designed to cloak the population in a blanket of communist ethics that included the promotion of the family, pronatalism, and respectability. Any plans for sweeping legal reform were put on hold until the economic situation had stabilized. In using family discourse as a moral cudgel to garner sympathy and bring discipline to a people undergoing rapid social and economic change, the regime highlighted homosexuality's alleged bourgeois origins—and its links to fascism—and drew with increasing vigor on Paragraph 175a to criminalize all acts of homosexual incitement and desire involving minors. The former minister of justice, Max Fechner, and the founding father of the Ministry of State Security (Stasi), Wilhelm Zaisser—both political opponents of SED leader Walter Ulbricht—fell victim to this homophobic rhetoric and were purged from their posts as "not only politically but morally degenerate." Conjuring the specter of sexual impropriety and seduction which had worked so well against Ernst Röhm in the early 1930s, the East German High Court charged Fechner with tempting "the still under 21-year-old witness G.—a member of the Guards' Battalion of the People's Police—to commit indecent sexual acts by unbuttoning his trousers and touching his genitals."[22] Same-sex desire challenged the regime's purity of purpose, while the government's heavy-handed response was eerily reminiscent of tactics honed by the Nazis a few years earlier. Despite efforts to distance the regime from that which came before, to the discerning citizen the state's response to homosexuality challenged if not totally undermined SED efforts to project an image of socialist humanism as the bedrock for a more enlightened form of governance.

Like the Nazis in the mid-1930s, East German leaders in the 1950s marshaled homophobia to project a sense of normalcy during moments of intense sociopolitical modernization and change to rid themselves of dissenters within the leadership.[23] East German leaders explicitly used Paragraph 175a to do so. At the same time that homosocial institutions like the People's Police were expanded to prop up the insecure regime, heightening the risk for homosexuality in this all-male institution, appeals to morality and justice helped formalize an ethics of collective citizenship and belonging that hinged on men's involvement in productive labor and healthful heterosexual relations.

From the summer of 1953 on, men and youths accused of besmirching the tenets of socialist citizenship became targets of especially exacting intervention, particularly if they were in any way linked to the SED, the People's Police, or mass organizations like the Free German Trade Union or the FDJ. The National People's Army (Nationale Volksarmee), founded in 1956, was so preoccupied with what men did in their private time that it routinely transferred and decommissioned "offenders" while simultaneously denying the existence of homosexuals in its ranks.[24] To safeguard the ideological chasteness of social policies, promote instructive examples of civic manhood, and secure productivity, authorities turned the private realm into a fertile site for intervention in the promotion of shared civic, sexual, and social ideals. They used a mix of social welfare and penal measures to reinforce the message that full and active citizenship must revolve around (re)productive labor and sexual restraint.[25] At the same time, drawing inspiration from Soviet pedagogue Anton Makarenko, who, in the early 1920s was one of the first in the Soviet Union to advocate temperance and the sublimation of sexual drives in the service of state building, youth services employed homes for juvenile offenders and workhouses like the *Struveshof* facility just outside Berlin to reeducate itinerant and criminal youth through a mix of socialist stewardship, agricultural labor, and industrial training.[26] Reeducation was anchored in the view that sexual desire shaped gender identity, was dangerously malleable, and required responsible sculpting.[27]

Socially conservative visions of sexual behavior surfaced in court cases and politicians' speeches as a central feature of appropriate socialist identification. They also reflected some East Germans' desire for a return to traditional values in a period of political upheaval.[28] For example, the remote district attorney's office that had been set up in mining towns in the Wismut region to prosecute crimes in highly secretive uranium operations reported that "unnatural desire" (*widernatürliche Unzucht*) endangered the "the health and purity of worker citizens."[29]

348

In 1958, Ulbricht reminded his audience at the Fifth Party Congress of the SED that the achievement of state socialism would require both the engagement and energy of all citizens. In outlining his Principles of Socialist Morals and Ethics—known idiomatically as the Ten Commandments—he underscored that "respect for family" was "a firm element of our world-view."[30] The Ten Commandments surfaced in facilities like *Struveshof* as essential features of reeducation programs linking heteronormative sexual ideals to healthy and active citizenship. The irony, of course, is that for the most endangered, the family idyll could only be enforced in the sterile environment of an institutional homosocial space, where, at least according to neurologist Hanns Schwarz, it took only one malcontent in a sleeping hall to unleash a "wellspring of infection"—a reference to seduction and the "disease" of homosexuality.[31]

Homosexual Deviance and the Moral Logic of a Heterosexual State

The Ministry of Justice, the police, and youth services received outside support in their attempts to police sexuality by linking normative (re)productive masculinity to the strength of the state. From the pages of magazines like *Junge Welt* and *Das Magazin* to the myriad sex education and advice manuals of the 1950s and early 1960s, a host of experts sought to shape the thoughts, minds, and actions of young East German citizens with regard to the moral economy of sex and preferred gender expression. While progressive-minded sex educators advocated against a "morality of the convent," discourses of responsible heterosexuality percolated into the 1964 juvenile justice statute, the 1965 family code, and the 1966 education reform act.[32] As evidenced in the extreme by the public explanations for Litfin's death at the Wall in August 1961, there could be no place, rhetorically or otherwise, for the unrepentant. Despite the talk of sexual openness in the 1960s, most experts agreed that homosexuals were effeminate and politically unreliable cosmopolitans who threatened to spread their malevolence to the innocent.

New Attempts at Reform and the Scientific Turn

In 1968, following the successes of new economic initiatives, East Germany decriminalized homosexuality among consenting adults. Both paragraphs 175 and 175a were removed from the criminal code, only to be replaced by a new ordinance "safeguarding" the sexual well-being of same-sex desiring young men under the age of eighteen. Police and welfare authorities were still licensed to intervene in the policing of age boundaries for sex acts between youths in addition to policing intergenerational infractions. While the age of majority for heterosexual encounters was set at fourteen, the new law cast increasing attention on same-sex sexual experimentation and for the first time included acts between girls.[33] In many ways, both subtle and explicit, decriminalization was a pyrrhic victory. The guarantees of sexual self-determination for adult men had been hard fought, but they came at a cost to male and female youths, who drew additional scrutiny for their sexual choices and actions.

Decriminalization certainly did not mean that the issue of male sexual deviance was off the table.[34] If anything, the opposite was true. To be sure, the 1960s marked an end to legal reformers' preoccupation with aberrant desire. However, as in Western nations, authority over the question changed hands from jurists and reform commissions to sociologists and criminologists, psychiatrists, and psychotherapists. Homosexuality was less a legal issue than a medical one, affirming, in a way, Magnus Hirschfeld's original line of argument. In the GDR, social scientists were enlisted to explain why the socialist norms formulated in the 1950s were not being adequately internalized in the 1960s, 1970s, and 1980s. Drawing on a strand within Marxist-Leninist ethics on socialist personhood, new research initiatives sought to decode the root causes of criminal motivation, marking the reemergence of the social and psychological sciences in matters of educational, youth, and criminal policy east of the Iron Curtain.[35]

The new emphasis on the inner workings of the socialist personality coincided with a change in priorities within the regime over how to balance liberalizing tendencies in legal reform with the feared increase in popular expectations for greater political freedom.[36] By 1971, with Erich Honecker's ascension to power, the ministries of health, justice, and education began to work more explicitly with psychologists and police to assess the reasons behind the continued "asociality" of select groups, such as alcoholics, rowdies, and the perpetually unemployed.[37] Frequently, they cited juvenile delinquency and homosexuality as risky behaviors in need of better management. Failure to demonstrate commitment to the socialist community was now interpreted as a psychological failing, thus securing a firm place for psychosocial definitions of same-sex attraction.[38] Homosexuality had been transformed into a condition to be pitied if not prosecuted, one that might be treated if not prevented. In the process, it morphed from a series of acts with some influence upon gender comportment into the basis of an identity.

Within a few years after decriminalization, homosexuality among adults became a topic positively discussed in the East German press, even as youth sexuality remained politically contentious. When sexologist Siegfried Schnabl described homosexuality as normal in his impassioned 1973 "Plea for a Minority" in the East German glossy paper *Das Magazin*, twenty-one-year-old student and later gay rights activist Klaus Laabs's "heart almost stopped beating" at the sight of an open and professional discussion of the issue.[39] Despite this new openness, gays and lesbians still needed to meet clandestinely in apartments and salons. But greater public discussion of homosexuality did not eradicate the confusion surrounding its root causes.[40] Even Schnabl's sympathetic approach contained the prospect of therapeutic intervention to help heal the afflicted.[41] In a 1978 forum in the magazine *Deine Gesundheit*, physicians Klaus Tosetti and Gerhard Misgeld humanized homosexuality as providing "everything the culturally developed person might hope for in life: sexual harmony, aesthetic taste, love, and the recognition of one's peers." Yet even as they proclaimed that homosexuality was "neither a sickness, nor something that made one ill," they advocated for greater research into its biological origins, since it could be a burden some people did not wish to bear.[42]

The 1970s and 1980s witnessed the slow liberalization of attitudes on matters of sexuality generally. Many East Germans continued to view gays as perverse, upholding traditional visions of men's and women's roles. Reflecting on the situation in 1981, one interviewee in an ethnography on queer East Germans claimed that hateful comments like "you should castrate that sow" were in fact "par for the course."[43] In the 1980s, a People's Police officer who had been let go from his post upon discovery of intimate letters in his locker was even told by his colleagues, "Hitler forgot to gas you."[44] The state's position did little to clarify matters. The age boundary between adolescent and adult continued to provoke controversy. As the 1981 commentary to the criminal code made plain, consensual sex between men might be tolerated, but it certainly was not condoned if one or both partners was under the age of majority. Homosexual acts were still judged "liable to compromise the formation of sexual-ethical norms . . . and the normal sexual development of young people."[45] Decriminalization had hardly challenged the social stigma that the heteronormative gaze attached to the allegedly deleterious impact of same-sex acts on fragile adolescent sexuality and the maintenance of family-based male social roles.

Claims to a public gay identity frequently met with scorn and sanctions. Men who opted to live outside the closet, who even embraced their homoerotic desire as a foundation of identity, were still denied positions within the government, the party, state bureaucracy, police, military, and mass organizations. Some were able to find employment in academia, the theater, and belle-lettres, but many more were forced into the second tier of employment. As nonindustrial workers denied party status, they worked in a substratum of the socialist utopia, making a living as bartenders, dancers, eulogists, and booksellers.

Some certainly felt relegated to this realm reluctantly, but others recognized a degree of freedom within their subcultural existence. As anthropologist Heidi Minning found in her interviews with East German gays and lesbians after 1989, those who identified publicly as gay (*schwul*) willingly worked in the arts and service professions, while men who sought to pass as straight often came from blue-collar occupations where a hardened heterosexual masculinity remained the norm.[46] Far from heralding the dawn of a new era, the 1970s and 1980s remained difficult years for East Germany's gays and lesbians, especially those beginning to organize for change.

Continuous Homophobia and Organized Protest

The suppression of benign forms of public sexual expression testifies to the vigor with which the regime cultivated homophobia into the 1980s. In 1975, the Aufbau publishing house deleted the eighth chapter of Thomas Mann's *Lotte in Weimar* in its reprint of the novel because of its unabashed depiction of homoeroticism.[47] In 1986, the central advertising agency, the Deutsche Werbe- und Anzeigengesellschaft (DEWAG), dropped all "contacts desired" advertisements from weekly newspapers.[48] Even ads in which women sought "pen pals" were censored.[49] Those who petitioned for redress, like Andreas T. and Lutz C. in 1986, were invited for a "conversation" with the local People's Police detachment, which duly informed the Central Committee's Department of Security of their investigation.[50] Student activist Klaus Laabs's position paper to the Humboldt University, criticizing its antiquated position on the burgeoning gay rights issue, caused the author's expulsion from the ruling party because of his "affront to collective purity."[51] Even the young American anthropologist John Borneman, in East Berlin researching everyday life behind the Iron Curtain, was monitored by Kurt Bach, a curious psychologist from Leipzig. Bach applied to the Ministry of People's Development for a temporary exit visa to travel to an international conference in Amsterdam and get a take on Borneman's ideas about the regulation of desire in the GDR.[52] In 1987, Bach had applied to the ministry for a temporary exit visa, claiming he would challenge Borneman's anti-GDR stance. Denied this opportunity, his paper was presented in absentia, in which he professed his belief that socialism held the possibility for destigmatizing 'unnatural desire.'"[53]

The 1980s saw a mixed picture in the GDR. Officials quashed attempts to commemorate pink triangle victims of Nazi atrocities at Buchenwald and Sachsenhausen, but in 1984 they allowed a Protestant church service in East Berlin led by vicar Eduard Stapel honoring the same prisoner group. To many activists it appeared that change was on the horizon. Homosexual working groups organized within the sanctuary provided by the Protestant churches. Yet many same-sex desiring men opted to continue meeting clandestinely, while many gay women remained wholly invisible to the state by living their lives without such self-defining labels as lesbian.[54] A 1985 Leipzig conference on psychosocial aspects of homosexuality began a period of "enlightenment from above," as medical experts and sexologists met with local gay and lesbian activists.[55] Even the Eleventh Party Congress of the SED in 1986 brought a glimmer of hope: the Party emphasized the place of the individual in socialist society in an attempt to reach out to an increasingly disgruntled population and remain in control of social change.[56] A thirty-five-page study on "The Situation of Homophile Citizens in the GDR," commissioned for the Party Congress by Egon Krenz, one of the more liberal members of the SED's Central Committee, outlined reasons why homosexuals should be welcomed into public life, citing the dangers that might ensue if they were forced underground. Underscoring the humanist dimension of socialism, the report cited the deleterious impact of continued marginalization, ranging from suicide, disease transmission (syphilis but not AIDS, since the GDR did not yet admit to the latter epidemic), and increased contacts with foreigners to clique-building, cruising, seduction, and blackmail. Homosexuality, the report said, as one of a variety of forms of desire, was naturally occurring and innate. It was the conditions in which it surfaced that determined whether any harm befell the individual, and by extension, society. Provided society accepted gays and the state created appropriate centers for socialization like group sexual counseling centers for "young people in the phase of Coming Out," university clubs, and social gathering spots instead of private salons, pubs, and bars, gays might be more readily integrated into society and enjoy greater citizenship rights as a "special and protected minority."[57] Although the study attempted to destigmatize homosexuality, it still provided a series of conditions for state recognition, chief of which was unfettered access to the subculture. In other words, this was not a celebration of difference in the service of socialist personality development but a call for greater institutionalization.

Despite all this, emboldened organizers used the opportunities presented in the 1980s to carve a space for greater sexual self-determination, demanding attention to the place of homosexuality in the GDR, asking for spaces to organize, the establishment of youth clubs and advice centers, and nondiscriminatory policies in the workplace.[58] Parents now sought compassion and redress in petitions to Erich Honecker's office when a loved one's situation appeared to contravene official policy.[59] The mixed-sex Sunday Club was founded in 1987 as an explicitly homosocial gathering space and entertainment venue. And by January 1989, the RosaLinde FDJ club became the first of its kind to receive official support for gay youth in Leipzig. Although this semblance of toleration may have chipped away at homophobia within some echelons of society, it still failed to control gay bashing in the capital, especially given the rise of right-wing activity and skinhead youth.[60] Nevertheless, gay men and women made good on the promise of liberalization and reform by reinterpreting the rhetoric of personality development as a means to lobby for public visibility. In the process, they tested the state's and society's commitment to inclusion and community.

As a new generation of sociologists, psychologists, and psychiatrists tapped into the discourse of personality, nowhere did this new research imperative have more sweeping influence than in the Stasi itself, which gleefully adopted methods from these research agendas. It was not uncommon for the state and the Stasi to employ research institutes for policy-driven initiatives, producing theses and dissertations on matters of crime, policing, philosophy, and sociology.[61] In 1983, Gerhard Fehr wrote a dissertation in the criminology department of East Berlin's Humboldt University, but his was no typical piece of scholarship. A Stasi operative, Fehr's commission included the elaboration of state policy under the cover of legitimate research.[62] Taking seriously the quest for scientific objectivity in revisiting the place of homosexuality in developed socialism, Fehr provided the Stasi with ample ammunition to better identify the now-public homosexual. Fehr's reach was wide: by one account, more than 150 Stasi moles who had infiltrated gay-friendly organizations within the Protestant churches knew the dissertation and its maxims.[63] His description of homosexual typologies revisited the time-honored issues of promiscuity, broken familial bonds, seduction, and infection. The language of risk resonated with fears of western contact, threats of loyalty and derision, and cronyism, since homosexuals "are active in all areas of society, and due to their joy in making contacts for sexual exploitation, are particularly of interest for class opponents and agents."[64] Curiously absent from the text of the dissertation but shaping its concerns was the rising wave of applications to leave the GDR, an increase in suicides, and the specter of AIDS, all of which the state security apparatus described as disproportionately affecting the nation's gays.[65] In the rhetoric of an embattled state in the 1980s, the image of gay men remained virtually unchanged. They were still portrayed as sickly, weak, and effeminate, prone to pacifist tendencies and venereal disease, and thus an "internal threat to the security of the GDR."[66]

Although the Stasi directed increasing attention toward the burgeoning gay and lesbian movements, there was a certain degree of *Realpolitik* at work, given the fraying edges of authority and mounting waves of citizen displeasure. The security apparatus, while hard-hearted, could also be notoriously fickle, changing priorities midstream when faced with new challenges. Fehr's dissertation gloried in demonizing homosexuals as sexual saboteurs; yet the use of agents to spy on the church movement had to rely on the quiescence of gay men and women forced to betray trust. Indeed, despite its own demonization of gays, the Stasi welcomed the use of same-sex desiring informers, even judging their abilities as uniquely sophisticated. As early as 1965, an operative report had maintained that gay men were particularly well suited to the "information service" due to inborn psychological qualities or deviance honed in youth. Naturally conspiratorial, "given their predisposition to fantasy and emotions," gay men, like the security service itself, were "discriminating, careful, and selective with whom they shared information and intimate exchanges." Those displaying an enhanced femininity were more capable of disarming women's reticence and gaining trust. The more manly men, by contrast, might use their physical attributes to engage in heterosexual sex without emotional attachment. "Typically of greater intelligence, rarely loners, socially engaging, and well connected," gay men were disarming and gallant, while probing and analytical. Since they were accustomed to extralegal treatment, they might be open to greater incidents of blackmail, but "no homosexual may be put under moral pressure or be easily influenced." In a scathing yet sophisticated gender analysis that married psychosocial categories with case studies, the operative put together an elaborate range of gender differences in sexual behavior, roles, and drives, suggesting the strengths and weaknesses of certain masculinities over others.[67] At the same time that the regime safeguarded heteronormative working-class manliness from the perils of the effete intellectual or lurking

355

homosexual, it was not above using all manner of men for security work, shedding insight into the hypocrisy of the state and the durability (and apparent usefulness) of the image of gays as politically duplicitous.

Clearly, the danger of seduction did not just surface in the otherwise well-intentioned insights of progressive sexologists or the warped thinking of Stasi operatives, but lurked in all discussions about male sexuality for the remainder of the twentieth century. Although research had taken the question of crime away from notions of inborn susceptibility toward a greater appreciation of "the psychological," important residues of strict biological determinism remained.[68] Certainly, the language of infection, seduction, and containment meant different things at different moments in history. But the conflation of homosexuality with treason or political degeneration remained a constant force through much of the GDR's history. In the 1980s, homosexual activists returned to this language of right to personality as a way to realize respect for individuation and desire and, as a result, were deemed a political danger. Still, despite the denigration of same-sex desiring men as leering seducers and unmanly individualists, the state at various points in its existence recognized the need to reach out to this marginalized group, while officially ostracizing homosexuality as decadent and anticollectivist.

In December 1988, the GDR amended its criminal code for the fifth and final time, removing the last official reference to homosexual derision. Homosexuality in all its forms was no longer criminal. Yet despite public pronouncements of toleration, in a research lab of East Berlin's Charité Hospital, endocrinologist Günter Dörner continued to search for ways to prevent the heartache of sexual "abnormality." Since the late 1960s, and with much international acclaim, Dörner had been suggesting that male rats that had been "feminized" with injections of female hormones demonstrated greater interest and capacity for being mounted, which he interpreted as meaning that men born with androgen deficiencies tended to exhibit feminine attributes and an increased predisposition to homosexuality. Holding the possibility of correcting this imbalance in utero, Dörner's work promised the near-total correction of anomalous desire before birth. This portion of Dörner's research, although controversial, managed to survive the Cold War and in 2002 garnered him the highest civilian honor in unified Germany, the coveted Cross of Merit (Bundesverdienstkreuz).[69]

Earlier, in the 1980s, Dörner had made another controversial suggestion—that stressful conditions during the Second World War negatively affected androgen secretions in the womb, causing an upswing of homosexual births in the ensuing generation.[70] In other words, more gay men are born in times of war than in times of peace, possibly explaining, at least in Dörner's mind, the burgeoning homosexual rights movements of the early 1970s. War ran counter to nature; armed conflict was so debilitating that it actually undermined the virility of the state in times of peace. Seduced by Nazi militarism and not the preying homosexual, Germans had unwittingly enabled the spread of homosexuality as a disease and infected ensuing generations.

When Dörner was honored, activist scholars with the Magnus Hirschfeld Society in Berlin voiced their opposition in letters to German president Johannes Rau, arguing that by calling homosexuality a condition to be prevented, Dörner was not only advocating discrimination but evoking images of euthanasia—with all of its National Socialist overtones. What was forgotten in the quest to rightly call attention to the implications of hormone research was the fact that the eponymous icon of the homosexual emancipation movement, Magnus Hirschfeld, likewise had toyed with eugenics as cofounder of the Medical Society for Sexology and Eugenics (Ärztliche Gesellschaft für Sexualwissenschaft und Eugenik).[71] In fact, Hirschfeld himself sought ways to "reorient" homosexuals through the implantation of "manly" testicles from healthy heterosexual men. This example suggests the need to view history in all its complexity, in recognition of the pervasiveness of eugenic thinking and gender stereotypes before, during, and after the Nazis, in liberal democracies and developed socialism.

Conclusion

We are just at the beginning of our quest to understand the complex and indeed contradictory place of homosexuality in the fractious twentieth century. Although it is assumed that the growth of human rights discourse out of the horror of genocide and the Holocaust led to the rise of social movements in the 1960s and the concomitant liberalization of sexual and gender norms, this chapter shows that for gay men in the GDR, there was no sexual revolution. Official homophobia remained state practice well past the legal reforms of the late 1960s. Men and their masculinities were constantly under surveillance in the "long postwar," suggesting that we need to be alert to the ways in which gender transgression—in this case, effeminacy and the threat of seduction—attracted the attention of the state as threats to heteronormative definitions of citizenship.

To be sure, German history has witnessed an elaborate mix of ideas on how best to control and manage "unnatural" forms of sexual expression, from legal and medical frameworks to eugenic, social hygiene, psychosocial, personality-driven, rights-based, and risk discourses. Expert knowledge played a key role, from Magnus Hirschfeld's gender variation to the Stasi's attempts to differentiate between friends and enemies on the basis of gender and sexuality. This pattern confirms what historians Greg Eghigian and Edward Dickinson both have pointed to in their respective work on modernity and sexuality: namely, that each of the post-1945 Germanys, whether a democratic welfare state or a welfare dictatorship, inherited, renegotiated, and redeployed biopolitical imperatives as vital elements of state-building.[72] Gendered norms and sexual constraints were essential components in the quest to manage and deploy citizen energy. At the same time that technocrats and Stasi operatives pathologized same-sex desiring men as hostile to the cause of building and then sustaining socialism, by the 1970s and 1980s gay men and women were using Marxist-Leninist ethics to forge a place for greater public engagement while advocating for a private sphere of intimacy and companionship. The web of power built by the insecure state not only helped create the conditions of its own demise but provided important, if limited, avenues of recourse for civil society.

While East German society may have been more liberal in certain matters of sexuality, to the bitter end the regime maintained churlish notions of sexual propriety as far as gay men were concerned, especially when its core political and military institutions were affected. The mechanisms of education, policing, treatment, and control succeeded in making the homosexual a subject of public concern, in some cases a focus for pity and not infrequently for animosity. But state involvement in the private lives of its citizens did not succeed in expunging alternative forms of sexual expression. On the contrary, in lending voice to a range of masculinities, from the normative to the abject, the effeminate to the mannish, these technologies of governance helped form a foundation for solidarity and social organization along the axis of sexual identity. In the unified Federal Republic of Germany, biological maxims remain part of the juridical and medical discussion of sexual freedom and aberrant sexual desire. Given the hydra that is sexual modernity, the East German case serves as an important reminder that although Magnus Hirschfeld taught us to strive *per scientiam ad justitiam* (through science to justice), we must do so in full recognition of all that the modern project entails, for better and for worse.

Notes

1. A longer version of this article appeared in *Feminist Studies* 36, no. 3 (Fall 2010): 553–77, and is published here with permission of the editors.

2. Werner Filmer and Herbert Schwan, *Opfer der Mauer* (Munich: Bertelsmann, 1991), 78–82; and Heiner Sauer and Hans-Otto Plumeyer, *Der Salzgitter Report: Die Zentrale Erfassungsstelle berichtet über Verbrechen im SED Staat* (Munich: Bechtle, 1991), 280.

3. *Berliner Zeitung*, August 31, 1961; and Elmar Kraushaar, *Hundert Jahre schwul: Eine Revue*. (Berlin: Rowohlt, 1997), 115.

4. *Neues Deutschland*, September 1, 1961.

5. *Neues Deutschland*, August 28, 1961.

6. Manfred Schönebeck, *DT 64-Streitlexikon "Mensch, Du!"* Heft 3, (Begleitmaterial zu der Ratgebersendung *"Mensch, Du – ich bin schwul!"* in Jugendradio DT 64), 1989.

7. Dagmar Herzog, *Sex After Fascism: Memory and Morality in Twentieth-Century Germany* (Princeton, NJ: Princeton University Press, 2005), 198–99; Mary Fulbrook, *The People's State: East German Society from Hitler to Honecker* (New Haven, CT: Yale University Press. 2005), 164.

8. See Simon Karlinsky, "Gay Life in the Age of Two Josephs: McCarthy and Stalin," *The Advocate* 366 (April 28, 1983), 37.

9. Greg Eghigian, "The Psychologization of the Socialist Self: East German Forensic Psychology and Its Deviants, 1945–75," *German History* 22 (2004): 181–205.

10. Gorky's 1934 essay "Proletarian Humanism," quoted in Siegfried Tornow, "Männliche Homosexualität und Politik in Sowjet-Russland," in *Homosexualität und Wissenschaft II* (Berlin: Verlag Rosa Winkel, 1992), 281; Klaus Mann, "Homosexualität und Faschismus," in *Heute und Morgen: Schriften zur Zeit*, ed. Martin Gregor-Dellin (Munich: Nymphenburger Verlagsbuchhandlung, 1969), 130–33.

11. Ben de Jong, "'An Intolerable Kind of Moral Degeneration': Homosexuality in the Soviet Union," *Review of Socialist Law* 4 (1982): 342.

12. H. Kilian, "Das Wiedereinleben des Heimkehrers in Familie, Ehe und Beruf," *Beiträge für Sexualforschung* 11 (1957): 32–4.

13. Ute Schneider, *Hausväteridylle oder sozialistische Utopie? Die Familie im Recht der DDR* (Cologne: Böhlau, 2004).

14. Verena Zimmermann, *Den neuen Menschen schaffen. Die Umerziehung von schwererziehbaren und straffälligen Jugendlichen in der DDR (1945–1990)* (Cologne: Böhlau, 2004).

15. Andrew Bickford, "The Militarization of Masculinity in the Former German Democratic Republic" in *Military Masculinities: Identity and State*, ed. Paul Higate (New York: Praeger, 2003), 157–74.

16. Günter Grau, "Ein Leben im Kampf gegen den Paragraphen 175: Zum Wirken des Dresdener Arztes Rudolf Klimmer, 1905–1977," in *100 Jahre Schwulenbewegung*, ed. Manfred Herzer (Berlin: Verlag Rosa Winkel, 1998), 46–64.

17. *Amtsblatt der Militärregierung Deutschland* 1 (1945): 11.

18. Günter Grau, "Im Auftrag der Partei: Versuch einer Reform der strafrechtlichen Bestimmungen zur Homosexualität in der DDR 1952," *Zeitschrift für Sexualforschung* 9 (1996): 109–29.

19. *Kammergericht Berlin* (1950), 129.

20. Wolfgang Bretschneider, *Sexuell aufklären rechtzeitig und richtig* (Leipzig: Urania, 1956); Hans Heinrich Muchow, *Sexualreife und Sozialstruktur der Jugend* (Reinbeck/ Hamburg: Rowohlt, 1959), 27–70; Kurt Saller, *Zivilisation und Sexualität* (Stuttgart: Ferdinand Enke Verlag, 1956).

21. Grau, "Im Auftrag der Partei."

22. Oberstes Gericht, 1Zst (1) 2/55.

23. Geoffrey Giles, "The Persecution of Gay Men and Lesbians during the Third Reich," in *The Routledge History of the Holocaust*, ed. Jonathan Friedman (London and New York: Routledge, 2011), 385–96.

24. Herzog, *Sex After Fascism*, 198–199; Fulbrook, *The People's State*, 164; Bickford, "Command Performance: Militarization, Masculinity, and the State in the German Democratic Republic and Post-Unification Germany" (Ph.D. diss., Rutgers University, 2002).

25. Jennifer V. Evans, "Repressive Rehabilitation: Sexual Delinquency, Youth Crime, and Retributive Justice in Berlin Brandenburg, 1945–58," in *Crime and Criminal Justice in Modern Germany, 1870–1960*, ed. Richard Wetzell (New York: Berghahn Books, 2014).

26. Bekämpfung der Jugendkriminalität, Thesen für die Bezirksbeauftragten zur Zentralen Arbeitsgemeinschaft für Jugendschutz zur Vorbereitung und Durchführung der Konferenzen über die Fragen des Jugendschutzes in den Bezirken, circa 1958, Bundesarchiv-Berlin (BArch), DC 4 Amt für Jugendfragen, Nr. 1401.

27. Thomas Lindenberger, "'Asoziale Lebensweise': Herrschaftslegitimation, Sozialdisziplinierung und die Konstruktion eines 'negativen Milieus' in der SED-Diktatur," *Geschichte und Gesellschaft* 32 (2005): 227–54.

28. Jennifer V. Evans, "The Moral State: Men, Mining, and Masculinity in the Early GDR," *German History* 23 (2005): 355–70.

29. Sächsisches Staatsarchiv Chemnitz (StAC), Bestand 32888, Bergbaustaatsanwalt 467, 21. August 1954.

30. Walter Ulbricht, "Grundsätze der sozialistischen Ethik und Moral," in *Zur Geschichte der Deutschen Arbeiterbewegung*, vol. 7, *Reden und Aufsätze, 1957–1959* (Berlin: JHW. Dietz Nachfolge, 1964), 376–78.

31. Hanns Schwarz, *Schriftliche Sexualberatung. Erfahrungen und Vorschläge mit 60 Briefen und Antworten* (Rudolstadt: Greifenverlag, 1959), 66.

32. Herzog, *Sex After Fascism*, 195–96; Gudrun v. Kowalski, *Homosexualität in der DDR* (Marburg: Verlag Arbeiterbewegung und Gesellschaftswissenschaft, 1987), 32.

33. Raelynn J. Hillhouse, "Out of the Closet behind the Wall: Sexual Politics and Social Change in the GDR," *Slavic Review* 49, no. 4 (1990): 587.

34. *Kahlschlag. Das 11. Plenum des ZK der SED 1965. Studien und Dokumente* (Berlin: Aufbau, 1991).

35. Eghigian, "The Psychologization of the Socialist Self," 191.

36. Jeremi Suri, "The Promise and Failure of 'Developed Socialism': The Soviet 'Thaw' and the Crucible of the Prague Spring, 1964–1972," *Contemporary European History* 15, no. 2 (2006): 133–58, 137.

37. Hans Szewczyk, "Dissoziale und asoziale Familien als Disposition zur kriminellen Entwicklung Jugendlicher," *Aktuelle Beiträge der Staats- und Rechtswissenschaft* (1970): 130–36.

38. Egighian, "The Psychologization of the Socialist Self, " 181–205.

39. Siegfried Schnabl, "Plädoyer für eine Minderheit," *Das Magazin* 12 (1973): 28–30; Klaus Laabs, "In eigener Sache, maskiert," in *Homosexualität in der DDR: Materialien und Meinungen*, ed. Wolfram Setz (Hamburg: Männerschwarm Verlag, 2006), 161.

40. Herzog, *Sex After Fascism*, 203.

41. Siegfried Schnabl, "Plädoyer für eine Minderheit," 28–30.

42. Klaus Tosetti and Gerhard Misgeld, "Homosexualität," *Deine Gesundheit* 2 (1978): 53, 54.

43. Jürgen Lemke, *Gay Voices from East Germany* (Bloomington: Indiana University Press, 191), 142.

44. SAPMO-BArch DY 30/1122 Abteilung Sicherheitsfragen. Letter from Jan H. dated May 25, 1989.

45. Autorenkollektiv, *Strafgesetzbuch der DDR, Kommentar* (Berlin: Staatsverlag der DDR, 1981), 386.

46. Heidi Minning, "Who Is the 'I' in "I Love You"? The Negotiation of Gay and Lesbian Identities in Former East Berlin, Germany," *The Anthropology of East Europe Review* 18 (2000), unpaginated.

47. Thomas Mann, *Lotte in Weimar* (Berlin: Aufbau-Verlag, 1975) discussed in Olaf Brühl, "Sozialistisch und schwul," in Setz, *Homosexualität in der DDR*, 89–152.

48. Bert Thinius, *Aufbruch aus dem grauen Versteck, Ankunft im bunten Ghetto?: Randglossen zu Erfahrungen schwuler Männer in der DDR und in Deutschland Ost* (Berlin: Bundesverband Homosexualität, 1994), 49.

49. Heidi Minning, "Who Is the 'I'?"

50. SAPMO-BArch DY 30/1152 Abteilung Sicherheitsfragen. See petitions from Andreas T. and Lutz C. dated August 20, 1986.

51. Bert Thinius, *Aufbruch aus dem grauen Versteck*, 45.

52. See the correspondence between Dr. Kurt Bach and various functionaries within the SED, November 13, 1987, in SAPMO-BArch, Abteilung Volksbildung des ZK der SED, DY 30 Nr. 5773.

53. Olaf Brühl, "Sozialistisch und schwul," 139; Bach's article is published as "Homosexualität in der DDR," *DornRosa* No. 13 (June 1988).

54. Heidi Minning, unpaginated. See also Ursula Sillig, *Un-sichtbare Frauen: Lesben und ihre Emanzipation in der DDR* (Berlin: LinksDruck Verlag, 1991).

55. Jean Jacques Soukup, *Die DDR: Die Schwulen*, 131.

56. Hillhouse, "Out of the Closet," 586.

57. SAPMO-BARch, DY 30/IV 2/2.039/4 Büro Egon Krenz. Vorbereitung des XI. Parteitages der SED vom 17. bis 21. April 1986. "Zur Situation homophiler Bürger in der DDR (Analyse des Phänomens und Lösungsvorschläge)," 7, 9, 35.

58. See Lutz Möbius, "Schön grell und bunt – aber nicht nur. Zur Geschichte des FDJ-Schwulenklubs 'RosaLinde' in Leipzig," in *Die DDR: Die Schwulen*, 59–62.

59. SAPMO-BArch DY 30/ 1315 Abteilung Sicherheitsfragen. 4.3.4. Eingabenbearbeitung im Sektor Ministerium für Staatssicherheit. August H to Erich Honecker, petition, May 22,1985.

60. Jim Steakley, "Gays under Socialism: Male Homosexuality in the GDR," *Body Politic* 29 (1976/1977): 15–18.

61. Greg Eghigian, "Homo Munitus: The East German Observed," in *Socialist Modern: East German Everyday Culture and Politics*, ed. Katherine Pence and Paul Betts (Ann Arbor: University of Michigan Press, 2008), 49–50.

62. Denis M. Sweet, "Bodies for Germany, Bodies for Socialism: The German Democratic Republic Devises a Gay (Male) Body," in *Gender and Germanness: Cultural Productions of Nation*, ed. Patricia Herminghouse and Magda Mueller (New York: Berghahn Books, 1998), 259.

63. Eduard Stapel, *Warme Brüder gegen Kalte Krieger: Schwulenbwergung in der DDR im Visier der Staatssicherheit* (Magdeburg: Landesbeauftragte für die Unterlagen des Staatssicherheitsdienstes der ehemaligen DDR Sachsen-Anhalt, 1999), 17.

64. Gerhard Fehr, "Zu einigen Aspekten der Entwicklung der Risikogruppe der männlichen Homosexuellen und der Risikogruppe der kriminellgefährdetetn, nicht lesbischen, weiblichen Jugendlichen und Jungenerwachsenen in der Hauptstadt Berlin," (PhD diss., Humboldt Universität zu Berlin, 1983), 115 and 116.

65. Eike Stedefeldt, "Zur weiteren Veranlassung: Ein Interview mit dem MfS-Offizier Wolfgang Schmidt" in Setz, *Homosexualität in der DDR*, 186.

66. BStU MfS HA XX ZMA 10050/12a 1983, 265 as cited in Stapel, *Warme Brüder gegen Kalte Krieger*, 77; and Günter Grau, "Sozialistische Moral und Homosexualität. Die Politik der SED und das Homosexuellenstrafrecht 1945 bis 1989," in Detlef Grumbach, *Die Linke und das Laster: Schwule Emanzipation und linke Vorurteile* (Hamburg: Männerschwarm Verlag, 1995), 138.

67. "Bericht über eine Ausarbeitung für das MfS-Berlin in der Zeit 1962/65 auf Anforderung des MfS-Offiziers Wolf vom MfS-Berlin, Bonn im Oktober/November 1965," in Setz, *Homosexualität in der DDR*, 205–36, primarily 205–9; and Florian Mildenberger, "Die Stasi und die Homosexuellen: Ein Überläufer berichtet (1965)," in Setz, *Homosexualität in der DDR*, 202–4.

68. Peter Hegarty and Felicia Pratto, "Sexual Orientation Beliefs: Their Relationship to Anti-Gay Attitudes and Biological Determinist Arguments," *Journal of Homosexuality* 41 (2001): 121–35.

69. Toni Brennan and Peter Hegarty, "Who Was Magnus Hirschfeld and Why Do We Need to Know?," *History and Philosophy of Psychology* 9 (2007): 12–28; Günter Grau, "Protest letter to the President of the Federal Republic of Germany," Johannes Rau, on the occasion of awarding the Federal Cross to Günter Dörner, December 4, 2002; available at http:www.hirschfeld.in-berlin.de.

70. Volkmar Sigusch, Eberhard Schorsch, and Martin Dannecker, "Official Statement by the German Society for Sex Research (Deutsche Gesellschaft fiir Sexualforschung e.V.) on the Research of Prof. Dr. Günter Dörner on the Subject of Homosexuality," *Archives of Sexual Behavior* 11(1982): 445–50.

71. Rainer Herrn, "On the History of Biological Theories of Homosexuality," *Journal of Homosexuality* 28 (1995): 31–56.

72. Edward Ross Dickinson, "Biopolitics, Fascism, Democracy: Some Reflections on Our Discourse about 'Modernity,'" *Central European History* 37 (2004): 1–48; Eghigian, "The Psychologization of the Socialist Self."

Contributors

Rebecca Boehling, formerly a professor of modern European history and director of the Dresher Center for the Humanities at the University of Maryland, Baltimore County, is now the director of the International Tracing Service (ITS) in Bad Arolsen, Germany. She has published on the Holocaust, post–World War II Germany, and German-American relations. Her books include *A Question of Priorities: Democratic Reforms and Economic Recovery in Postwar Germany* (1996) and *Life and Loss in the Shadow of the Holocaust: A Jewish Family's Untold Story* (coauthored with Uta Larkey, 2011). She is currently working on a comparative study of British, French, and US approaches to denazification in Allied-occupied Germany.

Friederike Brühöfener is a graduate student in the Department of History at the University of North Carolina at Chapel Hill. Her research interests include modern German and European history, cultural history, military history, and gender, with a special focus on the history of masculinities. Her dissertation, "Defining the West German Soldier—Military, Society, and Masculinity in West Germany, 1945–1989," studies the contested notions of masculinity that emerged from the creation of the Bundeswehr by the Federal Republic of Germany. She plans to extend the dissertation to a book entitled "Forging States, Armies, and Men: Military Masculinity, Politics, and Society in East and West Germany, 1945–1989."

Steve Estes is professor of modern US history at Sonoma State University, Rohnert Park, California. He has published on labor organization, education, the American South, race relations, and sexuality. His books include *I Am a Man!: Race, Manhood, and the Civil Rights Movement* (2005) and *Ask & Tell: Gay and Lesbian Veterans Speak Out* (2007), as well as *Raising Minority Academic Achievement* (coedited with Donna Walker and Sonia Jurich, 2001). His current book manuscript, "Too Proud to Whitewash: Charleston since the Civil Rights Movement," is under contract with the University of North Carolina Press.

Jennifer V. Evans is associate professor of history and graduate chair of the Department of History at Carleton University, Ottawa, Canada. Her research interests focus on twentieth-century Germany and the history of sexuality. In addition to articles on the regulation of same-sex sexuality in Nazi and post-1945 Germany, she has recently published the book *Life among the Ruins: Cityscape and Sexuality in Cold War Berlin* (2011), which explores the reemergence of the city's various subcultures in the aftermath of World War II. Currently, she is preparing a manuscript on the experiences of pink triangle victims after Hitler, while also working on research projects analyzing queer erotic photography in the 1970s and 1980s as a form of self-actualization.

Atina Grossmann is professor of modern European and German history and of women's and gender studies at The Cooper Union, New York. She has published extensively on the history of the Third Reich and the Holocaust, the history of sexuality, and postwar Germany. Her books include *Reforming Sex: The German Movement for Birth Control and Abortion Reform, 1920–1950* (1995); *Crimes of War: Guilt and Denial in the Twentieth Century* (coedited with Omar Bartov and Mary Nolan, 2002); *Jews, Germans, and Allies: Close Encounters in Occupied Germany* (2007); and *After the Nazi Racial State: Difference and Democracy in Germany and Europe* (coedited with Rita Chin, Heide Fehrenbach, and Geoff Eley, 2009). Her current project, "Soviet Central Asia, Iran, and India: Sites of Refuge and Relief for European Jews during World War II," examines the stories of transnational Jewish refugees.

Karen Hagemann is the James G. Kenan Distinguished Professor of History at the University of North Carolina at Chapel Hill. She has published widely on modern German and European history and cultural, political, military, and gender history. Her recent books include *Masculinities in Politics and War: Rewritings of Modern History* (coedited with Stefan Dudink and John Tosh, 2004); *Gendering Modern German History: Rewriting Historiography* (coedited with Jean Quataert, 2007, in German 2008); *Representing Masculinity:*

364

Citizenship in Modern Western Culture (coedited with Stefan Dudink and Anna Clark, 2007/2012); *Civil Society and Gender Justice: Historical and Comparative Perspectives* (coedited with Sonya Michel and Gunilla Budde, 2008/2011); *Gender, War, and Politics: Transatlantic Perspectives, 1775–1830* (co-edited with Gisela Mettele and Jane Rendall, 2010); and *War Memories: The Revolutionary and Napoleonic Wars in Modern European Culture* (coedited with Alan Forrest and Etienne François, 2012). Currently she is writing a monograph entitled "Revisiting Prussia's Wars against Napoleon: Nation, Political Culture, Memory" (to be published by Cambridge University Press) and preparing as the general editor the "Oxford Handbook on Gender, War and the Western World since 1650" (Oxford University Press).

Donna Harsch is a professor of history at Carnegie Mellon University, Pittsburgh. She has published widely on gender history, political mobilization and institutions, and political culture in twentieth-century Germany. Her books include *German Social Democracy and the Rise of Nazism* (1993) and *Revenge of the Domestic: Women, the Family, and Communism in the German Democratic Republic* (2007). Her current research compares popular health cultures, professional medicine, and public health policies in West and East Germany from the 1940s through the 1970s, focusing on basic health, the treatment of contagious disease, and the control of health-averse behaviors.

Laura McEnaney is Nadine Austin Wood Professor of American History at Whittier College in California. She works on women's and gender history and the history of the United States after World War II, and is the author of *Civil Defense Begins at Home: Militarization Meets Everyday Life in the Fifties* (2000). Currently she is finishing the manuscript of her second monograph, "World War II's "Postwar": A Social and Policy History of Peace, 1944–1953."

Joanne Meyerowitz is Arthur Unobskey Professor of History and American Studies and chair of American Studies at Yale University. She has published widely on twentieth-century US history, women's history, and the history of gender and sexuality. Her books include *Women Adrift: Independent Wage Earners in Chicago, 1880–1930* (1988); *How Sex Changed: A History of Transsexuality in the United States* (2002); and two edited volumes: *Not June Cleaver: Women and Gender in Postwar America, 1945–1960* (1994); and *History and September 11th* (2003).

Sonya Michel is professor of history, American studies, and women's studies at the University of Maryland, College Park. She has published extensively on twentieth-century American history, especially the history of women and gender, sexualities, and poverty and social welfare, both in the United States and from a comparative perspective. Her books include *Behind the Lines: Gender and the Two World Wars* (coedited with Margaret Higonnet, Jane Jenson, and Margaret Weitz, 1987); *Children's Interests / Mothers' Rights: The Shaping of America's Child Care Policy* (1999); *Engendering America: A Documentary History* (coauthored with Robyn Muncy, 2000); *Child Care Policy at the Crossroads: Gender and Welfare State Restructuring* (coedited with Rianne Mahon, 2002); *Civil Society and Gender Justice: Historical and Comparative Perspectives* (coedited with Karen Hagemann and Gunilla Budde (2008/2011); *Women, Migration, and the Work of Care: The United States in Comparative Perspective* (2011), which she edited; and "An *American* Dilemma? Race, Ethnicity, and Welfare States" (coedited with Pauli Kettunen and Klaus Petersen, manuscript in development). She is currently coauthoring a textbook entitled "Poverty and Social Policy in the United States: Historical, Comparative, and Transnational Perspectives," with Sarah Rose, Richard Scotch, and Laura Frader (under contract to Routledge).

Jennifer Mittelstadt is associate professor of history at Rutgers, The State University of New Jersey, New Brunswick. She writes on the political history of the twentieth-century United States, focusing on social policy and social politics, liberalism, second-wave feminism, and the military and militarization. Her publications include *From Welfare to Workfare: The Unintended Consequences of Liberal Reform, 1945–1965* (2005), and *Welfare in the United States: A History with Documents* (coedited with Premilla Nadasen and Marisa Chappell, 2009). She is currently writing a book on the US Army, social welfare, and politics in the late twentieth century.

Robert G. Moeller is professor of history at the University of California, Irvine. He has published widely on twentieth-century German and European history with a focus on social history, the history of women and gender, cultural history, and the history of memory. His books include *German Peasants and Agrarian Politics, 1914–1924: The Rhineland and Westphalia* (1986); *Protecting Motherhood: Women and the Family in the Politics of Postwar West Germany* (1993); *War Stories: The Search for a Usable Past in the Federal Republic of Germany* (2003); and *The Nazi State and German Society: A Brief History* *with Documents* (2010); as well as two edited volumes: *Peasants and Lords in Modern Germany: Recent Contributions to Agricultural History* (1986) and *West Germany Under Construction: Politics, Society, and Culture in the Adenauer Era* (1997). He also coedited *Histories of the Aftermath: The Legacies of the Second World War in Europe* (with Frank Biess, 2010). He is currently working on a history of the Federal Republic of Germany in the 1950s, focusing on how West Germans defined the basis for social solidarity and legitimate political identities in the aftermath of Nazism and defeat in war.

Kathleen J. Nawyn is a historian with the US Army Center of Military History. She holds a doctorate in modern European history from the University of North Carolina at Chapel Hill, where she wrote a dissertation titled "'Striking at the Roots of German Militarism': Efforts to Demilitarize German Society and Culture in American-Occupied Württemberg-Baden, 1945–1949."

Amy Rutenberg is assistant professor of history and social studies education at Appalachian State University, Boone, North Carolina. Her research interests include twentieth-century American history, women and gender, political history, and war and society. She recently defended her dissertation, "Citizen-Civilians: Masculinity, Citizenship, and American Military Manpower Policy, 1945–1975."

Angela Tudico earned her doctorate in US history at the University of Maryland at College Park, where she completed her dissertation, "'They're Bringing Home Japanese Brides': Japanese War Brides in the Postwar Era." She currently works at the National Archives at New York City.

Ulrike Weckel is professor of the history of journalism at Justus Liebig University, Giessen. She has published widely on modern German and European history, especially women in the Enlightenment, gender and the Third Reich, and film studies and visual history. Her publications include *Zwischen Häuslichkeit und Öffentlichkeit. Die ersten deutschen Frauenzeitschriften im späten 18. Jahrhundert und ihr Publikum* (1998); *Beschämende Bilder. Deutsche Reaktionen auf alliierte Dokumentarfilme über befreite Konzentrationslager* (2012); as well as the edited volumes *Zwischen Karriere und Verfolgung: Handlungsräume von Frauen im nationalsozialistischen Deutschland* (coedited with Kirsten Heinsohn and Barbara Vogel, 1997); *Ordnung, Politik und Geselligkeit der Geschlechter im 18. Jahrhundert* (coedited with Claudia Opitz, Brigitte Tolkemitt, and Olivia Hochstrasser, 1998); and *"Bestien" und "Befehlsempfänger": Frauen und Männer in NS-Prozessen nach 1945* (coedited with Edgar Wolfrum, 2003).

Alice Weinreb is assistant professor of history at Loyola University, Chicago, where she teaches courses in twentieth-century Europe, the history and politics of food in Europe, the Holocaust, and European environmental history. Weinreb previously taught at Utah State University and at Northwestern University, where she was a founding member of the Chicago Area Food Studies Working Group based at University of Illinois-Chicago. She has published articles in *Central European History, German Studies Review, Bulletin of the German Historical Institute*, and *Zeitschrift für Körpergeschichte*, as well as several anthologies, and has completed the manuscript for a book, "Modern Hungers: Food, War, and Germany in the Twentieth Century." Her next project will examine the postwar environmental movement in West Germany and the rise of a specifically German definition of a clean and healthy environment.

Index

abortions, 19–20, 301
abundance, government promises of, 88
Acheson, Dean, 193
Ackermann, Heinrich, 325
ACS (Army Community Service), 284
activism: antiwar rallies, 133; civil
    disobedience, 174; civil rights
    movement, 19, 187, 194–99, 302;
    gay rights movement, 306, 335, 336;
    homophile movement, 306, 335;
    homosexual rights movement (West
    Germany), 334–35; peace activism,
    173–78; women's movement, 19
Adenauer, Konrad, 146–51, 154, 327–28
Adenauer administration, 152, 155
Adenauer Cabinet, 237
Administration of Nutrition, Agriculture
    and Forestry (West Germany), 250n29
Admission of the Alien Fiancées or
    Fiancés of Members of the Armed
    Forces of the United States (P.L. 471,
    Fiancée Act), 214
Adorno, Theodor, 331
AFAP ("Army Family Action Plan"), 284
African Americans: in Chicago, 85, 86–87;
    family health issues of, 86–87; in Great
    Migration, 190; military service of,
    173, 176–77; military units, heroism

of, 186; soldiers, 43–44; veterans, self-
    perceptions of, 186, 189–91. *See also*
    race, masculinity, and citizenship in US
age of consent, 326, 344, 351
AIDS, 355
Ailey, Alvin, 305
airlines, confusion over Fiancée Act, 219
alcohol use by soldiers, 155–56, 158
Algiers, 215
Allies, 133–34, 146, 323–24
All-Volunteer Force (AVF), 26n44,
    165–66, 275, 276, 278
American Civil Liberties Union, 312
American consumer goods, West Berlin
    exhibition of, 257–58
*American Crucible: Race and Nation in the
    Twentieth Century* (Gerstle), 208–9
American Friends Service Committee, 229
American Law Institute, 309
American occupation zone. *See* German
    women and local politics under
    American occupation; German youth
    and changing ideals of manhood in
    occupied Württemberg-Baden; sex and
    sexual violence, war, and occupation in
    German post–World War II memory
    and imagination
American Social Hygiene Association, 81